Melville's Reading

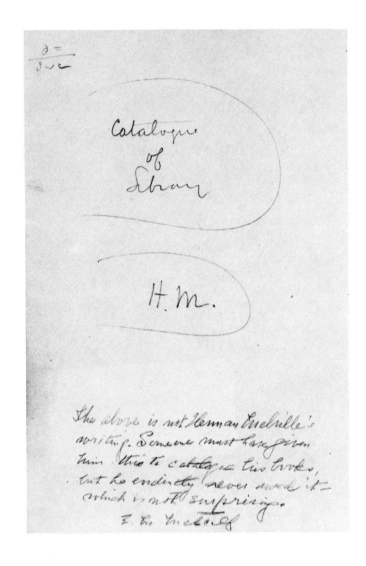

'Catalogue of Library H. M.'

From a bound blank book, approximately 21 x 14.4 cm., presented to
the Houghton Library by the late Eleanor Melville Metcalf, a granddaughter of Herman Melville. As her note points out, the inscription
is not in his hand; the writing is probably that of his brother Allan, a
likely donor of the volume. (MS Am 188.4; by permission of the
Houghton Library, Harvard University.)

MELVILLE'S READING

REVISED AND ENLARGED EDITION

Merton M. Sealts, Jr.

"I have swam through libraries. . . ."
—Ishmael, in *Moby-Dick*, Ch. 32

UNIVERSITY OF SOUTH CAROLINA PRESS

Manufactured in the United States of America

Library of Congress Cataloging-in-Publication Data

Sealts, Merton M.
    Melville's reading.

    Includes index.
    1. Melville, Herman, 1819–1891—Books and reading.
2. Melville, Herman, 1819–1891—Library—Catalogs.
3. Melville, Herman, 1819–1891—Sources. I. Title.
PS2388.B6S43   1988   813'.3   87-16186
ISBN 0-87249-515-9

For Jay Leyda

Contents

Preface to the 1988 Edition

This book is the second recension of *Melville's Reading*, which was initially published in successive issues of the *Harvard Library Bulletin* between 1948 and 1950 and subsequently revised for publication in book form sixteen years later, in 1966. Each version has been prepared in response to the emergence of additional books once owned by Herman Melville and the accumulation of other new evidence concerning his reading. The present volume is a major revision and enlargement of the 1966 edition that takes account of the most recent discoveries.[1] It also reflects a growing understanding of the interrelations between events of Melville's life in the world and his inner life in what he called 'the world of mind'—the world of the books he read and the books he wrote—that has developed over the last half-century of Melville scholarship and criticism.

Since 1966 we have seen the emergence of more books that once belonged to Melville—including his heavily annotated copies of Milton and Dante—and the startling discovery in 1983 of a veritable treasure trove of Melville family papers, which have since been added to the already rich Gansevoort-Lansing Collection in the Rare Books and Manuscripts Division of the New York Public Library. These papers afford new information concerning Melville himself and the books, magazines,

---

[1] It incorporates those later additions and changes reported first in two supplementary notes appearing in the *Harvard Library Bulletin* 19 (July 1971): 280–284, and 27 (July 1979): 330–335, and later in my *Pursuing Melville 1940–1980: Chapters and Essays* (University of Wisconsin Press, 1982), pp. 31–57 and 347–354.

and newspapers read by him or within his extensive family circle. This material has been used in revising the basic Check-List of Books Owned and Borrowed in Part II of this edition and in greatly broadening the discussion of Melville as reader that constitutes Part I. Although additional books and letters are likely to turn up in future years, and researchers will no doubt come across more minor sources of Melville's prose and poetry, it is clear that scholarship has now identified the main lines of his reading over the years and the principal literary sources of his successive books. These definitive findings are now brought together in this revised and enlarged edition of *Melville's Reading*.[2]

Like the original form of *Melville's Reading*, this new project would not have been undertaken without the urging of Jay Leyda, whose indispensable *Melville Log* will also be appearing in a revised and enlarged edition. I acknowledge with thanks the authorization to incorporate copyrighted materials previously published by the *Harvard Library Bulletin* and by the University of Wisconsin Press; the award of a Travel to Collections Grant by the National Endowment for the Humanities; the special permission of the New York Public Library to make use of the new Melville Family Papers in its Ganesvoort-Lansing Collection; and the authorization of the following institutions and individuals to list books and other materials now in their respective collections: Alan Abrams; Greg Bassett; the Berkshire Athenaeum; the Berkshire County Historical Society; Brown University: the John Hay Library; Kenneth W. Cameron; Christie's New York; Columbia University Libraries: the Rare Book and Manuscript Library; H. Richard Dietrich; John F. Fleming, Inc.; J. W. P. Frost; Peter R. Haack; Harvard College Library: the Houghton Library; Lansingburgh Historical Society; J. C. Levenson; Mrs. Roderick Marshall; H. Bradley Martin; the Massachusetts Historical Society; Jean F. Melvill; Howard S. Mott, Inc.; the Newberry Library; the New-York Historical Society; the New York Public Library (Astor, Lenox and Tilden Foundations); the New York Society Library; Princeton University Library; William Reese; the Rosenbach Museum and Library; George Rovere; Serendipity Books, Berkeley, California; Sotheby's, New York; the Stephen B. Luce Library (Maritime College, State University of New York, Fort Schuyler, Bronx, New York); University of Virginia Library: Alderman Library; Diane and Merrill Whitburn; Library of the Woodstock Theological Center of Georgetown University; and Yale University Library: the Beinecke Library.

The individuals I have named here and the staffs of the firms and in-

[2]I have drawn principally on major scholarly articles and books, making no attempt to mention *all* of the many source studies that have been published to date. These studies are listed and surveyed in *Melville's Sources*, a forthcoming book by Mary C. Bercaw; their most significant findings have for the most part been incorporated in the editorial apparatus of various scholarly editions of Melville's writings.

stitutions I have listed have been most generous in assisting me with this project. I should also like to acknowledge the help of Mrs. Paul W. Barden, Elizabeth Binnian, William F. Boni, Warren Broderick, Herbert Cahoon, Samuel M. Chambliss, Hennig Cohen, Harrison Hayford, the late Wilson Heflin, Mrs. Meredith M. Jack, Norman Kane, Walter Donald Kring, Jay Leyda, Alma A. MacDougall, Joel Myerson, the *New York Review of Books*, Hershel Parker, Rob Rulon-Mueller, M. Douglas Sackman, Donald Yannella, and—most especially—Ruth Mackenzie Sealts.

MERTON M. SEALTS, JR.

December 1986

Preface to the 1966 Edition (abridged)

This edition of *Melville's Reading* is a revision and enlargement of a study first published serially in the *Harvard Library Bulletin*, later offprinted, and now out of print.[1] . . . Many of the books listed in the original version . . . have passed into new hands, more volumes from Melville's own library have come to light, and later research has turned up further collateral information. For students of Melville generally as well as for scholarly specialists, librarians, and collectors, the resulting additions, corrections, and changes have been brought together in a book that 'points toward the future,' as the late Stanley Williams said of the original study.[2]

As author and compiler of *Melville's Reading*, I must assume full responsibility for the data it presents even as I acknowledge with appreciation the generous help received over the years from many persons, institutions, and business firms that have advised and in various ways assisted in its preparation and revision. The original articles would not have been undertaken without the urging of Jay Leyda. . . . He, Charles Olson, Henry A. Murray, and J. H. Birss, who had already located and

[1]'Melville's Reading: A Check-List of Books Owned and Borrowed,' *Harvard Library Bulletin 2* (1948): 141–163, 378–392; 3 (1949):119–130, 268–277, 407–421; 4 (1950: 98–109 (an offprint comprising all six installments appeared in 1950); and 'Melville's Reading: A Supplementary List of Books Owned and Borrowed,' 6 (1952): 239–247.

[2]Stanley T. Williams, 'Melville,' in *Eight American Authors: A Review of Research and Criticism*, ed. Floyd Stovall (New York: Modern Language Association of America, 1956), p. 253.

studied many of the volumes from Melville's library, generously put their findings at my disposal when I too joined the search. Melville's granddaughters and grandnieces—Mrs. Walter B. Binnian, Mrs. E. Barton Chapin, the late Mrs. Henry K. Metcalf, Mrs. A. D. Osborne, and the Misses Agnes, Helen, and Margaret Morewood—made readily available the books they had inherited, answering many a question that arose as investigation proceeded. Librarians, private collectors, and book dealers have also contributed valuable information since work began on the original study, which in the course of its serial publication served to locate a number of books previously unknown to scholars and to stimulate further investigation of aspects of Melville's reading.

For authorization to examine, record, and publish materials in their respective collections and for many other kindnesses I am indebted to the Berkshire Athenaeum, the Boston Athenaeum, Clifton Waller Barrett, Mrs. Walter B. Binnian, John H. Birss, Albert Boni, the late Mrs. L. A. Chambliss, Samuel M. Chambliss, Mrs. E. Barton Chapin, Dwight Francis, the Harvard College Library, Meredith M. Jack, Mrs. Meredith M. Jack, J. C. Levenson, Mrs. Benjamin H. Long, H. Bradley Martin, Jr., the late Mrs. Henry K. Metcalf, the Misses Agnes, Helen, and Margaret Morewood, Howard S. Mott, Henry A. Murray, the New York Public Library (material in the Henry W. and Albert A. Berg Collection is used here by special permission of the Library), the New York Society Library, Mrs. A. D. Osborne, the Princeton University Library, Rev. Edgar F. Romig, Miss Eleanor Romig, the Philip H. and A. S. W. Rosenbach Foundation, George Rovere, M. Douglas Sackman, the University of Virginia Library, the late Raymond Weaver, the late Carol V. Wight and Mrs. Wight, and the Yale University Library.

For assistance and suggestions concerning the search for materials I am also indebted to Lee Ash, Miss Dorothy C. Barck, Charles F. Batchelder, Jr., Mrs. Earle E. Bessey, Walter E. Bezanson, David Bortin, Bernard R. Bowron, William Braswell, Herbert Cahoon, Mr. and Mrs. John P. Comer, W. Walker Cowen, Miss Marjorie Lyle Crandall, the late Jesse B. Cross, the late Merrell R. Davis, Martin J. Faigel, Miss Elizabeth Foster, Vincent Freimarck, Donald Gallup, James Garfield, Miss Florence S. Garing, William H. Gilman, Mrs. Alfred Goldsmith, Harold Graves, Philip Hanson, the late Lathrop C. Harper, Carl Haverlin, Harrison Hayford, Wilson Heflin, James J. Heslin, Mrs. S. E. Hewett, Robert W. Hill, Tyrus Hillway, Miss Sylvia C. Hilton, Howard C. Horsford, Mark DeWolfe Howe, Miss Julie Hudson, the late William A. Jackson, Miss Carolyn Jakeman, Mrs. F. G. King, Wilmarth S. Lewis, Jay Leyda, William H. McCarthy, Jr., Mr. and Mrs. William H. Maas, T. O. Mabbott, Luther S. Mansfield, the late Henry K. Metcalf, Robert F. Metzdorff, Albert Mordell, Robert B. Newman, Mrs. Roy

Newman, Miss Leonora O'Herron, Leslie M. Oliver, Charles Olson, H. Thomas Osborne, Carola W. Paine, the late Victor Hugo Paltsits, Norman Holmes Pearson, David A. Randall, William H. Runge, James H. Sprinkel, Vincent Starrett, Richard C. Stavig, the late Arthur Swann, Earl Tannenbaum, Mrs. Robert J. Teddick, Milton Halsey Thomas, Willard Thorp, Mrs. Wesley Trimpi, Miss Louise Turpin, R. W. G. Vail, the late Carl Van Doren, Alexander O. Vietor, Howard P. Vincent, Miss Darthula Wilcox, Ralph E. Wilcoxen, James A. Williams, Mrs. Carroll A. Wilson, James I. Wyer, and John Cook Wyllie.

Institutions and business firms that have aided my research include the American Antiquarian Society, Athenaeum of Philadelphia, Bibliographical Society of America, Brooklyn Public Library, Carnegie Bookshop (New York City), Columbia University Library, Dartmouth College Library, Free Library of Philadelphia, General Society of Mechanics and Tradesmen (the Apprentices' Library) of New York City, Grace Church in New York, Harper and Row, Lawrence University Library, Leary's Book Store (Philadelphia), Library Company of Philadelphia, Library of Congress, Massachusetts Historical Society, Mercantile Library of New York, Mercantile Library of Philadelphia, New-York Historical Society, New York Public Library: Reference Department, New York State Library, Pageant Book Store (New York City), G. P. Putnam's Sons, Sailors' Snug Harbor (Staten Island, New York), Charles Scribner's Sons, Seven Gables Bookshop (New York City), Wellesley College Library, and John Wiley and Sons.

For assistance in other ways I am grateful to Wellesley College, to Lawrence College (now Lawrence University), and to the John Simon Guggenheim Memorial Foundation. A research grant from Wellesley while I was a member of its faculty made possible the travel and typing required for the original publication of this study. More recently, a leave of absence from Lawrence and the award of a Guggenheim Fellowship gave me the opportunity to revise and expand the basic material, and a research grant from Lawrence provided for the needed travel and incidental expenses.

The editorial guidance of George William Cottrell, Jr., formerly editor of the *Harvard Library Bulletin*, was invaluable in preparing for its original publication a manuscript that presented unusually thorny problems of style and format.

MERTON M. SEALTS, JR.

August 1965

Documentation

Since it has become customary for Melville scholars to refer to books that Melville owned and borrowed by citing numbered entries in Part II, the alphabetical 'Check-List of Books Owned and Borrowed' (e.g., 'Sealts No. 100'), this edition of *Melville's Reading*, like its predecessor of 1966, retains those numbers that were assigned at the time the first installment of the original articles went to press. Those articles conformed to the styling of the *Harvard Library Bulletin*, which has also been retained once again, though with some modifications. Thus documentation throughout the present volume is in line with the major recommendations of *The MLA Style Manual* (1985), which calls for (1) brief parenthetical references within the text to eliminate purely documentary footnotes and (2) a list of 'Works Cited' to provide full documentation of items referred to parenthetically.

Quotations of Melville's published works, cited parenthetically by short titles, are from (1) the nine volumes of *The Writings of Herman Melville* published to date in the Northwestern-Newberry Edition, and (2) those editions of *Moby-Dick*, of the works of Melville's later years, and of his letters and journals that have not yet been published in the Northwestern-Newberry Edition; these are listed under 'Works Cited.' Extracts from the letters and journals are cited by date to facilitate their location in both present and future editions as well as in Jay Leyda, *The Melville Log* (cited parenthetically as *Log*), which is also the acknowledged source of much information concerning events of Melville's life. Unpublished materials (notably correspondence) in the following collections are indicated by these abbreviations within the parenthetical references:

HCL   Harvard College Library: the Melville Collection
NL   Newberry Library: the Melville Collection
NYPL–D   New York Public Library: the Duyckinck Collection
NYPL–GL   New York Public Library: the Gansevoort-Lansing Collec-
             tion

Additional abbreviations employed only in the 'Check-List of Books Owned and Borrowed' are explained at the beginning of Part II.

PART I

MELVILLE AS READER

One must be an inventor to read well. As the proverb says, 'He that would bring home the wealth of the Indies, must carry out the wealth of the Indies.' There is then creative reading as well as creative writing.

—Emerson, 'The American Scholar' (1837)

Introduction

Melville's Library

Books, said Emerson in 'The American Scholar,' 'are for nothing but to inspire'; Herman Melville would surely have agreed. Emerson scorned 'the book-learned class, who value books as such'; Melville wrote of 'the heavy unmalleable element of mere book-knowledge' (*Pierre*, p. 283). Both men were creative readers as well as creative writers; both knew that a reader must indeed 'be an inventor to read well.' Though Emerson benefited from a university education, Melville's Ishmael was speaking for Melville himself when he declared in *Moby-Dick* that 'a whale-ship was *my* Yale College and my Harvard' (p. 101; emphasis added). But Melville family members were readers from an early age, and once Herman left the sea and became a creative writer he read omnivorously. To study the course of his reading, as Professor Herman Spivey recognized in reviewing the 1966 edition of this book, is to follow 'the self-education of a major writer.'

Melville's lifelong interest in books and reading is reflected in many of his fictional characters, in works from 'Fragments from a Writing Desk' (1839) to the posthumous *Billy Budd, Sailor*. As he wrote of his own Pierre, 'A varied scope of reading, little suspected by his friends, and randomly acquired by a random but lynx-eyed mind, . . . poured one considerable contributary stream into that bottomless spring of orig-

3

inal thought which the occasion and time had caused to burst out in himself' (*Pierre,* p. 283). And as F. O. Matthiessen observed in *American Renaissance,* 'The books that really spoke to Melville became an immediate part of him to a degree hardly matched by any other of our great writers in their maturity' (p. 122). Since the late 1930's, a succession of enlightening articles and monographs has demonstrated the stimulus of books—the Bible, the literature of travel, the prose cadences of Sir Thomas Browne, the poetry of Shakespeare and Milton, the thought of Plato and Bayle—in releasing his creative energies.[1]

The point of departure for many of these studies has been Melville's pencilings in volumes from his own library, for he was by no means a passive reader. As Walker Cowen, the most wide-ranging recorder of his marginalia, has explained, he responded actively to what he encountered on the printed page:

> When he came to statements he found particularly striking or ones with which he disagreed he did not hestiate to set down his own feelings in the margins. These markings and annotations are the record of an intimate dialogue between himself and the great writers. And because these marginalia were for his own use, they provide an unusually clear and direct view of his thinking. ('Melville's Marginalia: Hawthorne,' p. 279)

Although markings and annotation cannot indicate the full extent of Melville's response to an author, which in many instances became richer and deeper with consideration over time, it is fortunate for those interested in the man and his work that more than two hundred books from his library have survived and are available for study. These volumes constitute only a minor fraction of the many books he read and used, however, including more than a hundred others he is known to have acquired for himself and roughly a hundred more that he was recorded as borrowing. Melville never completed a projected catalogue of his own library (see the frontispiece); after his death in September 1891, the appraisers of his estate took only an approximate inventory, valuing at $600 his 'Personal books numbering about 1,000 volumes' (William Charvat, 'Melville's Income,' p. 252). Whether this figure included collected editions by general title or by individual volume is unclear, and whether the appraisers regarded copies of his own works as part of the library is unknown.

Some of these 'personal books' were kept at hand by Melville's widow, whose feelings about her husband's library are indicated by a quotation from another widow that she found and marked in one of them, Isaac Disraeli's *The Literary Character,* in 1895:

> 'My ideas of my husband,' she said, 'are so much associated with his *books,* that to part with them would be as it were breaking some of the last

ties which still connect me with so beloved an object. The being in the midst of books he has been accustomed to read, and which contain his *marks* and *notes,* will still give him *a sort of existence* with *me.'* (Check-List, No. 187: p. 205)

But her removal to smaller quarters in April 1892 had in fact made it necessary for Mrs. Melville to dispose of a portion of the library. A few books were presented to relatives and friends (Check-List, Nos. 284, 451.1, 539), but many more were sold early in that year. Her basis for determining which books to part with and which to keep is not known; as one of her granddaughters, the late Eleanor Melville Metcalf, once suggested, she may have given up some of the larger volumes simply because it was difficult to shelve them. This may explain why such books as Melville's folio Davenant and Jonson, bought in London in 1849 (Check-List, Nos. 176, 302), found their way into the second-hand market.

Books Retained in the Family

After Mrs. Melville herself died in 1906, nearly all of those books she had decided to keep remained with her surviving children, Elizabeth ('Bessie'), the unmarried daughter who died two years later, and Frances Melville Thomas (Mrs. Henry B. Thomas), who lived until 1938. Mrs. Thomas in turn gave a few books to Caroline W. Stewart, a school friend of her sister's who was the companion of the Thomas daughters, Eleanor (later Mrs. Henry K. Metcalf) and Frances (later Mrs. A. D. Osborne), on a European trip in 1901 (Check-List, Nos. 48, 49, 308). Eleanor Thomas gave another volume to the Rev. Samuel Hines Bishop (No. 543a). The remaining books that had been Melville's were subsequently divided among his four granddaughters: Eleanor, Frances, and their two younger sisters, Katherine (Mrs. Walter B. Binnian) and Jeannette (Mrs. E. Barton Chapin)—all now deceased.

In the 1940's and after, Mrs. Metcalf, Mrs. Binnian, and Mrs. Chapin presented most of their books to the Harvard College Library. Together with correspondence and manuscripts, these volumes comprise the extensive Melville Collection now housed in Harvard's Houghton Library, which has since been augmented by other gifts and purchases. Mrs. Osborne, after temporarily depositing books at both Harvard and Princeton, established the Osborne Collection in the New York Public Library. The Melville and Osborne Collections now hold 170 titles that were once Herman Melville's.

A few losses over the years should also be noted. Certain volumes kept in the Melville and Thomas families that were examined and described in earlier years by Mrs. Metcalf and by three pioneering Melville scholars, now deceased—Raymond Weaver, Robert S. Forsythe, and Charles Olson—can no longer be accounted for; in some instances these were part of multivolume sets now incomplete. (In the Check-List, see Nos. 15, 86a, 156, 383a, 404a, 456a, 469, 495a, 516.) Other books kept in the families that were listed in the first publication of this study (1948–1950) have also been lost (Check-List, Nos. 108–111 inclusive; 115, 432, 456, 507b).

A substantial number of Melville's books that had gone to other relatives during his lifetime are also extant. During the 1850's two of his sisters were married in Pittsfield—Catherine in 1853 to John C. Hoadley and Helen Maria in 1854 to George Griggs. Hoadley in particular became a close friend with whom Melville exchanged books and letters on literary matters. A number of these volumes have survived (Check-List, Nos. 100, 137, 296; see also No. 387a); others that Melville may have given Hoadley were presumably sold with Hoadley's library following his death in 1886.[2]

In 1855 Melville's mother and unmarried sister Frances Priscilla ('Fanny,' 1827–1885) left Pittsfield for Gansevoort, New York, to keep house for his uncle Herman Gansevoort, whose wife died in October. In later years Augusta, the other unmarried sister (1821–1876), joined them there. At least two books that belonged to Melville and later to Frances were given to a friend, Sarah Jane Vanderwerker, before Frances died (Check-List, Nos. 222, 404b). Other family books and papers kept at Gansevoort went to a sister, Catherine Melville Hoadley (1825–1905), and a cousin, Catherine Gansevoort Lansing (Mrs. Abraham Lansing, 1939–1918) of Albany. Mrs. Lansing in turn bequeathed her holdings to the late Victor Hugo Paltsits, long associated with the New York Public Library as Chief of the American History Division and Keeper of Manuscripts; Dr. Paltsits then presented them to the Library in 1919 as part of the extensive Gansevoort-Lansing Collection, comprising books and papers of the Gansevoort, Lansing, Van Schaick, Melville, and other related families. In 1929, drawing on these materials, he published his *Family Correspondence of Herman Melville 1830–1904 in the Gansevoort-Lansing Collection.*

This rich collection, which now includes fifteen books that were once Herman Melville's, has been augmented over the years by purchases and gifts, including a number of books from the Melville family inherited by Charlotte Hoadley (1858–1946), daughter of John C. Hoadley and Catherine Melville Hoadley. In 1983 the New York Public Library purchased a significant addition of Melville family papers that had belonged in turn to Augusta and Frances Melville, then passing outside the family when the property at Gansevoort was sold and remaining out of sight for nearly a century; their rediscovery is a story in itself (see John and Carolyn DeMarco, 'Finding the New Melville Papers'). This portion of the augmented collection comprises more than 500 letters exchanged between Augusta Melville and various members of her extended family as well as her friends. In the words of Susan Davis, the present Curator of Manuscripts, 'These letters describe in considerable detail the lives and daily activities of the writers,' men and women forming 'a fairly tightly knit circle who kept themselves apprised of each other's lives' ('More for the NYPL's Long Vaticans,' p. 5). No books came with the new papers, but there are many revealing references to what Melville and his immediate family were currently reading, from his early years until the 1860's.

In 1863, when Herman Melville, his wife, and their four children moved from Pittsfield to New York City, the Pittsfield property was sold to his brother Allan; with it went an undetermined number of books and papers—some of them Herman Melville's and some that had been left there by his mother and sisters. The house and its contents passed in turn to Allan's daughter Maria Gansevoort (Mrs. William) Morewood (1849–1935), who in 1874 had married the son of John and Sarah Morewood, Melville's neighbors and friends. William Morewood died in 1923. The Berkshire Athenaeum, Pittsfield's public library, has ten of Melville's books, including Field's *History of the County of Berkshire* (Check-List, No. 216), which Melville had acquired in 1850, the year when he bought Arrowhead, as he called the property, and gave to Allan in 1863 when his brother took title to the house. Some of the books now at the Athenaeum had formerly belonged to the late Agnes, Helen, and Margaret Morewood, granddaughters of Allan Melville. Two other items once in Miss Agnes Morewood's collection can no longer be accounted for (Check-List, Nos. 100, 179).[3]

Since most of Melville's surviving books, like his surviving manuscripts, date from the later decades of his life, it is possible that he disposed of a part of his existing library when he left Pittsfield in 1863, but efforts to trace other volumes have not been productive. Many books were sold at Arrowhead when it passed outside the Morewood family with the deaths of William and Maria Morewood. If any volumes that had been Herman Melville's were in the house, they were not discovered by Henry A. Murray when he examined the books there before Allan Melville's descendants disposed of the property. During my own first visit to Arrowhead in March 1941, when in the absence of its owners at that time the caretaker allowed me a limited view of the property, he recalled how he had once been instructed to burn a number of family papers—even though, as a Pittsfield acquaintance remarked, 'the *stamps* on old letters are worth money'! The caretaker may have been referring to one of the 'special series of bonfires' through which, in the words of Jay Leyda, Allan Melville's daughter sought to obliterate 'all traces of [Herman] Melville's brotherly and business relations with Allan' (*Log* 1: xiv–xv).

My own later inquiries concerning the public sale of household effects at Arrowhead, including books—inquiries addressed both to the auctioneer who conducted the sale and also to other persons in attendance—yielded only limited information: records were not kept either of the books sold or of their buyers. I learned that one buyer of books, Dr. Herschel C. Walker, formerly of Wynnewood, Pennsylvania, and later of New York, had taken some one hundred fifty to two hundred volumes a few days before the auction. Dr. Walker disposed of his own library in 1940, mostly to relatives, neighbors in Wynnewood, and employees. Of those books which I was able to trace—none of them Herman Melville's—two have since been stolen and are now unlocated (Check-List, Nos. 11a, 141a); another is in the Berkshire Athenaeum (No. 197a). Still other books from Arrowhead, such as a five-volume edition of the works of George William Curtis (New York, 1856) acquired by Milton Halsey Thomas, were clearly Allan Melville's, not Herman's.

Four other Melville association volumes have been fittingly returned to Pittsfield in more recent years and are now at Arrowhead in the collection of the Berkshire County Historical Society, the current owner of the property. Two of these came from Mrs. Binnian's family (Check-List, Nos. 12a, 232a[?], and two from M. Douglas Sackman (Nos. 223a[?], 436.1).

In his later years Melville himself may also have given books from his library to Sailors' Snug Harbor, a home for old seamen on Staten Island, New York. His younger brother Thomas served as its superintendent between 1867, after he retired from the sea, and his death in 1884. At least one book, Turnbull's *A Voyage Round the World*, which Herman Melville had bought in 1847 (Check-List, No. 530a), became part of the library there. Although Melville is known to have bought many such volumes in the 1840's and 1850's, relatively few works of maritime interest have turned up among his surviving books. It is possible that he presented other volumes to Sailors' Snug Harbor, just as his friend Evert Duyckinck, a trustee, gave a set of prints in 1877 (see Melville's letter to Duyckinck, 13 April 1877).

Other Books Given Away or Sold

Some of the books that once belonged to Melville but were given away or sold have been acquired both by private collectors and by various libraries. Among these libraries are the Berkshire Athenaeum and the Berkshire Historical Society, the Houghton Library, the New York

Public Library (books received with or acquired for its Berg, Duyckinck, and Gansevoort-Lansing Collections), the Newberry Library of Chicago, and the Brown, Columbia, Princeton, Virginia, and Yale University Libraries. But brief listings in sale catalogues of various dealers constitute all that is known of thirty other surviving volumes that are now in undisclosed locations. The provenance of books that did not come down through the family can be established only in part.

The volumes that Melville's widow determined to sell were offered in 1892 to John Anderson, Jr., whose shop at 99 Nassau Street in New York her husband had patronized. The late Charles Olson, who interviewed Anderson in 1934, made an intensive effort to trace these and other books that she sold. Oscar Wegelin, who as Anderson's young assistant had delivered orders to Melville's residence at 104 East 26th Street, told Olson in that same year that the total ran to at least 500 volumes—possibly more. This figure does not appear, however, in Wegelin's own *Colophon* article of 1935, 'Herman Melville as I Recall Him,' which in Olson's judgment was prompted by his own previous inquiries of the two men.

Anderson selected a number of what he considered the best books before calling in other dealers, but there is no surviving record of the price he paid or of exactly what titles he bought. Among Anderson's choices, it appears, were several volumes of Melville's poetry, including *John Marr and Other Sailors* (1888) and *Timoleon* (1891), which had been printed for private circulation in editions of twenty-five copies and are now regarded as rarities of great value. Wegelin's assertion that Anderson took 'the few remaining copies' of these works (p. 23) needs qualification, however, since Mrs. Melville still had copies on hand later in 1892. Her letter of 16 October to H. H. Ballard of the Berkshire Athenaeum mentions the titles of several of her husband's works that she had given that library, including both of these editions; the date 'Aug. 1892' appears in the Athenaeum copy of *John Marr*.

According to Wegelin, several unspecified items went from Anderson's shop into the collections of Thomas J. McKee, Henry C. Sturges, and Daniel Parish, Jr., but only two of them have been subsequently traced: a copy of *Timoleon* and a volume of Southey's *Oliver Newman* (Check-List, No. 482), each described in the extensive McKee sale catalogue of 1900–1902 (issued by Anderson) as carrying Melville's signature. The Southey, apparently the first Melville association volume to be so catalogued by a dealer, was again offered for sale in 1931 by Newark Galleries Inc., but its current ownership is unknown. As for titles sold by Anderson to Sturges and Parish, the Parish library is not represented among collections listed in McKay's *American Book Auction Catalogues* (1937), and no books autographed by Melville were noticed by Wegelin, as he told Olson, when he catalogued the Sturges library for auction in 1922.

For the books not taken by Anderson, Thomas E. Keane of 25 Ann Street 'greatly disappointed' Mrs. Melville, in Wegelin's words, with an offer of $100. Returning later to raise his bid, Keane found that she had already sold them to A. F. Farnell of Brooklyn, who took a 'cartload' to his shop at 42 Court Street; one of the volumes now at Princeton carries Farnell's sticker. Charles Olson 'had the Farnell lead from Anderson' before Wegelin's article appeared, as he told me in a letter. (In 'A Correspondence with Charles Olson' I have surveyed our exchange of information between 1940 and 1964 concerning Melville and his library.) 'All that Wegelin did,' Olson wrote, was to 'confirm' the Farnell lead. 'It was actually out of John Anderson[']s good brain that the story came.' In a later letter he added that Anderson had suggested to him in 1934 that Wegelin, who 'had been then his runner, might add facts to the story' ('A Correspondence. . . ,' pp. 106, 148).

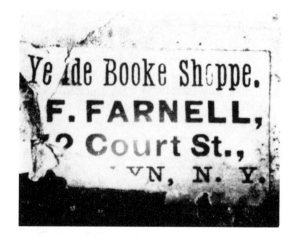

FROM FARNELL'S 'OLDE BOOKE SHOPPE'

Paper sticker from the Farnell shop in Brooklyn, placed inside the front cover of what had been Melville's copy of Macpherson's *Fingal* (Check-List, No. 343). (By permission of the Princeton University Library.)

Still further confirmation of that story came to me directly in an interview with the late Carol V. Wight at his home in Chatham, Massachusetts, on 17 January 1948. When still in his early twenties he had been a good friend of young Henry Farnell, the son of Alfred F. Farnell, had lived near the Farnell shop, and had spent much time among the books there, buying several titles on 14 April 1892 (Check-List, Nos. 95, 105, 112, 113, 369). At the time he heard that many 'theological' works acquired from Mrs. Melville were regarded as a dead loss and had been scrapped for waste paper; it was the preponderance of such works among Melville's books, he was told, that had led New York dealers to decline taking the entire lot.

Although Anderson, Keane, and A. F. Farnell are the only dealers mentioned by Wegelin in connection with Mrs. Melville's sale, the late Henry Farnell, in talking with Charles Olson in 1934, recalled that F. H. Bangs and Andrew Merwin of the New York auction house of Bangs & Co. had also evaluated the library; it may indeed have been their figure that was used by the appraisers of Melville's estate. And according to Douglas C. Parsonage, writing to me in behalf of the late Lathrop C. Harper (letter of 26 December 1947, Mrs. Melville sold still other books to the shop conducted by Mr. Harper and his elder brother, which they had opened in 1885 in the Astor House, Barclay Street, and which Melville himself had visited 'many times.' The purchase was handled by Francis Harper, and any records that may have been kept were destroyed when the two brothers later dissolved their partnership.

Olson, it should be added, was dubious concerning this account as well as Wegelin's, charging that Lathrop Harper 'had no such things to say' when the two of them talked in 1934 ('A Correspondence,' p. 106). As for the Farnell purchase, even though a sizeable portion may indeed have been scrapped, as Dr. Wight was told, the rapid and profitable movement of the books placed on sale made the whole transaction 'one of the best buys' of A. F. Farnell's career, as Wegelin remembered his telling Anderson some time later. But it was the younger Farnell, Henry, rather than his father who dealt with Mrs. Melville. The price she received, ten dollars higher than the figure of $110 mentioned by Wegelin, was recorded in Henry Farnell's diary as of 25 February 1892: 'Mr. Anderson telegraphed me to come to see a library—Went with him to Mrs. Melville 104 E. 26th st & bought the lot for $120.' Within the next two or three days, according to a further notation, books in the amount of $30 had already been resold to Michael Hennessy of Brooklyn, a writer for the New York *Times*.

Olson recorded Henry Farnell's words in 1934; long afterward he recalled that Farnell 'looked that diary up at home' rather than actually showing it to him ('A Correspondence,' pp. 133, 140). In an effort to locate the diary itself I addressed a letter of inquiry to H. A. Farnell & Co., Inc., a Brooklyn stationer. In response, its president, Louis H. Bornscheuer, who had joined 'the old firm' in 1906 and was executor of Henry Farnell's estate following his death in 1958, advised me that he had found no papers of any kind in the estate and did not recall ever seeing the diary. Farnell, he noted, had left no close relatives (letter of 31 May 1963).

Other Brooklyn buyers from the Farnell shop, as Henry Farnell reported to Olson, included James A. H. Bell, John E. Norcross, William E. Rawlins, Edward M. Smith, and Daniel M. Tredwell. Also among them was one of Melville's old teachers, Professor Charles E. West, formerly of Pittsfield and Albany, who had recently retired from the Brooklyn Heights Seminary. The libraries of three of these men, West, Hennessy, and Tredwell, were later catalogued for auction, but with no indication as to which of their books may once have been Melville's. Bell's collection of 10,425 volumes was presented to 'The Brooklyn Library'—now the Brooklyn Public Library—in 1898, three years before his death, but the accompanying manuscript catalogue, though it lists works *by* Melville that Bell had acquired, also fails to distinguish any association volumes bearing Melville's signature.

Olson, who saw one item at the Brooklyn Public Library that he believed to have been marked by Melville (an edition of Thomas Warton's *History of English Poetry*), was strongly persuaded that a sizeable number of Melville's books must have gone into the Bell Collection. But that collection long since ceased to be regarded as a separate entity by librarians on the Brooklyn staff, as I learned during several visits there (in 1941, 1947, and 1963), and my own attempts to link a number of books still on its shelves with Melville, through signature or markings, proved altogether fruitless ('A Correspondence,' pp. 96, 100, 134–137). Although I assume from what I learned at the Library that any book of Melville's which had come there as part of the Bell Collection was probably discarded years ago, it is still conceivable that something will yet turn up to justify Olson's persistent hope.

Melville in the Book Trade

Since the revival of Melville's fame in the 1920's and after, books from his library have become collector's items. By 1945, a single volume, imperfect in itself but containing Melville's extensive holograph notes, brought $2,100 when auctioned by Parke-Bernet Galleries, Inc., successor to the firm once headed by John Anderson, Jr. This was Owen Chase's *Narrative of the Most Extraordinary Shipwreck of the Whale-Ship Essex* (Check-List, No. 134), drawn upon for Melville's account in *Moby-Dick* of the destruction of the *Pequod*. Prices have continued to rise, both absolutely and in relation to books associated with other authors, during successive waves of the Melville revival. By the 1980's dealers were asking—and getting—prices in five and even six figures for such significant volumes as Melville's heavily annotated copies of Dante and Milton (Check-List, Nos. 174, 358b); books of less importance naturally bring lower prices. Even so, a present-day student cannot help remembering Melville's own need for money throughout most of his life and contrasting the low valuation of $600 put on his entire library at the time of his death. As Ishmael would say, 'Oh, Time, Strength, Cash, and Patience!'

Since Melville is recorded as buying many other books besides those that have so far been located, it seems likely that additional volumes from his library will continue to turn up in years to come, as they have done since the first publication of this study. In 1948 there was external evidence that Melville had owned at least 350 titles, of which 210 were known to have survived and 191 had been located; by 1966, 247 surviving books were known, with 219 located; the totals are now 269 titles surviving, 232 located. Of the surviving books included here in the alphabetical Check-List, I consider to be genuine all those I have seen myself, with the possible exception of the intriguing No. 223a; however, I am unable to vouch for those other books I have had no opportunity to examine—mostly titles listed at some time in various sale catalogues but now unlocated. There has been talk among book dealers and collectors that spurious items have been offered for sale as Melville association volumes; in Appendix A, 'Other Books Advertised as Melville's,' I have listed a few other titles that in my judgment do *not* warrant inclusion in the Check-List.

In Part II of this study, the known locations of those volumes I regard as authentic are indicated both in the entries by author and title within the Check-List of Books Owned and Borrowed and in the entries by location within the Analytical Index to the Check-List. Many of the most significant passages that Melville marked and annotated, though not recorded here, are quoted in Jay Leyda's *Melville Log,* which is being reprinted in a new and enlarged edition by Gordian Press. Walker Cowen's monumental transcriptions in his *Melville's Marginalia,* a 1965 Harvard doctoral dissertation that covers virtually all the books listed in the 1966 edition of *Melville's Reading,* will soon be available in book form from Garland Publishing Inc. 'The marginalia,' as Cowen has perceptively written, 'are the private journal' of Melville's discoveries as a reader, 'the documented history of [his] half-century struggle with himself and his art.'

> His acceptance and rejection and qualification of the truths others had wrung from the experience of their lives elevates these pages into something much greater than the sum of their biographical, critical, and literary parts. Each of the markings and annotations is the product of an exercise in discrimination. They are moral actions in the intellectual life of an artist who seeks, in the end, to discover himself.[4]

Notes

¹In *Melville's Sources,* a volume forthcoming from Northwestern University Press, Mary K. Bercaw lists the title of every work that has been suggested as an item used by Melville.

²The volume of Chatterton's *Poetical Works* that Melville gave Hoadley in 1854 (No. 137) is listed in the sale catalogue of Hoadley's library, but the inscription from Melville to Hoadley is not quoted; it would thus be impossible from the catalogue description alone to identify the book as one that had once been Melville's. That other books once in Melville's library were also included in the Hoadley sale seems quite likely: for example, No. 227 in the Charles F. Libbie and Co. *Catalogue of the Private Library of the Late John C. Hoadley . . . To Be Sold . . . Jan. 13 and 14, 1887* (Boston, 1887), p. 17, is the same title as No. 190 in the Check-List (unlocated), and may be the same copy.

³Writing on 1 February 1963 in response to an inquiry about books that I had previously examined at her home, Miss Agnes Morewood told me that she had since given some of the books to the Berkshire Athenaeum and sold others. 'I think [No. 100] was one I sold,' she wrote, and No. 179 was 'a question.'

⁴From Walker Cowen, *Melville's Marginalia* (1965), as extracted in 'Melville's "Discoveries": A Dialogue of the Mind with Itself,' p. 340.

I. 1819 – 1844

At Home, at School, and at Sea

A mong the books owned by Melville, kept by his widow, and later given in turn to a daughter and a granddaughter, there is a volume of extracts from Burton's *Anatomy of Melancholy* that was once part of his own father's library (Check-List, No. 103). In it is a note in Melville's hand, dated 'Pittsfield, July 7th 1851':

> I bought this book more than four years ago at Gowan[s]'s store in New York. Today, Allan [his brother, Allan Melville, Jr.] in looking at it, first detected the above pencil signature of my father's; who,—as it now appears—must have had this book, with many others, sold at auction, at least twenty five years ago.—Strange!

As we know, the senior Allan Melvill—to use the spelling he himself employed—had fallen on hard times before his death in 1832; evidently he had been obliged to sell much of his library in an effort to raise money. Since more than forty other books belonging to Melvill and his wife did not leave the family, it seems safe to assume that their total collection had been a substantial one. Certainly the Melvills fostered a love of reading in their eight children, who from their early years into maturity exchanged books among themselves and discussed their current reading in correspondence when they were separated. Reading aloud within the family circle, a practice established by Melville's

15

mother as early as the 1820's (Check-List, No. 304), was continued throughout Herman Melville's lifetime by his sisters and by his wife.

In two of Melville's works based in part on his own experience, *Redburn* (1849) and *Pierre* (1852), the youthful protagonists display a marked fondness for reading evidently nurtured within their boyhood homes. Before young Redburn went to sea, he tells us, he had read accounts of foreign countries 'in books of voyages . . . just as you read the Arabian Nights, which no one ever believes,' but once abroad he had looked in vain for the romantic persons, places, and events his reading had led him to associate with England (*Redburn*, pp. 41, 133). Redburn's father, like Allan Melvill, had been a European traveler, and Redburn specifically recalls his own fascinated interest in the large library case which during his father's lifetime had held 'long rows of old books . . . printed in Paris, and London, and Leipsic,' including a six-volume London edition of the *Spectator* and 'D'Alembert in French'; he also remembers their 'old family Plutarch' and 'an old copy of the Letters of Junius' that had belonged to his father (pp. 7, 67, 121). Of the nine 'old European and English guide-books' listed in Chapter 30 as 'among the odd volumes' in Redburn's father's library (p. 141), at least two had in fact been Allan Melvill's (Check-List, Nos. 402, 538).

Like Redburn, Pierre also had 'spent long summer afternoons in the deep recesses of his father's fastidiously picked and decorous library; where the Spenserian nymphs had early led him into many a maze of all-bewildering beauty.' Pierre specifically mentions the appearance of his father's set of the works of Plato (pp. 6, 249). However heightened these various passages may be, it seems by no means unlikely that in writing about Pierre and Redburn as youthful readers Melville was drawing upon recollections of his own boyhood, either at home in New York City or in the Albany library of his mother's brother Peter Gansevoort, as Henry A. Murray has suggested. The rather heavy-handed literary allusions in Melville's 'Fragments from a Writing Desk' (1839), contributed to a weekly newspaper shortly before his own first voyage and ten years before Melville wrote *Redburn*, are the tokens of his early familiarity with the writings of Shakespeare, Milton, Scott, Sheridan, Burke, Coleridge, Byron, and Thomas Moore; like his Redburn he also cites 'the Arabian Nights.' There is a quotation taken from a volume in the Melvill family library, Thomas Campbell's *The Pleasures of Hope* (Check-List, No. 118), but none of the other books mentioned here or in *Redburn* and *Pierre*, the two guidebooks excepted, is among the surviving volumes that once belonged to Allan and Maria Gansevoort Melvill. A list of French books charged to Allan Melvill in 1805 (see Appendix B.1) probably refers to items bought for resale in his importing business rather than for his own use.

Melville's Schooling (1824–1838)

By the time Melville wrote his 'Fragments from a Writing Desk' at the age of nineteen, he had not only completed his schooling but had also turned schoolmaster himself—at Pittsfield, Massachusetts, in 1837. William H. Gilman's pioneering study of Melville's formal education in his *Melville's Early Life and Redburn* (1951) has recently been revised and extended in articles by David K. Titus, 'Herman Melville at the Albany Academy' (1980), and John P. Runden, 'Columbia Grammar School: An Overlooked Year in the Lives of Gansevoort and Herman Melville' (1981). The findings of these three scholars deserve consideration in any account of Melville's development as a reader.

As we now know, Melville's schooling had begun in New York City when he was five years old. In December 1824 his mother drily reported that Herman 'does not appear so fond of his Book as to injure his Health,' and in 1826 his father described him as 'very backward in speech & somewhat slow in comprehension, but . . . as far as he understands men & things both solid & profound, & of a docile & amiable disposition' (*Log* 1: 20, 25). Until 1829 young Herman studied at the New-York Male High School, where like Redburn he may have 'spouted' Byron's 'Address to the Ocean' from its stage (*Redburn*, p. 122). In February 1828, when aged eight and evidently no longer 'backward in speech,' he won a prize as 'best Speaker in the introductory Department.' In that same year, according to a letter of 11 October to his maternal grandmother ('the third letter that I ever wrote'), his class was studying 'Geography, Gramar [*sic*], Arithmetic, Writing, Speaking, Spelling' as well as reading in 'the Scientific class book' (Check-List, No. 325a).

As Titus observes, the letter suggests that the boy was pursuing the standard elementary curriculum of the day. During the previous school year, when Herman was eight years old, he had been selected as a monitor. The school was then being conducted on the 'Lancastrian' plan 'whereby faculty taught student monitors, who then instructed other pupils,' but by 1831 the institution failed 'because of the difficulty of adapting the monitorial method to the higher subjects' (Titus, p. 5). Meanwhile, in 1829, both Herman and his older brother Gansevoort had been transferred to the Grammar School of Columbia College, as Runden has shown, with Gansevoort enrolling in the Classical Department on 14 May and Herman in the English Department on 28 September (p. 1). But Allan Melvill's business reverses led the family to move from New York to Albany in October 1830, and there both Gansevoort and Herman entered the Albany Academy.

Unlike the New-York Male High School, the Albany Academy was a 'classical school' that prepared students for college. It is probable that Melville himself, along with his Redburn, 'thought of going to college in time; and had vague thoughts of becoming an orator like Patrick Henry,' whose speeches Redburn 'used to speak on the stage' (*Redburn*, p. 36). From his entrance in 1830 until October 1831 Herman took the standard preparatory course in the Fourth Department, studying 'Reading and Spelling; Penmanship; Arithmetic; English Grammar; Geography; Natural History; Universal, Grecian, Roman and English History; Classical Biography; and Jewish Antiquities' (Titus, p. 6). One of his school texts survives, along with another volume he won as a prize in 1831 for 'Ciphering Books' in the standard arithmetic curriculum (Check-List, Nos. 380, 331). In 1863, when Melville was named a member of a committee to arrange for celebrating the Academy's semicentennial anniversary (see No. 81), a friend gave him a copy of another text used there during his student days (No. 390). The ubiquitous classical references in Melville's published writings, beginning with the 'Fragments' of 1839, suggest that his study of ancient history, biography, and literature during his school days left a lasting impression on both his thought and his art, as did his almost encyclopedic knowledge of both the Old and the New Testaments.[1]

For unknown reasons, young Herman left the Academy in October 1831, three months before his father's death, although his brothers Gansevoort and Allan continued in attendance there for a somewhat longer period. In 1832 he worked in Albany as a bank clerk; he then spent nearly a year with his uncle Thomas Melvill at Pittsfield. After a brief tenure at the Albany Classical School, where he wrote English compositions for Dr. Charles E. West in 1835, Herman returned to the Albany Academy for two quarters, from September 1836 until March 1837. As Titus has shown, his study of the 'Latin Language' at this time may have involved recitations in both Latin and Greek; his Redburn is aware of the Greek language's 'dual number' (*Redburn*, p. 269). Although Melville's knowledge of the classical languages must have been limited at best, his continued interest in the Latin derivation of English words is reflected in his own writing as late as the posthumous *Billy Budd, Sailor*.[2]

It is evident that neither the family library nor the school curriculum provided Melville with all his youthful reading. Along with what he was assigned in school, his Redburn remembered foggy Saturdays 'when school-boys stay at home reading Robinson Crusoe' (*Redburn*, p. 80). Melville too was obviously reading widely outside school hours. While the Melvilles were living in Albany, they had access not only to the personal library of Peter Ganesevoort but also to books drawn in his name from the Albany Library, of which he was a member.[3] Gansevoort Melville patronized the reading room of John Cook and held membership in the Albany Athenaeum; entries in a journal that he kept for the first three months of 1834 make it plain that books he borrowed were likely to be read and discussed by other members of the family as well (Check-List, Nos. 233b, 327a). On 29 January 1835 Herman Melville joined the newly formed Young Men's Association at Albany, and for two years he had access to its library of a thousand volumes. The library's records of books charged to members during this period are now lost, but both a manuscript catalogue and a printed version of 1837 still exist. Included in these compilations are works known to have influenced the 'Fragments' of 1839. The printed catalogue of 1837, in Gilman's words, 'forms the basis for Melville's first known reading list' (p. 74).[4]

At some unspecified time during Melville's youth, as he acknowledged in later years, the writings of Fenimore Cooper influenced him strongly. Although he never knew Cooper, Melville told Rufus Griswold in a letter of 19 December 1851 that 'the man, though dead, is still as living to me as ever.' Cooper's works, he wrote, were 'among the earliest I remember, as in my boyhood producing a vivid, and awakening power upon my mind.' None of Cooper's novels has turned up among his father's surviving books or his own, but Peter Gansevoort's library included a copy of *The Pioneers* (New York, 1823, in 2 vols; now in the New York Public Library), his sister Augusta had an 1826 edition of *The Last of the Mohicans*, and his brother Gansevoort was 'very well pleased' when he read *The Prarie* in 1834 (Check-List, Nos. 158.1, 158a). 'Long ago, and far inland,' Herman Melville wrote in 1850 of another of Cooper's novels, *The Red Rover*, 'we read in it our uncritical days' (No. 159).

Michael Rogin, who takes Melville's phrasing here quite literally, infers that he must have read the book not in the Albany area but during his visit 'far inland' at Galena, Illinois, in 1840. However this may be, Rogin's *Subversive Genealogy* stresses the lasting influence of what he calls Cooper's 'pirate works,' not only on Herman and his brother Gansevoort (who became a political expansionist in the 1840's) but also on young Philip Spencer, the central figure of the celebrated *Somers* mutiny of 1842 that Melville was to discuss in *White-Jacket* (1850) and to mention again in *John Marr* (1891) and *Billy Budd, Sailor* (see *Subversive Genealogy,* pp. 6 ff). Lieutenant Guert Gansevoort, a cousin of the Melvilles, had been second in command of the vessel when Spenser and two sailors were hanged as mutineers, and the Gansevoort and Melville families were naturally concerned when the *Somers* affair became a matter of public controversy. But Melville's writings never refer to Cooper's extended comments on the *Somers* case, published in 1844, and critics disagree concerning his own final judgment of the matter.

The purpose of Melville's trip to Galena in 1840 was a reunion with Major Thomas Melvill, Jr., and his family, with whom he had spent nearly a year at Pittsfield in 1833; the Melvills left Pittsfield for Illinois in 1837. Major Melvill too was interested in books; some indication of the character of his library is given by surviving booksellers' bills, which list twenty-one titles, many of them school texts, that he bought at intervals between 1814 and 1832 (see Appendix B.2); his nephew's acquaintance with any of these works has not been demonstrated, however. Another uncle, Peter Gansevoort, sent books to Melville in the fall of 1837 during his first term as a schoolmaster in the Pittsfield area (Check-List, Nos. 456a, 497), and on 31 December 1837 Melville wrote to say that he had found the books 'of eminent usefulness,' especially J. O. Taylor's *The District School*. As for American education on the common school level, the young teacher remarked that 'when reduced to practise, the high and sanguine hopes excited by its imposing appearance in *theory*—are a little dashed.'[5]

Melville did not continue teaching in 1838 but enrolled in the local academy at Lansingburgh, New York, where his mother had moved; there he studied engineering and surveying, apparently seeking to qualify himself for work on the Erie Canal. This was the last formal schooling he received. Though the position he sought never materialized, his study at the Lansingburgh academy was probably not without profit. In its library and scientific laboratories, as Gilman conjectured, Melville may well have 'laid the foundation for his mature interest in natural science' (p. 103).

The Years at Sea (1839–1844)

In June 1839, a month after publishing his 'Fragments from a Writing Desk' and with no other employment in sight, Melville signed aboard the merchant ship *St. Lawrence* with the rating of 'boy' for a cruise from New York to Liverpool. After five weeks in England, he returned with the ship on 1 October. He then resumed schoolteaching, this time at Greenbush, New York, but left his post at the end of one term when he failed to receive payment. His trip to Galena took place in the summer of 1840, and in the following December he signed for another voyage, sailing for the South Pacific aboard the whale-ship *Acushnet* early in January 1841. As Ishmael remarks in *Moby-Dick,* 'The transition is a keen one, I assure you, from a schoolmaster to a sailor' (p. 14).

'It was doubtless the stories of travel told by his father and a seafaring uncle which originally influenced Melville' to go to sea, according to Arthur Stedman, his literary executor. As for Melville's second voyage, in Stedman's words, he 'was again seized with the roving spirit, induced this time, perhaps, by the reading of Dana's "Two Years before the Mast," which appeared in 1840' ('Herman Melville,' p. 151). In *Redburn* Melville was obviously thinking of his father's seafaring brother-in-law John D'Wolf when young Redburn describes 'an uncle . . . who used to sail to a place called Archangel in Russia, and . . . was with Captain Langsdorff' (p. 35; see Check-List, Nos. 196, 197). In *Moby-Dick,* referring to Langsdorff's *Voyages,* Ishmael mentions Captain D'Wolf by name, adding, 'I have the honor of being a nephew of his' (p. 180). As for Dana's book, Melville himself wrote to its author, in a letter of 1 May 1850, of the 'strange, congenial feelings, with which after [his] first voyage, [he] for the first time read "Two Years Before the Mast." '

During this period between voyages Melville seems also to have read Jeremiah N. Reynolds's *Mocha Dick; or, The White Whale of the Pacific,* which was first published in the *Knickerbocker Magazine* for May 1839 and reprinted in 1840 (see Check-List, No. 438a). As Henry A. Murray has recently pointed out, he was to suggest through Ishmael's narrative in *Moby-Dick* that the image of a white whale had been 'influential in luring him to engage in the dangerous occupation of whaling.' When Melville ultimately came to write *Moby-Dick,* beginning in 1850, 'he evidently had the story of Mocha Dick in mind, because the name he chose for his whale was clearly derived from the earlier one' ('From Mocha to Moby,' pp. 6–7).

Neither *Redburn* nor *Moby-Dick,* as we know now, is a literal transcription of what befell Melville himself in 1839 and after, though like many of his works they convey a sense of their author's education and literary tastes as setting him off from his shipmates, for this same theme is repeated in each of the books that grew out of his observations of life among sailors and wanderers. *Typee* (1846), *Omoo* (1847), the setting of *Mardi* (1849), and the whaling background of *Moby-Dick* (1851) are all related to his life on shipboard and his sojourn in the Pacific islands; *Redburn* (1849) is based on his Liverpool voyage of 1839; *White-Jacket* (1850) is associated with his return from the Pacific in 1844 as a member of the crew of the American frigate *United States.* Stedman and earlier contemporaries of Melville, including members of his own family, read these books as largely autobiographical; twentieth-century scholars, however, have discovered how much they were heightened and extended not only by Melville's habitual literary allusions but also by his levies on earlier writers of travel narratives and accounts of whales and whaling, Dana and Reynolds included.

Melville apparently kept no journal during these years at sea, and nothing surviving from his library dates from this period. But in his own

MELVILLE'S FIRST READING OF DANA, 1840

The opening paragraph of Melville's letter of 1 May 1850 to Richard
Henry Dana, Jr. (Courtesy Massachusetts Historical Society.)

published works there are occasional passages that raise a special problem for the student of his reading. When the narrators of these works allude to books and authors, is Melville writing fact or fiction? Did he himself read what they report having read, and if so, did his own reading occur at the times and places described? Answers to these questions cannot be given without qualification. The *Acushnet* may have carried a ship's library, but the only list of books that has been located is in a manuscript log of a later voyage than Melville's;[6] in the opening chapter of *Typee,* based on his recollections of the *Acushnet,* it is said that the oppressive heat of the tropical latitudes made reading impossible: 'Take a book in your hand, and you were asleep in an instant' (p. 10).

In *Moby-Dick,* which also draws on Melville's memories of the *Acushnet,* there is only one passage that mentions reading as part of Ishmael's education at sea. This is his account of First Mate Owen Chase, one of the few survivors of the whale-ship *Essex,* which in 1820 had been rammed and sunk by an eighty-five-foot sperm whale. Ishmael states specifically that he had seen Owen Chase, had read Chase's published *Narrative* on shipboard in mid-Pacific, and had conversed with his son, 'all this within a few miles of the scene of the catastrophe' (pp. 178–179). At one time Ishmael's detailed assertion was regarded as pure fiction, intended by Melville to add detail and color to his book. Raymond Weaver, for example, suggested that he was 'using a technique learned from Defoe' (*Herman Melville,* p. 137). Later, with the recovery of Melville's own copy of Chase's *Narrative* (Check-List, No. 134), acquired in 1851 during the writing of *Moby-Dick,* it became evident that here at least Ishmael was speaking for Melville himself. According to the extensive manuscript notes bound into the volume, which have been reproduced in facsimile by both B. R. McElderry, Jr. (1963) and Thomas Farel Heffernan (1981), Melville had 'first become acquainted' with the story of the *Essex* in forecastle conversations aboard the *Acushnet.* When that ship later spoke a Nantucket whaler and the two crews met for a gam, the young man whom he erroneously described as a 'son' of Owen Chase—presumably William Henry Chase—handed him a copy of the *Narrative.* In Melville's words, reading 'this wondrous story upon the landless sea, & close to the very latitude of the shipwreck had a surprising effect upon me.' Still later, the notes continue, another speaking brought him a glimpse of a ship's captain whom he mistakenly took to be Owen Chase himself. He was, wrote Melville, 'the most prepossessing-looking whale-hunter I think I ever saw.' (As the late Wilson L. Heflin has shown in his 'Melville and Nantucket,' the ship was the *Charles Carroll* and its captain was not Chase but Thomas S. Andrews.)

On the ground that Melville's copy of Chase's *Narrative* corrobo-

he went to his chest & handed me a complete copy (same edition as this one) of the Narrative. This was the first printed account of it I had ever seen, & the only copy of Chace's narrative (regular & authentic) except the present one. The reading of this wondrous story upon the landless sea, & close to the very latitude of the shipwreck had a surprising effect upon me.

MELVILLE READS OWEN CHASE, 1841

In manuscript notes bound into his copy of Owen Chase, *Narrative of the . . . Shipwreck of the Whale-Ship Essex* (Check-List, No. 134), Melville recalls the 'surprising effect' of his first reading of the book, late in 1841, 'upon the landless sea.' (By permission of the Houghton Library, Harvard University.)

rates Ishmael's anecdote in *Moby-Dick*, it could be argued by analogy that other accounts of a similar nature in the earlier books are probably true to their author's experience. Certainly there are relevant examples in *Redburn*, as we have seen, and in *Omoo*, sequel to *Typee*, the narrator may well be speaking for Melville himself when he recalls his hunger for reading matter while he roved the South Seas and when he tells of his delight in finding a companion of kindred literary interests: a man known as Long Ghost, who 'quoted Virgil, and talked of Hobbes of Malmsbury, besides repeating poetry by the canto, especially Hudibras.' Again and again, we are told, he read through Long Ghost's Australian newspapers and battered books, 'including a learned treatise on the yellow fever,' and both men greedily devoured three volumes of Smollett's novels unexpectedly provided them by a Polynesian native (pp. 12, 36, 292–293). But as Hayford and Blair remark in their edition of *Omoo*, Long Ghost as Melville depicts him 'is remarkably like an exaggerated version of the narrator,' and as for the references to Virgil, Hobbes, Butler, and Smollett, the editors rightly observe that Melville 'often put into the manuscripts he was working on some sort of predated references to books that were currently interesting him' (pp. xxxv, 434).

More objective evidence of books known to be available to Melville in the early 1840's will be presented when Wilson Heflin's long-awaited book on Melville's whaling years is posthumously published. Using papers discovered by Edouard Stackpole, Professor Heflin reported in 1974, in his 'New Light on Herman Melville's Cruise in the *Charles and Henry*,' on the small library carried to the Pacific by the third whaleship on which Melville served; he was aboard this ship (the *Leviathan* of *Omoo*) for approximately six months, between November 1842 and May 1843, before beginning his homeward voyage on the *United States*. The library, bought by the ship's owners, Charles G. and Henry Coffin, before her sailing from Nantucket,

> consisted of thirty-seven books and two magazines (presumably bound volumes of several issues). The choice of these books—many of them juvenile, didactic, and sentimental in character,—seems to indicate in the Coffin owners, or their stationer, a shrewd assessment of the levels of literacy and taste among whalemen, plus a concerned effort to provide moral suasion. Dominant symbols in these volumes are home, fireside, country, and church. But this small library was intended to entertain, too. Much of it was popular fiction, including nautical yarns, romances, and adventure stories. There were also works of history (even one on banking) and biography. A good number of these volumes were published in the year of the ship's sailing. (p.11)

From the bill submitted to the Coffins by Andrew Macy, their stationer, Professor Heflin identified the individual titles (see Appendix C). In his words, 'These volumes must have proved most welcome' to 'this uncommonly literate and bookish young whaleman,' and the ship's library 'should certainly be taken into account among his early formative influences' (pp. 15–16).

THE SHIP'S LIBRARY OF THE *CHARLES AND HENRY*

Books available to Melville between November 1842 and May 1843; from the bill submitted to the ship's owners before its sailing from Nantucket. (Photo by Studio 13; reproduced by permission of Edouard A. Stackpole and the Nantucket Historical Association.)

Professor Heflin also discovered new evidence concerning the libraries aboard the frigate *United States,* on which Melville served between August 1843 and October 1844; his findings go well beyond the information previously published in 1939 by Charles L. Anderson in *Melville in the South Seas.* During Melville's tour of duty the *United States,* in addition to her regular officers' library, carried books for the use of enlisted men, selected in accordance with a 'List of Books to be allowed for the Libraries of seamen on board vessels of the Navy' proposed by the Board of Navy Commissioners on 31 May 1841. From this list the purser at the Norfolk Navy Yard, who saw to the provisioning of the frigate before her sailing, sent aboard the *United States* a seamen's library of more than a hundred volumes, including *Two Years Before the Mast, Robinson Crusoe,* 'Various narrations of imprisonment, shipwreck, perils and captivity,' 'Selections from [Harper's] Family Library' (117 volumes), and nine bound volumes of the *Penny Magazine.*[7]

What use Melville may have made of these books in 1843 and 1844 is difficult to say, since his treatment of books and reading in *White-Jacket,* the work based partly on his cruise in the *United States,* has little to do with any of these titles other than the *Penny Magazine.* He turned to the magazine again in 1849 as a useful source both for *White-Jacket* and for its immediate predecessor, *Redburn.* The records of Melville's reading during the later 1840's, after his career as an author had begun, are far more objective and complete than those from his earlier years at home, at school, and at sea.

Notes

[1]See Gerard M. Sweeney, *Melville's Use of Classical Mythology* (1975); Gail H. Coffler, *Melville's Classical Allusions* (1985); Nathalia Wright, 'Biblical Allusion in Melville's Prose' (1940) and *Melville's Use of the Bible* (1969).

[2]For examples, see three of the editorial notes in the 1962 Chicago edition: on 'sinister dexterity' (p. 139), 'prior to Cain's city and citified man' (p. 143), and 'the reactionary bite of that serpent' (p. 165).

[3]'Peter Gansevoort's borrowings for 1831 to 1836,' according to Gilman (p. 315, n. 134), are 'listed by shelf number in the "Loan Book of the Albany Library, Vol. II" (New York State Library, Albany). . . . In some months the number of books withdrawn (54 in one instance) suggests that he shared his privilege as a borrower, and it is very likely that Gansevoort and Herman took advantage of it.'

[4]'A manuscript catalogue of the library exists in the collection of the association's records,' Gilman adds (p. 316, n. 145), 'from which was printed a *Catalogue of Books in the Library of the Young Men's Association of the City of Albany* (Albany, 1837). Although this was not published until after Melville's membership had ceased, all the books listed were in the library by February 15, 1837, while Melville was still a member.'

[5]Melville's language here, as Jeanne C. Howes has pointed out ('Melville's Sensitive Years,' pp. 28–29), 'seems to echo' the resolutions of a convention held at Lenox, Massachusetts, on 13 September 1837 to discuss the state of the schools of Berkshire County; its actions were reported in the Pittsfield *Sun* of 21 September. Among those probably in attendance were Thomas Melvill, Jr., a member of the local school committee, 'whose interest and influence in common school education surely played a role in Herman's choice of a teaching career,' and Chief Justice Lemuel Shaw, Melville's future father-in-law; Melville himself may have been there as well. J. Orville Taylor, whose book Melville found useful in his teaching, was an Albany educator.

[6]The only list of books which has been located occurs in a manuscript journal kept by Ansell Weeks, Jr., entitled 'A Schedule of the Doings on Board Ship Acushnet July 18 1845' (Harvard College Library). The late Professor Wilson L. Heflin advised me in letters of 14 February and 4 April 1949 that of the titles in Weeks's journal a number were not published 'until after the ship was well into her second voyage,' in the words of his draft note concerning the journal, 'and at least two of them were not in print until a year or more after the termination of that voyage in January, 1848.' He concluded that pages of the journal 'provided space for the catalogue of a library, but hardly that of the whaler *Acushnet*.'

[7]Professor Heflin, in a letter of 9 December 1974 enclosing his annotated reproduction of the 1841 'List of Books,' told me that in discussing the books aboard the *United States* he also proposed to 'include the wardroom library (for officers) which could have been available to HM.' A full account of his findings about books available to Melville during his years at sea will be a part of his forthcoming book on Melville's whaling years.

2.   1844–1849

Typee, Omoo, and Mardi

*A*lthough Melville may once have regarded his years at sea as the formative period of his life, that was not his opinion by the time he came to write *Moby-Dick*. 'Until I was twenty-five,' he told Nathaniel Hawthorne in a much-quoted letter of 1? June 1851, 'I had no development at all. From my twenty-fifth year I date my life. Three weeks have scarcely passed between then and now, that I have not unfolded within myself.' By his own reckoning, then, his 'unfolding' had begun in 1844, when he was twenty-five. Having returned from nearly four years in the Pacific, he began writing his first book, *Typee* (1846), in which he looked back upon one segment of his life there and began to appraise the meaning of his experience.

Typee and Omoo

As a 'narrative of a four months' residence among the natives of a valley of the Marquesas Islands,' in the phrasing of its first English edition, *Typee* included 'incidents' which its author, according to his Preface, had often 'spun as a yarn' while still at sea (p. xiii). Again in *Omoo* (1847), the sequel written to capitalize on the success of *Typee*, Melville acknowledged his use of materials that he had 'verbally related' with some frequency, thus stamping them upon his memory (p. xiv). In each book he professed to be merely describing what he had seen in the

29

Pacific islands, disclaiming in *Omoo* any 'philosophic research' (p. xv) that might have explained the origin and purpose of the exotic native customs he had observed. The chronology of both narratives was less than exact, he acknowledged, because he had not kept a journal of his adventures in Polynesia. But as we now know, Melville was being disingenuous in comments such as these. In *Typee* he stretched the duration of his stay from a bare four weeks into the 'four months' claimed for his residence in the Typee valley, and for both books he engaged in considerable research, 'philosophic' or otherwise, to supplement his own recollections with borrowings from the writings of other men.

Although the resultant mingling of what he had read with what he had actually seen for himself is typical of Melville's subsequent writing, the extent of his departures from what he called 'the unvarnished truth' (*Typee*, p. xiv) was not realized until twentieth-century scholars began to explore both the events of his life and the records of his reading. In his own day, though a few doubters among the first English reviewers would not believe that such accomplished narratives could have been written by a common sailor, even members of his own family regarded them as straightforward autobiography, and this view of the books came to prevail during Melville's lifetime. Twentieth-century researchers, notably Charles R. Anderson in his *Melville in the South Seas* (1939), have shown, however, that the two works are neither unadorned fact nor out-and-out fiction but an imaginative combination of personal observation and literary borrowing. In the words of Leon Howard, reviewing the evidence in his Historical Note to the Northwestern-Newberry edition of *Typee* (1968), 'Melville drew his material from his experiences, from his imagination, and from a variety of travel books when the memory of his experiences failed him or when his personal observations were inadequate' (p. 291).

Both *Typee* and *Omoo* are indebted to books about the Pacific and its islands, ranging from older reports of the first voyagers into the South Seas—collected in *An Historical Account of the Circumnavigation of the Globe, and of the Progress of Discovery in the Pacific Ocean, from the Voyage of Magellan to the Death of Cook* (1836)—to William Ellis's *Polynesian Researches* (1833). For *Typee* he also depended on *A Visit to the South Seas* by the Rev. Charles Stewart (1831), 'which he probably had at hand from the beginning of his work,' as Howard remarked (p. 291), Capt. David Porter's *Journal of a Cruise . . . in the U.S. Frigate Essex* (1815), and Georg H. Von Langsdorff's *Voyages and Travels* (1813), which he would later quote in Chapter 45 of *Moby-Dick*. Melville's copies of these five works have apparently not survived, but though there is no specific external record of his buying or borrowing any of them it is clear from internal evidence that he had access to all five before he finished *Typee*.

For *Omoo* Melville once again took material from the *Circumnavigation*, from Stewart and Langsdorff, and especially from Ellis, whose *Polynesian Researches* became his principal source. He drew also on the Right Rev. Michael Russell's *Polynesia* (1843) and the six-volume *Narrative of the United States Exploring Expedition* (1845), a set which he later bought for himself (Check-List, No. 532). Although Melville's Preface acknowledges his use of *Polynesian Researches*, he seriously understates his actual debt, especially in the later pages of the book where he needed additional material to fill out his own limited experience and observation. In the words of Harrison Hayford, Ellis served him as 'historian, geographer, botanist, anthropologist, dictionary of native words common and proper, and even his eyes and ears' (Editors' Introduction to *Omoo*, 1969, p. xxv). Where Melville parted company with Ellis, however, was in the interpretation each writer gave of persons, places, and events. The most notable example of this difference concerned the missionary movement, which Ellis praised and Melville attacked, as he had previously done in *Typee*, with resulting cost to his standing among evangelical readers.

As Walter Blair has remarked, the very style of *Omoo* offers support for the narrator's 'implied claims about his background and learning.' The book is full of 'moderately learned allusions,' literary references 'to Butler, Smollett, Milton, Virgil, Pope, and Hobbes,' 'echoes of at least six plays of Shakespeare,' and 'dozens' of biblical 'quotations, paraphrases, or allusions'—all 'prophetic of the ornate and highly allusive style of *Mardi*' (Editors' Introduction to *Omoo*, 1969, p. xxxix). Given his background in a reading family and his own love of books from his boyhood onward, such lines of continuity between *Omoo* and his third book, *Mardi* (1849), are less surprising to the modern student than to his own contemporaries, who for the most part regarded the new work as a regrettable departure from his true vein.

Melville wrote most of *Typee* and *Omoo* in 1845 and 1846 during his residence with his mother and sisters at Lansingburgh. Family correspondence from these years frequently mentions the Melvilles' current reading, which included Dickens' *Dombey and Son* as reprinted in an Albany newspaper (Check-List, No. 180a) and such British publications as the *Times, Spectator,* and *Punch,* the *London Illustrated News,* and *Chambers's Edinburgh Journal,* sent to them by Gansevoort Melville, then Secretary of the American legation in London. Five books acquired by Melville's sisters during the Lansingburgh years have survived: Charlotte Brontë's *Jane Eyre,* Longfellow's *Voices of the*

Night, and novels by Elizabeth Grey and Julia Pardoe (Check-List, Nos. 87.1, 332a, 234.1 and 234.2, 396b).

In the winter of 1847 Herman Melville sought unsuccessfully to obtain a government office—evidently in anticipation of his marriage later in that year to Elizabeth Knapp Shaw of Boston; Elizabeth's father, Chief Justice Lemuel Shaw of the Supreme Judicial Court of Massachusetts, was an old family friend. On Melville's return from a visit to New York in the spring of 1847, as his mother reported, he brought additional reading matter: 'a great box & two trunks . . . filled with books' whose contents were established in a 'small front room' that he would use as 'a Library and Study' in which 'to begin a new work, on the "South Seas"—of course' (letter to Melville's sister Augusta, 19 May [NYPL–GL]).

Mardi

Some of the books that Melville had acquired in New York afford clues to his original intentions as he began a third book 'on the "South Seas" ' in the early months of 1847. Among his twelve known purchases in April and May, besides a dictionary and the *Narrative of the United States Exploring Expedition* (already used in *Omoo*), were four other books of voyages, as though he was planning another work like *Typee* and *Omoo* (Check-List, Nos. 550 and 532; 293, 372, 422, 530a). A fifth was Charles Darwin's journal of his cruise aboard the *Beagle* (No. 175), which Melville was to draw upon in 1854 for Sketches First and Fourth of 'The Encantadas.' Another group of unidentified purchases, among them three unnamed volumes of Harper's Family Library (Nos. 74, 75, 211), may also have dealt with Pacific travel, though there are of course other possibilities. The two remaining books, both of which have survived, are *The Vicar of Wakefield* and the second-hand copy of Burton that turned out to be a volume from his own father's library (Nos. 232, 103).

Nine of these twelve books are known only through entries in Melville's statements of account with his American publishers, Wiley and Putnam (succeeded by John Wiley) and Harper and Brothers. Melville and his lawyer brother Allan, his business agent in New York, received a professional discount on books bought from these firms; their purchases are recorded by date and usually by title in the statements rendered at intervals by each publisher. In some instances it is not certain whether individual titles were intended for Herman Melville, for Allan, or as gifts to relatives or friends. Since Allan's purchases were readily accessible to Herman as well, like those books belonging to other family members when all were part of a common household, such volumes are included in the alphabetical Check-List in Part II of this study. So too are books owned by Gansevoort Melville before his death in London on

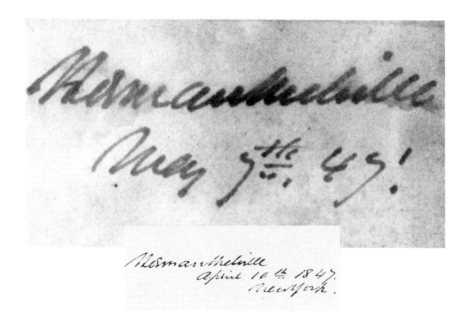

ADDITIONS TO MELVILLE'S LIBRARY, 1847

Melville's signature in ink in two of the volumes sent from New York to
Lansingsburgh in May 1847: Turnbull's *A Voyage Round the World* and
Goldsmith's *The Vicar of Wakefield* (Check-List, Nos. 530a, 232). (By
permission of the Stephen B. Luce Library, Maritime College, State
University of New York, and the Berkshire Athenaeum.)

12 May 1846; some of them are unmarked but others were subsequently
inscribed and annotated by Herman Melville and by other members of
the family.

The nature of most of the books that Melville is known to have acquired early in 1847 suggests that at the outset he intended his 'new
work' to be another narrative of Pacific adventure, however roman-
ticized in the telling, but both the scope of his reading and the character

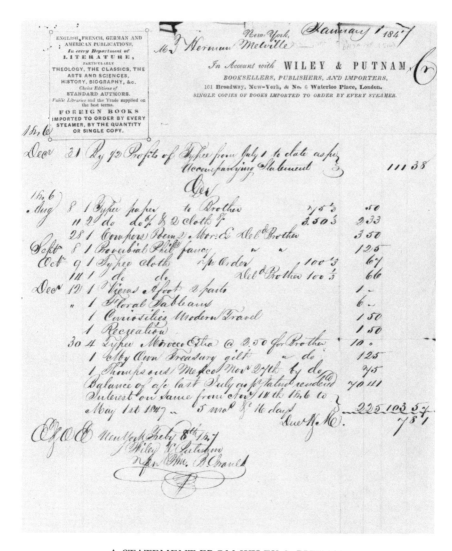

A STATEMENT FROM WILEY & PUTNAM

Statement of Melville's account with Wiley & Putnam, New York, 1
January 1847, showing charges for books. (By permission of the
Houghton Library, Harvard University.)

A STATEMENT FROM HARPER & BROTHERS

Statement of Melville's account with Harper & Brothers, New York, 31 July 1847, showing charges for books. (By permission of the Houghton Library, Harvard University.)

of the manuscript that became *Mardi* (1849) began to change markedly
after his removal to New York from Lansingburgh following his marriage in August 1847. He and his new wife set up housekeeping at 103
Fourth Avenue with the Allan Melvilles, also recently married. The
joint household, which included the four Melville sisters, their mother,
and their younger brother Thomas plus four domestics, totaled fifteen
residents by 1850, when Melville took his family, his mother and sisters
included, to Pittsfield (John M. J. Gretchko, 'Remnants of the U.S.
Census, 1850–1880').

The Melvilles led an active social life in New York that included
visits with friends and attendance at the theater and opera house, but
Herman himself reserved time each day for both reading and writing. A
letter of 23 December 1847 from his wife to her stepmother in Boston
outlines a typical day's program:

> We breakfast at 8 o'clock, then Herman goes to walk, and I fly up to put
> his room to rights, so that he can sit down to his desk immediately on his
> return. Then I bid him good bye, with many charges to be an industrious
> boy, and not upset the inkstand, and then flourish the duster, make the
> bed, &c in my own room [until] ding-ding goes the bell for luncheon. This
> is half past 12 o'clock—by this time we must expect callers, and so must
> be dressed immediately after lunch. Then Herman insists upon my taking a
> walk every day of an hours length at least. . . . At four we dine, and after
> dinner is over, Herman and I come up to our room, and enjoy a cosy chat
> for an hour or so—or he reads me some of the chapters he has been writ-
> ing in the day. Then he goes down town for a walk, looks at the papers in
> the reading-room &c, and returns about half past seven or eight. Then my
> work or my book is laid aside, and as he does not use his eyes but very
> little by candle light, I either read to him, or take a hand at whist for his
> amusement, or he listens to our reading or conversation, as best pleases
> him. For we all collect in the parlor in the evening, and generally one of us
> reads [a]loud for the benefit of the whole. Then we retire very early—at 10
> o'clock we are all dispersed—indeed we think that quite a late hour to be
> up. (*Log* 1: 266–267)

As the author of two successful books, Melville was soon moving
in New York literary circles, becoming one of the group of writers—the
'Knights of the Round Table'—who frequently gathered at 20 Clinton
Place, the home of Evert Duyckinck; as editor of Wiley & Putnam's Li-
brary of Choice Reading, Duyckinck had handled the details of the first
American edition of *Typee*. Early in 1847 Melville had already begun to
write occasional reviews for Duyckinck's new weekly journal, the
Literary World, and later in the year he contributed humorous articles
to the short-lived *Yankee Doodle* when Duyckinck's friend Cornelius
Mathews became its editor. Between 1847 and 1850 Melville presumably

MELVILLE'S FIRST BORROWINGS FROM EVERT DUYCKINCK

Leaf 12 of Evert Duyckinck's manuscript notebook 'Books Lent,'
showing the first volumes charged to Melville, probably in January or
February 1848: v. 2 of the *Works* of Rabelais and the *Narrative* of Captain
Charles H. Barnard. (Duyckinck Family Papers, Rare Books and
Manuscripts Division, The New York Public Library, Astor, Lenox and
Tilden Foundations. By permission.)

acquired reviewer's copies of six of the books he was asked to deal with for the *Literary World:* J. Ross Browne's *Etchings of a Whaling Cruise* and John Codman's *Sailors' Life and Sailors' Yarns* in 1847; Joseph C. Hart's *The Romance of Yachting* in 1848; Francis Parkman's *The California and Oregon Trail* and Fenimore Cooper's *The Sea Lions* in 1849; Cooper's *The Red Rover* in 1850 (Check-List, Nos. 88 and 149; 242; 397 and 160; 159).

Duyckinck himself had accumulated a notable private library that he made available to his intimates, Melville included, recording their borrowings in his memoranda of 'Books Lent'; over the years he listed twenty-nine widely varied titles charged to Melville, exclusive of whatever additional books and magazines the young author may have dipped into without actually withdrawing them.[1] During the year 1848, while *Mardi* was in progress, Melville borrowed three volumes of Rabelais, the *Narrative of the Sufferings and Adventures of Captain Charles H. Barnard,* the works of Sir Thomas Browne, a translation of Frithiof's Saga, and Anne Marsh-Caldwell's novel *Angela* (Check-List, Nos. 417, 38, 89, 500, 349). The influence of Duyckinck and his circle on what Melville himself called his unfolding can scarcely be overestimated. His use of Duyckinck's library, first explored by pioneering scholars such as Luther S. Mansfield, Willard Thorp, Perry Miller, and Merrell R. Davis, was especially important in his development.

As Melville gravitated to men who shared his interest in books and reading, so too did he find his way to the city's institutional libraries and bookstores. In January 1848, through Duyckinck's agency, he became a shareholder in the New York Society Library, which he had perhaps begun to use even earlier on payment of the fee asked of nonmembers.[2] As his wife reported, it was his daily habit to visit an unnamed 'reading room' for a look at 'the papers.' At that period the New York Society Library, then located on Broadway between Leonard Street and Catherine Lane, maintained two reading rooms, one reserved for newspapers and periodicals, the other a book room described as separated from the open-shelf room by two 'studies for those authors who desire to pursue their investigations with their authorities around them, or who wish to make new books on old Burton's recipe, "as apothecaries make new mixtures, by pouring out of one vessel into another." '[3]

By this time in his career Melville was thoroughly familiar with both 'old Burton' and his recipe, as we know from his authorial procedure in *Omoo.* The joint household on Fourth Avenue being a crowded one, the New York Society Library rooms may well have provided the young author with a welcome retreat as work on *Mardi* continued. While he held membership in 1848 he withdrew only two titles:

Bougaineville's *Voyage round the World* and Hartley's *Observations on Man* (Check-List, Nos. 85, 243), but here again, as with Duyckinck's books, he probably made far more extensive use of the library's facilities during his visits there than its record of withdrawals would indicate.

As Merrell Davis has shown in his detailed study of the composition of *Mardi,* the new work began to take on other dimensions early in 1848 as the scope of Melville's reading and writing reciprocally broadened beyond what he thought of as 'narratives of voyages'—that is, books like Bougaineville's or his own *Typee* and *Omoo.* For *Mardi*'s early chapters he continued to draw background material from Ellis's *Polynesian Researches* and other books of travel and adventure such as Frederick Debell Bennett's *Narrative of a Whaling Voyage,* which he probably owned; it was to serve him as a major source for *Moby-Dick.* The later chapters, however, clearly reflect his reading in general literature, which was now ranging from history and philosophy to poetry and drama. His surviving copies of Dante, Macpherson's *Fingal,* and Seneca's *Morals* (Check-List, Nos. 174, 343, 458), which date from this time, contributed in specific ways to the growing complexity of *Mardi;* Seneca, for example, is the 'antique Pagan' quoted in Chapter 124.

Among the varied titles that Melville bought from his publishers in late 1847 and 1848 are editions of Shakespeare (probably the poems), Cooke's *Froissart Ballads,* and writings of Montaigne, Defoe, Coleridge, Burton, Dante, and Thackeray (Check-List, Nos. 460a, 464, 158, 366, 177, 154, 102, 174, 512); the minds of Montaigne and Burton, like that of Sir Thomas Browne, he found to be especially congenial. The widening scope of his reading did not escape the attention of his friends. In 1847 Evert Duyckinck had thought of Melville in relation to other contemporary authors: parts of *Omoo* struck him as 'very much in the spirit of Dickens humorous handling of sacred things in Italy,' and later in that year he observed that Melville 'models his writing evidently a great deal on Washington Irving' (*Log* 1: 230, 253). But early in 1848 Duyckinck took note of a new development. 'By the way Melville reads old Books,' Duyckinck reported in a letter to his brother George on 18 March 1848. 'He has borrowed Sir Thomas Browne of me and says finely of the speculations of the *Religio Medici* that Browne is a kind of "crack'd Archangel" '—adding with apparent surprise, 'Was ever any thing of this sort said before by a sailor?' (*Log* 1: 273).

What Melville absorbed from *Religio Medici* is evident enough in *Mardi,* which echoes Browne, as Matthiessen recognized, 'to the length of ventriloquism' (*American Renaissance,* p. 123).[4] Browne led him in turn to the dialogues of Plato,[5] which became a major influence on the form and content of the middle chapters of the book, where the narrator and his Mardian companions engage in quasi-philosophical conversations that fill up chapter after chapter. Of the several speakers, each a voice for Melville's own literary interests at the time, Babbalanja the bedeviled philosopher, a kind of Mardian Socrates, is the most prominent; the others are Yoomy the poet and Mohi the chronicler or historian. Presiding is King Media, who as moderator must occasionally intervene to curb the excesses of his three talkative subjects, Babbalanja in particular.

Melville probably read Plato within the New York Society Library, which owned both the five-volume Taylor-Sydenham translation (1804) and also Taylor's version of *Six Books of Proclus on the Theology of Plato* (1816), a work that is parodied in chapters of *Mardi* satirizing obscure philosophical terminology (Sealts, 'Melville and the Platonic Tradition' and 'Melville's "Neoplatonical Originals" '). Neither Melville nor his characters deny *Mardi*'s literary indebtedness. 'Every thought's a soul of some past poet, hero, sage,' says Babbalanja (*Mardi,* p. 594), and the narrator, Taji, agrees:

> I am full with a thousand souls, . . . sometimes speaking one at a time, then all with one voice. . . . I list to St. Paul who argues the doubts of Montaigne; Julian the Apostate cross-questions Augustine; . . . Zeno murmurs maxims beneath the hoarse shout of Democritus; and though Democritus laugh loud and long, and the sneer of Pyrrho be seen; yet, divine Plato, and Proclus, and Verulam are of my counsel; and Zoroaster whispered me before I was born. (pp. 367–368)

Like the Mardian poet Lombardo, discussed in a late chapter that serves as a kind of apologia for *Mardi* itself, when Melville himself had 'set about' his third book 'he knew not what it would become.' Given the stimuli afforded by his residence in New York and the immediate effect of his voluminous reading in 1847 and 1848, he too 'did not build himself in with plans; he wrote right on; and so doing, got deeper and deeper into himself' (*Mardi,* p. 595). So Melville's own 'chartless voyage' had moved from his opening chapters of physical action to exploration of what Taji calls 'the world of mind' (pp. 556–557), modulating from narrative prose into poetry and allegory and mingling discussions of science with the philosophical dialogue. With respect to Melville's scientific knowledge, Tyrus Hillway observes that 'except for a smattering of elementary instruction in school,' most of his information 'came from his extensive personal reading'—chiefly in books and periodicals intended primarily for lay readers rather than for specialists. Even in fields where he read extensively when searching for source material, Hillway remarks, that reading was 'haphazard rather than systematic or thorough' ('Melville's Education in Science,' p. 411).[6]

In what Davis distinguished as still a third phase in the composition of *Mardi,* Melville paid more and more attention to the contemporary world of events, from the political upheavals of 1848 in Europe to the California gold rush; Michael Rogin's *Subversive Genealogy* has recently given new emphasis to the political implications of *Mardi* and its immediate successors, *Redburn* (1849) and *White-Jacket* (1850). Within *Mardi,* the major shifts in focus, as Melville himself realized, worked against the book's unity; like Lombardo's Koztanza, it 'lacks cohesion; it is wild, unconnected, all episode' (p. 597). But *Mardi* is nevertheless 'a rich book,' as Hawthorne was to say of it to Duyckinck, 'with depths here and there that compel a man to swim for his life'—'so good that one scarcely pardons the writer for not having brooded long over it, so as to make it a great deal better' (letter of 29 August 1850).

Hawthorne was kinder to *Mardi* than its published critics, British and American, who with few exceptions wrote it off as an out-and-out failure and called on Melville to abjure philosophizing in the future and provide them with more books like *Typee* and *Omoo.* Though Melville himself came to acknowledge the shortcomings of *Mardi,* he knew well enough that he had grown through writing it. 'Had I not written & published "Mardi," in all likelihood, I would not be as wise as I am now, or may be,' he remarked to Duyckinck (letter of 14 December 1849). If a choice were given him, moreover, he would rather produce more books like *Mardi* 'which are said to "fail" ' than go down to posterity as the author of *Typee*: the ' "man who lived among the cannibals" ' (letters to Lemuel Shaw, 6 October 1849, and Nathaniel Hawthorne, 1? June 1851).

To judge from Book XXI of *Pierre,* where Melville seems to be looking back over his own earlier writing, he identified his principal error in *Mardi* as too great a dependence on 'mere reading,' which he called more of an obstacle to an aspiring author than an accelerator; the one example cited of such an obstacle in the case of Pierre is Plato, a major influence on *Mardi*: 'Though Plato was indeed a transcendentally great man in himself, yet Plato must not be transcendentally great to him . . . so long as he . . . would also do something transcendentally great.' While composing *Mardi,* however, Melville was like the young Pierre in that he still

> did not see,—or if he did, he could not yet name the true cause for it,— that already, in the incipiency of his work, the heavy unmalleable element of mere book-knowledge would not congenially weld with the wide fluidness and ethereal airiness of spontaneous creative thought.

In short, he too had sought to 'climb Parnassus with a pile of folios on his back' (*Pierre,* pp. 283–284), and as a result his *Mardi* became

likewise overburdened with the heavy weight of unmalleable bookishness.

Notes

[1]Melville's use of Duyckinck's library was first studied by Luther S. Mansfield in his 'Herman Melville: Author and New Yorker, 1844–1851' (Ph.D. dissertation, University of Chicago, 1936). Chapter VII, 'Some Aspects of Melville's Reading,' was privately issued in 1938. The entries in Duyckinck's
'Books Lent' pertaining to Melville are transcribed and printed in Willard
Thorp, *Herman Melville* (1938), pp. xxvii–xxviii, n. Merrell R. Davis, *Melville's
Mardi* (1952), pp. 63–64, n. 9, gives more precise dates for some of these entries
by investigating Duyckinck's lendings generally.

In the alphabetical Check-List, Part II below, each of the entries based on
'Books Lent' has been expanded from Duyckinck's original notation with reference to Davis's findings, and the available edition of each title listed has been
identified where possible by consulting the various catalogues of Duyckinck's
library. These include *Lenox Library Short-Title Lists*, Nos. VIII and XII, prepared when the Duyckinck Collection was accessioned by the Lenox Library
beginning in 1878, and several manuscript lists compiled by Duyckinck himself
(NYPL–D): 'Catalogue of the Books of Evert A. Duyckinck' (1838), 'List of
Books' (undated), 'Catalogue of Books' (1856), and 'Books Lent.'

Duyckinck's own lists and his inscriptions in surviving books (NYPL–D)
show that when Melville began using his library in the 1840's it was not as large
as some Melville scholarship has implied. When given to the Lenox Library
after Duyckinck's death it contained 15,164 books and 1,596 pamphlets (H. M.
Lydenberg, *History of the New York Public Library*, pp. 101–102).

[2]Certificates on file at the library show that Melville held membership during the periods 17 January–11 September 1848 and 17 April–7 October 1850. *The
Alphabetical and Analytical Catalogue of the New York Society Library* (New
York, 1850) should be consulted as an indication of the books available to Melville for additional reading within the library building; editions of the four books
listed have been determined from this catalogue. For books charged to Allan
Melville, also a member at this period, see Check-List, Nos. 120a, 143.1, 352a.

[3]Quoted from the *New Yorker*, 28 November 1840, in A. B. Keep, *History
of the New York Society Library*, pp. 400–401.

[4]Brian Foley, 'Herman Melville and the Example of Sir Thomas Browne,'
illustrates those 'distinctive attributes' of Browne's prose style that Melville
adapted in both *Mardi* and *Moby-Dick*.

[5]As long ago as 1932 Cesar Pavese observed that 'the current at which
Melville drank most deeply, which lies at the roots of all seventeenth century
thought, was Platonizing rationalism, especially the rationalism of the English
essayists. Naturally, as with the Bible, he read Plato, and, I imagine, the Neo-
platonists and the mystics, from beginning to end. But the historical guise in
which these tendencies appeared to him was undoubtedly that of the English

seventeeth century. Thomas Browne was not only his teacher of style, but his spiritual father' ('The Literary Whaler (1932),' pp. 411–412).

⁶On the specific subject of geology, see the exchange between Tyrus Hillway and Elizabeth Foster in her 'Melville and Geology' (1945), his 'Melville's Geological Knowledge' (1949), her 'Another Note on Melville and Geology' (1951), and his 'Melville's Education in Science' (1974).

3. 1849

Redburn and *White-Jacket*

'Somehow, the books that prove most agreeable, grateful, and companionable, are those we pick up by chance here and there; those which seem put into our hands by Providence; those which pretend to little, but abound in much' (*White-Jacket*, p. 169). So Melville wrote in 1849, a pivotal year in his development, when he made key additions to his own library.

It was in just this spirit that Melville had begun browsing during the mid-forties in the bookshops and auction sales of New York. There, he recalled, he had once 'glanced at' a book by Emerson 'in Putnam's store,' as he told Duyckinck in 1849 (letter of 3 March), and had happened to buy what proved to be his father's copy of Robert Burton (Check-List, No. 103). The Burton he bought from William Gowans, who was both a bookseller and a publisher; in March 1849 he probably acquired Gowans's new edition of Plato's *Phaedon* in the Dacier translation—hence the French spelling of the title (Sealts, 'Melville and the Platonic Tradition,' pp. 297–298 and n. 30, p. 390). It may have been at this same time in 1849 that he also bought his two-volume set of Milton (inscribed 'N. Y. 1849') and the *Poetical Works* (inscription lacking) of 'the gentle and sequestered Wordsworth,' as he is called in *White-Jacket* (Check-List, Nos. 358b, 563a; *White-Jacket*, p. 40).

In the early months of 1849 Melville was in Boston with his wife to await the birth of their first child in February and the subsequent reception of *Mardi*; he made a brief trip to New York in March and returned there in April to write *Redburn* and *White-Jacket* in the late spring and summer. While in Boston Melville of course had access to the private library of his father-in-law, Lemuel Shaw, which was by no means limited to legal subjects (see Appendix C.3). Judge Shaw subscribed to such journals as the *North American Review* (to which he contributed), the *Christian Register,* the *Edinburgh Review,* and the *Quarterly Review*. He was also a frequent borrower—perhaps on Melville's behalf—from the shelves of the Boston Athenaeum, though there is no record of his having taken Melville there as a guest. Titles charged to Shaw at the Athenaeum during the several known periods of his son-in-law's visits to Boston have therefore been included in the alphabetical Check-List in Part II below.[1]

As we know from Melville's letters to Duyckinck, the extended stay in Boston with no new work as yet under his hand gave him an opportunity to read, to attend lectures and the theater, and of course to buy more books. After hearing Emerson lecture and finding him to be indeed 'a great man'—contrary to what New Yorkers were currently saying (letter of 24 February), he was moved to begin reading Emerson's essays in some depth (Sealts, 'Melville and Emerson's Rainbow,' p. 263 ff). 'Chancing to fall in' at a Boston dealer's with a seven-volume edition of Shakespeare 'in glorious great type' suited to his weak eyes (Check-List, No. 460), he was thereby enabled for what he called the first time to begin a really 'close acquaintance with the divine William.' He also reported another importance purchase, a four-volume set of Pierre Bayle's *Historical and Critical Dictionary* (No. 51), which he planned to 'sleep on . . . thro' the summer, with the Phaedon in one hand & Tom Brown[e] in the other' (letters of 24 February, 5 April 1849).

Most of the titles that Melville bought from Harper and Brothers during 1849 were probably intended as gifts: three sets of Macaulay's *History of England,* two copies of the Episcopal *Book of Common Prayer,* and a surviving volume that he inscribed to his sister Augusta, Cobb's *Miniature Lexicon* (Check-List, Nos. 335–337, 409, 148). But in March he made a significant purchase for himself: a set of Harper's Classical Library in thirty-seven volumes that included translations of major Greek and Roman historians, orators, poets, and dramatists— among them Homer in Pope's version and the tragedies of Aeschylus, Sophocles, and Euripides (No. 147). Although both the abundant classical allusions in *Mardi* and Melville's acquisition of these volumes reaffirm his long-standing interest in ancient history, literature, and philosophy, the possible influence of the authors included in the Classical Library has been studied only in part.

The late Charles Olson, who thought of Melville as another Homer ('He is Homer, and I seek to prove it'), and who also wrote eloquently on Shakespearean elements in *Moby-Dick*, was quick to observe that Melville must have been reading Greek tragedy in 1849 at the very time when he was making his 'close acquaintance' with the plays of Shakespeare (Sealts, 'A Correspondence with Charles Olson,' pp. 101, 107). In Matthiessen's formulation, Melville

> had just begun to meditate on Shakespeare more creatively than any other American writer ever has. This meditation brought him to his first profound comprehension of the nature of tragedy. This was the charge that released *Moby-Dick,* and that carried him in *Pierre* to the unbearable desperation of a Hamlet. (*American Renaissance*, p. 189)

The kind of reading that Melville began in 1849 thus struck far deeper than the books that had both inspired so much of *Mardi* and yet stood in the way of its success as a literary work. Though he had learned much, as he said, from writing and publishing such a book, he was still not ready for the pursuit of Moby Dick. Back in New York in April, aware of the critical verdict on *Mardi* and faced with the immediate need to turn out something more popular, he began casting about for a manageable subject. Meanwhile, from Duyckinck's library he borrowed Thomas Fuller's *The Holy State, and the Profane State* (Check-List, No. 221), from which he was to take the epigraph for *White-Jacket* (p. vii), and on or after 20 July he added three other titles: Cyrano de Bergerac's 'Voyage to the Moon'; Hawthorne's *Twice-Told Tales,* the source of an allusion in Chapter 68 of *White-Jacket;* and two volumes of the *Edinburgh Review* that he would be using in half a dozen other chapters (Nos. 172, 258, 200).

During the late spring and summer of 1849 Melville began the rapid composition of his fourth and fifth books, *Redburn* and *White-Jacket,* works which he later described to Judge Shaw as 'two *jobs,* which I have done for money—being forced to it, as other men are to sawing wood' (letter of 6 October 1849). For *Redburn,* written in less than ten weeks, he turned back to what he remembered of his own Liverpool voyage of 1839 as the basis for his narrator's story, once again mingling autobiographical elements with other materials either invented or drawn from his reading, as in *Typee* and *Omoo*. His considered methodology, to judge from a sentence in Chapter 24, was like that of sailors who make '*spun-yarn*': 'For material, they use odds and ends of old rigging called "*junk*," the yarns of which are picked to pieces, and then twisted

into new combinations, something as most books are manufactured'
(pp. 114–115). For *White-Jacket,* a longer and more ambitious work, he
drew on his service aboard the frigate *United States* in 1843–1844.

Redburn

Writing on 5 June to Richard Bentley, the London publisher of
Mardi, Melville described his next work as 'a thing of a widely different
cast . . .—a plain, straightforward, amusing narrative of personal
experience—the son of a gentleman on his first voyage to sea as a
sailor—no metaphysics, no conic-sections, nothing but cakes & ale.'
Though *Redburn* is a lesser work than *Mardi,* its greater narrative unity
made it far more readable and popular, then and now. With few exceptions the narrator, named Wellingborough Redburn, keeps the focus on
his own uncomplicated story, and neither the supporting characters nor
his own bookishness comes between him and the reader in the manner
of *Mardi.* That his account is anything but a literal report of Melville's
own Liverpool voyage was clearly demonstrated by the late William H.
Gilman, first in 'Melville's Liverpool Trip' (1946) and later in *Melville's
Early Life and* Redburn (1951).

In his fourth book Melville used his reading not only to fill out his
rapidly written narrative but also to give a sense of Redburn's situation
and to characterize him both as young protagonist and as older narrator.
His sources and methodology are the subjects of a classic essay by
Willard Thorp, 'Redburn's Prosy Old Guide-Book' (1966), and of
Thorp's later discovery of what Melville appropriated from the *Penny
Magazine* (which he had encountered aboard the *Charles and Henry*
during his years at sea) and from the *Penny Cyclopaedia* and the
Sailor's Magazine. (Thorp's findings are summarized in Hershel
Parker's Historical Note to the Northwestern-Newberry *Redburn,* pp.
329–332.) Walker Cowen has also suggested that for 'the poverty sections' of *Redburn* Melville may have drawn upon passages of the *Life
and Remarkable Adventures of Israel R. Potter* (Check-List, No. 407),
used in 1854–1855 for his own *Israel Potter* ('Melville's "Discoveries," ' p. 334).

By having his Redburn describe at some length the outward appearance of Adam Smith's *The Wealth of Nations* (pp. 86–87), copy the
elaborate title pages of actual guidebooks in Chapter 30, and in the next
chapter contrast the expectations aroused by his reading in *The Picture
of Liverpool* with his own visit to the city, Melville filled a substantial
number of pages, brought out sailor Redburn's youth and inexperience,
and enabled narrator Redburn to conclude that 'Every age makes its
own guide-books' (p. 157). This could be an echo of Emerson's remark
in 'The American Scholar' that 'each age . . . must write its own

books. . . . The books of an older period will not fit this.' That either
The Wealth of Nations or *The Picture of Liverpool* had accompanied
Melville himself on his own Liverpool voyage of 1839 is doubtful; that
he wrote *Redburn* ten years later with Adam Smith and a collection of
guidebooks before his eyes is manifest to any reader, though most of
the works named are not among his surviving books.[2]

Contrasting with these inappropriate volumes is the reading matter
supposedly favored by Redburn's shipmates: the 'Newgate Calendar,
and Pirate's Own' (p. 48), the *Three Spaniards* and Susanna Rowson's
well-known *Charlotte Temple* (p. 83), Blunt's 'extraordinary-looking
pamphlet . . . entitled the *Bonaparte Dream Book*' (p. 90), and two im-
pressive volumes loaned to Redburn by the sailor Max, 'an account of
Shipwrecks and Disasters at Sea, and . . . a large black volume, with
Delirium Tremens in great gilt letters on the back.' This last work, in
Redburn's words, 'proved to be a popular treatise on the subject of that
disease; and I remembered seeing several copies in the sailor book-stalls
about Fulton Market, and along South-street, in New York' (pp. 85–86).
Melville may of course have remembered some of these works from his
own days at sea, but American editions of several of them were not yet
available at the time of his own first voyage.[3] It seems more likely that
he had visited 'the sailor book-stalls' in 1849 to secure background
material for both *Redburn* and *White-Jacket*; in *White-Jacket* too the
sailors are said to prefer authors 'such as you may find at the book-
stalls along Fulton Market; they were slightly physiological in their nature' (*White-Jacket*, p. 169). By the same token, a reference in *Redburn*
to 'Mrs. Ellis's Daughters of England' (p. 110) may reflect the current
reading of his mother and sisters, which in 1850 included another work
by Mrs. Ellis, *Hearts and Homes* (Check-List, No. 202.1).

White-Jacket

White-Jacket too is anything but a literal version of Melville's own
experience, as various students of his years in the Pacific have now
made clear. As with *Redburn,* the reader must be careful not to mistake
fictionalized embellishment for established fact. Melville's unacknowledged literary appropriations for *White-Jacket* were far more numerous
and complex than his rather obvious borrowings for *Redburn*; according
to Willard Thorp's Historical Note to the Northwestern-Newberry edition, 'the number of his extensive pillages' for the later book 'is ex-
ceeded only by those in *Moby-Dick*' (p. 417). Thorp succinctly discusses more than a dozen major and minor sources that he and other
scholars have identified, including the *Edinburgh Review*; for one
example, the *Penny Cyclopaedia,* used earlier in *Redburn,* alone 'furnished fifteen passages or allusions in the chapters (60–63) recounting

Surgeon Cuticle's operation on the foretopman' (Thorp, p. 423)—an episode worthy of Melville's admired Smollett. Among the most important sources are various now-forgotten narratives by British and American seamen such as Henry Mercier (Check-List, No. 357a) that Melville 'skimmed off,' as Thorp puts it, for some of the most vivid passages in *White-Jacket*.

Perhaps the best illustration of Melville's artistic transformation of source material is Chapter 92, dealing with White-Jacket's fall from a yard-arm. This is an imagined episode developed from an incident in *A Mariner's Sketches* by Nathaniel Ames (1830) and wonderfully heightened by borrowings from Schiller's poem 'The Diver.' Melville acquired Bulwer Lytton's translation of Schiller's poems in 1849 (Check-List, No. 439), but whether he owned or borrowed *A Mariner's Sketches* is not known. The fullest treatment of White-Jacket's fall is by the late Howard P. Vincent in *The Tailoring of Melville's* White-Jacket (1970), a major critical work that studies Melville's use of sources 'in their totality rather than in isolation' (p. xi). Vincent stresses Melville's skill as a literary artist in *White-Jacket* and takes the book itself as a necessary prelude to *Moby-Dick*, begun in the following year.

Like the narrator in the earlier *Omoo*, the title character of *White-Jacket* is pleased to find friends on shipboard with literary interests akin to his own; such had been Melville's experience aboard the *United States*, and several of the figures in the book are based on men he had known there. White-Jacket immediately recognizes Nord (Oliver Russ) as 'a reader of good books' and would stake his very life on it, as he says, that Nord 'seized the right meaning of Montaigne.' One night he and Nord 'scoured all the prairies of reading; dived into the bosoms of authors, and tore out their hearts; and that night White-Jacket learned more than he has ever done in any single night since' (p. 51). The incomparable Jack Chase, who had served as captain of the main-top aboard the *United States*, appears in *White-Jacket* as a self-educated sailor who 'talked of Rob Roy, Don Juan, and Pelham; Macbeth and Ulysses; but, above all things, was an ardent admirer of Camoens' (*White-Jacket*, p. 14).[4] Along with Camoens, Chase also speaks familiarly of Shakespeare and Homer, Falconer's *Shipwreck*, Shelley, Byron, and Trelawny (pp. 270–271). As we know from Melville's dedication of the posthumous *Billy Budd, Sailor*, to Chase, the admiration he expressed in *White-Jacket* continued throughout his life.

Whether Chase in reality was as well read as Melville drew him in 1849 is impossible to determine, though it should be remembered that scholarship has shown Melville's own reading to be the source for much that he gives Chase to say about his earlier life at sea. In presenting him as a character who knows literature, like Long Ghost in *Omoo*, Melville may again have created a heightened version of his narrator who has read what he himself has been reading. Moreover, as Chase also harbors literary aspirations of his own, sensing something within himself that, 'under happier skies,' might have made him 'a Homer' (p. 271), he also expresses something of Melville's own ambition to produce a more worthy book than anything he had written between 1844 and 1849.

In direct contrast to Nord and Jack Chase is the *Neversink*'s chaplain, a 'transcendental divine' who like Melville knew both Plato and the German philosophers; 'White-Jacket himself saw him with Coleridge's Biographia Literaria in his hand' (p. 155), and he later observes that the chaplain 'pranced on Coleridge's *"High German horse"* ' (p. 167). In a typically obscure sermon to the men of the *Neversink* this ill-placed clergyman inappropriately

> enlarged upon the follies of the ancient philosophers; learnedly alluded to the *Phædon* of Plato; exposed the follies of Simplicius's Commentary on Aristotle's "De Cœlo," by arraying against that clever Pagan author the admired tract of Tertullian—*De Præscriptionibus Hæreticorum*—and concluded by a Sanscrit invocation. He was particularly hard upon the Gnostics and Marcionites of the second century of the Christian era; but he never, in the remotest manner, attacked the every-day vices of the nineteenth century, as eminently illustrated in our man-of-war world. (pp. 155–156)

As Anderson has shown, White-Jacket's satirical description of Sunday services on the *Neversink* does not square with a matter-of-fact sketch of religious activities written by the official Ship's Scribe of the *United States* (*Melville in the South Seas*, pp. 369–371). Like much of *White-Jacket*, which Melville presented as a generalized picture of naval life rather than a record of his own experiences, such a passage serves his purpose of exposing the American navy's disregard for the welfare of its common seamen. His own reading—not that of his years at sea but in works he had come upon more recently—helped him to drive home his point through satire and caricature; but in his portrait of the chaplain, a person far removed from the 'man-of-war world' he was depicting, he may also have been poking private fun at himself as the bookish author of *Mardi* and at his own inward voyage to 'the world of mind.'

In 1848, as we know, Melville himself had acquired a copy of *Biographia Literaria;* in 1849 his letters mention both the *Phaedon* and his recent purchase of Bayle's *Dictionary*; in *Moby-Dick* he was soon to reflect his own knowledge of the heretical 'Gnostics and Marcionites' in passages deriving in part from Bayle. As I have elsewhere remarked, 'Both the chaplain and Melville must also have been reading Andrews Norton' ('Melville and Emerson's Rainbow,' pp. 267–268), Norton being 'that distinctly *anti*-transcendental divine who in 1839 had attacked Emerson's Divinity School Address as "the latest form of infidelity." ' Thomas Vargish has traced the chaplain's citation of Tertullian's obscure tract to Melville's acquaintance with Norton's *magnum opus, The Evidences of the Genuineness of the Gospels* (1844) ('Gnostic Mythos in *Moby-Dick,*' p. 272). It would seem that Melville had looked into Norton as well as Emerson, either during or after his stay in Boston earlier in 1849.

Melville's private joke may be continued in Chapter 41 (pp. 167–169), where he lists the books that his White-Jacket supposedly read at sea. Those volumes he is said to have obtained from various members of the crew range widely, from 'a Negro Song-book' to 'a few choice old authors' like Beaumont and Fletcher, Jonson, and Marlowe, whose plays Melville would soon be buying for himself in London. But the works available from the ship's 'public library' are another matter. Titles such as Blair's *Lectures,* Locke's *Essays,* Machiavelli's *Art of War,* and Plutarch's *Lives* provide good reading, but they are 'not precisely adapted to tarry tastes,' as White-Jacket remarks. 'Who had the selection of these books, I do not know,' he says, 'but some of them must have been selected by our Chaplain.'[5]

There are other references to books in Chapter 24, 'Introductory to Cape Horn,' where White-Jacket/Melville recommends 'my friend Dana's unmatchable "Two Years Before the Mast" ' for 'the best idea' of the Cape (p. 99). As we now know, Melville himself had read Dana's book in 1840 (Check-List, No. 173), and *Two Years Before the Mast* clearly belongs in the alphabetical Check-List of books Melville owned and borrowed—not on the basis of the narrator's allusion in *White-Jacket* but on the objective evidence of his own letter to Dana previously quoted. What of the other books White-Jacket mentions in this same chapter? He refers to three 'remarkable and most interesting narratives' that record the 'disasters and sufferings' of Lord Anson's squadron during a celebrated passage around the Cape, adding, 'White-Jacket has them all' (p. 99). Melville himself, however, seems to have owned only one of these: John Byron's *Narrative* (Check-List, No. 113).[6] As Dennis Berthold has concluded, he 'may have discovered references to the other accounts there, since Byron's was the last published and specifically refutes the earlier versions' ('Factual Errors and Fictional Aims in *White-Jacket,*' p. 238, n. 15). In other words, White-Jacket's library and Melville's were by no means identical.

Book-Buying in Europe

In October 1849 Melville sailed for England to negotiate for the publication of *White-Jacket* there. Hoping also to travel on the Continent, he carried several European guidebooks borrowed from Evert Duyckinck's younger brother George, who had recently returned from abroad (Check-List, Nos. 77, 78, 166, 377). The journal of Melville's trip, which includes references to his shipboard reading of Dickens's *Pickwick,* Caroline Kirkland's *Holidays Abroad,* and an unnamed work of Charles Lamb (Check-List, Nos. 182, 311, 315), reports congenial discussions of literary and philosophical topics with others on board. George J. Adler, a German-American scholar introduced to him by the younger Duyckinck, soon became his 'principal companion.' Adler was 'full of the German metaphysics' and spoke of 'Kant, Swedenborg, &c.'; his personal philosophy struck Melville, who of course knew the *Biographia Literaria,* as 'Coleridgean.' Like Milton's fallen angels, the two men discoursed of 'Fixed Fate, Free will, foreknowledge absolute,' and over whisky punch and mulled wine they joined other shipboard friends to talk 'metaphysics,' discussing Hegel, Schlegel, and Kant and, like Coleridge and the chaplain of *White-Jacket,* 'riding on the German horse' (journal entries for 12, 13, 22, and 27 October).

As Melville prepared to land again in England after a lapse of ten years, he wryly compared his situation with what it had been in 1839: '—*then* a sailor, *now* H. M. author of "Peedee" "Hullabaloo" & "Pog-Dog" ' (entry for 4 November). His itinerary during November and December included libraries and bookshops as well as publishers' offices; while abroad he acquired over two dozen books by purchase or gift, listing their titles at the end of his journal. Other volumes were tempting but beyond his limited means: 'Saw many books I should like to buy—but can not,' runs a journal entry for 17 December, made in London. Reading favorable British notices of *Redburn* surprised him, since he himself belittled the book as mere 'trash,' written 'to buy some tobacco with' (entry for 6 November). Under other circumstances the favorable British reception of *Redburn* should have helped him place *White-Jacket,* but the troublesome issue of international copyright hampered his negotiations with a number of publishers. He finally signed an agreement with Richard Bentley, but was unable to secure a cash advance that would have financed his projected travel to Rome and the Mediterranean; he did manage to visit Paris, however, and to see the Rhine in Germany.

Apart from Melville's set of Shakespeare, his recently discovered copies of Wordsworth and Milton, and his volumes of Beaumont and Fletcher, Davenant, Marlowe, and Ben Jonson, relatively few of the books he bought in 1849 are known to survive. From the text of his journal, the itemized lists at the end, statements from his publishers, charges for books borrowed, and personal correspondence come many of the entries for the alphabetical Check-List. Some of the purchases he

MELVILLE'S 'BOOKS OBTAINED IN LONDON,' 1849

Melville's listing of 'Books obtained in London,' from his manuscript
'Journal of a Visit to London and the Continent.' (By permission of the
Houghton Library, Harvard University.)

'BOOKS OBTAINED IN PARIS' AND 'IN GERMANY,' 1849

Melville's listing of 'Books obtained in Paris' and 'Books obtained in Germany,' from his manuscript 'Journal of a Visit to London and the Continent.' (By permission of the Houghton Library, Harvard University.)

brought home from Europe in 1850 were presented as gifts—for example, a copy of Butler's *Hudibras* that he inscribed to Evert Duyckinck and a two-volume set of Chatterton's *Poetical Works* that he gave to John C. Hoadley in 1854 (Check-List, Nos. 104, 137); other books that he owned by this time were disposed of in later years when his interest waned, or when he secured better editions.

By 1854, when Melville gave his copy of Seneca's *Morals* to his brother Thomas, he probably owned his folio Seneca as well (Check-List, Nos. 458, 457), and of three titles that he gave his sister Fanny in 1862—the *Poetical Works* of Shakespeare, of Shenstone and Collins, and of James Thomson (Check-List, Nos. 464, 470, 515), at least two were by authors whose works he had recently purchased in newer editions (Nos. 156, 516). His surviving copies of Emerson's essays and poems (Nos. 203–206) all date from his later years, long after he read Emerson in 1849 and after. And it must be remembered that Melville knew—or knew of—many more authors and titles than those mentioned in correspondence or listed in records of purchases and library loans. Important as they are, therefore, these records tell much less than the full story of his voluminous reading during the years of his progressive unfolding; the records for 1850 and 1851, when he was writing *Moby-Dick,* are somewhat more revealing.

Notes

[1] Melville's name does not appear in either the ledgers or the guest register of the Athenaeum. Lemuel Shaw was a member from 1846 until his death in 1861; by 1851 he had withdrawn over a hundred books. The 35 titles charged to him during the known periods of his son-in-law's visits to Boston as chronicled in *The Melville Log* have been listed in terms of editions included in the *Catalogue of the Library of the Boston Athenaeum, 1807–1871* (1874–82); the editions available to him were identified with the assistance of Marjorie Lyle Crandall of the library staff when this study was first undertaken.

[2] *Redburn* describes his copy of *The Wealth of Nations* as an Aberdeen edition inscribed 'Jonathan Jones, from his particular friend Donald Dods, 1798'; no such volume is among Melville's own surviving books. Seven of the nine guidebooks Redburn mentions are identified in Thorp's article. *The Picture of Liverpool*, like *The Picture of London* (Check-List, No. 402), may actually have belonged to Melville and his father; if so, it has apparently not survived. Mrs. Metcalf, inquiring about it in a letter of 30 August 1919 to her mother, Frances Melville Thomas, was answered in a notation on the same letter (HCL): 'don't remember seeing it—many of the books were disposed of, when your grandmother left 26" st.'

[3] Maxine Moore, noting 'a spate of Napoleon dream books by various authors,' identifies as 'the most likely candidate . . . a popular volume by Mme

Camille LeNorman, or Marie Adelaide LeNormand, published in 1843' (*That Lonely Game,* p. 21, n. 12). With the 'account of shipwrecks and disasters' Keith Huntress in 'A Note on Melville's *Redburn*' has compared *Shipwrecks and Disasters at Sea; or, Historical Narratives of the Most Noted Calamities and Providential Deliverances Which Have Resulted from Maritime Enterprise. . . ,* reprinted in one volume (New York, 1844) from a three-volume Edinburgh edition (1812); Huntress has also suggested, though with some reservations, that '*Delirium Tremens*' might be an English work of 1830 by Andrew Blake. But the American edition of Blake's book (Washington, 1834), apparently unabridged, is a small pamphlet of only 24 pages, 8.6'' x 6.4'', and the second English edition (London, 1840), of 112 pages, is described as 'revised and much enlarged.' Max's 'large' volume is more likely a work of 483 pages (9.5'' x 6'') by James Root, *The Horrors of Delirium Tremens* (New York, 1844), a combined temperance tract and disquisition on theology; whether it was also 'black' with 'great gilt letters on the back' is unverified, however, for the only copies I have examined have been rebound.

⁴In *White-Jacket* Chase quotes somewhat inaccurately from Mickle's translation of the *Lusiads,* which he praises highly, saying that his father knew Mickle (p. 270); Melville's only surviving copy of Camões as translated by Strangford was acquired in 1867 (Check-List, No. 116). George Monteiro has a study of Melville and Camões in progress; see his 'Melville and Camões: A Working Bibliography' (1985).

⁵Keith Huntress, 'Melville's Use of a Source for *White-Jacket,*' points out that at least two of the titles mentioned in the 'Man-of-War Library' chapter are taken over from a literary source; Tyrus Hillway has shown that Melville also knew one of them directly: Mason Good's *Book of Nature*; see his 'Melville's Geological Knowledge' and particularly his 'Melville's Education in Science,' p. 417 and n. 26.

⁶The two earlier accounts are *A Voyage round the World . . . By George Anson,* compiled by Richard Walter (London, 1748 and subsequent editions), and *A Voyage to the South-Seas . . . Containing a Faithful Narrative of the Loss of His Majesty's Ship the Wager,* compiled by John Bulkeley and John Cummins (London, 1743 and subsequent editions).

4. 1850–1851

'Hawthorne and His Mosses' and *Moby-Dick*

Melville enjoyed 'a prosperous passage' back to New York from England, as he later reported; embarking from Portsmouth on Christmas morning, 1849, he 'carried the savor of the plumb-puddings & roast turkey all the way across the Atlantic' (letter to Richard Bentley, 27 June 1850). While still in Europe he had found time for only occasional reading, including 'a few chapters in Tristram Shandy' and all of that 'most wondrous book,' the ' "Opium Eater" ' of De Quincey (journal entries for 16 and 23 December), but during his five weeks at sea he had leisure for becoming acquainted with other works he was carrying home. On New Year's Day, 1850, for example, he turned to his prized folios of the older English dramatists, subsequently inscribing passages from Lamb's essays in his copy of Beaumont and Fletcher and making notes from his folio Ben Jonson at the end of his journal along with other references to De Quincey, Rousseau, Sir Thomas Browne, and Boswell on Dr. Johnson (Check-List, Nos. 316 and 53; 302; 180, 429, 90, 84; *Log* 1: 359–360).

Back in New York on 1 February, Melville began distributing gifts to his family and friends, including Evert Duyckinck, from whom he was soon borrowing books once again: Smollett's *Roderick Random* and Jean Paul Richter's *Flower, Fruit, and Thorn Pieces* in February, Carlyle's *Sartor Resartus* and *Heroes and Hero Worship* in June or July

59

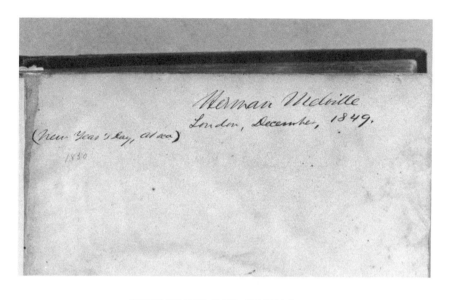

'NEW YEAR'S DAY, AT SEA,' 1850

Returning from Europe in January 1850, Melville began reading in books
he had bought while in London. This inscription is from his folio of
Davenant's works; there are similar inscriptions in his folios of
Beaumont and Fletcher and Ben Jonson (Check-List, Nos. 176, 53, 302).
(Reproduced through the courtesy of Howard S. Mott, Inc.)

(Check-List, Nos. 480, 424, 123, 122), and other titles later in the year.
On 17 April he renewed membership in the New York Society Library,
and on the twenty-ninth he withdrew two volumes on whaling by
William Scoresby: *An Account of the Arctic Regions* and *Journal of a
Voyage to the Northern Whale Fishery* (Nos. 450, 451).

At some time in the early months of 1850, perhaps while still on
shipboard, Melville had begun drafting his sixth book, which in writing
to his friend Dana on 1 May he referred to as the 'whaling voyage.' On
27 June, in a letter to Richard Bentley proposing the new work for publication in London, he characterized it as 'a romance of adventure,
founded upon certain wild legends in the Southern Sperm Whale
Fisheries.' Meanwhile, *White-Jacket,* like the earlier *Redburn,* was receiving the favorable notices denied *Mardi,* and its reviewers commonly
observed that in these later books he had fortunately returned to the
true vein he had abandoned in their predecessor. For Melville these
comments were an obvious warning: whatever his next book might become, it must not be another *Mardi.*

In May Melville had told Dana that he was 'half way' in his new work, and in June he expected it to be ready in 'the latter part of the coming autumn.' His further reading in the summer and fall of 1850, as he continued work on his manuscript, deserves special comment. From Harper and Brothers either he or his brother Allan bought Horace Greely's *Hints Toward Reforms* in May and other unnamed books in September (Check-List, Nos. 234, 81).[1] On 6 July he acquired a guidebook to London that had once belonged to his father: *Kearsley's Stranger's Guide, or Companion through London and Westminister* (Check-List, No. 304a), a work that he may have found useful when he came to write *Israel Potter* in 1854. The growing fascination with German literature and thought that he had already expressed—'riding the German horse,' as he called it, with reference to Coleridge's *Biographia Literaria* and his shipboard conversations with Adler—was shown once more by his purchase of Goethe's *Auto-Biography* in London (Check-List, No. 228) and his subsequent borrowing of both Richter and Carlyle from Duyckinck; Carlyle along with Coleridge was largely responsible for introducing many English-speaking readers of the day to contemporary German writers. Later in 1850 he also borrowed both Goethe's *Wilhelm Meister* and Carlyle's anthology *German Romance*, offering selected writings by Musaeus, La Motte-Fouqué, Tieck, Hoffman, and Richter (Check-List, Nos. 230, 121).

Melville's other borrowings from Duyckinck in the midsummer of 1850 were widely varied: Scogan's *Jests*; the poetry of Elizabeth Barrett, William Browne, and Alfred Tennyson; volumes of *Arcturus* and the *Democratic Review*; Thoreau's *A Week on the Concord and Merrimack Rivers*—perhaps as a follow-up to his earlier reading of Emerson; Sylvester Judd's novel *Margaret,* and a translation of *Lazarillo de Tormes* (Nos. 449; 92, 91, 504; 14, 531; 524; 303, 324). It should also be noted that his sister Augusta, who became a good friend of Duyckinck and his family during the New York years, had acknowledged Duyckinck's gifts of a number of books since 1848: Thackeray's *The Great Hoggarty Diamond* (1848), several volumes on Leigh Hunt in 1849, and Tennyson's *In Memoriam* and a novel by Grace Aguilar in July 1850 (Nos. 511a, 290b, 503a, 6a). In the fall of 1850 she borrowed his copy of *David Copperfield,* but apparently did not take it with her when she left New York for Pittsfield in October (No. 181). Some further indication of Augusta's taste in reading is afforded by her list of 'Books to be purchased,' which appears to date from this same period (Appendix B.4).

'Hawthorne and His Mosses'

In July 1850, seeking to escape the summer heat and a crowded household in New York, Melville took his wife and infant son Malcolm to the Berkshires of western Massachusetts, where they boarded with the widow and son of his late uncle Thomas at the Melvill farm near Pittsfield where Herman had worked as a boy. He soon began acquiring books of regional interest that were to yield material for his later writing: *A History of the County of Berkshire* and a volume on the Shakers, the latter bought during a visit to the Shaker village in nearby Hancock (Check-List, Nos. 216, 459a). More immediately important, however, was the copy of Hawthorne's *Mosses from an Old Manse* (1846) that was given to him on 18 July by his Aunt Mary Melvill (No. 248).

As we know, Melville had mentioned 'Hawthorne of Salem' in *White-Jacket* after reading Hawthorne's *Twice-Told Tales* during the summer of 1849, but the two authors had not then met; now, on 5 August 1850, their introduction took place during an all-day excursion in a congenial company that included Evert Duyckinck and Cornelius Mathews, who were visiting Melville, and Oliver Wendell Holmes, whose summer home was also near Pittsfield. Melville and Hawthorne took an immediate liking to one another, and in response Melville was prompted not only to hurry through his reading of *Mosses from an Old Manse,* marking it heavily as he read,[2] but also to complete an enthusiastic review of the book and an encomium of its author under the title of 'Hawthorne and His Mosses.' Mrs. Melville made a fair copy of the hastily written manuscript,[3] Melville corrected it, and Duyckinck carried it back to New York for publication in his *Literary World* on 17 and 24 August as the work of an unnamed 'Virginian Spending July in Vermont.'

In 'Hawthorne and His Mosses,' something of a sequel to the chapter on Lombardo and his writing in *Mardi,* Melville wrote prospectively rather than retrospectively about his own literary affiliations and ambitions; the review is at once a fictionalized narrative, designed to conceal its author's identity, and a challenging critical manifesto. The supposed 'Virginian' opens his story by establishing its setting in 'a fine old farm-house' in 'Vermont,' affirming that he had neither met Hawthorne nor previously read his *Mosses,* and telling how a 'cousin' had recently given him that volume as a replacement for Timothy Dwight's *Travels in New England,* the book he had been perusing in the hay-mow. The remaining pages move from an appreciation of Hawthorne into a discussion of Shakespeare, then on to a consideration of the possibilities open to the nineteenth-century American writer—by implication, to Melville himself, engaged as he was with the book that became *Moby-Dick.*

The special qualities in Hawthorne's tales and Shakespeare's plays that Melville elects to emphasize, thus expressing indirectly his own ideals as a writer, also reflect his familiarity with the literary criticism of British writers such as Coleridge, Lamb, and Carlyle. He specifically mentions Charles Lamb's *Specimens of English Dramatic Poets* (p. 253), which he had bought in 1849 (Check-List, No. 318), and his discussion of the staging of Shakespeare's *Richard III* clearly derives from Lamb's essay 'On the Tragedies of Shakespeare,' which he had subsequently read. Even more relevant is Carlyle's treatment of 'The Hero as Poet' in a book which Melville had borrowed from Duyckinck shortly before going to Pittsfield: *On Heroes, Hero-Worship, and the Heroic in History* (No. 122).

In celebrating Hawthorne's 'perfect ripeness,' Melville especially praises his tenderness and sympathy and his mingling of love and humor, all characteristics that Carlyle had distinguished in writing of Dante and Shakespeare. According to Carlyle, the *Divine Comedy* 'came deep out of the author's heart of hearts' (p. 82),[4] and Shakespeare could not have delinated 'so many suffering heroic hearts, if his own heroic heart had never suffered' (p. 97); according to Melville, an artist must have experienced suffering in order to depict it in others (p. 242). Melville wrote not only of Hawthorne's 'intricate, profound heart' but also of its complement: 'a great, deep intellect' (p. 242); Carlyle's poet must have 'intellect enough' as his 'first gift' (p. 94), and 'Shakespeare is the greatest of Intellects' (p. 96). These and other verbal parallels show how directly Melville was responding to his recent reading in authors such as Carlyle who had most powerfully affected him.[5]

Along with Hawthorne's attributes of both heart and intellect, melancholy and humor, height and depth, beauty and strength, Melville saw in his writings not only an 'Indian-summer sunlight' but also a 'power of blackness' that links him with Calvinistic 'Original Sin' as well as Shakespearean 'vital truth.' The 'mere critic' who probes only with his intellect, not with the intuitive truth of the heart, will miss these characteristic elements, Melville declares. Shakespeare's version of 'blackness,' he goes on to say, involves his probing 'at the very axis of reality' for truths that can be reported only 'covertly and by snatches.' Through his 'dark characters . . . he craftily says, or sometimes insinuates the things, which we feel to be so terrifically true, that it were all but madness for any good man, in his own proper character, to utter, or even hint of them. Tormented into desperation, Lear, the frantic king, tears off the mask, and speaks the sane madness of vital truth' (pp. 243–244).

As Charles Olson, F. O. Matthiessen, and later critics have shown, Melville's own 'dark characters' in *Moby-Dick* reflect the close reading of Shakespeare he had begun in 1849, as do the borrowed dramatic structure of certain chapters and the 'bold and nervous lofty language' of the book as a whole. Through Ahab and Ishmael he was able to speak his own 'vital truth,' thus addressing his earlier complaint to Duyckinck that 'an author can never—under no conceivable circumstances—be at all frank with his readers' (letter of 14 December

1849). *Moby-Dick* as it developed under the influence of both Shake-speare and Hawthorne reveals Melville's own preoccupation with black-ness, and its thematic pairings are analogous to the complementary qualities he had praised in Hawthorne—those 'unlike things' which he believed 'must meet and mate' to engender a successful work of art ('Art,' in *Poems*, p. 231).

Melville's linking of Hawthorne with the revered figure of Shake-speare, identifying both as masters of 'intuitive Truth,' startled readers of the *Literary World* by its seeming extravagance, but what is most striking to the twentieth-century student of the essay is its confident declaration that a 'noble-souled aspirant' of the nineteenth century in America—a Melville, say, as well as a Hawthorne—might go 'as far as Shakespeare into the universe' (p. 245). Such an affirmation is no mere echo of the literary nationalism of Duyckinck and Mathews and their 'Young America' movement. By this time in his career Melville was conscious of promptings within himself that might lead to 'the full flower of some still greater achievement' (p. 249) than the writings of his American contemporaries such as Irving, Cooper, and Dana—or of anything he himself had yet published.

Arrowhead

Melville's delight in his surroundings at Pittsfield and his awareness that Hawthorne had recently settled in the same area led him to pur-chase in September 1850 the Berkshire farm he was to call Arrowhead, which immediately adjoined the Melvill property where he had been staying. Had his aunt and cousin Robert not already sold Broadhall, as it was known, he would very likely have settled there. By October he and his wife and child, his mother, and his four sisters had moved from New York to Arrowhead, and in his new residence he became 'as busy as man could be. Every thing to be done, & scarcely any one to help me do it.' So he wrote to Evert Duyckinck on 6 October, noting that for the next month, during harvest-time, he expected 'to be in the open air all day, except when assisting in lifting a bedstead or a bureau.'

By early December, with the crops brought in and snow on the ground, Melville had eagerly resumed his writing. 'Can you send me about fifty fast-writing youths, with an easy style & not averse to polishing their labors?' he asked Duyckinck on 13 December. 'If you can, I wish you would, because since I have been here I have planned about that number of future works & cant find enough time to think about them separately.' His daily routine, he explained, began about eight in the morning, when he rose, went to the barn to feed the horse and cow, and then took his own breakfast. The rest of his schedule he reported as follows:

> I go to my work-room & light my fire—then spread my M.S.S on the table—take one business squint at it, & fall to with a will. At 2½ P.M. I hear a preconcerted knock at my door, which (by request) continues till I rise & go to the door, which serves to wean me effectively from my writing, however interested I may be. My friends the horse & cow now demand their dinner—& I go & give it to them. My own dinner over, I rig my sleigh & with my mother or sisters start off for the village—& if it be a Literary World day, great is the satisfaction thereof.—My evenings I spend in a sort of mesmeric state in my room—not being able to read—only now & then skimming over some large-printed book.

The old complaint that Melville later called 'the twilight of my eyes' (letter to Duyckinck, 26 March 1851) was to trouble him throughout the winter, making it almost impossible for him even to read after a day at his writing-table.

A comparable account of Melville's 'general method of literary work' during the Pittsfield years occurs in the biographical sketch written in 1891–1892 by his old friend J. E. A. Smith, the Pittsfield editor and compiler of Berkshire history. It was Melville's practice, Smith recalled, to

> shut himself up in his library, having his luncheon, if needed, placed at the door in order to avoid interruption. Often he submitted his manuscript to one of his sisters for revision. Probably it came from her hand somewhat toned down from what he left it in the heat of composition; but not essentially changed. This solitary labor continued until he was wearied, when he would emerge from his 'den,' join in family or social intercourse, indulge in light reading—which was not so very light; as it included much less of what we commonly call 'light literature' than it did of profound reviews, abstruse philosophy in prose or verse, and the like—visit or entertain his friends or otherwise enjoy himself: But no more formal or serious work for him until the next morning, although, consciously or unconsciously, his mind was always gathering material for it. ('Herman Melville,' pp. 130–131)

Smith's account, which differs in several ways from Melville's own, deserves further comment. It was Augusta Melville who made a fair copy of *Moby-Dick* for the printer during the winter of 1850–1851, as we know from her letter of 16 January 1851 (NYPL–GL) to her friend Mary Blatchford ('The mornings I pass in copying Herman's MS.'). Whether or not she 'toned down' her brother's draft chapters it is impossible to say, since the manuscript has apparently not survived. How much 'light reading,' as Smith called it, Melville himself was able to do of an evening would of course depend on the state of his eyes. More often, whenever he joined the family circle, he probably listened to whatever work was being read aloud, in accordance with long-standing custom. From Augusta Melville's letters we know two of the works that were read in this way during the first winter at Pittsfield. Melville's wife and son were in Boston from Thanksgiving until after Christmas, 1850, and his sister Helen was also away for a time, leaving 'a very small family, only four in number,' at Arrowhead: himself, his mother, and his sisters Augusta and Fanny. 'The long evenings we have improved by reading aloud,' Augusta told Mary Blatchford on 4 January 1851, finishing 'Schiller's "Ghost-Seer",' & several other interesting books' (NYPL–GL); Melville himself, it should be noted, later recalled 'the fearful interest' of Schiller's story (Check-List, No. 438a).

When Mrs. Melville came back to Pittsfield from her stay in Boston, she brought with her a copy of *David Copperfield* (Check-List, No. 181). This was reserved 'for evening reading' that began in mid-January after Helen Melville had also returned to Arrowhead (Augusta Melville to Helen Melville, 6 January, and to Mary Blatchford, 16 January, NYPL–GL). Dickens was evidently a family favorite; Melville himself had read *Pickwick Papers* on shipboard in 1849. In later years at Pittsfield, according to Mrs. Metcalf, he always referred to a 'certain local lady' as '*Mrs.* Pecksniff,' after the pompous male character in *Martin Chuzzlewit* (1843–44).

> Herman's mother could not have been sensitive to the resemblance, for she never questioned the authenticity of the name. One day the lady called: Mme Melville sailed in, and in her stateliest manner greeted her, 'How do you do, Mrs. Pecksniff?' The lady had read her Dickens, and never called again. Maria should have known her son better! (*Cycle and Epicycle,* p. 205)

If Melville joined the others for evening reading, as seems likely, then he may have been influenced to some degree by other authors and works that engaged his wife, mother, and sisters in the 1850's and after. Their correspondence of the Pittsfield years mentions a number of titles that might have caught his attention, such as William Starbuck Mayo's 'wild "Kaloolah" ' (as Augusta Melville called it) and his 'new work' of 1850, *The Berber* (Check-List, No. 353a). An excellent example is 'a very curious book, entitled "Two Years Among the Shakers" ' (No. 319a), which Augusta was reading in January 1851: 'How is it possible,' she asked Mary Blatchford in a letter of 16 January, 'to believe so much utter nonsense[?]' Melville himself may well have glanced at the book, along with his own copy of *A Summary View of the Millenial Church*

(No. 459a), as he drew the character of the Shaker Gabriel in *Moby-Dick*.

During the fifteen months that Melville and Hawthorne were Berkshire neighbors, from August 1850 to November 1851, the friendship between their families was to develop with great satisfaction on both sides. Sophia Hawthorne, who was delighted to find her husband 'mentioned with the Swan of Avon' in 'Hawthorne and His Mosses,' wrote Duyckinck on 29? August 1850 that the 'Virginian,' whoever he might be, 'is the first person who has ever in *print* apprehended Mr Hawthorne.' Duyckinck had provided the Hawthornes with copies of Melville's works, which interested them both; Hawthorne read them 'on the new hay in the barn' with 'a progressive appreciation of the author' (*Log* 1: 392, 391). By early September they had discovered that the Virginian was Melville, whom Mrs. Hawthorne characterized eloquently in her letters as 'a person of great ardor & simplicity. He is all on fire with the subject that interests him. It rings through his frame like a cathedral bell. His truth & honesty shine out at every point. At the same time he sees things artistically, as you perceive in his books' (*Log* 1: 924–925).

The two authors were soon exchanging visits. In their conversations, which sometimes 'lasted pretty deep into the night,' as Hawthorne noted, they talked of 'time and eternity, things of this world and of the next, and books, and publishers, and all possible and impossible matters' (*Log* 1: 419). As an overnight guest, Melville 'was very careful not to interrupt Mr Hawthorne's mornings,' the time his host reserved for writing; he 'generally walked off somewhere,' according to Mrs. Hawthorne, but on one occasion in early September 1850 he 'read Mr Emerson's Essays' (*Log* 2: 925)—probably *Representative Men,* his most recent collection (Check-List, No. 206a). On a later occasion, in March 1851, the two men evidently discussed Thoreau, whom Hawthorne had known in Concord and whose *Week on the Concord and Merrimack* Melville had been reading during the previous summer (*Log* 1: 407). Emerson may have figured as well when they tackled what Melville called 'the Problem of the Universe,' launching into 'metaphysics' and indulging in 'ontological heroics' (letters to Hawthorne, 16? April, 29 June 1851).

The direct influence of these conversations on Melville's thought and art as he worked on *Moby-Dick* is impossible to overestimate. His remarkable letters of 1850–1851, which show his preoccupation with the same philosophical topics that engage his Ishmael and Ahab, also make occasional references to Hawthorne's writings. Both Hawthorne and his wife gave various books to Melville and his son Malcolm: copies of Hawthorne's own works (Check-List, Nos. 245, 245a, 246, 257, 259,

260, 261) and other volumes that had belonged to Hawthorne's uncle
(Nos. 178a, 194). *The Scarlet Letter* was not among these gifts. Though
Melville had mentioned it by name in 'Hawthorne and His Mosses,'
there is no external evidence that he owned the book before 1870, when
he bought a copy of an 1850 printing (No. 253). When in 1851 he reread
Twice-Told Tales, in one of the volumes Hawthorne had given him, he
thought that 'they far exceed the "Mosses." ' So he wrote to Duyckinck on 12 February, remarking that though Hawthorne the man
lacked 'the plump sphericity' that 'roast-beef, done rare,' would provide, his literary works evince 'a quality of genius, immensely loftier, &
more profound too, than any other American has shown hitherto in the
printed form.' To Hawthorne himself on 16? April, in a private 'review' of the newly published work that had just been sent him, *The
House of the Seven Gables,* he declared: 'There is a certain tragic phase
of humanity which, in our opinion, was never more powerfully embodied than by Hawthorne.'

Moby-Dick

One resource Melville sorely missed as an author living in Berkshire was the 'long Vaticans [i.e., libraries] and street-stalls' (*Moby-
Dick,* p. 2) he had known in New York; 'They have no Vatican (as you
have) in Pittsfield here,' he told Duyckinck on 7 November 1851. The
local Pittsfield Library Association was open to him, but its holdings
were limited.[6] For the special titles needed as his work on *Moby-Dick*
progressed he found it necessary to place orders in the city with George
Putnam, who had imported at least one volume for him in July 1850:
Beale's *Natural History of the Sperm Whale* (Check-List, No. 52). Melville's brother Allan and his father-in-law Lemuel Shaw also assisted in
the collection of out-of-the-way materials for *Moby-Dick.* When Allan
Melville paid a New Year's visit to Pittsfield in January 1851, the 'principal contents' of a box of presents he had shipped from New York
were 'some very valuable books, for Herman's library,' as Augusta
Melville reported in a letter to her sister Helen on 6 January (NYPL–
GL). One of them, as we know, was the tenth volume of Cuvier's *The
Animal Kingdom,* covering the class Pisces (No. 171), a work that Melville drew on in a footnote to Chapter 42 of *Moby-Dick,* 'The Whiteness
of the Whale.' Perhaps the box also contained the bound blank book intended for a catalogue of Melville's library that unfortunately was never
undertaken (see the frontispiece, above).

At this same period Lemuel Shaw was attempting to secure books
concerning the island of Nantucket and its ships and men. In January
1851 he received from Thomas Macy of Nantucket a copy of Lay and
Hussey's *Narrative of the Mutiny, on Board the Ship Globe of Nan-*

tucket that he gave to Melville (Check-List, No. 323). He may possibly have added another book about the *Globe* affair, Hiram Paulding's *Journal of a Cruise of the United States Cruiser Dolphin . . . in Pursuit of the Mutineers of the Whaleship Globe,* which he had bought in 1831 (Appendix B.3). Attached to the front flyleaf of Melville's copy of the Lay and Hussey *Narrative* is a letter of 9 January 1851 from Thomas Macy to T. G. Coffin, through whom he had evidently received Shaw's request for books about Nantucket. Macy informed Coffin that he was sending the volume 'as a present to Judge Shaw,' adding that 'after the most dilligent search' he had 'not succeeded in finding a copy of the loss of Ship Essex'—i.e., Owen Chase's graphic *Narrative*—that had also been asked for. 'Should I hereafter succeed in procuring one,' he concluded, 'I will forward it,' either through Coffin or directly to Shaw. On 4 April 1851 Macy wrote to Shaw, sending him what he described as 'a mutilated copy' of the desired book—'the only copy that I have been able to procure.' In the book itself (No. 134) are Melville's inscription ('Herman Melville from Judge Shaw April. 1851.') and his extensive notes on the story of the *Essex,* which he cites in Chapter 45 of *Moby-Dick,* 'The Affidavit,' as corroborating 'the most marvellous event in this book' (p. 181), meaning the sinking of the *Pequod.* On 7 January 1852 Thomas Macy gave him a third book, Obed Macy's *History of Nantucket* (No. 345)—possibly in exchange for a copy of *Moby-Dick,* though no record of such a gift has come to light. Whether or not they met at that time is unknown.

The standard work on the whaling background of Melville's sixth book is *The Trying-Out of Moby-Dick* (1949) by the late Howard P. Vincent, which 'combines a study of the whaling sources of *Moby-Dick* with an account of its composition, and suggestions concerning interpretation and meaning' (p. 7). Additional findings with respect to other sources of the book are reported in the Explanatory Notes of the Hendricks House edition of *Moby-Dick* (1952), edited by Vincent in collaboration with the late Luther S. Mansfield (pp. 570–832). For Melville's writing 'on whales and whaling,' in the words of Mansfield and Vincent, he

> had need of whaling books for facts to weight his exposition. He said that he had "swum through libraries," but it is apparent that he read only five authors with care—Beale [Check-List, No. 52], Bennett, J. Ross Browne [No. 88], Cheever, and Scoresby [Nos. 450, 451]—and that there were more whaling authors he did not know than he knew. The whaling books were mostly read within a limited period and for the specific purpose of this novel.

'Of Melville's more general reading,' the editors went on to say,

Shakespeare perhaps had the most profound impact. But in *Moby-Dick* the influence of Carlyle was almost equally apparent; and De Quincey, Sir Thomas Browne, Goethe, Montaigne, Emerson, and Hawthorne helped importantly to shape ideas or phrasing. Melville, however, could get from books of such slight literary merit as Robert Southey's *The Doctor* and Thomas Hope's *Anastasius* [No. 282] abundant stimuli that set his mind to work. Far outranking all other books in its all-pervading influence was the King James version of the Bible, which Melville read and reread, annotated and marked in more than one edition. (pp. 570–571)

Later scholarship has not materially altered these generalizations—especially those concerning the 'whaling authors' Melville knew and did not know. But along with the influence of Shakespeare should be considered Melville's reading of other dramatic and epic poetry—Homer, Virgil, and Milton; the Greek tragedians; Shakespeare's own contemporaries such as Marlowe and Jonson—and of nineteenth-century dramatic criticism. Besides Montaigne and Sir Thomas Browne, Melville by this period was also indebted to other prose writers of the sixteenth and seventeenth centuries—notably Rabelais and Burton and Bayle. Browne had also led him to Plato, whose profound influence on *Moby-Dick* has recently been demonstrated by Michael Levin in 'Ahab as Socratic Philosopher' (1979) and in my own 'Melville and the Platonic Tradition' (1982). Between the writing of *Mardi,* with its overdependence on Plato, and the composition of *Moby-Dick,* as I observed in the latter essay,

> Melville developed from an author who entertained philosophical ideas into a full-fledged philosophical novelist. In *Mardi* the characters talk philosophy; in *Moby-Dick,* for good or for ill, both Ahab and Ishmael put their philosophy to the test of experience in the course of Ahab's doomed quest for Moby Dick. (pp. 315–316)

Other philosophical and religious motifs in *Moby-Dick* have been traced to Melville's knowledge—direct or indirect—of Edmund Burke's *A Philosophical Inquiry into the Origin of Our Ideas of the Sublime and Beautiful* (Check-List, No. 97) and of Gnostic, Zoroastrian, and Hindu thought (notably by Barbara Glenn, Thomas Vargish, Dorothee Metlitsky Finkelstein, and H. B. Kulkarni), and to his use of secondary sources such as Bayle's *Dictionary* (No. 51), Chambers's *Cyclopaedia* (No. 128), *Anthon's Classical Dictionary,* and John Kitto's *Cyclopaedia of Biblical Literature.* As Millicent Bell has justly remarked, 'One of the knottiest problems in considering Melville's use of his reading will always be the question of how much he read in original sources and how much he derived at second-hand' ('Pierre Bayle and *Moby Dick,*' p. 626). A good illustration is the set of 'Extracts' prefixed to *Moby-Dick,* quotations which afford 'a glancing bird's eye view of what had been promiscuously said, thought, fancied, and sung of Leviathan, by many nations and generations' (p. 2), from Genesis on down. Melville's model, according to Mansfield and Vincent, may have been the seven volumes of Southey's *The Doctor* (1834–1847), each of which opens with a 'Prelude of Mottoes.' 'Melville's own reading accounted for a large number of the quotations,' they observe, 'but many came to him from secondary sources'—particularly Cheever and Browne (pp. 579–580); others may have been given him by Evert Duyckinck, as Melville's letter to Duyckinck of 7 November 1851 may suggest. Investigation of the known sources of individual quotations—by Mansfield and Vincent and more recently by the Northwestern-Newberry editors—has in turn revealed passages used elsewhere in the book.

Recent scholarship has particularly emphasized the relation of *Moby-Dick* to the romantic tradition in both Europe and America. Since his youth Melville had known the poetry of Byron and the fiction of Cooper; since the late 1840's he had been reading and absorbing the writings of Wordsworth and Coleridge and Carlyle, Goethe and Schiller, Emerson and Thoreau. As Morse Peckham, a theorist of romanticism, remarked in 1966, 'It is as if Melville had absorbed all at once all stages of Romanticism up to his own time, and had presented them in *Moby-Dick* in inextricable confusion' ('Hawthorne and Melville as European Authors,' p. 59). Although significant findings have been published concerning his response in *Moby-Dick* to these individual authors and their works, much remains to be done,[7] not merely in terms of source-study but also with the object of seeing both Melville and his book as exemplars of romantic thought and art. Melville was above all an artist, a poet in prose. As a writer, Jay Leyda has observed, he 'used books for their music as well as for their ideas and information—everyone can hear the rhythms of Shakespeare, Browne, Carlyle in *Moby Dick*' (*Log* 1: xx). Moreover, he drew extensively in *Moby-Dick* on his growing familiarity with pictorial art, as admirably demonstrated in several recent studies. Larry J. Reynolds has shown that the striking image of the Catskill eagle at the conclusion of Chapter 96 derives from Melville's perceptive response to a well-known painting of 1849, Asher Durand's 'Kindred Spirits'; Robert K. Wallace has presented new evidence for his knowledge and use of the works of J. M. W. Turner; and Stuart M. Frank in *Herman Melville's Picture Gallery,* a fascinating book-length study, has identified and illustrated the sources of the 'pictorial' chapters of *Moby-Dick.*

Notes

[1]On 21 December 1849, while Melville was still abroad, Allan Melville had charged two titles to his brother's account with Harper and Brothers: a set of Thomas Chalmers's *Posthumous Works* and a volume of Montalba's *Fairy Tales from All Nations*—the latter a New Year's present for his cousin Catherine Gansevoort (Check-List, Nos. 127, 367).

[2]For a full report of the markings and annotations in Melville's copy of the *Mosses,* see Walker Cowen, 'Melville's Marginalia: Hawthorne.'

[3]On the composition and revision of 'Hawthorne and His Mosses,' see Sealts, Historical Note to The Piazza Tales *and Other Prose Pieces, 1839–1860,* pp. 471 ff.; page references that follow are to the text of the review as printed in this same volume. One indication of Melville's haste in writing is his erroneous statement that the 'courtly author' who once called Shakespeare 'an "upstart crow" ' was Henry Chettle rather than Robert Greene (p. 246); a marginal line in Melville's set of Shakespeare (I: xiv–xv) marks a correct account of Greene's epithet (Check-List, No. 460).

[4]Page references are to the 1846 Wiley and Putnam edition of *On Heroes,* one of the two editions owned by Duyckinck.

[5]Melville's fondness for the phrase 'blackness of darkness' (from Jude 4:13) may owe something to Carlyle's use of the expression in Book II, Chapter 4 of *Sartor Resartus,* also borrowed in the summer of 1850. Other phrasing in the essay is clearly traceable to his reading during 1849 and 1850: e.g., the twice-repeated figure of the plummet (pp. 242, 243) probably echoes *The Tempest* V.i.56–57, 'obscure' is used as a noun here ('the infinite obscure,' p. 244) as it is in *Paradise Lost* II.406: 'the palpable obscure'; the statement that Shakespeare 'has been approached' (p. 245) reflects Melville's reaction to an editor's remark that 'Shakespeare must ever remain unapproachable': 'Cant,' wrote Melville. 'No man "must ever remain unapproachable" ' (*Log* 1: 363–364; Check-List, No. 137: p. clx).

[6]Nonmembers were permitted to use the library on payment of a small fee. An 1853 catalogue, an 1853 supplement, and frequent announcements in local newspapers of new books acquired indicate the resources available there during Melville's residence in Pittsfield.

[7]Although both doctoral dissertations and scholarly essays have dealt with Melville's reading in each of these authors, no comprehensive study has yet been published relating his work to that of the British, German, and American romantics generally. In his chapter on Melville in Myerson's *The Transcendentalists: A Review of Research and Criticism* (1984), Brian Higgins surveys much of this work, justly concluding that 'an invaluable contribution to Melville research remains to be made by a scholar who is able to combine such factual information as is available with a comprehensive examination of Melville's works for all the evidence they yield about his response to American and European Transcendentalists and other philosophical idealists, including most notably Thoreau and Carlyle' (p. 361).

5. 1851–1853

Pierre

O n 1? June 1851, in the same remarkable letter to Hawthorne in which he took note of the continual 'unfolding' within himself that had begun in his twenty-fifth year, Melville expressed the fear that he had 'now come to the inmost leaf of the bulb, and that shortly the flower must fall to the mould.' The letter was written when he was physically tired from outdoor work, 'building and patching and tinkering' about the farmhouse as well as planting his corn and potatoes, so that by evening he felt 'completely done up.' Even more telling was his discouraged comment on *Moby-Dick,* begun early in 1850 and projected for completion in the following autumn, but still unfinished after a difficult winter. 'In a week or so,' he went on to tell Hawthorne,

> I go to New York to . . . work and slave on my "Whale" while it is driving through the press. *That* is the only way I can finish it now,—I am so pulled hither and thither by circumstances. The calm, the coolness, the silent grass-growing mood in which a man *ought* always to compose,—that, I fear, can seldom be mine. Dollars damn me; and the malicious Devil is forever grinning in upon me, holding the door ajar. My dear Sir, a presentiment is on me,—I shall at last be worn out and perish, like an old nutmeg-grater, ground to pieces by the constant attrition of the wood, that is, the nutmeg. What I feel most moved to write, that is banned,—it will

not pay. Yet, altogether, write the *other* way I cannot. So the product is a final hash, and all my books are botches.

'I'm rather sore, perhaps, in this letter,' he then acknowledged; 'but see my hand!—four blisters on this palm, made by hoes and hammers within the last few days.'

Melville had good reason to be uneasy as he surveyed his 'circumstances' in the spring of 1851. In buying Arrowhead, besides giving a mortgage he had also needed to borrow heavily, first from his father-in-law to acquire the property and more recently from an old friend in Lansingburgh to cover alterations. Farm work was not only physically tiring; it had also taken time and energy that might otherwise have gone into his writing, and with his new work still incomplete there was no income from that quarter, Harper and Brothers having declined to make the advance payment he had requested in April. Still more troubling were his mixed feelings about the book itself, which—as he must have realized—had developed more in the interdicted vein of *Mardi* than in the popular mode of *Redburn* and *White-Jacket*. Even in *Mardi* he had recognized that though an author such as his Lombardo is moved to write by the promptings of 'a full heart,' there is also a financial motive—'the necessity of bestirring himself to procure his yams' (p. 592). Now, as he complained to Hawthorne, the two impulses had been working at cross-purposes within himself: 'So the product is a final hash, and all my books are botches.'

As this letter reveals, the enthusiasm with which Melville began *Moby-Dick,* though it continued during his first weeks at Arrowhead, had now given way to doubt and discouragement. Throughout the early months of 1851 he evidently drove himself relentlessly to finish what he later called his 'ditcher's work with that book' (letter to Hawthorne, 17? November 1851). His wife, remembering his altered schedule of writing after the new year began, was to note that he

> wrote White Whale or Moby Dick under unfavorable circumstances— would sit at his desk all day not eating any thing till four or five o clock— then ride to the village after dark—Would be up early and out walking before breakfast—sometimes splitting wood for exercise. (Sealts, *The Early Lives of Melville,* p. 169)

On 29 June 1851, after returning from his trip to New York, Melville wrote Hawthorne to report that though the *'Whale'* was 'half through the press,' its conclusion remained to be written. 'The tail is not yet cooked,' as he put it—'though the hell-fire in which the whole book is broiled might not unreasonably have cooked it all ere this.' In late July, with writing and proofreading nearly done, he reluctantly accepted Richard Bentley's disappointing offer for the English edition, made with regard for the unsettled copyright question in Great Britain. By the end of July, having the book at last off his hands and looking forward as a farmer to the close of the haying season, he was proposing a Berkshire excursion with Hawthorne and a visit to Arrowhead by Evert and George Duyckinck, who came to Pittsfield in August. After their departure, with *Moby-Dick* scheduled for October publication in London and for November by the Harpers in New York, he was already making plans for his seventh book.

Pierre

Two editions of *Pierre,* the Hendricks House (1949) and the Northwestern-Newberry (1971), offer valuable discussions of the relation between Melville's recent reading and the direction his writing took during the winter of 1851–1852. Henry A. Murray, approaching the book in the earlier of these editions as Melville's 'spiritual autobiography in the form of a novel,' pointed out that since the autumn of 1849 he had been reading such revelatory works as

> Rousseau's *Confessions,* Goethe's *Autobiography,* De Quincey's *Autobiographical Sketches* and *Confessions of an Opium Eater,* [Carlyle's] *Sartor Resartus,* and, there are reasons to believe, [Thackeray's] *Pendennis* and [Borrow's] *Lavengro,* both of which are partial self-revelations. If to this list we add the autobiographical novels of Disraeli, who, omitting Byron, seems to have provided more raw material for *Pierre* than any other author, it is evident that Melville had ample encouragement to carry truthtelling further than he ever had before. (Introduction to *Pierre,* p. xxiv)

According to Murray, the title character of *Pierre* as he is presented in the early chapters reflects Melville's own youthful fascination with the figure of Lord Byron, known to him through Moore's *Life of Byron* as well as through Byron's own works (p. xli; see Check-List, Nos. 369, 112). Among other 'architects of Melville's early ideal self and so of the character of Pierre,' Murray mentions Benjamin Disraeli in particular and, to a lesser degree, 'Scott, Spenser, Moore, Cooper, and Bulwer-Lytton' (p.xli). In the characterization of Pierre, Thackeray's *Pendennis* (1850) and Shakespeare's *Romeo and Juliet* also figured, though the spirit of *Romeo and Juliet* that pervades the early chapters soon gives way to that of *Hamlet.* In Book IX Melville writes of young Glendinning: 'Dante had made him fierce, and Hamlet had insinuated that there was none to strike' (p. 170). In the central part of the book, according to Murray, Melville drew heavily on Disraeli's novels for both 'ore' and 'rubbish' (p. lxvii), but in 'the last phase of Pierre's career' Murray sees Byron once again—that 'prototype of the Romantic genius,' standing along with Melville's own Ahab among such 'heroic sufferers and malcontents' as 'Titan, Prometheus, Satan, Lear,

Timon, Cain, and Manfred' (p. lxxxvi).

Remarking on *Pierre's* eccentricities of grammar and style, Murray has a final comment on the influence of Melville's reading. 'The whole work,' he writes,

> seems to have been composed in a state of mind that requires some of the instrumentalities of poetry for its adequate expression. This is manifest very often in the imagery and not infrequently in the beat of the author's prose, which . . . is reminiscent at times of Thomas Browne's majestic style and, now and then, of the flowing cadences of De Quincey. The influence of Carlyle is also unmistakable. (p. xciv)

Murray's generalizations about the influence of various books and authors are documented in the detailed explanatory notes to his edition. Leon Howard's portion of the Historical Note to the Northwestern-Newberry edition particularly stresses the increasing influence of both Carlyle and Shakespeare on the latter half of *Pierre*—that part of the book which, in Howard's words, especially 'reflects Melville's intellectual and compositional experiences of the preceding year' (p. 372).[1]

Some of the most striking images in *Pierre* appear to derive from Melville's reading of Emerson, as pointed out in my 'Melville and Emerson's Rainbow' (pp. 270–271 and nn. 53–57, pp. 384–385). Other scholars have also suggested his possible use of Mme de Staël's *Corinne,* which he had obtained from Bentley while in London, and of Sylvester Judd's *Margaret,* which he borrowed from Evert Duyckinck in 1850 (Check-List, Nos. 486, 303). Howard considered *Corinne* a more likely possibility than *Margaret,* but found even closer parallels in Bulwer-Lytton's *Zanoni,* a book given Melville by his neighbor Sarah Morewood in September 1851, along with Harriet Martineau's *The Hour and the Man* (Nos. 334, 350), at the very time when he was thinking about his next book (Howard, pp. 370–372). Melville's continuing interest in Bulwer may be attested by Mrs. Morewood's later gift of a second novel, *Pilgrims of the Rhine,* in 1854 (No. 333); he may also have known Bulwer's *The New Timon* (1846), listed by his sister Augusta among her 'Books to be purchased' (Appendix B.4).

Still other works acquired by Melville in 1851 should also be mentioned here: a copy of Cornelius Mathews' new novel *Chanticleer* and a translation by his friend George Adler of Goethe's *Iphigenia in Tauris,* both sent to him in January (Check-List, Nos. 351a, 229), and volumes 4 and 5 of Richard Hildreth's *History of the United States,* shipped to him by Harper and Brothers in November (No. 272). By late 1851 he had evidently bought at least the third volume (1850) of the new Bohn edition of Plato (the edition cited in *Billy Budd, Sailor*): there are allusions to the *Banquet,* or *Symposium,* in his letter of 17? November to

Hawthorne and also in Book II of *Pierre* (Sealts, 'Melville and the Platonic Tradition,' pp. 319–320). Of the various books given Melville by Hawthorne, at least two—*Twice-Told Tales* and *The House of the Seven Gables*—he had not only read but also discussed in letters of 1851 to Duyckinck and to Hawthorne himself. *Pierre* is the first of his books to be written in the third person, like most of Hawthorne's fiction; Hawthorne's practice may have influenced this new departure. And like *Seven Gables* in particular, *Pierre* is a domestic romance dealing with several generations of a single family; as in Hawthorne's book, there is a family mansion, Saddle Meadows, and even a family secret— if one accepts Pierre's assumption that Isabel is his unacknowledged half-sister.

Besides the likely influence of Hawthorne and his writings, there may be a related factor at work: the possible appeal of an out-and-out romance to female readers, whom Melville's stories of the sea were not designed to attract. He himself repeatedly stressed the differences between his latest work and its predecessors; to Richard Bentley, for example, he emphasized its 'utterly new scenes & characters,' calling it 'a regular romance, with a mysterious plot to it, & stirring passions at work, . . . representing a new & elevated aspect of American life' (letter of 16 April 1852). Perhaps he was making a considered attempt in *Pierre* to 'write the *other* way'— for a popular and largely feminine audience. The women of his own household, as Melville surely knew, were drawn to such authors as Angela Marsh-Caldwell, Sarah Ellis, Grace Aguilar, and Elizabeth Sewell. *Moby-Dick,* on the other hand, was 'by no means the sort of book' for readers like Sarah Morewood, whom he warned away from it, and he was 'really amazed' when Sophia Hawthorne praised the new work: 'some *men* have said they were pleased with it,' he wrote, 'but you are the only *woman*' (letters of 12? September 1851, 8 January 1852).

If Melville was indeed writing a romance for women readers, that intention may explain his remark to Mrs. Hawthorne that his next book would be 'a rural bowl of milk' rather than another 'bowl of salt water.' It may also throw light on his later statement to Bentley that he believed *Pierre* to be 'very much more calculated for popularity' than anything of his that Bentley had yet published (letters of 8 January, 16 April 1852). For some modern critics, surprised by this claim for *Pierre,* Melville's words to Bentley must represent either a misconception of the audience of the day or a deliberately misleading attempt at authorial salesmanship. Others argue that his intentions shifted after he had undertaken the actual composition of *Pierre*—probably begun in November 1851, the month when the first American edition of *Moby-Dick* was published, and before the reviews of it reached Pittsfield.

Elizabeth Melville had given birth to a second son in October; in the early autumn her husband had crops to harvest and the winter's wood to cut. A 'joy-giving and exultation-breeding letter' from Hawthorne afforded him 'a sense of unspeakable security' because Hawthorne had 'understood' *Moby-Dick* (letter to Hawthorne, 17? November 1851). But on 21 November the Hawthornes left the Berkshires for a temporary residence in West Newton, and without Hawthorne's neighborly companionship and encouragement Melville was facing a lonely winter. Soon he was taking refuge in his writing. The pattern he followed with *Pierre* was like that of his labors on *Moby-Dick* during the previous winter and spring. Sarah Morewood, in writing to George Duyckinck on 28 December 1851, remarked that her neighborhood, being 'engaged in a new work,' was not leaving his study 'till quite dark in the evening—when he for the first time during the whole day partakes of solid food—he must therefore write under a state of morbid excitement which will soon injure his health' (*Log* 1:44)

Melville's mother, in a letter of 29 December to Augusta Melville (NYPL–GL), similarly reported that 'Herman is perfectly absorb'd by this book he is now writing,' adding that he was 'very angry' after hearing complaints in Pittsfield that *Moby-Dick* 'is more than Blasphemous.' As he also saw the published reviews of the book, both English and American, he must have soon realized that readers who 'understood' his 'Whale' as the Hawthornes did were exceptional. Even the *Literary World,* in a long two-part notice of *Moby-Dick* probably written by Evert Duyckinck, concentrated its praise on Melville's treatment of whales and whaling but raised objections to his portrayal of both Ahab and Ishmael: Ahab, conceived in the spirit of German melodrama as a 'Faust of the quarter-deck,' struck the reviewer as 'too long drawn out,' and Ishmael's 'piratical running down of creeds and opinions' troubled Duyckinck, reminding him of 'the conceited indifferentism of Emerson, or the run-a-muck style of Carlyle.'[2]

Though not all reviewers were hostile to *Moby-Dick,* Duyckinck's strictures and other negative criticisms at home and abroad served to confirm Melville's worst fears about the book; some commentators contend that he materially altered the second half of his next work by way of response. Certainly *Pierre* in its published form is considerably longer than he had projected it would be, and its protagonist's delayed emergence as a writer of books is somewhat unexpected. Whatever the case, the narrator's treatment of Pierre's career as an author is particularly relevant to a study of Melville's own reading and writing. His comments on Pierre's 'juvenile' authorship, for example, amount to a virtual critique of Melville's first three books. Early literary success, the narrator tells us, commonly owes less to any true originality on an author's part than to 'some rich and peculiar experience in life, embodied in a book,' just as Melville had embodied his South Sea experience in *Typee* and *Omoo*. When young Pierre 'immaturely attempts a mature work,' like Melville himself in *Mardi,* the narrator finds him trying to make 'mere reading' serve instead of 'spontaneous creative thought,' with the dominating influence of Plato mentioned as a case in point (pp. 259, 282–284).

Later, in Book XXII, we see Pierre in the very posture of Melville himself in the year 1851, laboring over his latest manuscript 'from eight o'clock in the morning till half-past four in the evening,' stopping only for the sake of his failing eyes (pp. 303, 301). As Pierre composes his new book, moreover, he begins to lash out at writers who had presumably nurtured him in the past. 'Away, ye chattering apes of a sophomorean Spinoza and Plato,' he writes. 'Tell me not, thou inconceivable coxcomb of a Goethe, that the universe can not spare thee and thy immortality' (p. 302). This is not simply an isolated outburst by Melville's protagonist, for in a similar passage the narrator also attacks these same writers, arraigning them along with other 'philosophers and their vain philosophy':

> Plato, and Spinoza, and Goethe, and many more belong to this guild of self-imposters, with a preposterous rabble of Muggletonian Scots and Yankees, whose vile brogue still the more bestreaks the stripedness of their Greek or German Neoplatonical originals. (p. 208)

As we know, Melville himself had been a devoted reader of Plato and his modern successors—Carlyle (a Scot), Emerson (a Yankee), and Goethe (a German), the very figures whose supposedly malign influence on *Moby-Dick* had been singled out in Duyckinck's recent review, which must have affected him deeply.[3] Critics had been objecting to Melville's philosophizing since the time of *Mardi,* as he well knew. In *Moby-Dick* there is even some foreshadowing of these passages in *Pierre* when Ishmael, contrasting idealist with empirical philosophers, advises his reader to 'throw *all* these thunderheads overboard' (p. 277; emphasis added).[4] Now in *Pierre* Melville was not merely answering Duyckinck's charges; he was also repudiating philosophy generally— and so turning his back on what had been a major component of his reading and writing. 'For there is no faith, and no stoicism, and no philosophy,' according to Book XXI, that will 'stand the final test of a real impassioned onset of Life and Passion. . . . For Faith and philosophy are air, but events are brass. Amidst his gray philosophizings, Life breaks upon a man like a morning' (p. 289).

After *Pierre*

With the completion of *Pierre* in the spring of 1852, a disillusioned Melville had indeed come to the inmost leaf of the bulb, though his family may have been slow to realize where his reading, thinking, and writing had taken him. The modern reader who is familiar with the correspondence of his domestic circle at Arrowhead during the preceding year must be struck by the contrast in both subject matter and tone between the cheerful, matter-of-fact letters penned by his closest relatives and the books he was striving to write, alone in his upstairs study. Apart from the brief comments on his working habits that are quoted above, there was seemingly little conception of his struggles to finish either *Moby-Dick* or *Pierre*.[5] Now, unable to come to terms for *Pierre* with Richard Bentley, who refused to accept the book without extensive revisions, he was obliged to settle for its English publication only in the form of imported American sheets. Bentley's private reaction to the book foreshadowed its public reception, for though the reviews of *Moby-Dick* had been mixed, those of *Pierre*, published in New York by Harper and Brothers in late July of 1852, were unanimously hostile. Criticism went far beyond the objections previously raised against any of Melville's earlier works, *Mardi* included, to attack it on moral as well as aesthetic grounds and even to question the sanity of its author. By publishing such a book, Melville was warned in print, he had jeopardized his future as a professional writer.

One can only speculate about the reactions of Melville's family, both to the devastating reviews and to the book itself. Elizabeth Melville, who had a difficult recovery from her second pregnancy, may have known little about *Pierre* while it was still in manuscript, her husband's sister Helen having served as its copyist (*Log* 1: 441). But Melville, like his Pierre, had once again 'directly plagiarized,' not only from his reading but 'from his own experience' (*Pierre*, p. 302), and his wife, with her penchant for reading his published works as autobiography, must have seen obvious parallels, not only between Pierre's way of writing and her husband's but also the many resemblances between various members of the Glendinning family and their counterparts among the Melvilles and Gansevoorts.[6] What either she or her mother-in-law knew, or suspected, about such parallels between fiction and fact may have something to do with the family's curious reticence with regard to *Pierre*, both in correspondence of the 1850's and in later years.[7] Long afterward, when in 1901 Elizabeth was sent proof of a projected article on Melville, she requested a significant change:

> I should like to amend one statement where it is said that the reception of 'Pierre' had any part in causing my husband to lead 'a recluse life'—in fact it was a subject of joke with him, declaring that it was but just, and I know that however it might have affected his literary reputation, it con-

cerned him personally but very little. (Dorothy V. B. D. R. McNeilly, 'The Melvilles and Mrs. Ferris,' p. 6)

Reliable or otherwise, this comment by Mrs. Melville is all that is known concerning Melville's own reaction to the reception of his seventh book.

According to Melville himself, when he responded on 17 July 1852 to Hawthorne's gift of *The Blithedale Romance* (Check-List, No. 245) and to a note inviting him to visit the Hawthornes in Concord, where they had recently settled, he had done no writing after finishing *Pierre*. 'For the last three months & more,' he told Hawthorne, he had been 'an utter idler and a savage—out of doors all the time.' He had just returned from a two-week excursion to the islands of Nantucket, Martha's Vineyard, and Naushon with his father-in-law, who held court on the islands. While on Nantucket he himself talked with Captain George Pollard, who had been master of the ill-fated *Essex*. Because of this absence, he explained to Hawthorne, he had 'not yet got far into' *Blithedale,* but he could see already that Hawthorne had 'most admirably employed materials which are richer than I had fancied them'—presumably an allusion to Hawthorne's own experiences as a member of the Brook Farm community.

Melville's next letter to Hawthorne, written on 13 August 1852, is the first of a series dealing with the tribulations of a woman of Nantucket, Agatha Hatch Robinson, who had been deserted by her sailor husband. During his recent travels he had heard of her situation from a New Bedford lawyer, who at his request sent him a document giving further details of her case. He had considered writing 'a regular story to be founded on these striking incidents,' he told Hawthorne, but on second thought had decided that the materials were more in Hawthorne's vein than his own; he accordingly forwarded the lawyers document to Concord with comments on its appropriate treatment should Hawthorne care to make fictional use of it. Hawthorne seems not to have replied—either about the story of Agatha or about the copy of *Pierre* that had presumably been sent to him in return for *Blighedale* —by 25 October,when Melville again wrote. In this letter, besides offering more suggestions for the story of Agatha Robinson should Hawthorne 'be engaged upon it,' he recommended a new book, J. E. A. Smith's *Taghconic; or Letters and Legends about Our Summer Home* (Check-List, No. 478), describing it as a ''Guide-Book'' to Berkshire' and remarking, 'you figure in it, & I also.' The book includes chapters by various hands, Sarah Moorewood among them, but Melville, in his mother's words, had 'not contributed one line, tho often requested to do so' (*Log* 1: 461).

Early in December, having visited Hawthorne in Concord while on his way to Boston, Melville agreed in his next letter with Hawthorne's suggestion that he himself should write the story of Agatha, which apparently occupied him during the winter of 1852–1853. Meanwhile, however, the severe reviews of *Pierre* that appeared in the summer and fall had raised serious doubts among his relatives about his future as an author. Following the national election of November 1852, when Hawthorne's friend Franklin Pierce was chosen for the presidency, the possibility of a foreign consulship for Melville under the new administration was discussed 'again & again' within the family. His mother reported this possibility to her brother Peter Gansevoort, observing in a letter of 20 April 1853 that Hawthorne had promised to help by receiving letters written in Melville's behalf and by speaking personally to Pierce. Melville himself 'dislikes asking favors from any one,' she noted, and 'therefore postponed writing from time to time, until he became so completely absorbed by his new work, now nearly ready for the press, that he has not taken the proper, & necessary measures to procure this earnestly wished for office' (*Log* 1: 464, 468).

On 22 May 1853 Melville's wife gave birth to their third child, Elizabeth. In early June, when he went to New York to see Peter Gansevoort off for England, he took with him for submission to Harper and Brothers a book-length manuscript—presumably the 'Agatha' story—that he was 'prevented from printing,' as he put it in a subsequent letter to the firm on 24 November. In view of his perennial need for money, heightened now by the poor sales of *Pierre,* and of his family's growing concern for his physical and mental condition, the rejection of his latest manuscript must have been a severe blow. As Elizabeth Melville later remembered, 'We all felt anxious about the strain on his health in Spring of 1853' (Sealts, *The Early Lives of Melville,* p. 169).

The family's increasing anxiety is reflected in Maria Melville's letter of 20 April to her brother, which urged him to 'lose no time' in pressing her son's candidacy for a consulship, 'as every day counts.' 'A change of occupation,' she told Peter Gansevoort, 'is necessary' for Herman, who 'would be greatly benefited by a sojourn abroad.' He

> would then be compelled to more intercourse with his fellow creatures. It would very materially renew, & strengthen both his body & mind.
>
> The constant in-door confinement with little intermission to which Hermans occupation as author compels him, does not agree with him. This constant working of the brain, & excitement of the imagination, is wearing Herman out. (*Log* 1: 469)

But the hoped-for appointment did not materialize, despite the best efforts of Peter Gansevoort, Lemuel Shaw, Allan Melville, and a number of friends and acquaintances that included both Hawthorne and Richard Henry Dana. There was one new development, however: during or after Melville's visit to New York in June, when his latest manuscript was rejected, the Harper brothers persuaded him to become a contributor to *Harper's New Monthly Magazine*.[8]

Notes

[1]One book charged to Melville's account with the Harpers on 9 February 1852—possibly by Allan Melville—had no discernible influence on *Pierre*: John S. Springer's *Forest Life and Forest Trees* (1851), which deals with winter camp life and lumbering operations in Maine (Check-List, No. 484).

[2]The Norton *Moby-Dick*, pp. 613–616, reprints this installment of Duyckinck's review.

[3]Much has been written about Melville's response to the notice and its effect on *Pierre*. As a subscriber to the *Literary World* he would of course have seen each installment shortly after its publication. During a visit to New York early in 1852 he sent Duyckinck a note of 9? January thanking him for a New Year's gift; though he declined an invitation to meet he promised 'to call though at some other time—not very remote in the future, either.' But on 14 February he addressed a brusque note to 'Editors of Literary World' canceling his subscription, following it on 16 April with a second note to the same effect (reproduced in 'A New Melville Letter'). Meanwhile he had written into *Pierre* both a pun on the Duyckinck name (p. 107: 'the diving and ducking moralities of this earth') and an episode based on his own refusal to contribute to the Duyckinck's *Dollar Magazine* (pp. 253–254: Pierre's scorn for 'the personal profaneness of gentlemen of the Captain Kidd school of literature'). The Duyckincks in turn published a devastating review of *Pierre*.

[4]Melville adapted his much-quoted passage from Emerson's contrast of the philosophies of Locke and Kant in 'The Transcendentalist' (Sealts, 'Melville and the Platonic Tradition,' pp. 318–319).

[5]James C. Wilson, basing his judgments on an examination of the Melville Family Papers recently acquired by the New York Public Library, takes issue with the position of biographers such as Newton Arvin and Edwin Haviland Miller concerning Melville's family relations. He concludes that 'Melville was not estranged from his family, that family relations at Arrowhead were fairly normal and reasonably happy—at least outwardly. Melville's buried emotions might have surfaced in his fiction or in his more private conversations with Hawthorne, but the Melville Family Papers do not reveal him as a brooding, obsessive, narcissistic presence. . . . On the contrary, . . . he was an active and usually agreeable participant in the life of the family *while* he wrote the fiction and cultivated the most important intellectual relationship of his life with Hawthorne' ('Melville at Arrowhead,' p. 242).

My own study of these and related documents of the 1850's, though it confirms Wilson's general impression, has led me to emphasize the differences as well as the points of contact between Melville and his family, and also to sense a growing inwardness in Melville himself that especially manifested itself during and after the early months of 1851.

[6]Two parallels are especially pertinent. As Murray has recently shown in 'Allan Melvill's Bye-Blow,' Herman Melville's father had reputedly fathered an illegitimate daughter some years before his marriage, as Pierre believes the elder Glendinning to have done, and Lemuel Shaw as a family friend had made inquiries concerning the story. Moreover, we are told that Glendinning during his last illness had 'wandered in his mind' and finally 'died a raver,' leading Pierre to fear 'his own hereditary liability to madness' (pp. 70, 178, 287). In fact, Allan Melvill had died under similar circumstances when Herman, like Pierre, was twelve years of age, and Shaw had been apprised of the situation at that time.

[7]All that Elizabeth Melville set down about the book in her family memoranda of 1861 was that her husband 'Wrote "Pierre" published 1852' (Sealts, *The Early Lives of Melville*, p. 169). In 1892, the year after his death, when she arranged for a reprinting of J. E. A. Smith's serialized biographical sketch of Melville, she omitted much of what Smith had originally written about *Pierre*.

[8]See the letter of 27 July 1853 from Hope Savage Shaw to Samuel H. Savage, quoted in Frederick J. Kennedy and Joyce Deveau Kennedy, 'Additions to *The Melville Log*,' p. 8; Sealts, Historical Note to The Piazza Tales *and Other Prose Pieces*, p. 481.

6. 1853–1856

The Magazine Pieces,
Israel Potter, The Piazza Tales

*M*elville's decision to become a magazine writer, made chiefly out of his pressing need for money after the Harpers had declined his eighth book-length manuscript, opened a new chapter in his professional career. From 1844 until the summer of 1853, except for his occasional pieces for the *Literary World* and *Yankee Doodle*, he had been a writer only of books. In 1851 he had refused Evert Duyckinck's request that he contribute to *Holden's Dollar Magazine* and in 1852 he had evidently not responded to other invitations from the publishers of *Putnam's Monthly Magazine* in New York and *Bentley's Miscellany* in London. At the same time, however, he was well aware that the American reading public preferred those authors 'who write those most saleable of all books nowadays—i e—the newspapers, & magazines,' as he remarked ruefully to Richard Bentley in his letter of 20 July 1851.

Melville obviously had no objection to seeing long excerpts from his own works included in advance notices of his books and in later reviews. A recent example had been the appearance in *Harper's* for October 1851 of an entire chapter of *Moby-Dick,* 'The Town-Ho's Story' (Ch. 54), a self-contained episode that served as an advertisement for the book, a month before its American publication. Other segments of his earlier works could also have been printed as independent stories or sketches, as the Harpers may well have realized. Now, after the failure of *Pierre*, it would be prudent for them to recruit Melville as an anonymous contributor to their new magazine rather than to risk bringing out another book with his name on the title page.

As for Melville, who had previously thought of publishing *Pierre* 'anonymously, or under an assumed name,' as he had suggested to Richard Bentley in his letter of 16 April 1852, the prospect of writing both anonymously and in shorter forms might well have seemed attractive by 1853, given the energy it had cost him to turn out eight book-length manuscripts in roughly as many years, plus the repeated disappointments he had suffered with *Moby-Dick*, with *Pierre*, and with his recently rejected work. By 13 August 1853 he had three new magazine pieces ready for the Harpers: probably 'The Happy Failure' (1854), 'The Fiddler' (1854), and 'Cock-A-Doodle-Doo!' (1853). By September he had also completed a longer story, 'Bartleby, the Scrivener' (1853), for *Putnam's Monthly Magazine*, a younger rival of *Harper's* that also published its contributions anonymously. But he had not yet given up the idea of another still longer work, for on 24 November he wrote the Harpers to say that he had 'in hand, and pretty well on towards completion, another book—300 pages, say—partly of nautical adventure, and partly—or, rather, chiefly, of Tortoise Hunting Adventure.'

The Harpers responded favorably to Melville's request for an advance payment of $300 for the new book, but a disastrous fire at their New York publishing house seems to have interfered with further negotiations for the projected work. He may have adapted some of the material on 'Tortoise Hunting' for 'The Encantadas,' which he sent to George Palmer Putnam in the following February; the ten component sketches appeared serially in the issues of *Putnam's Magazine* for March, April, and May 1854. Between July 1854 and March 1855, *Putnam's* also serialized his *Israel Potter*, which was then reprinted as Melville's eighth published book. By May 1856 a total of fourteen tales and sketches by Melville, apart from *Israel Potter*, had appeared in *Harper's* and *Putnam's* magazines; he had also written an additional piece, 'The Two Temples,' that remained unpublished after George Putnam and his editor, Charles F. Briggs, rejected it. In 1856 the new firm of Dix and Edwards, which had recently bought *Putnam's Magazine*, reprinted five of his contributions in *The Piazza Tales*, his ninth published book, along with a new title piece, 'The Piazza,' that Melville wrote especially for the volume.

Despite his uncertain health, Melville had worked productively for the past three years, earning an estimated total of $1,329.50 for his magazine writing alone, which yielded him five dollars per printed page (Sealts, Historical Note to The Piazza Tales *and Other Prose Pieces,*

1839–1860, p. 494); most contributors were paid a dollar or two less. But times were hard, and though reviews of the collected *Piazza Tales* were generally favorable, the receipts from sales failed to meet the costs of production.

Sources of the Magazine Pieces

One reviewer of *The Piazza Tales,* writing in the Newark, New Jersey, *Daily Advertiser* for 18 June 1856, hailed Melville's book as a return to 'the real Typee and Omoo vein,' complaining that his more recent works had been 'the fruits of his reading rather than of his imagination.' There was some justification for this last remark, as even Melville himself had admitted with respect to *Mardi,* but it would be a mistake to suppose that his reading had not contributed substantially to his magazine writing. Scholarly investigation of these pieces in recent years, as I have summarized it elsewhere,

> has now established Melville's principal sources in his own observation of the contemporary scene (some of it recorded in his earlier journal-entries), his wide knowledge of general literature, and his reading of more specialized materials ranging from narratives of Pacific voyages to newspaper and magazine articles of the day that added both substance and topical interest to his writing.
>   The investigation of Melville's use of these varied source materials helps to explain what George William Curtis meant in 1855 when he applauded one of the stories as 'thoroughly magazinish.' (Historical Note to The Piazza Tales *and Other Prose Pieces, 1839–1860,* p. 513)[1]

Curtis's remark confirms the sagacity of George Putnam and the brothers Harper in soliciting manuscripts from Melville and paying for them at premium rates; it also suggests that Melville himself became a better judge of popular taste as a magazine writer than he had been as the author of *Pierre.* He evidently took profitable notice of what contemporary newspapers and magazines of the 1850's were carrying, and learned to pattern his own pieces accordingly, with respect to both form and content. He began buying monthly numbers of *Harper's* when it first appeared in June 1850, and at Pittsfield in September 1851 he became a regular subscriber (Check-List, No. 240), though there may have been some delay in receiving the magazine. In a letter of 5 November 1851 (NYPL–GL) from his mother to his sister Augusta, who was then with the Allan Melvilles in New York, it was reported that Herman had 'bought at the Village'—Pittsfield—the October number, which included 'The Town-Ho's Story,' and that Allan had sent the November issue to Arrowhead. 'We have up to May 1851,' Maria Melville noted, but not the issues for June through September, 'which we would like to have.'

Melville presumably subscribed as well to *Putnam's,* which began publication in January 1853, though there is no record of his term of subscription (No. 413).

Among other periodicals that Melville read at least occasionally is
Littel's Living Age, an eclectic Boston weekly that reprinted fiction,
poetry, and comment from foreign periodicals. In the summer of 1856
he spoke with his friend J. E. A. Smith about an article on Cooper,
Dana, and himself, 'A Trio of American Sailor-Authors,' copied from
the *Dublin University Magazine* in the *Living Age* for 1 March 1856
(Check-List, No. 327.1). The Melvilles probably saw some or all of the
local Pittsfield newspapers: the *Sun* (see No. 216), the weekly *Culturist
and Gazette,* and the *Eagle,* for which Smith was a writer and—in 1854
and after—an editor. They also subscribed for a time to the New York
Herald; Maria Melville, in her letter of 5 November 1851 quoted above,
complained, that 'We have not had a Herald or any paper for ten days
past,' and Melville himself, in a later notation inside the front cover of
his notebook of 'Lecture Engagements' (HCL), wrote, 'Herald stops
Jan 7ᵗʰ 1854.' On occasion he read other metropolitan newspapers, at
Pittsfield or elsewhere. The New York *Times* or *Tribune,* the
Springfield, Massachusetts, *Republican,* and the Albany *Evening
Tribune, Evening Journal,* and *Argus* all provided material at various
times for one or another of the magazine pieces. Like the monthly magazines, with their comments on literature, art, and current events at
home and abroad, the newspapers kept him abreast of what was taking
place in the world beyond Berkshire.

What I have called Melville's 'own observation of the contemporary scene' is evident in a number of these short pieces in his abundant
references—overt and otherwise—to persons, places, and events he
knew at first hand. As his relatives must have been aware and as some
reviewers shrewdly guessed, many of the characters in his short fiction
were based on men and women he knew at various times and places in
his career. He himself was to remark in *The Confidence-Man* that any
writer of fiction must necessarily 'pick up' most of his characters 'in
town,' for the city is 'a kind of man-show,' where he 'goes for his
stock, just as the agriculturist goes to the cattle-show for his' (p. 238).
And since Melville never excelled at originating plots, a number of his
stories, like his earlier books, are elaborations of personal experience,
sometimes as recorded in his journal and frequently supplemented by
material drawn from his reading.

In this connection, several contemporary authors contributed in a
special way to Melville's writing for the magazines. Both nineteenth-
century reviewers of *The Piazza Tales* and twentieth-century critics
have seen resemblances between his shorter fiction and the sketches

and tales of Irving, Poe, Hawthorne, Lamb, and Dickens. Although no single work by any of these contemporaries can be considered a primary source of a given piece by Melville, he not infrequently followed the lead of others in terms of plotting, characterization, and technique of narration. As we know, Melville had been reading Hawthorne, Lamb, and Dickens since 1849. In 1850 his 'Hawthorne and His Mosses' in effect dismissed Irving as merely an imitator of Goldsmith, but when he turned to shorter fiction in 1853 he himself found Irving a useful model. His friend Richard Lathers gave him a new set of Irving's works in June of that year; in August he reciprocated with an abridged version of Abraham Tucker's *The Light of Nature Revealed* (Check-List, Nos. 292a, 529). Melville's only known copy of Poe's works is a later edition acquired in 1860 and given to his wife in 1861 (No. 404a), but his caricature of Poe as the peddler in Chapter 36 of *The Confidence-Man* shows his familiarity with the man and his writings.

A brief review of the stories and their sources, in the approximate order of their composition, will illustrate the foregoing generalizations. What seem to be Melville's first two magazine pieces of 1853, 'The Happy Failure' and 'The Fiddler,' are set respectively along the Hudson River—which Melville knew well from his years in Albany and Lansingburgh—and in New York City. The title character of 'The Happy Failure' has been said to resemble two of his kinsmen whose careers were relatively unsuccessful: Thomas Melvill, Jr., and Herman Gansevoort; the 'uncle' of the story and his black servant Yorpy are also like Poe's Legrand and Jupiter in 'The Gold-Bug.' Another experience of failure befalls the narrator of 'The Fiddler' when his 'poem' is 'damned,' and he must therefore learn to live '*With* genius and *without* fame.' According to Donald Yannella in a recent essay, 'Writing "the *other* way," ' the narrator's situation is like Melville's own after the mixed reception of *Moby-Dick* and the outright failure of *Pierre,* when he turned to magazine fiction much as the narrator takes up 'fiddling'; Yannella also suggests that Standard and Hautboy, the supporting characters, may be patterned after Evert Duyckinck and Cornelius Mathews.

The next two stories of 1853, 'Cock-A-Doodle-Doo!' and 'Bartleby, the Scrivener,' are longer and more fully developed narratives, one set in rural Berkshire and the other in a New York lawyer's Wall Street office—a locale Melville knew well, his brother Allan being a Wall Street lawyer. Both stories deal once more with characters out of step with their environments; both make knowing references to current events; both reflect Melville's general reading. The Berkshire narrator in particular alludes freely to classical and biblical topics, names *Tristram Shandy* and *The Anatomy of Melancholy*, parodies a poem by Wordsworth, and echoes *Hamlet* and *Paradise Lost*. As contemporary comment suggested, the lawyer-narrator in 'Bartleby' and his forlorn clerk may have been patterned after living models; the supporting characters could easily have come from the pen of Dickens, Lamb, or Irving. The idea for 'Bartleby' may have been suggested to Melville by an advertisement in the New York *Times* and *Tribune* for 18 February 1853 that quoted the first chapter of a novel by James A. Maitland: *The Lawyer's Story,* in which a lawyer hires an extra copying clerk. The concluding references in 'Bartleby' to the Dead Letter Office in Washington pick up another topic of interest that had been featured in newspapers of the early 1850's.

Between the late summer of 1853 and the following spring, Melville composed three two-part sketches that Jay Leyda has called 'diptychs': they all feature contrasting episodes, one American and the other English. The first part of 'Poor Man's Pudding and Rich Man's Crumbs,' which has a Berkshire setting like that of 'Cock-A-Doodle-Doo!,' may be a parody of Catharine Maria Sedgwick's *The Poor Rich Man and the Rich Poor Man* (1836). The second part is based directly on journal entries Melville had made in London in 1849. Both sections of 'The Two Temples' come primarily out of Melville's personal observation: his familiarity with two New York churches and his acquaintance with the sexton of one of them, Isaac Brown, plus his rewarding visit to a theater while he was in London. 'The Paradise of Bachelors and the Tartarus of Maids' begins with recollections of bachelor friends in London and closes with a graphic but symbolic description of an American paper mill, recalling an actual excursion to a paper factory that Melville had made in 1851 and revealing his close familiarity with Berkshire geography.

The ten sketches comprising 'The Encantadas,' written in 1854, are based primarily on recollections of Melville's visit to the Galapagos Islands during his whaling years, supplemented by material drawn from at least six books of Pacific voyages written by David Porter, James Colnett, 'that excellent Buccaneer' William Cowley, James Burney, the naturalist Charles Darwin, and Amasa Delano. Some or all of these works were in his library at Pittsfield. He had used Porter's *Journal* as early as *Typee* and bought Darwin's journal of his voyage on the *Beagle* in 1847 (Check-List, No. 175); he was to draw more extensively on Delano's *Narrative of Voyages and Travels* in 'Benito Cereno' (1855) and on James Burney's five-volume *History of the Discoveries in the Pacific Ocean* in his lecture of 1858, 'The South Seas.' The account in Sketch Eighth of the ordeal of Hunilla, the Chola widow, elaborates on reports carried in Albany and Springfield newspapers during November of 1853; Melville may have enriched his treatment of her story by recalling the case of Agatha Hatch Robinson. Most of the poetic epigraphs for the several sketches came from a still unidentified edition of the works of Edmund Spenser;[2] the others are from the poetry of William Collins and from Melville's surviving copies of Thomas Chatterton's works and the plays of Beaumont and Fletcher (Nos. 137, 53).

There are primary sources for two of Melville's longer contributions to *Putnam's: Israel Potter*, written in 1854, and 'Benito Cereno,' composed a year later, both being adaptations and expansions of narratives by other writers. For *Israel Potter* Melville used an 1824 pamphlet ascribed to the real-life Potter but presumably written for him by its publisher, Henry Trumbull (Check-List, No. 407). Melville had acquired the pamphlet before his European trip of 1849, when he bought an old map of London (No. 330a) for possible use in 'serving up' Potter's story at some future time. When he came to construct his serialized novel, as Walter E. Bezanson has observed in his Historical Note to the Northwestern-Newberry edition of *Israel Potter*, he 'moved in and out of his sources so frequently' that the finished story 'offers a rare opportunity to watch him at work.'

> Four books were successively open beside him during the writing of thirteen of his twenty-six chapters: Henry Trumbull's *Life* . . . ; Robert C. Sands's compiled *Life and Correspondence of John Paul Jones* (New York, 1830); James Fenimore Cooper's *History of the Navy of the United States of America* (New York, 1853); and Ethan Allen's *A Narrative of Colonel Ethan Allen's Captivity* (first published in Philadelphia, 1779).
>
> In addition, he read widely in Benjamin Franklin's collected writings, made minor use of a few other books, and refreshed his memory of England and Paris with his own journal. (p. 184)

One of the 'other books' was the two-volume *Life* of the painter Benjamin Haydon (Check-List, No. 262), which Melville bought on 7 April 1854 while in New York for his brother Allan's birthday; a passage in the first volume was the germ of Chapter 23 of *Israel Potter* (*Log* 1: 486). For his adaptation of Trumbull's pamphlet, as Bezanson points out, he had already changed the narrative mode from first person to third and proceeded to move Potter's birthplace from Cranston, Rhode Island, to the Berkshire region of Massachusetts, thus preparing the way for his own 'prelude of "poetic reflection"' on the Berkshire country' and his further use of Field's *History of the County* . . . and Smith's *Taghconic* (Historical Note, pp. 186–187; Check-List, Nos. 216, 478; for chapters set in England, see Nos. 304a, 330a).

At some time in 1854 Melville wrote two shorter pieces, 'The Lightning-Rod Man' and 'The 'Gees.' As local newspapers testify, the Berkshires had been invaded by salesmen of lightning-rods in the fall of 1853; the late Helen Morewood repeated to Jay Leyda a story her father had told of an actual encounter between Melville and one of these itinerants. 'The Lightning-Rod Man' alludes to Cotton Mather's *Magnalia Christi Americana,* of which the Pittsfield Library Association had a copy; the late Margaret Morewood remembered another copy at Arrowhead. In view of the narrator's satirical reference to his visitor as a 'pretended envoy extraordinary' from the gods, it may be significant that in the spring of 1854 Melville urged his sister Helen to read 'Plutarch on the Cessation of the Oracles' (Check-List, No. 404.2). 'The 'Gees,' which draws on Melville's first-hand knowledge of Portuguese sailors during his years at sea, may have been suggested by a review article in *Putnam's Monthly* for July 1854 that dealt with supposedly fixed racial distinctions; Melville's satirical sketch anticipates his chapter on Indian-hating in *The Confidence-Man* (1857).

Perhaps the least characteristic of Melville's stories is 'The Bell-Tower,' submitted to *Putnam's* in the spring of 1855, which somewhat resembles the work of Hawthorne and Poe. Its setting in Renaissance Italy may reflect Melville's familiarity with Machiavelli's *Florentine Histories* (Check-List, No. 340a) and the *Autobiography* of Benvenuto Cellini. Other suggested sources include articles on Albertus and Agrippa in Bayle's *Dictionary,* Mary Shelley's *Frankenstein: or, The Modern Prometheus,* and Hawthorne's 'The Minotaur' in his *Tanglewood Tales* (Nos. 51, 467, 256).

For 'Benito Cereno,' Melville enlarged upon Chapter 18 of *A Narrative of Voyages and Travels in the Northern and Southern Hemispheres* (Boston, 1817) by a Yankee sea captain, Amasa Delano; he had previously used this book in 'The Encantadas.' As G. Thomas Tanselle has suggested ('Two Melville Association Copies,' pp. 184–186), it may well have been called to his attention in March 1853 by Henry F. Hubbard, who had been one of his shipmates aboard the *Acushnet* in 1841 and had since settled in California. Hubbard came to Pittsfield for a reunion with his sister Sarah, who had married Amasa Rice, a Pittsfield farmer. The mother of Henry and Sarah Hubbard was a fourth cousin of Amasa Delano; since Melville presented Hubbard with a copy of *Moby-Dick* during his visit to Arrowhead, it is even possible that Hubbard returned the favor with a copy of *Voyages and Travels,* though the particular volume owned by Melville has not come to light. The Northwestern-Newberry edition of *The Piazza Tales,* which reproduces Delano's eighth chapter in facsimile, also discusses Melville's adaptation and enlargement of his narrative.

Three pieces written between the summer of 1854 and the summer or fall of 1855, 'Jimmy Rose,' 'I and My Chimney,' and 'The Apple-Tree Table,' are best discussed as a group. All three are domestic narratives related in the first person; all have settings in houses that Melville knew well, Broadhall and Arrowhead, though he shifted their locations for fictional purposes. The title character of 'Jimmy Rose,' another of Melville's worldly failures, has attributes of Melville's father, his grandfather, and especially his uncle Thomas Melvill, Jr. The features of Jimmy's old house in the city—notably the parlor adorned with 'genuine Versailles paper'—clearly identify it as a re-creation of Broadhall, where Major Melvill had lived during his Pittsfield years.[3] 'I and My Chimney' describes the imposing central chimney of a farm-house very much like Arrowhead, though the threatened removal of the chimney may have been suggested by a similar alteration at Broadhall in 1851 after its sale to the Morewoods. The narrator of 'I and My Chimney,' who takes to 'oldness in things,' is like the story-tellers in works of Irving, George William Curtis, and perhaps of Hawthorne; his domineering wife could have come out of any number of Irving's writings. Essentially the same couple, along with their two daughters and "Biddy the girl,' reappear as city dwellers in 'The Apple-Tree Table,' a story significantly subtitled 'Original Spiritual Manifesta-tions.' But though the wife of 'I and My Chimney' is interested in such current fads as 'Swendenborgianism, and the Spirit Rapping philosophy, with other new views,' her skeptical counterpart in 'The Apple-Tree Table' does not believe in 'spirits' and spirit-rapping as her daughters do. Her husband, the narrator, half accepts what he reads in Cotton Mather's *Magnalia*; she, however, puts her trust in 'Professor Johnson, the naturalist.'

The latter two stories are especially interesting to the student of Melville's reading, since both effectively combine literary borrowings with personal experience to form well-integrated narratives. 'I and My Chimney' reflects Melville's knowledge of Giovanni Battista Belzoni, the Egyptologist whose machine for regulating the waters of the Nile may have previously suggested the uncle's 'Great Hydraulic-Hydrostatic Apparatus' in 'The Happy Failure.' The story also draws on Irving's 'Legend of the Arabian Astrologer' in *The Alhambra*, the evident source of a much-quoted image in Book XXI of *Pierre*: the de-scent into the pyramid (p. 285). What Melville writes of the pyramidal chimney also echoes what Henry Thoreau had written of the chimney he constructed at Walden; so Pamela Matthews has persuasively demonstrated in 'Four Old Smokers: Melville, Thoreau, and Their Chimneys.' And as Thoreau remarks in the concluding chapter of *Wal-den* (1854), 'Every one has heard the story which has gone the rounds of New England, of a strong and beautiful bug which came out of the dry leaf of an old table of apple-tree wood'—the very story on which Melville based 'The Apple-Tree Table.' Reading *Walden* in 1854 or 1855 probably sent Melville back to at least one of two works associated with his stay at Broadhall in 1850: Dwight's *Travels in New England* and *A*

History of the County of Berkshire, which offer versions of the same story. In his annotated copy of the *History* (Check-List, No. 216), a number of passages are marked, some used in 'The Apple-Tree Table' and others in the earlier *Israel Potter.*

Recapitulation: 'The Piazza'

The dialectic of old and new, spiritualism and naturalism, that runs through 'I and My Chimney' and 'The Apple-Tree Table' is a sign that in the magazine fiction of the mid-1850's Melville was doing more than merely writing to please the public. His earlier stories had expressed his concern for the poor and oppressed; 'Temple First' and 'The Lightning-Rod Man' satirize contemporary religionists of differing stripes; 'The Tartarus of Maids' and 'The Bell-Tower' show his distrust of industrialization and technology; 'Benito Cereno,' as commentators now recognize, is an oblique comment on those prevailing attitudes toward blacks and slavery in the United States that would ultimately precipitate civil war between North and South. Some modern readers take 'I and My Chimney'—the very story that Curtis termed 'thoroughly magazinish'—as an allegorical treatment of the divided state of the Union in the 1850's. But at the same time the chimney represents something very personal to Melville, and the search for some reputed 'unsoundness' within it may recall the examinations, physical and mental, that he himself was reportedly obliged to undergo in the years after *Pierre.*[4]

In late January or early February 1856, before 'I and My Chimney' and 'The Apple-Tree Table' appeared in *Putnam's,* Melville wrote 'The Piazza' as a title piece for the five earlier stories from the magazine that are collected in *The Piazza Tales.* His narrator opens his story with an epigraph from Shakespeare's *Cymbeline* and specifically reminds the reader of *Hamlet, Macbeth,* and *A Midsummer Night's Dream.* Following a familiar Melvillean pattern, he employs numerous biblical and mythological references and alludes also to 'old wars of Lucifer and Michael' in *Paradise Lost,* to Emerson's poem 'The Problem,' and to Don Quixote—Melville had bought a translation of Cervantes' work in September 1855 (Check-List, No. 125). The story of his disillusioned attempt 'to get to fairy-land' is counterpointed by his direct reference to 'one Edmund Spenser, who had been there—so he wrote me'; the lonely girl Marianna whom he encounters on his journey recalls both Shakespeare's dejected Marianna in *Measure for Measure* and Tennyson's 'Marianna' and 'Marianna in the South.'

This opening narrative, which once more uses both Arrowhead and the nearby Mount Greylock as its setting, establishes a characteristic tone for what is to follow, much as Hawthorne's account of the old manse at Concord prepares the reader for the tales collected in his *Mosses from an Old Manse*. Melville may well have been rereading both Hawthorne and his own 'Hawthorne and His Mosses' when he made the decision to introduce his own collection with 'The Piazza.' One writer, Helmbrecht Breinig, takes 'The Piazza' as Melville's new evaluation—even his parody—of Hawthorne and 'a more skeptical re-valuation' of what he had previously written about Hawthorne's tales in 1850 as he himself was working on *Moby-Dick* ('The Destruction of Fairyland,' p. 268). Certainly 'The Piazza' reflects the altered tenor of his more recent reading and writing, looking forward to the chastened mood in which he was to compose *The Confidence-Man* much as 'Hawthorne and His Mosses' reflects the ebullience with which he began *Moby-Dick* six years before. The narrator of 'I and My Chimney' closes his story 'standing guard over [his] mossy old chimney'; the narrator of 'The Piazza' walks 'the piazza deck, haunted by Marianna's face, and many as real a story.'

Notes

[1] The following discussion of sources for Melville's magazine fiction other than *Israel Potter* is primarily based on materials I collected between 1965 and 1978, when my service as volume editor for the Northwestern-Newberry edition of The Piazza Tales *and Other Prose Pieces, 1819–1860*, was terminated; I have added references to more recent scholarship. Further information and documentation as assembled by my successors will be found in the notes to in-dividual prose pieces in the Northwestern-Newberry volume.

[2] Melville did not acquire his surviving copy of Spenser until 1861 (Check-List, No. 483). Penny L. Hirsch, after making a line-by-line collation between the epigraphs and editions of Spenser available in 1854, reports in 'Melville's Spenser Edition for *The Encantadas*' that he 'used a text based on that of John Upton's two-volume edition of *The Faerie Queene* (London, 1758). The closest such text . . . was the one in Volume II of Robert Anderson's *Poets of Great Britain* (London and Edinburgh, 1792–93). Very possibly the edition Melville ac-tually had in hand was some later one, perhaps American, based on Anderson.'

[3] Evert Duyckinck had described Broadhall in 1850 as 'an old family man-sion, wainscoted and stately, with large halls & chimneys—quite a piece of mouldering rural grandeur. . . . Herman Melville knows every stone & tree & will probably make a book of its features' (*Log* 1: 383). As I have pointed out in 'The Ghost of Major Melvill,' Melville's description of the house in 'Jimmy Rose' anticipates his description of Broadhall itself in his later 'Sketch of Major Thomas Melville, Jr.'

[4] As Mrs. Melville later recalled, 'In Feb 1855' her husband 'had his first at-tack of severe rheumatism in his back—so that he was helpless—and in the following June an attack of Sciatica—Our neighbor in Pittsfield Dr. O. W. Holmes attended & prescribed for him' (Sealts, *The Early Lives of Melville*, p.

169). Similarly, the narrator-protagonist in 'I and My Chimney' is 'crippled up as any old apple tree' with sciatica. On the relation of the story both to family 'secrets' that Melville had alluded to in *Pierre* and to concern for his own mental health, see note 6 to the preceding chapter and also my 'Melville's Chimney, Reexamined.'

7. 1856–1860

The Confidence-Man and the Lectures

A number of changes occurred in the household at Pittsfield between Melville's purchase of Arrowhead in 1850 and his publication of *The Piazza Tales* in 1856. A second son and two daughters were born: Stanwix in 1851, Elizabeth in 1853, and Frances in 1855. Two of Melville's sisters married and joined their husbands; Catherine became Mrs. John Hoadley in 1853 and Helen married George Griggs in 1854. Following the death of Mrs. Herman Gansevoort in October 1855, Melville's mother and his sister Frances Priscilla remained at Gansevoort, New York, to keep house there for his Uncle Herman. Still at Arrowhead until the fall of 1856, Agusta Melville, the other unmarried sister, not only acted as Herman's copyist for the magazine pieces and *The Confidence-Man* but also kept in touch with a wide circle of relatives and friends through correspondence and occasional visits. The letters she preserved are the nucleus of the Melville Family Papers now in the New York Public Library.

Despite their failure to obtain a consular position for Melville in 1853, members of his family continued their efforts to get him away from his desk for the sake of his failing health. One recurrent suggestion was that he husband his energies by becoming a public lecturer. Writing to Augusta on 10 February 1854, his mother sent 'this message to

Herman'—a message evidently prompted by John Hoadley during her recent visit with the Hoadleys at Lawrence, Massachusetts:

> That *one Lecture* prepared by himself can be repeated seventy times with success. That . . . all the lecturers *now* prepare one lecture & travel the country with this one for the whole season, are feasted[,] made much of, & seldom less than fifty dollars are given to the lecturer. . . . This is the present style of enlightening the many who have no time to devote to reading & research—
>
> & now my dear darling Herman all your friends, relatives & admirers, say that you are the very man to carry an audience, to create a sensation, to do wonders. to close this subject I will only request you to think over this *not* new subject when in a happy hopeful state of mind, and there is a chance of your coming to this wise conclusion, to do that thing, which at once, and by the same agreeable act, will bring us fame & fortune. (NYPL–GL)

Although Melville was unwilling at this time to accede to his mother's request, 'this *not* new subject' was kept alive within the family, and two years later, after his return from a trip abroad, he would at last consent to try his hand at lecturing.

Meanwhile, however, he had continued his work for the magazines, despite recurrent disabilities. In February 1855 he was helpless with rheumatism; in June, when he suffered an attack of sciatica, Dr. Oliver Wendell Holmes, his summer neighbor, 'attended & prescribed for him'; in September he was reported by the *Berkshire Eagle* as 'just recovering from a severe illness' (*Log* 2: 498, 502, 507). It may have been in August that Melville in turn visited Holmes in the company of Maunsell Field and the artist Felix Darley, whom Melville probably knew through the Duyckincks. As Field recalled, Holmes and Melville talked at length, 'with the most amazing skill and brilliancy,' on a subject that Melville had been reading about since the time of *Moby-Dick* and perhaps even earlier: 'East India religions and mythologies' (*Log* 2: 506). Also in August, it should be noted, either Melville or perhaps his brother Allan obtained two books on a widely different subject, Panama, from the Harpers: *Waikna* by E. G. Squier and *Panama in 1855* by Robert Tomes, another member of the Duyckinck circle (Check-List, Nos. 485, 528).

As Melville's health worsened during the mid-fifties, so did his finances. The Harper fire, he estimated, had cost him around a thousand dollars in lost royalties, leaving him indebted to the firm, and he had fallen behind in paying even the interest due on another outstanding obligation: a note of $2,050 that was scheduled to mature on 1 May 1856. In April he took steps to sell all or part of his farm, putting it in the hands of a New York broker and also running an advertisement in the

Pittsfield *Sun*. By July he had sold the western half 'upon pretty good terms' (*Log* 2: 514, 517), and with further help from Lemuel Shaw he was able to pay off the note. Worries over money had previously led him to think of collecting his stories from *Putnam's* in *The Piazza Tales*. On 22 May 1856, when he wrote to apprise his father-in-law of his financial assets and liabilities, he reported that he had 'certain books in hand which may or may not fetch in money. My immediate resources are what I can get for articles sent to magazines' (Patricia Barber, 'Two New Melville Letters,' p. 421). One of the 'books in hand' was obviously *The Piazza Tales,* which, he explained, was 'to be published this week'; the other must have been *The Confidence-Man,* which was to appear a year later as his tenth book.

The Confidence-Man: His Masquerade

The organizing concept of a single masquerading 'confidence man,' one who victimizes in turn a whole series of gullible but representative Americans, had apparently come to Melville as early as the spring of 1855. At that time he read one or more newspaper articles about a criminal finally arrested in Albany after cleverly obtaining money from trustful victims in a number of American cities; the man's earlier exploits had been widely publicized by New York newspapers and periodicals, including the Duyckincks' *Literary World*, before Melville left for the Berkshires in 1850. The first of the later articles, appearing in the Albany *Evening Journal* for 28 April 1855 under the heading 'The Original Confidence Man in Town.—A Short Chapter on Misplaced Confidence,' was followed by other stories in the *Journal*, the Albany *Argus*, and the Springfield, Massachusetts, *Republican*. As Melville developed the manuscript that became *The Confidence-Man* he obviously used some or all of these reports in delineating his title character and illustrating his methods.

This development presumably began during the summer or fall of 1855; there are several close parallels between certain chapters of *The Confidence-Man* and 'The Apple-Tree Table,' which was probably composed at that time. Some of the component episodes that seem self-contained may have been drafted originally as magazine pieces; for example, the story in Chapter 40 of China Aster's undoing by 'a friendly loan,' which is uncomfortably close to Melville's own situation in the spring of 1856. But as his writing continued he evidently began to bring his materials together in a unified book about American society, setting it aboard a Mississippi steamboat in what was then thought of as 'the West.' In the course of his 1840 visit to the Thomas Melvills in Galena, Illinois, he had probably traveled the Mississippi on a steamboat; more recently he had remarked in *Israel Potter* that 'the western spirit is, or will yet be . . . the true American one' (p. 149). A rejected passage of eloquent description headed 'The River'—originally 'The Mississippi' (pp. 496–499)—may at one time have stood at or near the beginning of his manuscript.

Much of *The Confidence-Man* must have been 'in hand' by late April or early May of 1856, when Melville proposed a new work to Dix and Edwards—perhaps for serialization in *Putnam's*; on 29 June George William Curtis advised the firm to 'decline any novel from Melville that is not extremely good' (Alma A. MacDougall, 'The Chronology of *The Confidence-Man* and "Benito Cereno," ' p. 3). Revision and copying were completed during the summer of 1856. Although *The Confidence-Man* was never serialized, arrangements for its publication in book form were made with Dix and Edwards before Melville sailed for Europe in the following October.

Most of Melville's principal sources are identified in the detailed Explanatory Notes to Elizabeth Foster's indispensable edition of 1954. In the well-chosen words of her Introduction, 'Streams more diverse than those the Mississippi musters, flow into *The Confidence-Man.*'

> The Bible, *Pilgrim's Progress,* Shakespeare, and *Paradise Lost* mingle with all varieties of picaresque fiction, from coney-catching anecdotes to *Don Quixote*; Hawthorne's fine-wrought allegorical stories intermix with the raw histories of frontier settlement, Indian massacres, river bandits, steamboat con men; the wisdom of the ancients, Lucian's irony and Tacitus' pessimism, flow beside the brash confidence of the new Western world, the Wall Street spirit, sentimental optimism, Emerson's blind faith. The opposites in *The Confidence-Man* are as paradoxical as the blubber and poetry of *Moby-Dick.* (pp. xciv–xcv)

Of all of these contributory streams, the Bible—Old Testament, New Testament, and the apocryphal books—may be the most significant, for biblical themes and scriptural phrases are virtually omnipresent in *The Confidence-Man.*

The Editorial Appendix of the Northwestern-Newberry edition of *The Confidence-Man* (1984) discusses two other sources in detail. One, previously identified in the Foster edition (pp. 334–341), is the sixth chapter of Judge James Hall's *Sketches of History, Life, and Manners, in the West* (Philadelphia, 1835), which the editors reproduce in facsimile (pp. 502–510). For the treatment of Indian-haters and Indian-hating in Chapters 26 and 27 Melville appropriated Hall's chapter, much as he had pillaged Henry Trumbull's narrative for *Israel Potter* and a chapter from Amasa Delano's *Voyages and Travels* for 'Benito Cereno.' The other source is one of several versions of a description of the Mississippi by Timothy Flint that is demonstrably a source for 'The River.' Since 'the actual work in whose pages Melville found Flint's account is not yet identified,' the editors print relevant excerpts from the Introduction to his *A Condensed Geography and History of the Western States; or, The Mississippi Valley* (Cincinnati, 1828), designating those words or phrases which Melville used or paraphrased in 'The River' (pp. 514, 515–518).

The Northwestern-Newberry edition also cites other probable sources identified in recent scholarship: Dickens's *American Notes* (1842) and *Martin Chuzzlewit* (1844); the *Life* of Phineas Taylor Barnum, first published in 1855; and various minor works concerning rogues of the West that Melville may have read or read about. As his analogy for a truly 'original' character in fiction—Hamlet, Don Quixote, Milton's Satan—he instanced Barnum's 'revolving Drummond light, raying away from itself all round it' (p. 239). At least two of his own characters—the 'mystic' of Chapters 36–37 known as 'Mark Winsome' and the unnamed peddler of Chapter 36—clearly derive from his knowledge of Ralph Waldo Emerson and Edgar Allan Poe and their writings. The 'Goneril' of Chapter 12 is much like the actress Fanny Kemble Butler, whose readings of Shakespeare he had attended at Boston in 1849 and who later became a Berkshire resident. He had also heard a lecture by Emerson in 1849 and may have attended another at Pittsfield on 13 March 1856, while still at work on his manuscript; for *The Confidence-Man*, it has been said, Emerson's essay on friendship is required reading. Other figures, most notably Henry Thoreau, have also been nominated as the originals of various characters in the book, as the Northwestern-Newberry Historical Note observes, but 'only the most confident of critics could accept them all.' Indeed, 'a critic deficient in confidence might even declare that except for Emerson not one . . . was beyond reasonable doubt used as a model by Melville—or, if in part so used, meant to be recognized' (p. 292).

Return to Europe, 1856–1857

'I suppose you have been informed by some of the family, how very ill Herman has been.' So Lemuel Shaw wrote to his younger son Samuel on 1 September 1856, mentioning Elizabeth Melville's 'great anxiety' for her husband as expressed in her letters. What she had reported is familiar:

> When he is deeply engaged in one of his literary works, he confines him[self] to hard study many hours in the day, with little or no exercise, & this specially in winter for a great many days together. He probably thus overworks himself & brings on severe nervous affections. He has been advised strongly to break off this labor for some time, & take a voyage or a journey, & endeavor to recruit. (*Log* 2: 521)

Although Shaw did not say so in his letter, it was he who financed the voyage that Melville began in October 1856. During his absence Elizabeth and their daughters were to stay in Boston with the Shaws; two of his sisters were to care for the boys; the house at Pittsfield would remain closed.

In preparation for his trip Melville probably assembled a number of European guidebooks, such as the 'Continental Guide' he had bought in Paris in 1849, the 'Book of the Continent' given him by Murray, and perhaps the same handbooks for central and northern Italy he had borrowed from George Duyckinck seven years before (Check-List, Nos. 157a, 378, 375, 377). As for historical background, he had long been familiar with ancient history and knew Gibbon's *Decline and Fall of the Roman Empire*, to which he would allude while in Rome (No. 223b), and as numerous references in *The Confidence-Man* attest, he had been rereading the Latin classics in translation. He had also been enjoying Boccaccio: shortly before his departure, when he spent an evening in New York with Evert Duyckinck, he 'cited a good story from the Decameron' and also 'instanced old Burton as atheistical' (Nos. 71a, 102, 103). Duyckinck found Melville to be in good spirits, 'charged to the muzzle with his sailor metaphysics and jargon of things unknowable,' and termed the evening 'an orgy of indecency and blasphemy' (*Log* 2: 523).

Melville sailed from New York to Glasgow and spent some time in Scotland and England before proceeding to the Mediterranean. In England he stayed for a few days with the Hawthornes; Hawthorne was then serving as American consul at Liverpool. 'We soon found ourselves on pretty much our former terms of sociability and confidence,' Hawthorne noted in his journal, adding that Melville had not been well:

> He has been affected with neuralgic complaints in his head and limbs, and no doubt has suffered from too constant literary application, pursued without too much success, latterly; and his writings, for a long while past, have indicated a morbid state of mind. (*Log* 2: 528)

Their subsequent conversations took a familiar turn. As Hawthorne remarked, in a much-quoted passage that strikingly characterizes Melville's thinking during his most productive years,

> Melville, as he always does, began to reason of Providence and futurity, and of everything that lies beyond human ken, and informed me that he had 'pretty much made up his mind to be annihilated;' but still he does not seem to rest in that anticipation; and, I think, will never rest until he gets hold of a definite belief. It is strange how he persists—and has persisted ever since I knew him, and probably long before—in wandering to and fro over these deserts. . . . He can neither believe, nor be comfortable in his

unbelief; and he is too honest and courageous not to try to do one or the other. If he were a religious man, he would be one of the most truly religious and reverential; he has a very high and noble nature, and [is] better worth immortality than most of us. (*Log* 2: 529)

Melville sailed from England to the Mediterranean, visiting Turkey, Egypt, Palestine, Greece, and Italy, and then proceeded northward to London by way of Germany and the Netherlands. The revealing journal of his travels, which would become a major source for his lecture on 'Statues in Rome' in 1857 and later for his long narrative poem *Clarel* (1876), records a gradual improvement in his health, in spite of occasional discouraging setbacks, but reports no resolution of the religious problems he had discussed with Hawthorne. Unlike the journal of 1849, this journal mentions almost no reading en route: only an 'account of Jaffa' in *Sailing Directions* in December 1856 and an unnamed 'book on Palestine' and 'Dumas's "Diamond Necklace" ' in January 1857 (Check-List, Nos. 434a, 78a, 193). Certainly there was nothing to compare with the enthusiastic book-buying of 1849: in Italy Melville bought additional guidebooks that may also have been useful for 'Statues in Rome'—Braun's *Handbook of the Ruins and Museums of Rome* and Valery's *Historical, Literary, and Artistical Travels in Italy* (Nos. 86.1, 533)—but he referred to neither of these works in the journal.

Melville as Lecturer

Before Melville's return from abroad in May 1857, his relatives had already begun another campaign to find alternative work for him, preferably in the customs service. During a week in Boston, when he told the junior Lemuel Shaw that though improved in health he was still 'not perfectly well,' he affirmed that he wished 'to get a place in the N. Y. Custom House' instead of resuming his writing (*Log* 2: 579, 580). Once back in Pittsfield he again advertised his farm for sale, placing notices in both the *Eagle* and the *Sun*. His intention was to move to a house in Brooklyn, New York, but his plans changed when he failed to secure a customs appointment and no buyer for Arrowhead appeared. Times were hard in 1857, and there were many business failures; Melville's current publishers, Dix and Edwards, soon dissolved partnership without paying him royalties for either *The Piazza Tales* or *The Confidence-Man*. Short of resuming work for the magazines, there seemed to be only one alternative: to seek what his mother called 'fame and fortune' on the lecture circuit, as she and John Hoadley had long been urging.

For his first season as a lecturer, which opened on 23 November 1857 with an engagement at Lawrence, Massachusetts, one that Hoadley probably arranged, Melville chose to speak on 'Statues in Rome.'

This was hardly an ideal subject for popular audiences, as he soon learned from newspaper reports, but one that he himself found congenial, given his recent visit to Italy, his long-standing familiarity with ancient history, and his growing interest in art. In composing 'Statues in Rome,' he 'probably turned for reference to one or more of the standard guidebooks on Italy,' but together with what he 'remembered directly of his visit,' Melville's journal was 'the primary "source" ' for his first lecture. So I wrote in my *Melville as Lecturer* (pp. 9, 10), which records passages both from the journal and from various guidebooks that correspond most closely to the content or phrasing of the lecture.[1]

Beginning with his early 'Fragments from a Writing Desk' in 1839, Melville had frequently alluded in his writings to Roman art and architecture. His probable model in the first 'Fragment' had been the last quarter of Byron's *Childe Harold's Pilgrimage,* which is once again evoked and quoted in 'Statues in Rome' much as it was in contemporary guidebooks on Italy. In the lecture Melville also introduced lines of poetry from Milton and Burns. His discussion of various portrait busts reflects his knowledge of Demosthenes, Julius Caesar, Seneca, and Plato, gained from their own works and from his reading in Plutarch, Cicero, and especially Tacitus. Gibbon's *Decline and Fall* was the book 'that of all others may have brought to a focus the miscellaneous knowledge of Roman life and times' that he 'acquired from such authors' (*Melville as Lecturer,* p. 11).

The contrast between art and science that runs through 'Statues in Rome' is introduced by Melville's opening allusions to Burns and Linnaeus; it is rounded out in his final paragraphs when he sets the Vatican Museum against the Washington Patent Office as the respective indices of the ancient world and the modern. As recognized in some of the newspaper accounts of his lecture, Melville's own preference was for ancient art over modern science and technology. Neither his chosen subject nor his fondness for art and antiquity struck a popular chord with most of his listeners, however; they wanted something more modern and lively. Melville responded in preparing for his second lecture season by returning—doubtless with considerable reluctance—to the locale of *Typee* and *Omoo.* By calling his lecture 'The South Seas,' as he must have realized, he was reminding potential listeners of his own identity as the 'man who lived among the cannibals'—the very identity he had tried to escape in writing *Mardi, Moby-Dick,* and *Pierre.*

Melville opened 'The South Seas' by expressing his 'lingering regard for certain old associations' (p. 410), among them the writings of Charles Lamb, who had worked for the South Sea Company in London, and such voyagers as William Dampier, John Harris, James Burney,

and James Cook. He evidently had Lamb's 'The South-Sea House' at
hand as he wrote his introductory paragraphs. Burney's *Chronological
History of the Discoveries in the South Sea or Pacific Ocean* (1803–
1817) was his principal source for his later discussion of Balboa, Magellan, and Mendaña, and he also drew on his own *Typee* for descriptive
passages. An allusion to the Hawaiian legend of Kamapiikai came from
William Ellis's *Narrative of a Tour through Hawaii, or Owhyhee* (London, 1827), and the account of tattooing was possibly indebted to
Charles Wilkes's narrative in the *United States Exploring Expedition*
(Check-List, No. 531), as one reviewer shrewdly suspected. The lecturer may have quoted *The Faerie Queene,* as one of the newspaper reports implies; he did make a pointed reference to Anne Radcliffe and
her romances, as Melville had recently done in both 'The Apple-Tree
Table' and his journal of 1856–1857; and he included a disparaging allusion to 'compensation—a very philosophical word' (p. 420) that recalls
Melville's earlier jabs at Emersonianism in *Pierre* and *The
Confidence-Man.*

What a reviewer of 'Statues in Rome' had recognized as Melville's
'affection for heathenism' is reaffirmed in the conclusion to 'The South
Seas,' where he spoke of his hope for the Pacific islands: that 'these
Edens . . . , many being yet uncontaminated by the contact of civilization, will long remain unspoiled in their simplicity, beauty, and purity'
(p. 420). When two young Hawaiian-Americans from Williams College
made a visit to Arrowhead in April 1859, they found Melville 'disgusted
with the civilized world and with our Christendom in general and in particular.' Though they wished to hear him talk of 'Typee and those
Paradise islands, . . . he preferred to pour forth his philosophy and his
theories of life' and to discourse of Aristotle and Plato. 'The ancient
dignity of Homeric times,' he reportedly said,

> afforded the only state of humanity, individual or social, to which he could
> turn with any complacency. What little there was of meaning in the reli-
> gions of the present day has come down from Plato. All our philosophy
> and all our art and poetry were either derived or imitated from the ancient
> Greeks. (*Log* 2: 605)

Melville's praise of Greek philosophy, art, and poetry is linked both
to his recent visit to Greece and to his reading and writing of the 1850's;
his comment on Plato, for example, echoes Emerson in *Representative
Men.* He had evidently been buying volumes of the new Bohn edition of
Plato, the source of allusions in both *Pierre* and *The Confidence-Man*
(Sealts, 'Melville and the Platonic Tradition,' pp. 319–320, 326–327), and
in November 1858 George Duyckinck had given him a five-volume set
of Homer's works in Chapman's translation (Check-List, Nos. 276–278).

THE VISION OF DANTE.

Hell.

CANTO I.

ARGUMENT.

The writer, having lost his way in a gloomy forest, and being hindered by certain wild beasts from ascending a mountain, is met by Virgil, who promises to show him the punishments of Hell, and afterwards of Purgatory; and that he shall then be conducted by Beatrice into Paradise. In follows the Roman poet.

IN the midway[1] of this our mortal life,
I found me in a gloomy wood, astray
Gone from the path direct: and e'en to tell,
It were no easy task, how savage wild
That forest, how robust and rough its growth,
Which to remember[2] only, my dismay
Renews, in bitterness not far from death.
Yet, to discourse of what there good befel,
All else will I relate discover'd there.
How first I enter'd it I scarce can say,
Such sleepy dulness in that instant weigh'd
My senses down, when the true path I left;

[1] *In the midway.*] That the era of the Poem is intended by these words to be fixed to the thirty-fifth year of the poet's age, A.D. 1300, will appear more plainly in Canto xxi. Convivio, human life is compared to an arch or bow, the highest point of which is, in those well framed by nature, at their thirty-fifth year. Opere di Dante, edit. Ven. 8vo, 1793. t. i. p. 195. [2] *Which to remember.*] "Even when I remember I am afraid, and trembling taketh hold on my flesh." Job xxi. 6.

B

CHRONOLOGICAL VIEW.

(xlviii)

A.D.
1316 Louis X. of France dies, and is succeeded by Philip V. John XXII. elected Pope. Par. xxvii. 53.
Joinville, the French historian, dies about this time.
1320 About this time John Gower is born, eight years before his friend Chaucer.
1321 July. Dante dies at Ravenna, of a complaint brought on by disappointment at his failure in a negociation which he had been conducting with the Venetians, for his patron Guido Novello da Polenta. His obsequies are sumptuously performed at Ravenna by Guido, who himself died in the ensuing year.

DANTE, HOMER, AND WALTER SAVAGE LANDOR

In his copy of Dante (Check-List, No. 174), pp. xlviii – l, Melville inscribes adaptations of Pope's version of *Odyssey* 11.273 – 276 and Landor's *The Pentamoron,* adding penciled dates: 'A.D. 1858' and 'Sep. 22. 1860.' (Photo courtesy of Christie's.)

His own poems on Greek art and architecture, though not published until 1891 in *Timoleon,* seem to derive from these years following his return from the Mediterranean. Writing to Duyckinck on 6 November 1858, following an attack of eye trouble that had kept him from reading, Melville announced his intention of comparing Chapman's rendering of the Greek with Pope's: 'As for Pope's version (of which I have a copy) I expect it,—when I shall put Chapman beside it—to go off shrieking, like the bankrupt deities in Milton's hymn.' The intended comparison evidently began shortly thereafter: Melville's annotations in his volumes both of Chapman's Homer and of Cary's Dante (No. 174) include quotations from Pope's version of the *Odyssey,* and one of them, in the Dante, is dated '1858.'[2]

Melville was generally more successful with 'The South Seas' during his second lecture season than he had been with 'Statues in Rome' a year before, the larger eastern cities being especially receptive, but audiences in Illinois and Wisconsin had difficulty with both his topic and his voice. Several local newspapers carried openly hostile reports, contrasting his performance with that of the popular Bayard Taylor; 'Lecturing,' said the Rockford *Republican,* 'is evidently not his forte, his style as well as the subject matter being intensely "Polynesian" and calculated to "Taboo" him from the lecture field in the future' (*Log* 2: 603).

Notices of this kind may explain Melville's inability to secure more than three engagements during his third lecture season, in 1859–1860; another probable factor was his illness in the fall of 1859, just when bookings for the coming winter were in progress. His new subject, 'Traveling: Its Pleasures, Pains, and Profits,' was possibly suggested by William Hazlitt's essay 'On Going a Journey,' Hazlitt being a favorite writer of Melville's later years. We travel, Hazlitt wrote, 'to be free of all impediments and of all inconveniences; to leave ourselves behind, much more to get rid of others'; in the lecture Melville spoke of travel as being 'a new birth' (p. 423). He referred specifically to Washington Irving's 'The Voyage,' which opens *The Sketch-Book,* and observed that one 'may perhaps acquire the justest of all views by reading and comparing all writers of travels.'

> Great men do this, and yet yearn to travel. Richter longed to behold the sea. Schiller thought so earnestly of travel that it filled his dreams with sights of other lands. Dr. Johnson had the same longing, with exaggerated ideas of the distinction to be reflected from it. (p. 423)

In such literary references Melville was expressing his devotion to both reading and traveling. His notebook of lecture engagements (HCL) includes a few entries concerning reading during his lecture tours, recording his purchase of newspapers, the *Police Gazette,* and unspecified 'Books' bought on 4 January 1859, probably in Albany (Check-List, No. 83). But lecturing, unlike traveling, yielded him more pain than either pleasure or profit. In his three seasons on the platform he was paid a grand total of $1,273.50 in fees; 'against this had to be charged not only the expense of travel during 1856–57 but also the physical effort and emotional stress which lecturing demanded' (*Melville as Lecturer,* p. 117). Meanwhile, writing poetry rather than either lectures or fiction had attracted him more and more, and when he left on another voyage for his health in 1860 a collection of his verse was being copied for submission to a publisher during his absence.

Melville's growing interest in poetry is reflected in his book-buying during the late 1850's, which included Child's *English and Scottish Popular Ballads,* George Herbert's *The Temple,* and the works of Robert Herrick (Check-List, Nos. 143, 270, 271); he also received a copy of Emerson's *Poems* as a gift (No. 206). In June 1859 he bought for his brother Allan a copy of *The Poets of the Nineteenth Century,* compiled by Evert Duyckinck and his friend the Rev. Robert Wilmott; later in the year he ordered two additional books for Allan: Thomson's *The Land and the Book* and the Countess d'Orsay's novel *Clouded Happiness* (Nos. 558a, 523, 395). He also renewed his own subscription to *Harper's Monthly Magazine* and subscribed to both the *Monthly* and *Harper's Weekly* for his mother at Gansevoort (Nos. 240, 241).

The *Meteor* Voyage

In May 1860, following his abbreviated third lecture season, Melville accepted an invitation to accompany his seafaring brother Thomas on a voyage around Cape Horn aboard the clipper ship *Meteor,* of which his brother was the recently appointed master. In anticipation of Melville's absence, Lemuel Shaw engaged to cancel all of his outstanding notes: the arrangement called for Melville to convey the Arrowhead property to Shaw, who in turn would make it a part of Elizabeth Melville's prospective inheritance upon her father's death. Melville also left his manuscript poems in the hands of Allan Melville and Evert Duyckinck with instructions concerning their publication.

From Duyckinck he had borrowed all or part of two multivolume works on art for his previous winter's reading: in November, Lanzi's three-volume *History of Painting in Italy* and Vasari's five-volume *Lives of the Most Eminent Painters, Sculptors, and Architects* (Check-List, Nos. 320, 534), which testify to his growing interest in art. In January 1860, when he presumably returned these books, he took four volumes of *The Tatler* and, in Chalmers's *The British Essayists,* three of *The Ob-*

server and three of *The Looker-On* (Nos. 494 and 126). To Duyckinck he remarked at the time that 'the mealy mouthed habit of writing of human nature of the present day would not tolerate the plain speaking of Johnson, for instance, in the Rambler' (*Log* 2: 613). During one of these visits he presumably joined other friends of Duyckinck as subscribers who made possible the publication of a translation of Fauriel's *History of Provençal Poetry* (1860) by George Adler (No. 211a). In Boston during February he bought the works of another seventeenth-century English poet, Andrew Marvell (No. 351).

Aboard the *Meteor* in May Melville took with him 'a good lot of books,' including 'plenty of old periodicals—lazy reading for lazy latitudes' (letter to Evert Duyckinck, 28 May 1860). Among the books, as shown by his notations in individual volumes, were his copies of Béranger's *Songs,* the New Testament and Psalms, Campbell's *Sketches of Life and Character,* Dante, Hawthorne's *Marble Faun* (given him by Sarah Morewood), his five volumes of Chapman's Homer, Milton, Schiller's *Poems and Ballads,* and Wordsworth (Check-List, Nos. 58, 65, 117, 174, 247, 276–278, 358b, 439, 563a). Thomas Melville had at least one title: a bound volume of *Littell's Living Age* for July through September 1850 (No. 327.2). Melville's manuscript journal for 18 June 1860 reads in part: 'Spent the day dipping into the "Quarterlies," ' but adds: 'Find methodical reading out of the question' (*Log* 2: 619).

Melville left the *Meteor* at San Francisco, giving up his earlier idea of crossing the Pacific with his brother, and returned home by way of Panama. Duyckinck, he learned, had been unable to place the projected volume of poems, having tried at least two publishers: Charles Scribner and the firm of Rudd & Carleton; Melville had previously told Allan, 'Don't have the Harpers' (*Log* 2: 616). By this time it seemed clear to Melville that his career as a professional writer was over. Checked and

MELVILLE REREADS MILTON IN 1860

Dated inscriptions in his copy of *The Poetical Works* (Check-List, No. 358b). (From *Melville Society Extracts* 58 [May 1984]: 16.)

underscored in a book he had read while aboard the *Meteor,* Homer's *Batrachomyomachia* (Check-List, No. 276: p. 133), is this line:

The work that I was born to do is done!

Notes

[1]Since the manuscripts of Melville's three unpublished lectures have apparently not survived, they are discussed in terms of the texts reconstructed from contemporary newspaper accounts, first printed in *Melville as Lecturer* (1957) and reprinted with revisions in the Northwestern-Newberry edition of The *Piazza Tales and Other Prose Pieces, 1839–1860* (1987). The revised texts are cited parenthetically.

Although my survey of Melville's sources for all three lectures is documented in *Melville as Lecturer,* it should be said that the notes to 'Statues in Rome' in that volume include no references to Braun's *Handbook* (Check-List, No. 86.1), which I did not identify as Melville's until I came to annotate Elizabeth Melville's memoranda in preparing *The Early Lives of Melville* (1974); in *The Early Lives,* see p. 175 and note 50, p. 250.

[2]Melville must have taken his quotations from Pope's translation as published in Harper's Classical Library (Check-List, No. 147); the *Odyssey* is not included in his copy of Pope's *Poetical Works* (No. 405). The fact that he dated one of his inscriptions '1858' argues against the contention of Davis and Gilman that he 'appears not to have read Chapman thoroughly' until 1860 (*Letters,* p. 191, n. 1).

8. 1860–1876

Battle-Pieces and *Clarel*

R eferring to Melville's later career, Raymond Weaver in 1921 called
the final chapter of his *Herman Melville* 'The Long Quietus';
Willard Thorp's phrase in 1937 was 'Herman Melville's Silent Years.'
Stanton Garner, however, spoke in 1982 of 'The Melville Who Awaits
Discovery,' and his title is a fitting one, for there is much still to be
learned about the later Melville. Though he published four books at
intervals during the last three decades of his life, he no longer considered himself a professional writer, and while he continued to send and
receive letters, the volume and frequency of his correspondence were
much diminished. There were apparently no more letters to and from
Hawthorne and relatively few to the Duyckincks; none are as revealing
as those written earlier, when his career as an author was in the ascen-
dant. Given these circumstances, it is fortunate for those interested in
Melville that most of his surviving manuscripts—some of them still unpublished in 1987—date from this late period; so too do many of the
books from his library, which include not only works of literature and
biography but also studies in art and philosophy. His annotation and
markings in volumes that he bought between 1860 and 1891 provide
valuable indications of his private thinking on a variety of topics, sup-

plementing and sometimes clarifying what he chose to reveal to his correspondents and his readers.

1860–1866: *Battle-Pieces*

Melville's first published book of poetry, *Battle-Pieces and Aspects of the War* (1866), is his considered response to four years of war between the states, 1861 to 1865. He had returned from San Francisco in November 1860 to find the country in crisis. South Carolina seceded from the United States in December following Abraham Lincoln's election to the presidency. Other Southern states followed, and in February 1861 they formed their own Confederate government. Lincoln could not be inaugurated until March, and meanwhile the federal administration under James Buchanan seemed paralyzed. On 12 April 1861, barely a month after Lincoln took office, Confederate batteries at Charleston, South Carolina, began open warfare by firing on Fort Sumter. Against this ominous background Melville had to find a new direction for his own career.

Melville's family was aware that his health had not benefited from his most recent travels, and in February 1861 his brother Allan initiated an unsuccessful campaign to secure a consular post for him at Florence from the new Lincoln administration. Herman himself went to Washington in pursuit of the appointment but was called home by word of the serious illness of Lemuel Shaw, which soon proved to be fatal. Deprived of Shaw's personal and financial support, which had sustained him and his family for so many years, Melville was facing a crisis of his own, with his health uncertain and his prospects of employment dim. During the remaining months of 1861 he spent much time with relatives, away from Pittsfield; in December he closed Arrowhead and passed the winter in Boston and New York, where he suffered another attack of rheumatism in January 1862.

Reading and occasional writing were evidently Melville's principal occupations during this period. He had bought at least one book during his brief stay in San Francisco: Mackay's *Book of English Songs* (Check-List, No. 342). In January 1861 he gave his copy of Poe's works to his wife (No. 404a); in the ensuing months he continued his study of poetry, acquiring the poetical works of Leigh Hunt, Shelley, Tennyson, and Thomson and a new edition of Spenser (Nos. 290a, 469, 508, 516, 483). In October he bought Sir Henry Taylor's *Notes from Life,* and later, as a gift from the author, he received *A Voyage to the North Pacific* by his uncle John D'Wolf (Nos. 495.1, 196). To Augusta he gave what had been their cousin Priscilla's copy of an 1828 literary annual, *The Bijou* (No. 66). Meanwhile, he had been writing verse of his own, some of it while still aboard the *Meteor* (*Log* 2: 624).

Scholarship has not yet established the time at which Melville composed two poems based in part on his visit to Italy in 1857, but these months immediately following his return from San Francisco seem a likely possibility. 'At the Hostelry' includes 'a running retrospect touching Italian affairs' (*Poems*, p. 313). 'Naples in the Time of Bomba' grew out of his journal entries for 19–21 February 1857; 'Bomba' was Ferdinand II, King of the Two Sicilies, whose death in 1859 may have prompted Melville to write the poem. 'At the Hostelry' is a Landor-like imaginary conversation among several great painters of the past; Melville's familiarity with these men and their works may reflect his reading in the art historians Vasari and Lanzi in 1858–1860 and Vasari again in 1862 (Check-List, Nos. 534, 534a, 320). Although he never published either poem, he kept the two manuscripts at hand for use in a projected prose-and-verse volume that he occasionally worked at as last as 1890 (Sealts, 'Melville's Burgundy Club Sketches').

While 'rheumatism-bound' in New York, Melville wrote to Evert Duyckinck on 1? February 1862 requesting the loan of 'some of those volumes of the Elizabethan dramatists' in Dodsley's *Select Collection* (Check-List, No. 188). 'Is Dekar [i.e., Thomas Dekker] among the set?' he asked. 'And Webster? . . . Send me any except Marlowe, whom I have read' (No. 348). In New York he also resumed his old habit of book-buying, with special emphasis on a variety of nineteenth-century poets. As Walter Bezanson has observed, the rejection of his projected volume of poetry in 1860 led him 'to increase his study of poets and poetry' as possible models of craftsmanship for his own verse (Introduction to *Clarel*, pp. xxviii–xxix). At this time he acquired poetry by Matthew Arnold, Lord Byron, Charles Churchill, William Collins, Abraham Cowley, Robert Fergusson, Heinrich Heine, Thomas Hood, possibly John Keats, James Clarence Mangan, Thomas Moore, and Henry Kirk White (Nos. 21, 112, 144, 156, 160a, 215, 268, 279, 305, 347, 370, 556).

Melville also bought a number of prose works in 1862: seven volumes by Isaac Disraeli, Emerson's *Essays*, Hazlitt's *Lectures on the English Comic Writers,* and Madame de Staël's *Germany* (Nos. 184–187, 204–205, 263b, 487); later in the year he acquired the *Works* of Jean de La Bruyère, which included characters by Theophrastus (No. 314). In Pittsfield he gave still other books to his sisters and elder daughter. His set of Spenser (No. 483) went to Helen Melville Griggs and his copies of Cooke's editions of Shakespeare and Collins, Shenstone, and Thomson (Nos. 464, 470, 515) to Frances Priscilla Melville; Bessie Melville received Mrs. Hemans's *Poetical Works* (No. 269) as a Christmas gift.

Either while still in New York or after his return to Pittsfield, Melville heavily marked and annotated a number of his recent purchases, especially when he found passages that seemed to speak to his own condition. In Hood's *Poetical Works*, for example, he marked, checked, and underlined a statement by Monckton Milnes that Hood's poetical vigor had advanced 'just in proportion as his physical health declined' (1: x–xi)—a statement applicable to his own situation since the late 1850's. In May 1862, unable to work the farm, he once more advertised Arrowhead for sale, again with no success; in November he closed the house for the winter and moved into the village. While on a trip back to Arrowhead with his friend J. E. A. Smith he was painfully injured when both men were thrown from their wagon; Melville suffered a dislocated shoulder along with numerous bruises, and for some weeks he was once more seriously ill. In the following spring Allan Melville agreed to buy the property as a summer residence, and in October 1863 Herman and Elizabeth moved permanently to a house in New York that had been Allan's. To obtain better schools for the children may have been one reason for their decision to leave Pittsfield, as Arthur Stedman was to state in 1892 ('Herman Melville,' p. 152), but there were obviously other considerations as well. At least the family finances had improved with the settlement of Lemuel Shaw's estate. By February 1864 Melville was able to reduce his debt to Harper and Brothers by making a payment of $200 on his account, and by November 1865, as royalties on his Harper publications accumulated, the balance stood in his favor. Other legacies to Herman and Elizabeth paid off the mortgage on the New York house and covered necessary repairs (*Log* 2: 654, 676, 663).

During 1863 the Melvilles lost two good friends: George Duyckinck died in March and Sarah Morewood in October. In June of that year, when Melville attended the fiftieth anniversary celebration of the Albany Academy, he presumably received a copy of the anniversary program as well as the present of one of his old school-books (Check-List, Nos. 8a, 390). In this same year, if not even earlier, he began to compose individual poems that would later become part of *Battle-Pieces* (*Log* 2: 662, 665), but in December he lacked 'spirit enough' to 'scribble anything' about an unnamed book sent him by Evert Duyckinck (No. 79). In April 1864 he directly experienced military life and action during a visit to the Union Army of the Potomac with his brother Allan. Their cousin Henry Gansevoort, then a field officer in the Thirteenth New York Cavalry stationed at Vienna, Virginia, introduced Herman to Brigadier General Robert O. Tyler, who presented him with copies of Jean Paul Richter's *Titan* and the *Comedies* of Terence (Check-List, Nos. 425, 509). When Melville later read *Titan* he called it 'a little better than "Mardi" ' (letter to Henry Gansevoort, 10 May 1864).

While at the front, as Stanton Garner has shown in 'Melville's

Scout Toward Aldie,' Melville found material for a poem he was to write for *Battle-Pieces* by joining a Union scouting party; during his visit he probably heard a story about the verdict and sentence imposed by a recent drumhead court that he may well have recalled long afterward in writing his *Billy Budd, Sailor*. For the experience of camp life he paid a price, however: on returning to New York he suffered 'an acute attack of neuralgia in the eyes.' Shortly thereafter he was 'much shocked' by news of Hawthorne's sudden death on 19 May 1864 (*Log* 2: 668, 669). In response he may have written his poem 'Monody,' though its seeming application to Hawthorne lacks specific documentation. Just at this time, in June 1864, he acquired *The Poems of Elizabeth Barrett Browning*, whose work he had known since 1850 (Check-List, Nos. 93, 92). Together with the poetry of Arnold and Emerson, Mrs. Browning's verses were to prove a significant influence on his own writing.

It was in the spring of 1865, by his own testimony, that Melville began to think of a collection of his war poetry. 'With few exceptions,' according to his prefatory note to *Battle-Pieces,* the individual poems 'originated in an impulse imparted by the fall of Richmond,' which had surrendered to Federal troops on 3 April 1865. Among the pieces he had composed before that time was 'The Frenzy in the Wake,' written, as he explained, 'while yet the reports were coming North of Sherman's homeward advance from Savannah.' In addition to his own excursion to the front in 1864 he had been following the course of the war through newspapers and through the battlefield reports and on-the-spot sketches carried in *Harper's Weekly* (Check-List, No. 241).[1] *The Rebellion Record*, another publication that he himself cited in a note to 'Rebel Color-bearers at Shiloh,' became a major source for *Battle-Pieces*: in each of its first eight volumes (1860–1864) he had access to a 'Diary of Events,' a selection of newspaper stories and official accounts of military operations, and a miscellaneous section of 'Poetry, Rumors and Incidents.' Hennig Cohen, whose Introduction and notes to his edition of *Battle-Pieces* (1964) constitute the most detailed study of Melville's sources that has so far been published, concludes that Melville drew upon *The Rebellion Record* 'for at least twenty poems'—especially for raw facts 'concerning the first years of the war, when his interest had been relatively slight, and which were then as much as five years in the past' (p. 16).

While working on *Battle-Pieces* Melville bought, in August 1865, a book by one of Sherman's staff officers: Major George Nichol's *The Story of the Great March*. In July 1866, when he was probably writing the noble prose Supplement that concludes his volume, he purchased John W. Draper's *Thoughts on the Future Civil Policy of America,* which may have helped him to formulate his own compassionate views

on the country's prospects after the war (Check-List, Nos. 384a, 190).[2]
The poetry of *Battle-Pieces* is rich with literary allusions; Cohen's Introduction emphasizes 'the Bible, especially the Old Testament; Milton,
particularly his treatment of the revolt of Satan; and Shakespeare, notably, crucial passages from the tragedies' (p. 11).

As Cohen also points out, Melville thought of his main title for the
book in terms of pictorial art, as when he had referred in *Moby-Dick* to
Garneray's whaling pictures as 'sea battle-pieces' (*Moby-Dick,* p. 230).
Among sources for the poetry, in Cohen's words, were

> the paintings in the great collections of Europe which he had seen on his
> trips abroad, the art exhibitions he attended in New York, the prints which
> he found such pleasure in collecting, and the sketches of military life which
> he saw in *Harper's Weekly.* (p. 12)

In London on 1 May 1857 Melville had seen Turner's 'well known
painting' of what his note to 'The Temeraire' calls 'that storied ship.'
More recently, at the National Academy Exhibition in April 1865, he
had been impressed by two paintings that suggested other poems for his
volume: 'The Coming Storm' by Robert Swain Gifford and 'Jane
Jackson, Formerly a Slave,' by Elihu Vedder. In later years he was to
collect not only prints but also a variety of books on art, augmented by
gifts such as Ruskin's *Modern Painters,* probably given him by Allan at
about this time, and the volume on *Vatican Sculptures* sent to him from
Rome in 1866 by its author, Robert Macpherson (Nos. 431, 344).[3]

Melville quotes Plutarch and Froissart in his notes to *Battle-Pieces*;
in the Supplement he alludes to a variety of writers, from Machiavelli to
the Scottish authors Robert Burns, Sir Walter Scott, and James Hogg,
and in its conclusion he echoes Aristotle's *Poetics* by calling the war a
'great historic tragedy' that may instruct 'our whole beloved
country'—North and South—'through terror and pity.' To the allusions
identified by Cohen may be added another: a probable recollection of
Thoreau's chapter on 'Brute Neighbors' in *Walden,* with its memorable
description of a battle among ants. In a chorus of 'The Armies of the
Wilderness' Melville writes:

> *Were men but strong and wise,*
> *Honest as Grant, and calm,*
> *War would be left to the red and black ants,*
> *And the happy world disarm.*
>
>   (*Poems,* p. 66)[4]

1866–1876: *Clarel*

During 1866, in anticipation of the publication of *Battle-Pieces* in
August, Harper and Brothers published five poems from the volume in

Harper's Monthly, but without attributing them to Melville or paying him for their use. In July, after he had finished work on the book and gone to Gansevoort to see his mother and sisters, he was described as 'looking thin & miserable' (*Log* 2: 681). The reviewers were less than enthusiastic about Melville as a poet, and by December, he was told, the publishers had shipped barely 500 copies (*Log* 2: 684). In that same month, having received the government office he had long been seeking, he began work as a federal Inspector of Customs under Henry A. Smythe, the Collector at New York, whom he had met during his Mediterranean trip of 1856–1857 and to whom he owed his nomination. When his mother visited him in the following February she reported his health as 'much better since he has been compelled to go out daily to attend to his business'; his Albany cousin Catherine Gansevoort inferred that 'intercourse with his fellow creatures' had made him 'less of a misanthrope' (*Log* 2: 686).

The strain of preparing *Battle-Pieces* for the press had taken its toll not only upon Melville but also upon his family. In May 1867 Elizabeth Shaw Melville's half-brother Samuel Shaw wrote from Boston to her pastor in New York, Henry Whitney Bellows, concerning a family crisis. Her situation at home, Shaw declared, had been 'a cause of anxiety' to the Shaws 'for years past'; a separation from her husband was now being urged by her friends and her family physician, and 'the Melvilles also, though not till quite recently,' had expressed their willingness to help. Her 'real position,' Shaw declared, is that of a wife who is 'convinced that her husband is insane,' and in his own opinion she would have left Melville 'long ago' if she had not feared 'the censure of the world upon her conduct' (Walter D. Kring and Jonathan S. Carey, 'Two Discoveries Concerning Herman Melville,' pp. 139–141). The separation did not take place, either then or later, but in the following September the Melvilles' elder son, Malcolm, who was living at home, died in his bed of a self-inflicted pistol shot to the head. Members of the coroner's jury, which rendered a verdict of suicide, later expressed their belief that his act was neither premeditated nor consciously done.

What the events of this year meant to Elizabeth and Herman Melville can never be fully known. Their relatives were circumspect in their comments following Malcolm's death; Herman's brother Thomas observed only that 'they feel poor Mackie's loss deeply,' and Catherine Gansevoort, expressing her pity for them, remarked that 'both Cousin Herman & Lizzie are of such nervous temperaments I should fear for *their peace of mind*' (*Log* 2: 692, 690). Later in the year Herman was once again ill with back trouble, but he soon returned to work. In January he was listed among the 'probable contributors' to *Putnam's Magazine,* a revived version of the old *Putnam's Monthly,* but he seems not to have published there. During the next eight years, while continuing in the customs service, Melville established a quiet routine of reading and writing during his leisure hours that led ultimately to the publication in 1876 of *Clarel: A Poem and a Pilgrimage in the Holy Land*, an outgrowth of his own visit to Palestine in 1857.

Walter Bezanson, in the Introduction to his irreplaceable edition of *Clarel* (1960), has this to say about the beginning of the poem:

> At some definite point between the end of the War and 1870, when he began to purchase books for his work, he made the crucial decisions which enabled him to go ahead with *Clarel*. It is possible, since we have no documents on the matter, that this was merely the moment when he found circumstances right for beginning a project which had been maturing in his mind for a decade, and for which he had been grooming himself by the study and practice of verse. This would imply a surer sense of pattern than seems to emerge from this period in Melville's life. In either case, there is speculative evidence that Melville had written something like a quarter or a third of his poem by 1870.

According to Bezanson, 'The best hypothesis would seem to be that Melville began his poem about 1867' (p. xxxiii). Agnes Dicken Cannon, however, is 'convinced that he did not devise a meter for *Clarel* and actually begin work on the poem until after he had read Arnold's essay "On Translating Homer" ' in *Essays in Criticism,* which he bought in 1869 and apparently reread in 1871 ('On Translating *Clarel*,' n. 1, pp. 177–178; Check-List, No. 17).

Whenever Melville may have begun to plan or actually to write his poem, it is clear that he did not buy books specifically about the Holy Land until 1870; there is no special pattern in his acquisitions during the three preceding years. In January 1867 he thanked Charles Warren Stoddard for a copy of his *Poems*; in May he bought Strangford's translation of the poems of Camoës, marking passages in both English and Portuguese; in October he bought Bryant's *Poems* (Check-List, Nos. 490b, 116, 94). In 1868, besides attending a reading by Charles Dickens in March, he acquired Hawthorne's *Our Old Home, The Men of the Time*—a volume of 1852 in which a sketch of his own life had appeared, Sa'adi's *Gûlistân,* the *Shelley Memorials,* and also an unidentified book (Nos. 249, 356, 434, 466, 79a). In June 1868 he gave *The Poetry of Love* to his sister Frances Priscilla (No. 404b). The acquisitions of 1869, besides *Essays in Criticism,* include Jeremy Taylor's *Holy Dying* and two volumes of the *Poems* of Winthrop Mackworth Praed, of which he gave a volume apiece to Frances Priscilla and Augusta Melville (Nos. 495a, 408).

It was in the early 1870's, with *Clarel* obviously in mind, that Melville began gathering books dealing with the Mediterranean and Near East, especially Palestine; Bezanson compares his acquisition of books on whaling in 1850 and 1851 as he was writing *Moby-Dick* (p. xxxv). The books he bought in 1870 include W. H. Bartlett's *Forty Days in the Desert* and *The Nile Boat;* Davenport Adams's *The Buried Cities of Campania* (which he subsequently gave to his daughter Frances); John Macgregor's *The Rob Roy on the Jordan;* and especially Arthur Penryhn Stanley's major work on *Sinai and Palestine in Connection with Their History* (Nos. 48 and 49; 4, 340, 488). Stanley's book, according to Bezanson, was 'the most solid account' of Palestine 'with which we know he worked, and the one from which he borrowed most heavily' (p. xxxv).

In this same year, 1870, Melville also acquired other books not directly related to the poem, including two albums illustrating works of Schiller given him by Ellen Marett Gifford, his wife's cousin (Nos. 440, 441). He bought John Aubrey's *Miscellanies; Eugénie Grandet,* the first of many volumes of Balzac he was to acquire over the years; Hazlitt's *Criticisms on Art* and *The Literary Works of Sir Joshua Reynolds,* marks of his continuing interest in painting; an illustrated *Life of William Blake* by Gilchrist; Emerson's *The Conduct of Life;* William Habington's *Castara;* Hawthorne's *American Note-Books,* his *Scarlet Letter,* and possibly his *English Note-Books* as well; another work by Hazlitt, *The Round Table;* and James Howell's *Instructions for Forreine Travel* (Nos. 21a, 28, 263a, 423, 224, 203, 236, 250, 253, 251; 265, 285b). In September Melville gave John Hoadley a facsimile edition of the poems of Robert Burns, and as Christmas gifts he bought for his daughters Mrs. Jameson's *Characteristics of Women* and Tennyson's *The Holy Grail* and for his wife another work by Bartlett, *Walks about the City and Environs of Jerusalem* (Nos. 100, 295, 503, 50).

Between 1871 and 1875 there is little external evidence concerning Melville's progress with *Clarel* other than his purchase in 1872 of Edward H. Palmer's *The Desert of the Exodus* (Check-List, No. 396). These were not easy years for him or for his wife. His health was not robust, Elizabeth was said to look 'prematurely old,' and their surviving son Stanwix suffered from 'a demon of restlessness' that made him a wanderer at sea and on land, periodically leaving his family and once again returning (*Log* 2: 728, 733). In 1872, the year of their silver wedding anniversary, a disastrous fire in Boston caused Elizabeth to lose an annual income of $500 from property there that she had inherited from her father, just at the time when her husband, with other federal employees of the New York Custom House, suffered a reduction in stipend and heard rumors of possible removals from office. Within the larger family circle there was a succession of deaths: Henry Gansevoort died in 1871; Allan Melville, John D'Wolf, and Melville's mother in 1872; Susan Gansevoort in 1874. Maria Melville, who had been living at

Gansevoort, died at the home of Thomas Melville on Staten Island; Thomas, who retired from the sea in 1864, became Governor of Sailors' Snug Harbor, a home for retired seamen, in 1867 and married in June 1868.

Herman Melville's reading between 1871 and 1875 was various. His continuing interest in Hawthorne, anticipating his characterization of Vine in *Clarel*, is again shown by his acquisition in 1871 of *The Snow-Image* and in 1872 of the *French and Italian Note-Books* and *Septimius Felton*, the latter a birthday gift from his wife (Check-List, Nos. 255, 252, 254). He had come to regard Matthew Arnold as 'his most serious poetic contemporary,' Bezanson rightly notes, 'and his reading of the *Poems* in 1862, and of *New Poems* in 1871 [Nos. 21, 20], turned out to be a major resource for *Clarel*' (p. xxix; see also Bezanson's 'Melville's Reading of Arnold's Poetry').

In 1871 Melville acquired two works on art: James Jackson Jarves's *The Art Idea*, given him by John Hoadley, and *The Works of Eminent Masters in Painting, Sculpture, Architecture, and Decorative Art* (Check-List, Nos. 296, 564). In 1872 he bought Horace Walpole's *Anecdotes of Painting in England* (No. 543a) and in 1874 and 1875 he gave his wife King's *Handbook of Engraved Gems* and *The Wonders of Engraving* by Georges Duplessis (Nos. 308, 195). In 1872 he was rereading Davenant, and in 1875 he autographed a book that had belonged to his father, William Tennant's *Anster Fair* (Nos. 176, 500a).

Other books that Melville bought for himself between 1871 and 1875 include William R. Alger's *The Solitudes of Nature and of Man; Arichandra*, a Tamil drama; Robert Bell's collection of *Songs from the Dramatists;* Bunyan's *Divine Emblems; Three Dramas* by Calderon, in which he marked passages in both English and Spanish;[5] Fitzgerald's *Polonius;* either the *Life, Letters, Lectures, and Addresses* or the *Sermons* of Frederick William Robertson; the *Diary, Reminiscences, and Correspondence of Henry Crabb Robinson;* a new edition of Shakespeare's sonnets; Shelley's *Essays, Letters from Abroad, Translations and Fragments;* another copy of Tennyson's *In Memoriam* that he subsequently gave to his daughter Elizabeth; Thackeray's *Ballads;* and Christopher Wordsworth's *Greece: Pictorial, Descriptive, and Historical* (Nos. 11, 14.1, 56, 941, 114, 218, 427, 428, 465, 468, 505, 511, 563).

As presents during the years when he was at work on *Clarel* Melville selected *The Words of Wellington* for his son Stanwix; Quarles's *Emblems* for his daughter Elizabeth; and a number of books for his daughter Frances: Burgess's *Old English Wild Flowers*, Goldsmith's *The Deserted Village*, Grimm's *German Popular Stories, Pearls of Shakespeare,* and Tegg's *Wills of Their Own* (Check-List, Nos. 554; 414; 96,

231, 234b, 462, 499). In 1868 or after he gave two books to his sister
Frances Priscilla: Bloomfield's *The Farmer's Boy* and Tennyson's *The
May Queen* (Nos. 70, 507). In 1872 he presented to his brother Thomas
a set of Chambers's *Cyclopaedia* that his uncle Herman Gansevoort had
given him in 1846 (No. 128). In 1875 he gave Montalambert's *Life of
Saint Elizabeth* (No. 368) to his cousin Catherine Gansevoort, who had
become Mrs. Abraham Lansing in 1873.

Melville finished composing *Clarel* in 1875. The most immediate
source for the poem was his own journal of 1856–1857, where he had
entered his first-hand impressions of the land and people of Palestine;
Bezanson has traced more than a hundred direct borrowings from the
journal that Melville 'blended constantly with Biblical events and citations.'

> The Bible, as Nathalia Wright has skillfully demonstrated, had long been
> Melville's primary literary resource, and its uses for the present narrative
> were unique. In the most literal sense the Bible was *the* basic historical
> guide to Palestine, as all travelers' handbooks were quick to acknowledge.
> The several hundred scriptural allusions in *Clarel* were not always drawn
> directly from the Bible, however. Melville worked also with commentary
> or concordance at hand. Or again, if he was using John Murray's excellent
> *A Handbook for Travellers in Syria and Palestine,* as is probable, he found
> Biblical allusions cited there. So too with most travel books he was plun-
> dering: apt quotation from Scripture was a standard convention of Holy
> Land literature.

'If in one sense Melville's travel experience lay back of the demands he
now made on the Bible as a source,' Bezanson concludes, 'in another
sense the Bible lay back of his experience and that of all other travelers
he read' (p. xxxiv).

Next to the journal and the Bible, Stanley's *Sinai and Palestine*
also contributed significantly to *Clarel;* Bezanson tallies 'some sixty
markings and many subsequent borrowings' (p. xxxv). In addition, Melville 'moved in and out of' both 'classics and popular works on the
Holy Land.'

> Probably he scanned the writings of Josephus. . . . He read with special de-
> light the medieval pilgrimages in the Bohn Library collection, building one
> canto . . . from a saint's legend there, and pored over at least one ripe old
> seventeenth-century folio of wonders, George Sandys' *A Relation of a
> Journey* . . . [Check-List, No. 436a]. He was familiar with the lives and
> writings of such . . . travelers as Volney, Chauteaubriand [No. 136],
> Lamartine, and Burckhardt. Recollections of earlier readings in *Vathek,
> Anastasius* [Nos. 54, 282], and *The Talisman* gave him moods to create or
> criticize, and a relative ease with the vocabulary of Eastern romance. He

made at least minor appropriations from Kinglake's *Eothen*, Warburton's *The Crescent and the Cross*, and Curzon's *Visits to Monasteries in the Levant*.

But as Bezanson cautions, 'We cannot always tell precisely from which book Melville was drawing, for most of the works he used were themselves composites of other books' (p. xxxv).

One other area of reading not related to the literature of travel should also be mentioned here. Like his more thoughtful contemporaries in England and on the continent, if not his own countrymen, Melville was well aware of the crisis of religious faith brought on during the nineteenth century by the twin challenges of new scientific theories and the so-called 'Higher Criticism' of the Bible. No partisan of science himself, he had nevertheless read Darwin's *Journal* as early as 1847 (Check-List, No. 175) and drawn on it in Sketch Fourth of 'The Encantadas' in 1854; he was sufficiently acquainted with Darwin's subsequent theorizing to refer to him knowingly in the poem. He also knew, or knew of, the *Roman History* by the German historian Barthold Georg Niebuhr and the *Life of Jesus* by the German biblical critic David Friedrich Strauss. 'Heartily wish Niebuhr & Strauss to the dogs,' he had written in his Mediterranean journal on 5 February 1857. '—The deuce take their penetration & acumen. They have robbed us of the bloom'; in *Clarel* Rolfe complains that 'Zion, like Rome, is Niebuhrized' (I.xxxiv.19). How Melville himself was affected by these problems of belief had been apparent to Hawthorne when they talked at Liverpool in 1856. Together with the contributions of Melville's reading to the poem, the religious and philosophical dimensions of *Clarel* deserve the emphasis they are given in Bezanson's comprehensive Introduction. Whatever strictly religious and theological works Melville may have had at hand while he was writing *Clarel* is simply not known. It should be remembered, however, that his library reportedly included many 'theological' works that were scrapped after his death as unsuitable for resale.

Another dimension of the poem is more personal. Bezanson's comprehensive Introduction analyzes Melville's portraits of his younger self and of Hawthorne, in the characters of Rolfe and Vine, and his dramatic study of their respective strengths and weaknesses. Also noteworthy, in view of Melville's personal history, is his handling of what Bezanson calls 'the darker elements' in Rolfe and in himself that are 'channeled into the striking series of monomaniacs' among the subordinate characters of the poem (p. lxxxvii). As *Clarel* thus brings to a focus the major concerns of Melville's life and thought in the 1870's, it is, like *Moby-Dick* and *The Confidence-Man* before it, a summation of his inner development to the time of its composition.

Notes

[1]During the war years the Melvilles were reading both *Harper's Weekly* and *Harper's Monthly* and sending copies to Augusta and Maria Gansevoort Melville at Gansevoort. Elizabeth's letters to Augusta in 1863 express her vexation when numbers of the *Weekly* with installments of Wilkie Collins's serial *No Name* were delayed in the mails or missing (Check-List, Nos. 240, 241, 156a; letters of 11 February, 8 and 22 March, 16 April 1863, in NYPL–GL). Herman sent his mother the number for 3 September 1864, mentioned in her letter of 9 September to Catherine Gansevoort Lansing (NYPL–GL). At Christmas in 1865 he presented bound volumes of the *Weekly* to his wife and children.

[2]Melville may have given the Draper volume to John Hoadley; see p. 14 above, note 2.

[3]At this time, while Melville's mother was visiting from Gansevoort, the family was 'reading aloud' from books by Adeline Whitney and Charlotte Yonge (Check-List, Nos. 556a, 556b, 567).

[4]Melville's rhyming of 'disarm' with 'and calm' is a clue to his pronunciation of words ending in '-arm.'

[5]Melville had evidently acquired some fluency in both Spanish and Portuguese (cf. No. 116) during his years at sea. On one occasion in 1851 he had greeted Hawthorne in Spanish (*Log* 1: 418).

9. 1876–1891

John Marr, Timoleon, and Billy Budd, Sailor

*T*he publication of *Clarel* was financed by a gift for that purpose from Peter Gansevoort, whose death in Albany on 4 January 1876 occurred just as Melville was making arrangements with G. P. Putnam and Sons in New York for printing the volume. Soon after returning from his uncle's funeral he began receiving proofs, which required 'every minute' of his time away from work; his wife, who helped with proofreading, had to ask his relatives not to visit until the task was finished. As she explained to Catherine Lansing on 2 February, Herman 'is in such a frightfully nervous state . . . that I am actually *afraid* to have any one here. . . . If ever this dreadful *incubus* of a *book* (I call it so because it has undermined all our happiness) gets off Herman's shoulders I do hope he may be in better mental health' (*Log* 2: 747). The situation at home was further complicated by the fatal illness of Augusta Melville, which began in mid-February while she was visiting her brother Thomas on Staten Island; she died in April, three days before the death of Dr. Augustus Kinsley Gardner, the Melvilles' family physician, and two months before the publication of *Clarel* on 2 June 'after a series of the most vexatious delays' (*Log* 2: 748).

Except for one English review in the *Academy*, the few notices that *Clarel* received showed little appreciation or even understanding of

Melville's poem. He was probably not surprised, remembering the indifferent reception of *Battle-Pieces*; in his prefatory note to the more demanding *Clarel* he had already dismissed the book, 'content beforehand with whatever future awaits it,' and afterward, in a letter of 10 October 1884 to his English correspondent James Billson, he termed it 'eminently adapted for unpopularity.' Elizabeth Melville's later statement that the book was 'withdrawn from circulation' by her husband has recently been confirmed: a newly reproduced letter reveals that on 27 March 1879 he authorized the Putnam firm to send over two hundred copies to be pulped, and the publisher in fact did so on 18 April of that year.[1]

The death of Augusta Melville was another in the long series of losses for the Melvilles that had begun following their return to New York in 1863. As J. E. A. Smith was to remark in his later biographical sketch, 'death followed death among their relations and dearest friends in such rapid succession that there was scarcely a year when the family could be said to be out of mourning' ('Herman Melville,' p. 137). Melville's old friend Evert Duyckinck, whom he had been regularly visiting, died in 1878; Elizabeth's stepmother, Hope Savage Shaw, in 1879. During the early 1880's they received word from Galena of the deaths of Robert Melvill and his mother; in 1884 they lost both Thomas Melville and Elizabeth's half-brother Lemuel, and in 1885 Frances Priscilla Melville died.[2] There were two deaths in 1886: their wandering son Stanwix died in San Francisco in February, the second month of his father's retirement from the customs service; John Hoadley died in October. In 1888 both George and Helen Griggs died, and in 1890 Allan Melville's widow. These losses cast their shadow over much of Melville's later writing.

Life within the immediate family was quiet during the late 1870's and 1880's. Frances, the younger daughter, became engaged in 1878 and was married in 1880; three of her four children were born while Melville was still alive, and in after-years the two eldest, Eleanor and Frances, were to write affectionate reminiscences of their grandparents. Melville and his wife experienced recurrent bouts of illness; she frequently had ' "run down" turns,' as she called them, and their unmarried daughter Elizabeth ('Bessie') was crippled by arthritis: in 1879 Mrs. Melville complained to Catherine Lansing of 'the weak and prostrated condition that Bessie and I suffer from . . . nearly all the time' (*Log* 2: 771, 772). Each year both mother and daughter left the city to escape hay fever, and sometimes Melville joined them in the mountains or at the seashore during his two-week vacation. While his mother and sisters were alive he had made occasional holiday trips to Gansevoort and Albany; in later years Catherine Lansing frequently visited the Melvilles in New York.

The family paid the last of several visits to Pittsfield in 1885, and in 1888 Melville went alone to Bermuda. At home in New York he enjoyed his books, his collection of prints, and his private writing; his other hobbies were taking long walks and growing roses.

While Allan Melville was alive he had taken care of his brother's business affairs; in later years it was Elizabeth who managed the family finances, which for a time were precarious. As she had explained their difficult circumstances in 1872, writing to Catherine Lansing, 'Herman from his studious habits and tastes being unfitted for practical matters, all the *financial* management falls upon me' (*Log* 2: 729). But beginning in 1876, with the death of Peter Gansevoort, a series of legacies gradually eased the situation and ultimately made it possible for Herman to retire at sixty-six: in 1885 he resigned his customs post on 31 December. By this time his wife was allowing him $25 each month for buying books and prints (Eleanor Melville Metcalf, *Herman Melville*, p. 265), but it was rumored in the New York book trade that he spent more on his purchases than the family liked (Oscar Wegelin, 'Herman Melville as I Recall Him,' p. 22). According to family tradition, he often bought as 'presents' for his wife and children certain volumes that he wanted at hand but felt he could not afford for himself (Metcalf, *Herman Melville,* pp. 258–259); his gifts of several books useful for *Clarel* and a number of works on the various fine arts would seem to substantiate this report.

Melville obviously enjoyed prowling the bookstores and looking for bargains there: in August 1876, for example, he found at a Nassau Street shop 'a good set of the poet Chaucer' at $4.00 that he 'snapped up immediately' for Abraham Lansing; in October he bought for Lansing another eight-volume set in the 'same edition as mine—Bell's' (*Log* 2: 753, 756; Check-List, Nos. 140, 138 and 139). Either in 1876 (when he was in Philadelphia for the Centennial Exposition) or at some later period he is said to have visited the Philadelphia shop of Moses Polock (A. S. W. Rosenbach, *Books and Bidders,* p. 6). Between 1875 and 1880 he was seen browsing from time to time at Albert L. Luyster's Fulton Street bookstore in New York, and in later years at the stores of John Anderson, Jr., and Francis P. and Lathrop C. Harper (Frederick J. Kennedy, 'Dr. Samuel Jones and Herman Melville'; Wegelin, 'Herman Melville as I Recall Him'; letter from Douglas G. Parsonage, writing to me in behalf of Lathrop C. Harper, 26 December 1947).

As in earlier days, Melville continued to read newspapers and magazines; according to family tradition, as reported by Mrs. Metcalf, he subscribed to the New York *Herald* because it contained the best shipping news. He also saw on occasion copies of the Albany *Journal* and *Argus,* 'Frank Leslie's Illustrated paper,' and the New York *Evening*

Post (*Log* 2: 746, 759 and 791, 764; Check-List, No. 392). In 1885 both the New York *Tribune* and the Boston *Herald* printed his poem 'The Admiral of the White,' which was later to appear in full as 'The Haglets' in his *John Marr and Other Sailors* (1888).

Melville also depended on libraries for some of his reading matter. From comments in his letters it is known that he at least visited the new Lenox Library following its opening for public use in 1877, and had met its librarian 'two or three times' by August 1878 (*Log* 2: 763, 768, 771). This was the year of Evert Duyckinck's death, when the Lenox Library began to accession his books and manuscripts—now constituting the New York Public Library's Duyckinck Collection. After undertaking the posthumous *Billy Budd, Sailor,* which began as a short ballad about the time of his retirement but grew into his final novel, he sought material for it in at least one reference library that is yet to be identified (see Appendix D: 'The Library Call Slips'). From 20 November 1889 until his death on 28 September 1891 he was again a member of the New York Society Library, then located at University Place, having been willed a share, 'free from all annual payments,' by his wife's cousin Ellen Marett Gifford.[3]

During 1890 and 1891 Melville was charged at the New York Society Library with fifty-one books, some clearly for his own use but most of them probably intended for his wife and daughter or for family reading aloud. These books are listed here for reference in the order of their charging, with inclusive dates of withdrawal and return given as they are recorded in the Library's ledgers; each title is preceded by its entry number in the alphabetical Check-List in Part II below.

> *1890.* 217: Edward FitzGerald, *Works* (1–18 April); 264: William Hazlitt, *Political Essays* (18–26 April); 354, Lucia Mead, *Memoirs of a Millionaire* (26–30 April); 535: Gillan Vase, *Through Love to Life* (30 April–9 May); 99: Clara Louise Burnham, *The Mistress of Beech Knoll* (9–20 May); 400: Bliss Perry, *The Broughton House* (20–31 May); 223: Théophile Gautier, *The Romance of the Mummy* (20–31 May); 297: Douglas Jerrold, *The Mutiny at the Nore. A Nautical Drama* (31 May–13 June); 286: William Dean Howells, *A Hazard of New Fortunes* (31 May–13 June); 452 and 453: Sir Walter Scott, *Peveril of the Peak* and *Quentin Durward* (13–23 June); 200a: Amelia Edwards, *Debenham's Vow* (20 October–5 November); 233a: 'Grace C. E.' [unidentified] (25 October–5 November); 45 and 46: Amelia Barr, *Jan Vedder's Wife* (5–12 November) and *The Last of the McAllisters* (12–15 November); 287: William Dean Howells, *The Shadow of a Dream* (15–19 November); 415: Josiah Quincy, *Figures of the Past* (15 November–9 December); 164: F. Marion Crawford, *A Cigarette-Maker's Romance* (19–24 November); 162: Joseph S. Coyne, *The Old Chateau . . . A Drama . . .* (22 November–4 December); 542: Lucy Walford, *Pauline* (4 December–2 January 1891).

1891. 163: Christopher Pearse Cranch, *The Bird and the Bell* (8–10 January); 10: Francesca Alexander, *Christ's Folk in the Apennine* (10 January–4 February); 106: Edwin L.

Bynner, *The Begum's Daughter* (17–19 January); 491: Richard Henry Stoddard, *The Lion's Cub* (19–21 January); 426: Morley Roberts, *In Low Relief* (19–30 January); 59: Sir Walter Besant, *Children of Gibeon* (30 January–12 February); 220: Octavius Brooks Frothingham, *Boston Unitarianism, 1820–1850* (30 January–5 February); 443: Arthur Schopenhauer, *Counsels and Maxims* (5–12 February); 41: Amelia Barr, *The Bow of Orange Ribbon* (12 February–2 March); 301: Richard Johnston, *Widow Guthrie* (14 February–2 March); 43: Amelia Barr, *Friend Olivia* (2–13 March); 338: Justin McCarthy, *The Ladies' Gallery* (2–14 March); 561: Katherine Woods, *Metzerott, Shoemaker* (13–21 March); 168: Julie Cruger, *A Successful Man* (26–27 March); 2: Abigail Adams, *Letters* (21 March–8 April); 473: Abigail Adams Smith, *Journal and Correspondence of Miss Adams* (21–27 March); 42 and 40: Amelia Barr, *Feet of Clay* (27 March–8 April) and *A Border Shepherdess* (27 March–9 April); 477: Elizabeth Smith, *Heart of Gold* (8–9 April); 68: Richard Doddridge Blackmore, *Lorna Doone* (8–9 April); 560: Ellen Wood, *The Mystery. A Story of Domestic Life* (9–18 April); 47: Amelia Barr, *Master of His Fate* (9–18 April); 267: Annie Hector, *A Woman's Heart* (18–28 April); 44: Amelia Barr, *The Household of McNeil* (18–28 April); 389: Margaret Oliphant, *Effie Ogilvie* (28 April–14 May); 310: Ellen Kirk, *A Daughter of Eve* (28 April–14 May); 510: Mary Virginia Terhune, *With the Best Intentions* (14–25 May); 167: Julie Cruger, *A Diplomat's Diary* (14–21 May); 309: Rudyard Kipling: *The Light That Failed* (21 May–5 June); 39: Amelia Barr, *The Beads of Tasmer* (25 May–5 June); 67: William Black, *A Princess of Thule* (5–27 June).

The borrowings stopped in late June 1891; in July Dr. Everett S. Warner began his final attendance on Melville, whose death occurred on 28 September.

Melville's Library, 1876–1891

Among surviving books that Melville acquired in his late years are a number bearing his characteristic marks and notes but not his autograph—books unlikely to be identified as his had they not been kept in the family. The absence of an identifying signature may account for the seeming disappearance of other volumes he is known to have read and which he probably owned, such as 'the "Mermaid Series" of old plays' that occupied him during the last weeks of his life, and 'in which he took much pleasure' (Check-List, No. 358). The quoted words are from young Arthur Stedman (Introduction to *Typee*, 1892, p. 163), who came to know Melville in 1888 and assisted Mrs. Melville after her husband's death as his literary executor. Melville's library as Stedman knew it 'was composed of standard works of all classes, including, of course, a proportion of nautical literature' (Introduction to *Typee*, p.

163).[4] Only a relatively small number of the books known to survive can be classed as 'nautical literature,' however; if others were given to Sailors' Snug Harbor, either by Melville himself or by his widow (like Turnbull's *Voyage*, Check-List, No. 530a), they may yet turn up among volumes now in storage.

Although Stedman also emphasized Melville's absorbing interest in philosophy, the surviving works by philosophers are again few in number: two works by Aristotle, published by Bohn in 1889–1890 and 1872, respectively, and at some time rebound uniformly with *The Lives and Opinions of Eminent Philosophers* by Diogenes Laertes, published in 1853 (Nos. 14a, 14b, 183a); and five works by Schopenhauer. (The Bohn edition of Plato that is cited in *Billy Budd, Sailor,* has seemingly not survived.) Between 5 and 12 February 1891, as we know, Melville borrowed a translation of Schopenhauer's *Counsels and Maxims* from the New York Society Library and subsequently bought that same title for himself, along with *Religion: A Dialogue, Studies in Pessimism, The Wisdom of Life,* and a three-volume edition of *The World as Will and Idea* (Nos. 443–448). According to Stedman, he was reading Schopenhauer during his last illness.

'In addition to his philosophical studies,' Stedman also wrote, Melville

> was much interested in all matters relating to the fine arts, and devoted most of his leisure hours to the two subjects. A notable collection of etchings and engravings from the old masters was gradually made by him, those from Claude's paintings being a specialty. (p. 161)[5]

Most of his books on painting and the fine arts are among those volumes lacking his autograph and notation of his date of purchase. In addition to volumes already mentioned, including works he gave to his wife and daughters, the following authors and titles are therefore listed alphabetically, preceded by their respective entry numbers in the Check-List, and with their dates of publication indicated in parentheses:

> 72: Bohn, *A Guide to the Knowledge of Pottery, Porcelain, and Other Objects of Vertu* (1857); 87: Brock-Arnold, *Gainsborough [and Constable]* (1881); 169: Cundall, *The Landscape and Pastoral Painters of Holland: Ruisdael, Hobbema, Cuijp, Potter* (1891); 192: Dullea, *Claude Gelée le Lorrain* (1887); 219: Forsyth, *Remarks on Antiquities, Arts, and Letters . . . in Italy* (1824); 233: Gower, *The Figure Painters of Holland* (1880); 263: Haydon and Hazlitt, *Painting and the Fine Arts* (1838) (and 263a: Hazlitt, *Criticisms on Art,* 1843, bought in 1870); 283: Hope, *The Costume of the Ancients* (1875); 291: a single volume of *The Illustrated Magazine of Art* (1853); 298: Jewitt, *The Ceramic Art of Great Britain* (1878); 360–364: Mollett, *Meisonnier* (1882), *The Painters of Barbizon: Corot, Daubigny,*

Dupré (1890), *The Painters of Barbizon: Millet, Rousseau, Diaz* (1890), *Rembrandt* (1882), and *Sir David Wilkie* (1881); 365: Monkhouse, *Turner* (1879); 412: Pulling, *Sir Joshua Reynolds* (1880); 451.1: Scott, *The Renaissance of Art in Italy* (1883); and 489: Stephens, *A Memoir of George Cruikshank* (1891).

Also prominent among the surviving books are Melville's collection of volumes by and about Balzac, which he apparently began in 1870 with *Eugénie Grandet* (Check-List, No. 28). By 1891 he had acquired fourteen other works by Balzac himself in the translation by Katherine Prescott Wormeley, buying them either individually or perhaps as a set (Nos. 22, 24–27, 29–37); some of these volumes are among the books lacking his usual signature and indicated date of purchase. He also bought books on Balzac by Edgar Saltus and H. H. Walker, and in 1889 his wife gave him Balzac's *Correspondence* as a birthday present (Nos. 436, 543; 23). His interest in Matthew Arnold, which had begun in the 1860's, continued into the 1880's with his purchase of *Culture and Anarchy, Literature and Dogma,* and *Mixed Essays* (Nos. 16, 18, 19); on 20 December 1885, in a letter to his English correspondent James Billson, he remarked on 'that prudential worldly element, wherewithall Mr. Arnold has conciliated the conventionalists.'

Since Melville's other purchases for himself cannot always be dated, those surviving books that he probably bought during the years 1876–1891 are listed here, in alphabetical order, for convenient reference; dates of publication are given in parentheses:

178: Defoe, *History of the Plague* . . . (1881); 290: Victor Hugo, *The Literary Life and Poetical Works* (1883); 314a: La Fontaine, *Fables* (1879); 321: La Rochefoucauld, *Reflections and Moral Maxims* (187–); 341: Charles Mackay, *The Lost Beauties of the English Language* (1874); 356a: Ada Isaacs Menken, *Infelicia* (1868); 387: Evangeline O'Connor, *An Analytical Index to the Works of Nathaniel Hawthorne*; 391 and 392: Omar Khayyām, *Rubáiyát* (1878, 1886); 435a: H. S. Salt, *The Life of James Thomson* (1889); 471: Richard Brinsley Sheridan, *The Plays* (1887); 501–502, 506: Tennyson, *The Holy Grail* (1870), and *Maud* (1855); 539: Samuel Waddington, ed., *The Sonnets of Europe* (1886).

From relatives Melville received a number of other books. In 1877 and 1878 the Lansings gave him John Hoadley's *Memorial of Henry Sanford Gansevoort,* what Mrs. Lansing termed 'the Oriskany & Schuylerville Centennial Volumes,' and an almanac (Check-List, Nos. 273, 394, 491b, 553). In 1883 Julian Hawthorne visited Melville in search of material for his *Nathaniel Hawthorne and His Wife*; in June 1885 Elizabeth Melville bought the book for her husband (No. 244). Her other gifts to him, along with Saltus's *Balzac* mentioned above, include a volume of Rossiter Johnson's *Little Classics* in 1882, *A Book About Roses* in 1884, and Drake's *Tea Leaves,* a book on the Boston Tea Party, in 1886 (Nos. 299, 275a, 498).

Melville's own choice of books for gifts to others during these same years is of interest in itself. For his wife in 1886, for example, he chose as a birthday present four books that had been published in London in 1847, the year of their marriage: Carleton's *The Natural History of the "Hawk" Tribe,* Reach's *London on the Thames,* Smith's *The Natural History of the Ballet-Girl* and *The Natural History of the Gent* (Check-List, Nos. 120, 418, 474, 475); he may also have given her Edward Perkins' *Na Motu: or, Reef-Rovings in the South Seas,* in November (No. 399); at Christmas his choice for her was Keddie's *Childhood a Hundred Years Ago* (No. 306). To Bessie, the unmarried daughter, he gave *A Book of Reference to Remarkable Passages in Shakespeare* in 1877, Addison's *Sir Roger de Coverley* in 1883, Loftie's *Views in Scotland, Views in the English Lake District,* and probably *Views in North Wales* in 1886 and after, as well as Tillotson's *Gems of Great Authors* (1880)—no date of gift indicated (Nos. 461, 5; 329, 330, 328; 526). The copy of Murphy's *Sporting Life in the Far West* that he bought in 1880 (No. 374) was very likely a gift for Stanwix Melville. To his first granddaughter, Eleanor Melville Thomas, he gave Keddie's *Landseer's Dogs and Their Stories* in 1891 (No. 307). And at some unspecified time he gave to Fanny M. Raymond a book by Richard Grant White: *National Hymns. How They Are Written and How They Are Not Written* (No. 556.1b).

Melville probably knew White as a fellow worker in the customs service at New York, where at least five writers were employed during his tenure there. As the Springfield *Republican* had remarked in 1868, 'Herman Melville, Barry Gray, Richard Grant White, Charles F. Briggs and Richard Henry Stoddard are all clerks [*sic*] in the New York custom house' (*Log* 2: 951), and Melville was acquainted with the other three men. He already owned at least one book by Briggs, *The Trippings of Tom Pepper* (Check-List, No. 86a), and had known him as the editor of *Putnam's Monthly Magazine* in the 1850's when he himself was a contributor. He and Stoddard had previously met, as Stoddard afterwards recalled; their casual relationship in later years is outlined in mv 'Melville and Richard Henry Stoddard.' In 1883 and 1884 Melville received from their author four books by Robert Barry Coffin ('Barry Gray'): *Castles in the Air, Matrimonial Infelicities, My Married Life at Hillside,* and *Out of Town* (Nos. 150–153).

Other books that came to Melville unsolicited include Samuel Samuels, *From the Forecastle to the Cabin,* in 1887 (apparently from Harper and Brothers), and two works by John W. Palmer, *After His*

Kind and *The Golden Dagon,* in 1889. In a letter to Palmer of 23 March 1889 Melville remarked that his wife was concluding her reading aloud to him of the latter book (Check-List, Nos. 436.1, 396.1, 396.2). In 1884 his English correspondent James Billson sent the first of a series of books by and about the poet James Thomson that came from Billson, from J. W. Barrs, and from Henry Stephens Salt: *Vane's Story,* followed by *The City of Dreadful Night, Essays and Phantasies, Satires and Profanities, Shelley, A Poem:* [*and*] *an Essay on the Poems of William Blake,* and *A Voice from the Nile* by Thomson and Salt's *Life of Thomson,* a volume Melville had previously bought for himself (Nos. 521, 517–520, 522; 435, 435a);[6] these books occasioned extensive comments in Melville's letters concerning not only Thomson but the general state of contemporary literature and society.

Between 1885 and 1890 Billson sent Melville a copy of the *Academy* with Robert Buchanan's poem 'Socrates in Camden,' which celebrates both Whitman and Melville; a 'semi-manuscript' copy of the *Rubáiyát*; a novel by Marcus Clark, *For the Term of His Natural Life*; and an issue of the *Scottish Art Review* containing Salt's essay on Melville (Check-List, Nos. 1, 393, 146, 455). Melville also corresponded with the English novelist William Clark Russell, who in 1890 sent *An Ocean Tragedy,* the new novel he had dedicated to Melville; also in Melville's library was Russell's *Horatio Nelson and the Naval Supremacy of England* (Nos. 433, 432).

Between 1888 and 1890 Melville was visited at his home by both Arthur Stedman and his father, Edmund Clarence Stedman. The elder Stedman, finding that they had a common interest in the writings of Richard Henry Horne, loaned Melville three of Horne's tragedies along with the *Lays and Legends* of George Walter Thornbury; after Melville's death his widow gave Stedman her husband's copy of Horne's *Exposition of the False Medium and the True* (Check-List, Nos. 285, 525, 284). Melville 'said so much of Whitman' to Stedman that the latter showed him his own treatment of the poet in *Poets of America* (No. 488a). Arthur Stedman, who knew both Whitman and Melville and was editing selections from Whitman's prose and poetry, probably told Melville more about Whitman.[7] Other comments on Whitman occur in Melville's letters to his English correspondents, along with remarks on William Blake, Richard Henry Dana, and John Keats (*Log* 2: 793, 806; 799, 811 f; 799; 787).

Melville's Late Manuscripts

On 10 January 1886, at the beginning of Melville's retirement, his wife wrote of him to Catherine Lansing: 'He has a great deal unfinished work at his desk which will give him occupation, which together with his love of books will prevent time from hanging heavy on his hands' (*Log* 2: 796). Much of this 'unfinished work' involved selecting, preparing, and supplementing existing materials for one or more projected volumes of verse. 'The Haglets' in his privately printed *John Marr and Other Sailors* (1888) had already appeared in part as 'The Admiral of the White' in newspapers of 1885, as noted above, and other sea pieces in that volume may also have been in manuscript before his retirement began. Melville's second privately printed collection, *Timoleon* (1891), includes eighteen pieces headed 'Fruit of Travel Long Ago'—his Mediterranean trip of 1856–1857—that he had presumably salvaged from the unpublished volume of 1860, together with another existing piece, 'The Age of the Antonines,' a version of which he had sent to John Hoadley in 1877.

Among other compositions of earlier years that drew Melville's attention after 1885 were 'At the Hostelry' and 'Naples in the Time of Bomba,' also deriving from his Mediterranean trip; these manuscripts had been on hand since the early 1860's if not earlier. In 1876, after completing *Clarel,* he had begun drafting prose headnotes for the two poems that would introduce their respective narrators: the Marquis de Grandvin, a personification of wine, and his friend and disciple Major Jack Gentian, a Union veteran of the Civil War. The work lapsed in the later 1870's, but during his retirement Melville made further additions to and revisions of the projected volume, once tentatively entitled 'Parthenope.' As the book took form, however, the prose sketches threatened to eclipse the poetry, and he ultimately determined to drop them altogether, as he explained in a new prefatory note to the poems that was written about 1890.[8]

Melville's several portraits of Jack Gentian are worth attention as reflections not of his reading but of his past experience. To a degree Gentian is another partial self-projection like Ishmael in *Moby-Dick* and Rolfe in *Clarel,* embodying both characteristic traits and other attributes he would have been pleased to call his own. Melville had made Pierre of 'double Revolutionary descent' (*Pierre,* p. 20), as he was himself; so too is Jack Gentian. The Major recalls a childhood in New York, his friends of the stirring days there during the Mexican War, and his travels abroad; he has a high regard for Scripture and for the writings of Shakespeare and Hawthorne; he has tried but failed to obtain a consular appointment in Italy. Though in all these respects Gentian is like Melville, he differs in being both a Civil War veteran and a bachelor, and here he resembles Melville's late cousin Henry Gansevoort, dead since 1871. Jack Gentian has lost an arm in battle, much as Jack Chase in *White-Jacket* had lost a finger—or Ahab in *Moby-Dick* a leg. Gentian's pride in his hereditary badge of the Society of the

Cincinnati—an organization formed by officers of an earlier war, the American Revolution—leads Melville as narrator to recall a favorite uncle, the late Herman Gansevoort, who had also inherited the Cincinnati badge.

In 1870 Melville had contributed a sketch of another uncle, Major Thomas Melvill, Jr., to J. E. A. Smith's *History of Pittsfield, 1800–1876*, published in 1876. There is something of both Melville and his uncle Thomas in the prose introduction to the title poem of *John Marr and Other Sailors*—and perhaps something too of their seemingly Burkean view of the French Revolution in *Billy Budd, Sailor*.[9] The prose sketch of John Marr, a former seaman who compensates for his isolation in the present by calling up companions out of the past, sets the tone for the whole volume, which is filled with recollections of persons and places that Melville himself had known during his years at sea. In *Timoleon*, assembled three years later, both the descriptive pieces grouped as 'Fruit of Travel Long Ago' and lyrics such as 'Monody' are also retrospective, but still other poems are indebted to Melville's reading as well as to personal experience. The title piece is based on Plutarch's Life of Timoleon; 'After the Pleasure Party' turns on a celebrated figure in Plato's *Symposium, or Banquet,* which Melville had probably read once again in Shelley's translation in 1873 or after (Check-List, No. 468). 'The Age of the Antonines,' as he told Hoadley in a letter of 31 March 1877, was 'suggested by a passage in Gibbon (Decline & Fall)' (No. 223b), and still other pieces have historical, literary, and religious or mythological referents. Melville planned one further collection of retrospective verse, 'Weeds and Wildings, Chiefly, With a Rose or Two,' that was to include both old and new compositions, but this was left unpublished at his death in 1891.

Melville's practice of writing prose headnotes, begun with the Burgundy Club pieces and continued in both the *John Marr* volume and 'Weeds and Wildings,' figures in the genesis of several of his minor prose manuscripts that deserve more study than they have so far received. 'Rammon,' as Eleanor Tilton believes, was probably written in 1887 or 1888 'for the already composed lyric "The Enviable Isles," ' though in that case the verse was subsequently removed from the composite piece for use in the *John Marr* volume ('Melville's "Rammon," ' p. 86). 'Daniel Orme' may have been drafted as an introduction to another lyric intended for the *John Marr* volume. In the words of F. Barron Freeman, this prose sketch 'reveals a fairly common attribute of Melville's last writings: a frequent harking-back to the milieu of *White-Jacket* and, perhaps, to his own experiences aboard the frigate *United States*'; Freeman errs, however, in stating that Melville wrote the sketch for inclusion in *Billy Budd* but later 'omitted' it from his story

('The Enigma of Melville's "Daniel Orme," ' pp. 211, 209). A third prose piece, 'Under the Rose,' seems to be linked in some way to the rose poems in Melville's 'Weeds and Wildings.' For this collection he composed several prose headnotes; the longest, which pays tribute to Washington Irving, was written to introduce 'Rip Van Winkle's Lilac.'

Billy Budd, Sailor

The major work of Melville's last years, *Billy Budd, Sailor,* grew out of a prose headnote to a sailor ballad he had written for the *John Marr* volume; as with the Burgundy Club sketches, the prose came to overbalance the verse and take on a life of its own. As demonstrated in the Chicago edition of 1962, the story developed in three major stages, focusing in turn on Billy Budd, a merchant sailor impressed aboard the British man-of-war *Bellipotent*, on John Claggart, the ship's master-at-arms, and on Edward Fairfax Vere, her captain. Melville was still making significant revisions in the manuscript during his last illness. While he was composing the pieces that were intended for *John Marr* he was reliving his own days at sea and may well have been rereading his earlier books—*White-Jacket* in particular.[10] *Billy Budd, Sailor,* like the lyric 'Tom Deadlight' in *John Marr,* is set aboard a British warship in the days before steamships, though the *Bellipotent* of the story greatly resembles the American *Neversink* of *White-Jacket.*

Billy Budd himself, as I have remarked elsewhere, is 'reminiscent of all youthful, unenlightened, and even "savage" characters in Melville's writings from *Typee* onward, and John Claggart is a further development of such figures as Jackson in *Redburn* and Bland in *White-Jacket;* Captain Vere's affiliations, however, 'are chiefly with the work of Melville's later years,' from *Battle-Pieces* and *Clarel* to the Burgundy Club sketches (Sealts, 'Innocence and Infamy,' pp. 413–414, 414–415). Concerning Claggart's mingled envy of and antipathy toward innocent Billy, various scholars have seen analogies in scriptural stories (Cain and Abel, Saul and David), in Shakespeare's Iago and Othello, and in Milton's Satan as he looks upon Adam and Eve in the Garden. Others find parallels in Plutarch's Timophanes and Timoleon, in Balzac's *The Two Brothers* (Check-List, No. 37), and even in the supposed youthful rivalry between Melville himself and his older brother Gansevoort.

The narrator of *Billy Budd, Sailor,* whose references to his past match events in Melville's own life, is given to invoking the Bible, the classics—including 'the authentic translation' of Plato (p. 75), and 'one of Hawthorne's minor tales,' 'The Birthmark' (p. 53), all favorites of Melville himself. Vere too is 'as apt to cite some historical character or incident from antiquity' (originally 'cite some allusion to Plutarch, say,

or Livy') 'as he would be to cite from the moderns' (pp. 63, 315: Leaf
87). As with Melville in his last years, Vere's 'isolated leisure' was welcome to one who 'loved books,' for in his chosen 'line of reading he
found confirmation of his own more reserved thoughts—confirmation
which he had vainly sought in social converse' (p. 62). However Melville may have judged Vere, it seems clear that once again he had
endowed a character with some of his own attributes: both, for example, were strict disciplinarians, given to moodiness and irascibility that
were interpreted by others as signs of outright insanity. (The parallels
are explored most fully by Peter L. Hays and Richard Dilworth Rust in
' "Something Healing." ')

For the historical background of *Billy Budd, Sailor,* the conflict between Great Britain and France in the 1790's and the Nore Mutiny of
1797, Melville went to at least two sources: at an unidentified library he
took notes from *The Naval History of Great Britain* by the British naval
historian William James, which is cited in Chapter 3 (Appendix D;
Check-List, No. 294a), and among his own books he used the *Life of
Nelson* by Robert Southey, which Mrs. Melville described as 'kept for
reference' for the story (No. 481). He may also have consulted Joseph
Allen's *Battles of the British Navy,* which is apparently referred to in a
manuscript notation (p. 428), but Clark Russell's book on Nelson, not
published until 1890 (No. 432), probably came to him too late to be of
much use.

To Russell himself in 1886 Melville had praised Dana's *Two Years
Before the Mast* (*Log* 2: 799–800), which had appeared in a new
'author's edition' in 1869; William H. Bond, noting that Billy Budd's
stammer is like that of Dana's Sam as he is presented in the 1869 edition, has proposed that work as a 'cue' for *Billy Budd, Sailor* ('Melville
and *Two Years Before the Mast*'). Among other possible sources, one
suggested by Stanton Garner, as previously noted, is the story of a
drumhead court that Melville probably heard while visiting the Union
front during the Civil War. B. R. McElderry, Jr., and Richard and Rita
Gollin have called attention to parallels both in Douglas Jerrold's
Black-Ey'd Susan and *The Mutiny at the Nore* (Check-List, No. 297)
and in Captain Marryat's *The King's Own*; John Bryant has cited
Charles F. Briggs's *Working a Passage* ('Three Earlier Treatments of
the *Billy Budd* Theme'; 'Justice in an Earlier Treatment of the *Billy
Budd* Theme'; 'Melville and Charles F. Briggs').

Hayford and Sealts in the Editors' Introduction to their 1962
Chicago edition of the story mention Cooper's *The Two Admirals* and
Wing and Wing and refer to possible 'unsuspected analogues' in American naval history, Melville's own experience in the American navy, and
various pieces of minor sea literature (pp. 30–33). Although Melville did

not take the controversial *Somers* mutiny affair of 1842 in the American navy as his point of departure for *Billy Budd,* as some earlier scholars had thought, the Chicago editors acknowledge that it 'was certainly a cogent analogue' in the last stage of its composition, with its emphasis on Captain Vere and his role (p. 30); there is, however, no evidence to indicate whether or not Melville saw articles in American magazines of 1887 and 1888 that renewed popular discussion of the *Somers* affair, and no agreement concerning his final judgment of the case.

Interpretations of *Billy Budd, Sailor,* have been many and various and seem destined to remain so; a more appropriate subtitle might be 'The Ambiguities,' as with the earlier *Pierre,* rather than 'An Inside Narrative.' The story has been read not only as a work of fiction but as a religious allegory, a personal testament, and an ironic political statement. Where some readers have emphasized the analogue of the *Somers* case, others have examined Billy's trial and sentence with reference to British naval history and law, charging Vere—or even Melville himself—with ignorance of or wilful departures from orthodox naval procedures. The narrator's role, an apparent shift in his presentation of Vere during the last phase of composition, and the unfinished state of the manuscript itself have all been matters of disagreement. Much recent criticism has focused on Captain Vere, whom every reader must judge—so the narrator tells us—not by external standards but 'by such light as this narrative may afford' (p. 102).

As these successive chapters on Melville's life and writings have shown again and again, the problem of interpreting any of his works is complicated by his inveterate habit of linking material from his reading with both personal reminiscence and imaginative projection. His final work of fiction draws once more on such old favorites as the Bible and the classics, Plato and Montaigne, Shakespeare and Milton, the verse of Dibdin and Tennyson, the prose of Hawthorne and of 'a writer whom few know' (p. 114)—obviously Melville himself, whose own life and writings contributed as much or more to the story than anything he read in literature, philosophy, or history. Although *Billy Budd, Sailor,* can be approached and enjoyed on its own terms alone, it will always attract students of Melville as the last work of his varied career as a student, sailor, reader, thinker, prominent author, obscure customs inspector, and creative artist. To engender true artistry, he wrote in 'Art' (*Poems,* p. 231), such 'unlike things' as 'instinct and study' must 'meet and mate,' as they do once more in this retrospective product of his final years.

Notes

[1] Letter to the *New York Times Saturday Review*, 5 October 1901, as quoted in Sealts, *The Early Lives of Melville*, p. 78; letter to G. P. Putnam and Sons, 27 March 1879, reproduced from a Swan catalogue in 'Collecting Melville et al.,' *Melville Society Extracts* 66 (May 1986): 14.

[2] When Frances Priscilla Melville's estate was settled in 1886, with Abraham Lansing as executor, the Melvilles received not only substantial legacies but also items of furniture from Gansevoort; the property itself passed into other hands. Herman had apparently not visited there since 1883 (*Log* 2: 783), and was probably unaware that the family papers belonging in turn to his late sisters Augusta and Frances Priscilla were still extant. After their reemergence in 1983, as noted in the Introduction above, they became a part of the New York Public Library's Gansevoort-Lansing Collection.

In a letter of 15 August 1954, Jay Leyda told me of his then recent visit to Gansevoort and examination of the Sunday School library at the Dutch Reformed Church, where Augusta Melville had catalogued its acquisitions between 1858 and her death in 1876. Included, along with religious books, were volumes of *The Youth's Friend*, acquired at different times but constituting 'a continuous run from 1831 to 1838—years that fit the Melville children perfectly,' but there is no indication as to whether or not these books came from the Melville sisters.

[3] Melville's letter of 17 November 1889 concerning his new certificate of membership, addressed to Simeon E. Baldwin of New Haven, executor of Mrs. Gifford's estate, is reproduced in *Melville Society Extracts* 58 (May 1984): 7. Baldwin later sent the Melvilles his *Brief Memorial of Philip Marett*, acknowledged in Elizabeth Melville's letter to him of 3 March 1891 (Check-List, No. 21d).

[4] J. E. A. Smith wrote of 'Mr. Melville's curious library which had been so gathered that he was its soul' ('Herman Melville,' p. 136). To Oscar Wegelin, Melville 'was hardly a collector in the sense in which the term is employed today. . . . Melville's was a reader's and a student's library' ('Herman Melville as I Recall Him,' p. 22). Lathrop C. Harper remembered 'no rarities, no special association copies,' in the 'miscellaneous and unimportant lot' that his brother Francis was said to have bought from Mrs. Melville (letter of 26 December 1947 from Douglas C. Parsonage).

[5] Among Melville's contemporaries, Smith, 'Herman Melville,' p. 136, also mentions Melville's 'rare and story telling engravings.' Robert K. Wallace, 'Melville's Prints and Engravings at the Berkshire Athenaeum,' offers a valuable discussion of Melville's interest in pictorial art and a catalogue of items surviving from his collection.

[6] The various gifts from Billson, Barrs, and Salt were tabulated by Mrs. Melville in her memoranda; see Sealts, *The Early Lives of Melville*, pp. 171–172. She gave to Arthur Stedman the copy of Salt's *Life of James Thomson* (1889) that Melville had previously bought for himself 'at a time when he was a very poor man,' as Stedman told Salt in 1892 (Check-List, No. 435a).

[7] I have discussed Melville's relations with the Stedmans in *The Early Lives*

of Melville, pp. 47–64, and have summarized in 'Melville and Whitman' what little the two writers apparently knew of one another.

[8]For the chronology of these pieces and a discussion of their significance, see my 'Melville's Burgundy Club Sketches.' At some time during his retirement, Melville also composed a rough draft of still another prose introduction to the two poems that is yet to be published. The manuscript is enclosed in a folded sheet he had originally labeled 'Timoleon' and then [cancelled] 'Left out of Timoleon'; on this sheet as reversed and refolded his wife wrote 'House of the Tragic Poet prefatory to Jack Gentian &c' (HCL).

[9]See R. R. Palmer, 'Herman Melville et la Révolution Française,' and Stanton Garner, 'The Picaresque Career of Thomas Melvill, Junior.'

[10]Melville was said to lack copies of his own works during his later years until supplied by John Anderson (*Log* 2: 787–788, 827); he may indeed have needed to replace copies of *Omoo*, *White-Jacket*, and *Moby-Dick*, all of which had gone out of print by 1887. Hayford and Sealts, p. 135, remark that in *Billy Budd, Sailor*, there are episodes 'so closely resembling passages in Melville's earlier works as to raise the question whether he was deliberately borrowing from them or had read them so recently that he unconsciously echoed even their phrasing'—as he did that of *White-Jacket* in calling his granddaughter Eleanor 'Tittery-Eye': see Sealts, *The Early Lives*, p. 179, and n. 4, p. 252. In 1890, with some prospect of a new London edition of *Typee* in view, he dictated notes for desired revisions (*The Early Lives*, p. 72).

PART II

BOOKS OWNED AND BORROWED

. . . this mere painstaking burrower and grub-worn of a poor
devil of a Sub-Sub appears to have gone through the long Vaticans and street-stalls of the earth, picking up whatever random
allusions . . . he could anyways find. . . .
  —'Extracts. (Supplied by a Sub-Sub Librarian.)' *Moby-
  Dick*, p. 2

Content of the Check-List

Scope

The Check-List that follows is composed of the titles of books owned and borrowed by Herman Melville and his immediate family, as revealed by the records of Melville's reading examined in Part I above. Its various entries fall in three general classes: books owned that have survived, books owned that have apparently not survived, and books borrowed. The term 'books' has been taken to include printed books and pamphlets, exclusive of copies of Melville's own works, and both single issues and bound volumes of periodicals, but not newspapers, broadsides, or portfolios of drawings unaccompanied by text. Books considered as owned by Melville include those purchased by him, those presented to him by friends or relatives, and those he reviewed, since review copies were presumably furnished him. Other titles, even though mentioned in his own writings or demonstrated to be 'sources' of his own work, have been omitted unless a definite record of his owning or borrowing them has been found.

The list includes books owned or borrowed by his immediate relatives during a period of residence in his household, as such books were readily accessible to him, but those evidently acquired or borrowed by relatives at a later date are omitted unless the volumes subsequently became part of the family library through inheritance or gift. Volumes of doubtful status during Melville's lifetime have been so indicated. Books borrowed from the library of the Boston Athenaeum by his father-in-law, Lemuel Shaw, during Melville's known visits to Boston are also included. Following the listings is an analytical index of entries in each of the categories mentioned.

Arrangement

For convenience in reference and citation, the entries in the Check-List are combined in one alphabetical catalogue and numbered consecutively. Author headings and principles of arrangement have in general been based on the *Catalog of Books Represented by Library of Congress Printed Cards* and the later *National Union Catalog: Pre-1956 Imprints.* Entries were numbered at the time the first installment of the original articles went to press; additions and changes made since that time have been entered in alphabetical sequence and given the numbers of the entries immediately preceding plus a suffix letter (or a suffix decimal if the addition precedes an entry already bearing a suffix letter: 556, 556.1, 556a). No quantitative significance is to be attached to the numbers themselves.

An effort has been made to supply information within the body of each entry rather than in appended notes, and at the same time to keep the entries clear and concise. Every entry consists of two parts: the first gives the author heading, the title or short title, the imprint in abbreviated form, and the number of volumes if more than one, plus an indication of Melville's holding in the case of incomplete sets; the second states the relation of the book to Melville or his close relatives, its location if the book has survived, and the source of information if it was borrowed or if it has apparently not survived. (The full titles of published sources cited in abbreviated form will be found in the list of Works Cited.)

No attempt has been made here to give detailed bibliographical descriptions of each volume or to reproduce every title page in full; such information, in most cases available elsewhere, is beyond the scope of this study. All listings have been made as nearly uniform in general style as possible, but certain variations have been necessary between books that have survived and those known only through references in contemporary records of purchases, gifts, and loans.

Books Owned That Have Survived

In addition to author headings, titles, imprints, and holdings, rebinding is indicated if apparently dating from the period of Melville's ownership. The following information is given when applicable in the second portion of each entry:

1. *Quotation of inscriptions relative to ownership, including the*

date and manner of acquisition. The conditions under which this list has been assembled have unfortunately precluded identification of the handwriting of all inscriptions, particularly in those books belonging to private collectors which the compiler has not seen, or when there was no opportunity for comparison with examples of known hands.

2. *Indication of the presence of marking or annotation.* For purposes of this list, 'marking' refers to underscoring, marginal lining, or checking of passages; 'annotation' refers to notes or comments written in the margins or elsewhere; volumes both 'marked' and 'annotated' are listed only as 'annotated.' In the absence of full quotation of passages marked or annotated, which is impracticable here, most scholars will wish to determine by personal examination of the books (or reproductions of such passages in other scholarly publications) the importance of the passages concerned. For this reason, neither quantitative nor qualitative distinctions have been made; the presence of a single mark or word has therefore sufficed in a few instances to establish a volume as 'marked' or 'annotated,' although such extreme cases are exceptional.

3. *Present location, if known.* In some cases, however, surviving volumes are known only through entries in modern sale catalogues. The catalogues have been cited in such instances and their descriptions fully quoted if the information called for above is not provided in the catalogue entries. The same principle has been followed in the case of surviving books examined and described at some time by a scholar or bibliophile but now unlocated. Certain entries, for example, are based wholly or in part on notes made available by the late Raymond Weaver shortly before his death in April 1948. The notes concern books that he examined and described in collecting materials for his pioneer biography of Melville, published in 1921. Some were single-volume works; others were volumes now lacking in several incomplete sets in the Melville Collection of the Harvard College Library. Surviving books that have not been examined by the compiler are marked with a number sign (#); all others have been checked by him for inscriptions, marking, and annotation.

Other Books Owned, and Books Borrowed

Author headings, titles, and imprints have been specified wherever possible in listing both books owned that have apparently not survived and books borrowed; the sources of acquisition or loan are also mentioned where known; titles, dates, and prices are quoted from contemporary records; and the records themselves are cited. Exceptional cases are as follows:

1. Where a contemporary description is so illegible or vague as to defy identification by author and title, entry has been made under the

first word or initial of the description concerned (e.g., No. 233a: 'Grace C. E.').

2. Under 'Book' and 'Books' have been listed a few unnamed purchases and gifts so described in contemporary records, together with five fragments apparently cut from the flyleaves of books belonging to Melville. Nos. 73a–83 are entries of this type.

3. Most of the other books in these categories have been identified not only by author and title but also by edition. Many titles were available in but one edition in Melville's day. If not, the fact of acquisition from a named publisher at a stated price has frequently provided a definite clue in the case of books owned; contemporary list prices quoted in advertisements, publishers' catalogues, and Roorbach's *Bibliotheca Americana* have proved valuable in following such clues except where the books were bought at second hand. Where other scholars have established the editions Melville used on the basis of internal evidence, that fact is also indicated (e.g., Nos. 51, 366).

As for books borrowed, if the borrowing was from a library that was catalogued, it has usually been possible to specify particular editions of known titles by reference to that library's catalogues of the period. Some titles, however, were not catalogued, particularly those loaned by private individuals; others were available in more than one edition. If the edition owned or borrowed must have been one of only two or three available at the time, these alternative identifications have been indicated; if many possible editions were available, only the author heading and short title have been given.

Abbreviations and Symbols

Certain recurring citations have been made in abbreviated form. The location of surviving books and manuscripts listed or cited has been indicated by symbols if the material is in a library; the known location of items belonging to private collectors has been shown by giving the last name of the collector. These names and symbols are listed here for convenient reference.

Abrams	The collection of Alan Abrams, Windsor, Ontario.
Bassett	The collection of Greg Bassett, College Park, Maryland.
BCHS	Berkshire County Historical Society, Pittsfield, Massachusetts.
BeA	Berkshire Athenaeum, Pittsfield, Massachusetts.
BoA	Library of the Boston Athenaeum. Ledgers for 1846–61, listing books borrowed by Lemuel Shaw, have provided information on books available to Melville during his visits to Shaw's residence in Boston.
BUL	Brown University: the John Hay Library.

CUL	Columbia University Libraries: the Rare Book and Manuscript Library.
Dietrich	The collection of H. Richard Dietrich, Jr., Chester Springs, Pennsylvania.
Fleming	John F. Fleming, Inc., New York City.
GMJ	Entry of the date indicated in Gansevoort Melville's Journal.
Haack	The collection of Peter R. Haack, West Newbury, Massachusetts.
HCL	Harvard College Library: the Houghton Library, exclusive of material designated HCL–H, HCL–J, HCL–L, HCL–W, and HCL–WP.
HCL–H	Harvard College Library: the Houghton Library. Statement of Melville's account with Harper and Brothers rendered as of the date indicated (e.g., 'HCL–H, 31 Jul 1847'), showing purchases of Harper publications made by him and by his brother Allan.
HCL–J	Harvard College Library: the Houghton Library. Entry of the date indicated (e.g., 'HCL–J, 23 Dec 1849') in Melville's journals.
HCL–L	Harvard College Library: the Houghton Library. List of the books acquired by Melville in Europe, entered on facing pages of the journal of his European trip in 1849–50.
HCL–W	Harvard College Library: the Houghton Library. Statement of Melville's account with John Wiley, rendered as of the date indicated (e.g., 'HCL–W, 1 Jul 1847'), showing purchases of books of various American and English publishers made by him and by his brother Allan.
HCL–WP	Harvard College Library: the Houghton Library. Statement of Melville's account with Wiley and Putnam, rendered as of the date indicated (e.g., 'HCL–WP, 1 Jan 1847'), showing purchases of books of various American and English publishers made by him and by his brother Allan.
Levenson	The collection of J. C. Levenson, Charlottesville, Virginia.
LHS	The Lansingburgh Historical Society, Lansingburgh, New York.
Marshall	The collection of Mrs. Roderick Marshall, Oxford, England.
Martin	The collection of H. Bradley Martin, New York City.
Mott	Howard S. Mott, Inc., Sheffield, Massachusetts.
NL	The Newberry Library, Chicago.
NYHS	The New-York Historical Society, New York City.
NYPL	The New York Public Library, Astor, Lenox and Tilden Foundations, exclusive of material designated NYPL–B, NYPL–BL, NYPL–D, NYPL–F, NYPL–GL, NYPL–L, and NYPL–O.
NYPL–B	The New York Public Library: the Henry W. and Albert A. Berg Collection.

NYPL–BL	The New York Public Library: Evert A. Duyckinck's manuscript notebook entitled 'Books Lent' (the Duyckinck Family Papers, Duyckinck Collection).
NYPL–D	The New York Public Library: the Duyckinck Collection, exclusive of NYPL–BL.
NYPL–F	The New York Public Library: the Ford Collection.
NYPL–GL	The New York Public Library: the Gansevoort-Lansing Collection.
NYPL–L	The New York Public Library: *Lenox Library Short-Title Lists*, VIII and XII, constituting the posthumous catalogue of Evert Duyckinck's library.
NYPL–O	The New York Public Library: the Osborne Collection.
NYSL	The New York Society Library. Ledgers for 1847–50 (Shares M–Z: 'Allan Melville' and 'Herman Melville') and 1890–92 (Shares M–W, p. 59) record titles borrowed by Allan and Herman Melville.
PUL	Princeton University Library.
Reese	The collection of William Reese, New Haven, Connecticut.
Rosenbach	The Rosenbach Museum and Library, Philadelphia, Pennsylvania.
Rovere	The collection of George Rovere, Agawam, Massachusetts.
SBL	Stephen B. Luce Library, Maritime College, State University of New York, Fort Schuyler, Bronx, New York.
Serendipity	Serendipity Books, Berkeley California.
Sotheby	Sotheby's, New York City.
UVL–B	University of Virginia Library: the Barrett Collection, Alderman Library.
UVL–S	University of Virginia Library: the Stone Collection, Alderman Library.
Weaver	The estate of the late Raymond Weaver.
Whitburn	Diane and Merrill Whitburn: Pride and Prejudice Books, Ballston Lake, New York.
Woodstock	Library of the Woodstock Theological Center, Georgetown University, Washington, D.C.
YUL	Yale University Library: the Beinecke Library.
#	Surviving books not examined by the compiler.

Certain entries include other notations. The phrase 'Present location unknown' is used with respect to books formerly in the collections of Melville descendants that the compiler has been unable to trace. The phrase 'Last reported in the collection of ———' is used with respect to books listed in the 1966 edition of *Melville's Reading* when recent letters of inquiry to their owners at that time have been returned as undeliverable.

Check-List of Books Owned and Borrowed

A

1. The Academy and Literature. London, 1869–1916. Melville's holding: v. 28, no. 693 (15 Aug 1885).

Melville's letter of 5 Sep 1885 to James Billson acknowledges the gift of 'a copy of "The Academy," received the other day, containing a poem by Robert Buchanan— "Socrates in Camden." '

2. Adams, Abigail (Smith). Letters of Mrs. Adams, the Wife of John Adams. With an Introductory Memoir by Her Grandson, Charles Francis Adams . . . Second Edition. Boston, Little and Brown, 1840. 2 v.

'Mrs. Adams Letters (1–2)' borrowed from NYSL 21 Mar–8 Apr 1891.

3. Adams, John. America and France. The Intire Message of the President . . . Covering the Full Powers to, and Dispatches from, the Envoys Extraordinary of the United States, to the French Republic . . . Boston, Russell, [1798?].

'A[llan] Melville'; 'George Griggs 1855'. (NYPL–GL)

4. Adams, William Henry Davenport, The Buried Cities of Campania; or, Pompeii and Herculaneum, Their History, Their Destruction, and Their Remains . . . London, Nelson, 1869.

'Miss. Fanny Melville from her Father. New York, March 2^d 1870 [Melville's hand].'; 'To Eleanor [Mrs. Metcalf]'. (HCL)

5. Addison, Joseph. Sir Roger de Coverley, Reimprinted from the Spectator; with Illustrations by Chas. O. Murray. London, Low [etc.], [1882?].

'Miss Bessie Melville from her Father. New Year's Day 1883 [Melville's hand]'; 'Katharine G. Binnian.' (HCL)

Adler, George J.: see Nos. 211a, 229.

Aeschylus: see No. 147.

6. Aesopus. Fabulae Aesopi Selectae, or, Select Fables of Aesop; with an English Translation . . . by H. Clarke . . . First Boston Edition . . . Boston, Hall, 1787.

'Allan Melvill's . . . Amherst Academy 1793 Albany'. Annotated. (NYPL–GL)

6a. Aguilar, Grace. The Vale of Cedars: or, The Martyr. New York, Appleton, 1850.

Augusta Melville's letter of 20 Jul 1850 to Evert Duyckinck (NYPL–D) thanks him 'for "The Vale of Cedars" '.

7. Aikin, John. Letters to a Young Lady on a Course of English Poetry . . . New York, Osborn, 1806.

'Maria Gansevoort Melville Albany December 1ˢᵗ 1814'; "Miss Augusta Melville from Her Mother'; 'To Lottie Hoadley—from her Aunt Fanny. Gansevoort. Jun.[?] 17. 1878'. (BeA)

8. Akenside, Mark. The Pleasures of Imagination . . . New York, M'Dermut and Arden, 1813.

'Miss Maria Gansevoort from her friend A[llan] M[elvill].' Marked; one marginal correction. (HCL)

8a. Albany Academy. Celebration of the Semi-Centennial Anniversary of the Albany Academy. Albany June 23, 1863. Albany, Munsell, 1863.

Presumably furnished Melville as an alumnus and member of the committee on arrangements for the celebration, which he attended.

9. Alemán, Mateo. Guzman de Alfarache . . . 3 v. Rebound.

Edition unidentified. 'Guzman 3 vol.' bought in London for 2[3?] shillings, rebound (HCL–J, 18 Dec 1849; HCL–L).

10. Alexander, Francesca. Christ's Folk in the Apennine. Reminiscences of Her Friends among the Tuscan Peasantry . . . Edited by John Ruskin . . . New York, Wiley, 1888.

'Christs Folk' borrowed from NYSL 10 Jan–4 Feb 1891.

11. Alger, William Rounseville. The Solitudes of Nature and of Man; or, The Loneliness of Human Life. [2nd ed.] . . . Boston, Roberts, 1867.

Annotated. (HCL)

11a. Alison, Sir Archibald, Bart. History of Europe, from the Commencement of the French Revolution in 1789, to the Restoration of the Bourbons in 1815 . . . New York, Harper, 1842–43. 4 v. Holding of Allan Melville, Jr: v. 1–3 only [?]. #

V. 1–3: 'Allan Melville [Jr] New York [printed label]'; one v. annotated: 'Shp M. P & E—In one week—Clark J. Austin'. (Stolen from the collection of Mrs. Meredith M. Jack, Haverford, Pa.)

Alison, Sir Archibald, Bart.: see also No. 359.

12. Allen, William. A Sermon Preached on Sunday, the Third of April, at the Funeral of Mrs. Fanny Lame Fleury, Wife of Thomas Melvill, Jun. Esq, Who Died in Pittsfield, Massachusetts, April 1, 1814, Aged 32 Years . . . [Pittsfield, 1814?].

(HCL; a second copy is in NYPL–GL)

12a. American Unitarian Association. Hymn and Tune Book for the Church and the Home. Revised Edition. Boston, American Unitarian Association, 1877.

Stamped 'Melville' on front cover; title page lacking. (BCHS)

Anacreon: see No. 147.

13. Andrews, James. Floral Tableaux . . . London, Bogue, 1846.

12 Dec 1846: '1 Floral Tableaux

[$6]–' (HCL–WP, 1 Jan 1847).

14. Arcturus, a Journal of Books and Opinion . . . New York, 1841–42. Borrowed by Melville: v. 1 (1841).
'Arcturus vol 1' borrowed from Evert Duyckinck in 1850 (NYPL–BL: 39th listing for 1850).

14.1. Arichandra, the Martyr of Truth: a Tamil Drama Translated into English by Muṫu Coomàra Swàmy. London, Smith, Elder, 1863. #
'To Rear Admiral, Sir Rodney Mundy, K.C.B. from the author, with his compliments.'; 'H. Melville, Nov. 17, '71 N.Y.' Annotated by the late Roderick Marshall. (Marshall)

14a. Aristotle. The Organon, or Logical Treatises . . . With the Introduction of Porphyry. Literally Translated, with Notes, Syllogistic Examples, Analysis, and Introduction. By Octavius Freire Owen, M.A. . . . London, Bell 1889–90. 2 v. Rebound.
Binding uniform with Nos. 14b, 183a. (HCL)

14b. ——. Aristotle's Treatise on Rhetoric, Literally Translated, with Hobbes' Analysis, Examination Questions, and an Appendix Containing the Greek Definitions. Also, The Poetic of Aristotle, Literally Translated, with a Selection of Notes, an Analysis, and Questions. By Theodore Buckley, B.A. . . . London, Bell and Daldy, 1872. Rebound.
Annotated. Binding uniform with Nos. 14a, 183a. (HCL)

15. Arnold, Sir Edwin. The Poems . . . New York, Hurst, [1879]. #
Marked. (Examined by Raymond Weaver; present location unknown)

16. Arnold, Matthew. Culture & Anarchy, an Essay in Political and Social Criticism; and Friendship's Garland, Being the Conversations, Letters, and Opinions of the Late Arminius, Baron von Thunderten-Tronckh . . . New York, Macmillan, 1883.
Marked. (HCL)

17. ——. Essays in Criticism . . . Boston, Ticknor and Fields, 1865.
'H. Melville July 10, '69 N.Y.'; 'H. Melville Feb 13, '71 N.Y.' Annotated. (HCL)

18. ——. Literature & Dogma; an Essay towards a Better Apprehension of the Bible . . . New York, Macmillan, 1881.
'Eleanor M. Thomas [Mrs. Metcalf]'. Annotated. (HCL)

19. ——. Mixed Essays, Irish Essays, and Others . . . New York, Macmillan, 1883.
Marked. Contains newspaper clipping. (HCL)

20. ——. New Poems . . . Boston, Ticknor and Fields, 1867.
'H. Melville Feb. 13, '71. [erased:] N.Y.' Annotated. (HCL)

21. ——. Poems . . . A New and Complete Edition. Boston, Ticknor and Fields, 1856.
'H. Melville N.Y. Ap. 6, 1862'. Annotated. Contains newspaper clipping of Arnold's 'A Wish' with reference to No. 20 as 'in Press'; notation '1867' at the top. (BeA)

'Atlas of the Heavens': see Nos. 75a, 101a.

21a. Aubrey, John. Miscellanies upon Various Subjects. Fourth Edition. London, John Russell Smith, 1857.
'H. Melville June 21 '70 N.Y.' Annotated. (UVL–B)

21b. Austin, Gilbert. Chironomia; or A Treatise on Rhetorical Delivery . . . London, Cadell and Davies, 1806.
'Gansevoort Melville London 1846'; 'John C. Hoadley—from his sisters Augusta & Fanny Melville'. (NYPL–GL)

21c. Austin, James Trecothick. An Oration, Pronounced at Lexington, Mass. In Commemoration of the Independence of the United States of America, and the Restoration of Peace. 4th July, 1815 . . . Boston, Rowe and Hooper, 1815.
'A[llan]. Melville'. (HCL)

B

21d. Baldwin, Simeon Eben. A Brief Memorial of Philip Marett. Read by Simeon E. Baldwin before the New Haven Colony Historical Society, September 22d, 1890. New Haven, Tuttle, Morehouse & Taylor, Printers, 1890.
Unlocated. Philip Marett (1792–1869) was the father of Ellen Marett Gifford (18?–1889), a cousin of Elizabeth Shaw Melville and benefactor of her family. In a letter of 3 Mar 1891 (Baldwin Family Papers, Yale University Library; quoted by authorization of the Library), Mrs. Melville thanked Baldwin 'for the very interesting "Memorial" which you were kind enough to send me. . . . Both my husband and I have read with great interest this appreciative and friendly "Memorial" and he begs to add to mine his thanks and regards.'

22. Balzac, Honoré de. Bureaucracy: or, A Civil Service Reformer. [Tr. by Katharine Prescott Wormeley.] Bos-

ton, Roberts, 1889.
Marked. (NYPL–O)

23. ———. The Correspondence of Honoré de Balzac; with a Memoir by His Sister, Madame de Surville; Translated by C. Lamb Kenney; with Portrait and Facsimile of the Handwriting of Balzac. London, Bentley, 1878. 2 v.
V. 1, 2: 'Herman from Lizzie [Mrs. Melville] Aug 1–1889'. Annotated. Contains clipping on Balzac. (NYPL–O)

24. ———. The Country Doctor. [Tr. by Katharine Prescott Wormeley.] Boston, Roberts, 1887. (NYPL–O)

25. ———. Cousin Bette. [Tr. by Katharine Prescott Wormeley.] Boston, Roberts, 1888. (NYPL–O)

26. ———. Cousin Pons. [Tr. by Katharine Prescott Wormeley.] Boston, Roberts, 1886.
'Mrs. Herman Melville The Florence New York'. (NYPL–O)

27. ———. The Duchesse de Langeais, with An Episode under the Terror, The Illustrious Gaudissart, A Passion in the Desert, and The Hidden Masterpiece. [Tr. by Katharine Prescott Wormeley.] Boston, Roberts, 1885.
'H. Melville 104 E. 26 St N.Y.' (NYPL–O)

28. ———. Eugenie Grandet; or, The Miser's Daughter. From the French of Honoré de Balzac. Translated by O. W. Wight and F. B. Goodrich. New York, Rudd and Carleton, 1861.
'H. Melville Dec 1, 1870 N.Y.' Annotated. (NYPL–O)

29. ———. Fame and Sorrow, with Colonal Chabert, The Atheist's Mass, La Grande Bretèche, The Purse, La

Grenadière. [Tr. by Katharine Prescott Wormeley.] Boston, Roberts, 1890. Marked. (NYPL–O)

30. ———. Louis Lambert. With an Introduction by George Frederic Parsons. [Tr. by Katharine Prescott Wormeley.] Boston, Roberts, 1889. (NYPL–O)

31. ———. The Magic Skin. With an Introduction by George Frederic Parsons. [Tr. by Katharine Prescott Wormeley.] Boston, Roberts, 1888.
'H. Melville N.Y.' (NYPL–O)

32. ———. Modeste Mignon. [Tr. by Katharine Prescott Wormeley.] Boston, Roberts, 1888.
(NYPL–O)

33. ———. Père Goriot. [Tr. by Katharine Prescott Wormeley.] Boston, Roberts, 1885.
Annotated. (NYPL–O)

34. ———. Seraphita. With an Introduction by George Frederic Parsons. [Tr. by Katharine Prescott Wormeley.] Boston, Roberts, 1889.
Marked. (NYPL–O)

35. ———. The Shorter Stories and Tales . . . Translated . . . by Philip Kent, B.A. New York, Arundell Print, [18–].
Annotated. Contains clipping on Balzac. (NYPL–O)

36. ———. Sons. of the Soil. [Tr. by Katharine Prescott Wormeley.] Boston, Roberts, 1890.
Annotated. (NYPL–O)

37. ———. The Two Brothers. [Tr. by Katharine Prescott Wormeley.] Boston, Roberts, 1887.
Marked. (NYPL–O)

Balzac, Honoré de: see also Nos. 436, 543.

Bard, Samuel A. [pseud.]: see Squier,

Ephraim George (No. 485).

38. Barnard, Charles H. A Narrative of the Sufferings and Adventures of Capt. Charles H. Barnard, in a Voyage round the World . . . New York, Bliss [etc.], 1829; *or,* New York, Callender, 1836.
'Barnard Narrative G. Tomes' borrowed from Evert Duyckinck in Jan or Feb 1848 (NYPL–BL, the second book charged to Melville; see Davis, *Melville's* Mardi, p. 64). Not in NYPL–L; apparently George Tomes's copy.

39. Barr, Amelia Edith (Huddleston). The Beads of Tasmer . . . New York, Bonner, 1891.
'Beads of Tasmer' borrowed from NYSL 25 May–5 Jun 1891.

40. ———. A Border Shepherdess; a Romance of Eskdale . . . New York, Dodd, Mead, [ᶜ1887].
'Border Shepherdess' borrowed from NYSL 27 Mar–9 Apr 1891.

41. ———. The Bow of Orange Ribbon; a Romance of New York . . . New York, Dodd, Mead, [ᶜ1886].
'Bow Orange Ribbon' borrowed from NYSL 12 Feb–2 Mar 1891.

42. ———. Feet of Clay . . . New York, Dodd, Mead, [ᶜ1889].
'Feet of Clay' borrowed from NYSL 27 Mar–8 Apr 1891.

43. ———. Friend Olivia . . . New York, Dodd, Mead, [ᶜ1889–90].
'Friend Olivia' borrowed from NYSL 2–13 Mar 1891.

44. ———. The Household of McNeil . . . New York, Dodd, Mead, 1890.
'Household McNeill' borrowed from NYSL 18–28 Apr 1891.

45. ———. Jan Vedder's Wife . . . New York, Dodd, Mead, [1885].
'Jan Vedders Wife' borrowed from

NYSL 5–12 Nov 1890.

46. ———. The Last of the McAllisters . . . New York, Dodd, Mead, 1889.
'Mc Allister' borrowed from NYSL 12–15 Nov 1890.

47. ———. Master of His Fate . . . New York, Dodd, Mead, [ᶜ1888].
'Master of His Fate.' borrowed from NYSL 9–18 Apr 1891.

48. Bartlett, William Henry. Forty Days in the Desert, on the Track of the Israelites; or, A Journey from Cairo, by Wady Feiran, to Mount Sinai and Petra . . . Fifth Edition. New York, Scribner, [186–?].
'H. Melville Jan 31, 70 N.Y.'; 'Caroline W. Stewart. From Mr. Melville's library.' Annotated. (NYPL–GL)

49. ———. The Nile-Boat; or, Glimpses of the Land of Egypt . . . Fifth Edition. New York, Scribner, [186–?].
'Caroline W. Stewart from Mr. Melville's library.' Annotated. (NYPL–GL)

50. ———. Walks about the City and Environs of Jerusalem . . . London, Virtue, [186–?].
'Mrs. Herman Melville from H. M. Xmas 1870 New York.' (NYPL–GL)

51. Bayle, Pierre. An Historical and Critical Dictionary . . . (Tr. by Jacob Tonson.) London, Harper, [etc.], 1710. 4 v.
'I bought a set of Bayle's Dictionary the other day, & . . . intend to lay the great old folios side by side & go to sleep on them . . .' (Melville to Evert Duyckinck, Boston, 5 Apr 1849). That Melville owned and used the 4-v. Tonson translation is demonstrated by James Duban, 'The

Translation of Pierre Bayle's *An Historical and Critical Dictionary* Owned by Melville.'

52. Beale, Thomas. The Natural History of the Sperm Whale . . . To Which Is Added a Sketch of a South-Sea Whaling Voyage . . . in Which the Author Was Personally Engaged . . . [2nd ed.] London, Van Voorst, 1839.
'Herman Melville New York, July 10ᵗʰ 1850'; 'Imported by Putnam for me $3.38.' Annotated. (HCL)

53. Beaumont, Francis. Fifty Comedies and Tragedies. Written by Francis Beaumont and John Fletcher . . . London, Martyn [etc.], 1679. Rebound.
'Beaumont & Fletcher folio' bought in London for 14 shillings (HCL–J, 14 Nov 1849; HCL–L). 'Herman Melville London, December, 1849. (New Year's Day, at sea)'; '1850'. Annotated. (HCL)

Beaumont, Francis: see also No. 358.

54. Beckford, William. Vathek: An Arabian Tale . . . With Notes, Critical and Expository. The Castle of Otranto. By Horace Walpole. The Bravo of Venice [by Heinrich Zschokke] Translated by M. G. Lewis. London, Bentley, 1849. (Standard Novels, no. 41.)
'Vathek (1 vol)' presented by Richard Bentley in London, 1849 (HCL–L), probably on 19 Dec; cf. No. 282. Books obtained from Bentley are listed in HCL–L after No. 330a, bought on 18 Dec, and before No. 228, inscribed 'Dec 25. 1849.'

Beever, Susanna: see No. 461.

55. Bell, Nancy R. E. (Meugens), 'Mrs A. G. Bell.' Raphael, by N.

D'Anvers [pseud.]. New York, Scribner and Welford, 1880. (HCL)

56. Bell, Robert, ed. Songs from the Dramatists . . . London, Parker, 1854. '*1855*. Mitford. 1854.'; 'Mitford's copy with autograph & ms. notes on fly-leaf'; 'H. Melville N.Y. 1873'. Annotated. (NYPL–O)

57. Bellegarde, Jean Baptiste Morvan de. Politeness of Manners and Behaviour in Fashionable Society. From the French of the Abbé de Bellegarde . . . Third Edition. Paris, [Printed by Charles], 1817. 'Allan Melvill'; 'Herman Melville'. Annotated. (NYPL: Rare Book Division)

58. Béranger, Pierre Jean de. The Songs of Béranger, in English. With a Sketch of the Author's Life. Philadelphia, Carey and Hart, 1844. 'H. Melville'; 'Pacific Ocean Sep 4th 1860 19° S. L.'; 'Abraham Lansing Xmas, 1876.' (NYPL–GL)

59. Besant, Sir Walter. Children of Gibeon . . . Leipzig, Tauchnitz, 1886. 2 v. 'Children Chibeon [*sic*]' borrowed from NYSL 30 Jan–12 Feb 1891.

60. Bible. English. 1810. Authorized. The Holy Bible . . . Philadelphia, Carey, 1810. 'Catherine Gansevoort, To her beloved Daughter, Maria Gansevoort Melvill [final 'e' deleted]. October 11th 1817. Albany'. Annotated. (NYPL–GL)

61. Bible. English. 1845. Authorized. The Holy Bible . . . Oxford, Oxford University Press, 1845. 'Elizabehth K[napp] Shaw [later Mrs. Melville] from her friend. L[ucy]

M[elville] Nourse August 4.th 1847.' Annotated by Mrs. Melville. (HCL)

62. Bible. English. 1846. Authorized. The Holy Bible . . . Together with the Apocrypha . . . Philadelphia, Butler, 1846. 2 v. in 1. 'Herman Melville March 23d 1850. New York.' Annotated. (Martin)

Bible. O.T. Psalms. Dutch. 1715: see No. 63.

62a. Bible. O. T. Psalms. English. 1796. The Psalms of David, with Hymns and Spiritual Songs, Having the proper Metre prefixed to each. Also, The Catechism, Compendium, Confession of Faith and Liturgy, of the Reformed Church in the Netherlands. For the Use of the Reformed Dutch Church in North-America. Albany, Charles R. and George Webster, 1796. Stamped 'Maria Gansevoort' on front cover. (NL)

Bible. O. T. Psalms. English. 1844: see No. 65.

63. Bible. N. T. Dutch. 1715. Het Nieuwe Testament . . . Amsterdam, van Reyschoote [etc.], 1715. De CL Psalmen des Propheten Davids . . . Amsterdam, Hasebroek [etc.], 1715. 2 v. in 1. 'Helen. M[aria] Melville Griggs from her Mother M[aria] G[ansevoort] Melville. Gansevoort August 4 1863.' (NYPL–GL)

64. Bible. N. T. English. 18–. Authorized. The New Testament . . . London, Eyre and Spottiswoode, [18–]. Melville's autograph pasted to flyleaf. Marked. (HCL)

65. Bible. N. T. English. 1844. Authorized. The New Testament . . . The Book of Psalms . . . New York,

American Bible Society, 1844. 2 v. in 1.

'From Aunt Jean [added by Mrs. Melville: '(Melville)'] 1846.'; 'C[ape] H[orn] 2'. Annotated. (HCL)

66. The Bijou; or Annual of Literature and the Arts. London, Pickering, 1828.
'Herman to Augusta [Melville] Pittsfield June 1861. Originally Priscilla's' [i.e., their cousin Priscilla Melvill's]. (HCL)

67. Black, William. A Princess of Thule. A Novel . . . New York, Harper, 1874; *or,* Philadelphia, Coates, [18–].
'Princess of Thule' borrowed from NYSL 5–27 Jun 1891.

68. Blackmore, Richard Doddridge. Lorna Doone. A Romance of Exmoor . . . New York, Putnam, 1890. 3 v.
'Lorna Doone' borrowed from NYSL 8–9 Apr 1891.

68a. Blake, John Lauris. First Book in Astronomy Applied to the Use of Common Schools . . . Boston, Lincoln and Edmands [etc.], 1831.
'To Master Thos. Melville for his attention to me, in preserving and restoring my Hymnbook, to show that acts of kindness may not always go unrewarded. H. B. Tuttle'; 'To Thomas Melville July 29, 1839 "An *undevout* astronomer is *mad*" [from Edward Young, *Night Thoughts,* 'Night IX,' line 771] T. C. *July*'. (BeA)

Blake, William: see Nos. 224, 520.

69. Blake, William P. Catalogue of Books, for Sale or Circulation, by W. P. & L. Blake, at the Boston Book-Store . . . Boston, Blake, 1798.
'A[llan] Melville'. (NYPL–GL)

70. Bloomfield, Robert. The Farmer's

Boy; a Rural Poem . . . London, [?], 1858. #
Described as containing an inscription 'in Herman Melville's Autograph Handwriting, presenting [it] to his Sister, Fanny,' together with No. 507, an 1868 edition of Tennyson's *May Queen* (American Book Auction, Catalogue 61, 26 Jan 1945, Lot 196).

Blumer, Edith (Walford): see No. 554.

71. Boaden, James. An Inquiry into the Authenticity of Various Pictures and Prints, Which, from the Decease of the Poet to Our Own Times, Have Been Offered to the Public as Portraits of Shakespeare . . . London, Triphook, 1824. Rebound.
'H. Melville'; 'This very valuable work, containing five different portrat [*sic*] of Shakespeare, (including a *true* copy of the famed Chandos portrait) sold for only 65 cents at Cooley K[eese] & H[ill]'s auction [191 Broadway, New York] June 27th '48. The leaves were uncut. [Inserted here by Mrs. Melville: 'Bound by'] H. M.' Bound in is a broadside of a performance of Farquhar's *Beaux' Stratagem* at the Drury Lane Theatre, London, 5 Jun 1818. (HCL)

71a. Boccaccio, Giovanni. The Decameron.
Either owned or borrowed by Melville. Visiting Evert Duyckinck in 1856, Melville 'cited a good story from the Decameron the *Enchantment* of the husband in the tree' (*Log* 2: 523, quoting from Duyckinck's diary, 1 Oct 1856).

72. Bohn, Henry George. A Guide to the Knowledge of Pottery, Porcelain, and Other Objects of Vertu. Comprising an Illustrated Catalogue of the

Bernal Collection . . . To Which Are Added an Introductory Essay on Pottery and Porcelain, and an Engraved List of Marks and Monograms . . . London, Bohn, 1857.
Annotated. (NYPL–O)

73. Book of the Poets. The Modern Poets of the Nineteenth Century. London, Scott [etc.], 1842.
'Augusta [Melville], from her aff' C. V. R. T[hayer] September 15th 1846.' (BeA)

73a. Book [unidentified].
'Herman Melville from his Aunt, Priscille [i.e., Priscilla] Melville, Boston, March 1846.' The inscription, described as 'Signature and two lines, apparently cut from a book, 1½ X 7½ inches,' is quoted in Kenneth W. Rendell, Inc., Catalogue 44: *Autograph Letters, Manuscripts & Documents* (62 Bristol Road, Somerville, Mass., Jan 1970), Lot 121.

74. ———.
'Herman Melville April 7, 1847 New York'. An autograph apparently cut from the flyleaf of a book; no purchases by Melville on 7 Apr 1847 are known. (Formerly in the collection of Mrs. Henry K. Metcalf; present location unknown)

75. ———.
'Herman Melville April 10, 1847'. An autograph apparently cut from the flyleaf of a book; for Melville's purchases on 10 Apr 1847 see Nos. 103, 175, 211, 293, 372, 550. (Weaver)

75a. ———.
'Herman Melville Esq with the respect of Evert A Duyckinck Aug 30. 1848.' An inscription apparently cut from the flyleaf of a book ('possibly

an Atlas of the Heavens'—note in Mrs. Metcalf's hand; see No. 101a). (BeA)

76. ———.
'Herman Melville October 1849.' An autograph apparently cut from the flyleaf of a book; for possible identifications—books read by Melville late in 1849—see Nos. 182, 311, 490. (Weaver)

77, 78. ———.
Two unidentified guidebooks borrowed from George L. Duyckinck before Melville's departure for Europe in Oct 1849 were returned, along with No. 166, on 2 Feb 1850, as noted in Melville's letter to Evert Duyckinck of that date.

78a. ———.
Either owned or borrowed by Melville. 2 Jan 1857: 'Spent day reading a book on Palestine' (HCL–J).

79. ———.
With a letter of 31 Dec 1863 Melville returned to Evert Duyckinck an unnamed book he had apparently been asked to review: 'I have read it with great interest. As for scribbling anything about it, . . . I have not spirit enough.'

79a. ———.
'H. Melville Oct. 10, 1868.' An autograph apparently cut from the flyleaf of a book. (NYPL: Rare Book Division, pasted in a copy of the first American edition of *Omoo*)

80. Books [unidentified].
In his letter to Peter Gansevoort of 31 Dec 1837 Melville acknowledges his uncle's gift of 'books,' one of which (No. 497) he names. Cf. also No. 456a.

81. ———.
24 Sep 1850: 'Books [$]8 43'

(HCL–H, 29 Apr 1851). For a possible identification see No. 272.

82. ――――.
1 Feb 1851: 'Books [$]3 05' (HCL–H, 29 Apr 1851). For a possible identification see No. 272.

83. ――――.
4 Jan 1859: 'Books [$]6.62'. Entry in Melville's notebook of lecture engagements (HCL).

84. Boswell, James. The Life of Samuel Johnson, L.L.D. . . . [London, Murray, 1839? *or* (from the same plates), London, Bohn, 1848?] 10 v.
Edition unidentified. 'Boswell's Johnson (10 vol. 18 mo)' bought in London for 21 shillings (HCL–J, 19 Dec 1849; HCL–L).

85. Bougainville, Louis Antoine de, Comte. A Voyage round the World. Performed . . . in the Years 1766, 1767, 1768, and 1769 . . . Translated from the French by John Reinhold Forster, F.A.S. London, Nourse [etc.], 1772.
'Bougaineville Voys' borrowed from NYSL 17 Jan–21 Feb 1848.

86. Bradford, John M. The Fear of the Lord, the Hope of Freedom. A Sermon, on the Present Struggle of the Dutch for Emancipation; Delivered . . . Albany, February 18th, 1814. Albany, Hosford, 1814.
'from Miss M[aria] G[ansevoort]— A[llan] Melville'. (NYPL–GL)

86.1. Braun, Emil. Handbook of the Ruins and Museums of Rome. A Guide for Travellers, Artists and Lovers of Antiquity. Brunswick, Frederick Vieweg; Rome, J. Spithöver, 1856.
Probably acquired by Melville while in Italy in 1857. Mrs. Melville in a later memorandum cited 'Brauns

Handbook' along with No. 375; see Sealts, *The Early Lives of Melville*, p. 175.

86a. Briggs, Charles Frederick. The Trippings of Tom Pepper; or, The Results of Romancing. An Autobiography. By Harry Franco [pseud.]. [V. 1]: New York, Burgess, Stringer, 1847; v. 2: New York, Graham, 1850. 2 v.
Melville's holding: v. 1 only ⚹
Described as 'The Trippings of Tom Pepper by Harry Franko 1847— Flyleaf, "Melville." ' (Present location unknown. Information on Nos. 86a, 383a, and 456a comes from rough notes obtained from the late R. S. Forsythe by J. H. Birss, c. 1933, and communicated at that time to William Braswell. No further information on the books has been found among that portion of Forsythe's notes accessible to Birss.)

British Dramatists: see Nos. 188, 358.

British Essayists: see Nos. 127, 359, 493, 494, 565.

87. Brock-Arnold, George Moss, Gainsborough [and Constable]. New York, Scribner and Welford, 1881. (HCL)

87.1. Brontë, Charlotte. Jane Eyre: An Autobiography. Edited by Currer Bell [pseud.]. New York, Harper & Brothers, 1848. #
'Augusta Melville from L[emuel]. Shaw [Jr.] 184?'; 'Augusta Melville—from Lemuel—'; 'Fanny Melville from her sister Augusta'. (LHS)

87a. Broughton, Thomas Duer. Selections from the Popular Poetry of the Hindoos. Arranged and Translated by Thomas Duer Broughton. London, Martin, 1814.

'H Melville'. Marked. (CUL)

88. Browne, John Ross. Etchings of a Whaling Cruise, with Notes of a Sojourn on the Island of Zanzibar. To Which Is Appended a Brief History of the Whale Fishery . . . New York, Harper, 1846.

In a note to Evert Duyckinck of 2 Feb 1847 Melville wrote: 'I have procured the book you spoke of from the Harpers—& shall find much pleasure in making it the basis of an article for your paper'. The note is pasted to the manuscript (NYPL–D) of Melville's review of Browne's book, which appeared in Duyckinck's *Literary World* 1, no. 6 (6 Mar 1847), 105–106.

89. Browne, Sir Thomas. Sir Thomas Browne's Works, Including His Life and Correspondence; Edited by Simon Wilkin . . . London, Pickering, 1835–36. 4 v.

'Sir Thos Browne vol 2' and later '2 vols' borrowed from Evert Duyckinck after mid-Feb 1848 (NYPL–L, the third book charged to Melville; Davis, *Melville's* Mardi, p. 64), and before Duyckinck's letter of 18 Mar 1848 to his brother George (NYPL–D), which mentions the loan.

90. ———. The Works . . . With Alphabetical Tables. [1st collected ed.] London, Basset [etc.], 1686. 4 pt. in 1 v.

'Sir Thomas Browne folio [added: '1686']' bought in London for 16 shillings (HCL–J, 19 Dec 1849; HCL–L).

91. Browne, William. [Brittania's Pastorals. V. 1 and 2 of] The Works . . . London, Davies, 1772. 3 v. [now bound together]; *or,* Brittania's Pastorals . . . London, Clarke, 1845.

'Browne's Brit Pastorals' borrowed from Evert Duyckinck in 1850 (NYPL–BL: 36th listing for 1850).

92. Browning, Elizabeth (Barrett). Poems . . . London, Bradbury and Evans, 1844. 2 v.

'Miss Barrett's Poems 2 v' borrowed from Evert Duyckinck in [Aug or Sep?] 1850 (NYPL–BL: 35th listing for 1850). A manuscript copy of 'The Cry of the Human' signed 'Elizabeth Barrett', which Cornelius Mathews presented to Mrs. Melville on 15 Aug 1850, is in HCL.

93. ———. The Poems . . . A New Edition . . . New York, Francis, 1860. 2 v.

V. 1, 2: 'H Melville'. V. 1: 'N.Y. June 1864'. Annotated. (NYPL–O)

Browning, Robert: in No. 564, p. 190, is an annotation by Melville citing the ' "Pictor Ignotus" of Browning'.

94. Bryant, William Cullen. Poems . . . Collected and Arranged by the Author. New York, Appleton, 1863.

'H. Melville Oct 12. 1867 N.Y.' Annotated. (NYPL–O)

Buchanan, Robert: see No. 1.

94a. Bunyan, John. Divine Emblems, or, Temporal Things Spiritualised, &c. With Preface by Alexander Smith . . . London, Bickers & Son, [186–].

'H. Melville 1871 N.Y.' (NL)

95. ———. The Pilgrim's Progress, from this World to that which is to come.

Edition unknown. Melville's copy, purchased from Farnell with other books from Melville's library (Nos. 105, 112, 113, 369) by the late Carol V. Wight, was apparently lost in the New England hurricane of 1938.

96. Burgess, Joseph Tom. Old English Wild Flowers . . . London, Warne, 1868.
'Fanny Melville A Birth-day gift March 2, 1874. N.Y.' (NYPL–O)

97. Burke, Edmund. A Philosophical Inquiry into the Origin of Our Ideas of the Sublime and Beautiful with an Introductory Discourse concerning Taste . . . Philadelphia, Johnson, 1806.
'H. Gansevoort'. Received by Mrs. Metcalf with other books from Melville's library. (HCL)

98. Burnet, John. A Treatise on Painting . . . London, Carpenter, 1834–37. 4[?] v. in 1.
'P. [*sic*] Burnet on Painting' charged to Lemuel Shaw by BoA 24 Feb–28 Apr 1849; Melville was in Boston 30 Jan–10 Apr.

99. Burnham, Clara Louise (Root). The Mistress of Beech Knoll; a Novel . . . Boston, Houghton, Mifflin, 1890.
'Mistress Beech Knoll' borrowed from NYSL 9–20 May 1890.

99a. Burns, James Drummond, comp. The Evening Hymn . . . London, Nelson, 1857.
'Augusta Melville New York October 1860'. Apparently owned by Melville or Mrs. Melville after Augusta's death. Annotated by Augusta Melville. (HCL)

100. Burns, Robert. Poems, Chiefly in the Scottish Dialect . . . Kilmarnock, Printed by J. Wilson, 1786 [Newport, R.I., Brown, 1870].
Reprint and facsimile of 1786 edition. 'Presented by Herman Melville to J. C. Hoadley, Sepr. 1870.–' (Formerly in the collection of Miss Agnes Morewood; present location unknown)

101. ———. The Poetical Works . . . With Memoir, Critical Dissertation, and Explanatory Notes, by the Rev. George Gilfillan . . . Edinburgh, Nichol, 1856. 2 v.
'H. Melville N.Y.' Marked. (HCL)

101a. Burritt, Elijah Hinsdale. Atlas, Designed to Illustrate the Geography of the Heavens . . .
Edition unidentified. Mrs. Metcalf remembered that in the Melville household in New York City there was a large atlas in paper covers, creased in the middle and kept with Chambers's *Cyclopaedia* (No. 128 or No. 128b), containing plates of the constellations in soft colors; she did not recall the exact title. According to John M. J. Gretchko (letter of 24 Jun 1978), the Perkins Observatory, Delaware, Ohio, has an edition of Burritt's *Atlas* (New York, F. J. Huntington, c. 1835), that fits Mrs. Metcalf's description. See also No. 75a.

102. Burton, Robert. The Anatomy of Melancholy . . . New York, Wiley, 1847.
8 Feb 1848: '1 Burtons Anatomy of Melancholy—[$]2.—' (HCL–W, 1 Jul 1848).

103. ———. Melancholy; as It Proceeds from the Disposition and Habit, the Passion of Love, and the Influence of Religion. Drawn Chiefly from . . . Burton's Anatomy of Melancholy . . . London, Vernor and Hood, 1801.
'A[llan] Melville'; 'Herman Melville April 10th 1847.' 'I bought this book more than four years ago at Gowan's store in New York. Today Allan [Melville, Jr.] . . . first detected the above pencil signature of my father's who . . . must have had this book, with many others, sold at

auction, at least twenty five years ago.—Strange! Pittsfield July 7th 1851'. (HCL)

104. Butler, Samuel. Hudibras. The First [–Third and Last] Part. Written in the Time of the Late Wars. Corrected and Amended. With Several Additions and Annotations . . . London, Baker, 1710. 3 pts. in 1 v.; rebound.

'Hudibras 18 mo. (old)' bought in London for 2 shillings (HCL–J, 17 Nov 1849; HCL–L) 'at Stribbs's in the Strand' (letter to Evert Duyckinck, 2 Feb 1850, NYPL–D). 'L. Duval'; 'R. Miles 1765'; 'Evert A Duyckinck from H. M. Feb 2^d 1850. 85 years after that Miles the old Englishman, in silk small clothes, bought the work at some stall—*you* own it now—who will own it next?' (NYPL–D: Rare Book Division)

105. ———. Hudibras . . . 2 v.
Edition unknown. Melville's copy, along with No. 95, was apparently destroyed in the New England hurricane of 1938.

106. Bynner, Edwin Lasseter. The Begum's Daughter . . . Boston, Little, Brown, 1890.

'Begum's Dau.' borrowed from NYSL 17–19 Jan 1891.

107. Byron, George Gordon Noël Byron, 6th Baron. The Complete Works . . . Paris, Galignani, 1842.

'Augusta Melville from her friend Howard Townsend March 1855'; 'Aunt Helen [Helen Maria Melville Griggs] to Minnie [Maria Gansevoort Hoadley]. 1888'. (NL)

107a. ———. The Bride of Abydos.
4 Jan 1834: read by Gansevoort Melville. (GMJ)

108. ———. Don Juan . . . London,

Murray, 1837. 2 v.
'Elizabeth K[napp] Shaw [later Mrs. Melville] from her brother Lemuel July 1847.' (Nos. 108–111 were formerly in the collection of Mrs. Henry K. Metcalf; present location unknown)

109. ———. Dramas . . . London, Murray, 1837. 2 v.
'Elizabeth K[napp] Shaw from her brother Lemuel July 1847.' (See No. 108)

110. ———. Miscellanies . . . London, Murray, 1837. 3 v.
V. 2: 'Elizabeth K[napp] Shaw. from her brother Lemuel July 1847.' (See No. 108)

111. ———. Tales . . . London, Murray, 1837. 2 v.
'Elizabeth K[napp] Shaw from her brother Lemuel July 1847.' (See No. 108)

112. ———. The Poetical Works . . . Boston, Little, Brown, [1853?]. 10 v.
V. 1, 5: 'H Melville'. '103 E. 10th St.' V. 1: 'Carol Wight April 14. 92'. Binding uniform with No. 369. From the character of the marking and annotation it would appear that this edition was read by Melville after his trip to the Near East in 1856–57 and during his study of versification in 1858–59 or after. Cf. No. 369. (HCL)

Byron, George Gordon Noël Byron, 6th Baron: see also No. 369.

113. Byron, John. The Narrative of the Honourable John Byron . . . Containing an Account of the Great Distresses Suffered by Himself and His Companions on the Coast of Patagonia, from the Year 1740, till Their Arrival in England, 1746. With a

Description of St. Jago de Chili, and
the Manners and Customs of the In-
habitants. Also a Relation of the Loss
of the Wager, Man of War, One of
Admiral Anson's Squadron. Written by
Himself. Second Edition. London,
Baker and Leigh, 1768.
    'George Savage Antigua'; 'G^t[?]
Hall'; 'Carol Wight'. Annotated [by
Melville?]; engraving with facsimile
signature 'Henry Melvill' laid in: cf.
HCL–J, London, 16 Dec 1849:
'walked to St: Thomas's Church,
Charter House . . . to hear my
famed namesake (almost) "The
Reverend H Melvill." ' Purchased
from Farnell with other books from
Melville's library (Nos. 95, 105, 112,
369) by the late Carol V. Wight.
(HCL)

C

Caesar, Caius Julius: see No. 147.

114. Calderón de la Barca, Pedro.
Three Dramas of Calderón, from the
Spanish. Love the Greatest Enchantment, The Sorceries of Sin, and The
Devotion of the Cross. By Denis Florence MacCarthy. Dublin, Kelly, 1870.
    'H. Melville Sep. 10, '74 N.Y.' Op-
posite a publisher's advertisement
Melville noted: 'by same Translator.
In another Vol. published about
1873 appear "Life's a Dream",
"Vision of St. Patrick", & The
"Wonder Working Magician"—The
first analysed by Dean Trench, the
2^d previously published by McCarthy with other dramas, the last not
appearing in former vols. Also, the
"Two Lovers of Heaven." ' Annotated; passages in both English and
Spanish marked. (NYPL–O)

115. Cameron, Lucy Lyttleton (Butt).
The Fruits of Education; or, The Two
Guardians . . . New York, Gilley,
1828.
    'Elizabeth K[napp] Shaw [later Mrs.
Melville] Presented by her Mother.
1830–'; [added in pencil] 'January
1st'. (Formerly in the collection of
Mrs.Henry K. Metcalf; present location unknown)

116. Camões, Luiz de. Poems, from
the Portuguese of Luis de Camoens.
With Remarks on His Life and Writings. Notes, etc. etc. By Lord Vis-
count Strangford . . . New Edition.
London, Carpenter, 1824. #
    'H. Melville N.Y. May 17th 1867'.
Annotated; passages in both English
and Portuguese marked. (Levenson)

116a. Campan, Jeanne Louise Hen-
riette Genest. Memoirs of the Private
Life of Marie Antoinette, Queen of
France and Navarre . . . [Philadelphia,
Small, 1823?].
    21 Nov 1823: Maria Gansevoort
Melvill wrote to Peter Gansevoort
(NYPL–GL): 'Pray for your
amusement and improvement pro-
cure a new work lately published
entitled   Memoirs   of   Marie
Antoinette—written by Madame
Campan—Sister of Our Old Friend,
Monsieur Genet.'

117. Campbell, Alexander. Sketches of
Life and Character . . . Edinburgh,
Edinburgh Printing and Publishing Co.,
1842. Recased.
    'H. Melville from Allan [Melville,
Jr.]. 1849'; 'Thomas Melvill [*sic*]
from Herman At sea. June, 1860.';
'Thomas Melville June 1860'. Anno-
tated [by Herman Melville?].
(NYPL–GL)

118. Campbell, Thomas. The Pleasures
of Hope, and Other Poems . . . New

York, Longworth, 1811.
'Miss Maria Gansevoort from her friend A[llan] M[elvill] Albany 11 March 1814'. Annotated. (NYPL–GL)

119. The Canons of Good Breeding; or, The Handbook of the Man of Fashion. By the Author of "The Laws of Etiquette" . . . Philadelphia, Lea and Blanchard, 1839.
'Ganesvoort [Melville] London 1846'. Annotated. The history of this book after Gansevoort Melville's death is unknown; cf. Nos. 21b, 266a. (NYPL–GL)

120. Carleton, John William. The Natural History of the "Hawk" Tribe . . . [London, Bogue, 1848?].
Associated with No. 474. (HCL)

120a. Carleton, William. Traits and Stories of the Irish Peasantry. Philadelphia, E. L. Carey & H. Hart, 1834. 2 v.
'Traits & Stories Irish 1.2.' borrowed from NYSL by Allan Melville, Jr., 7–29 May 1850.

121. Carlyle, Thomas, tr. German Romance: Specimens of Its Chief Authors; with Biographical and Critical Notices . . . Boston, Munro, 1841. 2 v.
'Carlyles Germ Rom 2 v' borrowed from Evert Duyckinck in [Aug or Sep ?] 1850 (NYPL–BL: 34th listing for 1850). V. 1: Carlyle's Preface, Musæus ('Dumb Love,' 'Libussa,' 'Melechsala'), Fouqué ('Aslauga's Knight'), Tieck ('The Fair-Haired Eckbert,' 'The Trusty Eckart,' 'The Runenberg,' 'The Elves,' 'The Goblet'); v. 2: Hoffman ('The Golden Pot'), Richter ('Army-Chaplain Schmelzle's Journey to Flætz,' 'Life of Quintus Fixlein').

122. ———. On Heroes, Hero-Worship, and the Heroic in History. Six Lectures: Reported, with Emendations and Additions by Thomas Carlyle. New York, Appleton, 1841; *or*, New York, Wiley and Putnam, 1846.
'Hero Worship' borrowed from Evert Duyckinck in [Jun or Jul?] 1850 (NYPL–BL: 16th listing for 1850).

123. ———. Sartor Resartus: The Life and Opinions of Herr Teufelsdröckh . . . Boston, Munroe, 1840; *or*, New York, Wiley and Putnam, 1847.
'Sartor Resartus' borrowed from Evert Duyckinck in Jun or Jul?] 1850 (NYPL–BL: 15th listing for 1850.

Carlyle, Thomas: see also No. 359.

124. Cervantes Saavedra, Miguel de. Don Quijote . . .
Edition unspecified. 'Don Quixote 1. 2. 3' charged to Lemuel Shaw by BoA 8–21 Jul 1854; Melville was in Boston sometime in Jul (see No. 411). BoA owned translations by Smollett (4 v., Dublin, 1796) and Motteux (5 v., Edinburgh, 1822) as well as editions in the original Spanish.

125. ———. Don Quixote de la Mancha. Translated from the Spanish of Miguel de Cervantes Saavedra, by Charles Jarvis, Esq. Carefully Revised and Corrected. With Numerous Illustrations by Tony Johannot . . . Philadelphia, Blanchard and Lea, 1853. 2 v.
V. 1: 'H. Melville Sep 18. '55'. Annotated. (HCL)

126. Chalmers, Alexander, ed. The British Essayists; with Prefaces, Historical and Biographical, by A. Chalmers . . . Boston, Little, Brown, 1856–57. 38 v. Borrowed by Melville:

v. 32–37.
'Tatler [No. 494], Observer [v. 32–34] Looker On [v. 35–37] 10 vols' borrowed from Evert Duyckinck for Melville's 'winter reading at Pittsfield' in 1860 (NYPL–BL; Duyckinck's diary, NYPL–D, 26–31 Jan 1860). NYPL–L lists 'British Essayists,' v. 32–37 only.

127. Chalmers, Thomas. Posthumous Works . . . Edited by the Rev. William Hanna . . . New York, Harper, 1848–50 [v. 1, 1849]. 8 v.
21 Dec 1849: '8 v. Chalmers [$]6.' (HCL–H, 22 Feb 1850).

128. Chambers, Ephraim. Cyclopaedia: or, An Universal Dictionary of Arts and Sciences . . . London, Knapton [etc.], 1728. 2 v.
Fragment of title page only survives (BeA): 'Herman Gansevoort'; 'to Herman Melville 1846'; 'to Capt. Thomas Melville 1872.'

128a. Chambers's Edinburgh Journal. London, 1833–44; Edinburgh, 1844–
Melville's holding: v. 5, no. 121 (25 Apr 1846) only?
Receipt mentioned in letter of 23 May 1846 from Melville to Alexander W. Bradford.

128b. Chambers's Encyclopedia: A Dictionary of Useful Knowledge for the People. London, W. & R. Chambers, 1868. 10 v.
Possibly owned by Melville or his family; see No. 101a. In a manuscript sketch of her husband's career Mrs. Melville wrote: 'It is erroneously stated in Chambers' Encyclopedia that "in 1860 Herman M. left his farm and made a voyage round the world in a whaling vessel" '; *Chambers's* article on Melville (VI, 397), after giving the er-

roneous date of 1860 for the publication of *Israel Potter,* continues: 'when he left his farm in Massachusetts and embarked in a whaling vessel on a voyage round the world.' One American edition of *Chambers's* (Philadelphia, Lippincott, 1875 and 1891) mentions no such voyage; another (New York, Collier, 1886) reads: 'In 1860, he embarked in a whaling-vessel for a new tour round the world' (V, 321).

129. Chamisso, Adelbert von. Peter Schlemihl . . . Translated by Sir John Bowring . . . With Plates by George Cruikshank . . . Third Edition . . . New York, Denham, 1874. Rebound.
A Cruikshank engraving tipped in. Marked. (HCL)

130. Channing, William Ellery. The Works . . . Eighth Complete Edition, with an Introduction . . . Boston, Munroe, 1848. 6 v.
V. 1–6: 'Elizabeth [Shaw Melville], with the best [v. 2: 'kind', v. 4: 'sincere good', v. 6: 'kindest'] wishes of her affectionate father Lemuel Shaw.' Annotated by Mrs. Melville. Contains clipping on Channing. (NYPL–O)

131. ———. A Sermon, Preached at the Annual Election, May 26, 1830, before His Excellency Levi Lincoln, Governor, His Honor Thomas L. Winthrop, Lieutenant Governor, the Honorable Council, and the Legislature of Massachusetts . . . Boston, Dutton and Wentworth, 1830.
'For Mr Allan Melvill New York from his Father T[homas] M[elvill]'; '19 Sept 1830'; 'Allan Melvill from TM'. (NYPL–GL)

131a. Channing, William Ellery (1817–1901). Poems . . . Second Series. Boston, Munroe, 1847.

Maria Gansevoort Melville, in a letter of 8 Feb 1847 to Augusta Melville (NYPL–GL), reports that Herman, then in Washington, 'was shewn a very pretty volume of Poetry by M^r W E Channing' that included ' "The Island of Nukehava" '; Allan Melville would 'send up the volume' from New York to Lansingburgh.

Chapman, George: see Nos. 276, 277, 278.

132. Chapone, Hester (Mulso). Letters on the Improvement of the Mind. Addressed to a Lady . . . Boston, Wells and Wait, 1809.

'Miss Maria Gansevoort [later Mrs. Alan Melvill] from A[llan] M[elvill] Ballstone-Spa 12th Augt 1814'. Annotated. (HCL)

133. Chase, Owen. Narrative of the Most Extraordinary and Distressing Shipwreck of the Whale-Ship Essex, of Nantucket; Which Was Attacked and Finally Destroyed by a Large Spermaceti-Whale, in the Pacific Ocean; with an Account of the Unparalleled Sufferings of the Captain and Crew . . . New York, Gilley, 1821.

Borrowed from a 'son' of Owen Chase in the South Pacific late in 1841 (Melville's notes in No. 134).

134. ———. Narrative . . . New York, Gilley, 1821.

Pp. 123–128 missing; bound in are a letter from Thomas Macy to Lemuel Shaw, 'Nantucket 4 ṁ 1851' (cf. No. 323), and manuscript notes by Melville. 'Herman Melville from Judge Shaw April. 1851.' Annotated. (HCL)

135. Chasles, Philarète. Anglo-American Literature and Manners: From the French of Philarète Chasles . . . New York, Scribner, 1852.

'M^rs J J Audubon—from Mr Mallory—'; 'E[lizabeth] S[haw] Melville 105 East 18th st.' Annotated by Mrs. Melville. (HCL)

136. Chateaubriand, François Auguste René, Vicomte de. Memoirs of Chateaubriand, Written by Himself . . . London, Colburn, 1848.

'Chateaubriand's Memrs.' charged to Lemuel Shaw by BoA 31 Mar–28 Apr 1849; Melville was in Boston 30 Jan–10 Apr.

137. Chatterton, Thomas. The Poetical Works . . . With Notices of His Life, History of the Rowley Controversy, a Selection of His Letters, and Notes Critical and Explanatory . . . Cambridge, Grant, 1842. 2 v. Rebound.

'Chatterton 2 [vol]' bought in London for 5 shillings (HCL–J, 18 Dec 1849; HCL–L). V. 1, 2: 'Herman Melville London Dec: 19. 1848.' V. 1: 'Bought at a dirty stall there, and got it bound near by.' V. 2: 'To My Brother^x John C Hoadley Pittsfield, Jan 6th 1854 ^xPresented in earnest token of my disclaimer as to the criticism of the word "friend" used on the fly-leaf of the "Whale".' Annotated. (NYPL–B)

138. Chaucer, Geoffrey. Poetical Works . . . Edited with a Memoir by Robert Bell . . . London, Parker, 1854–56. 8 v.

Melville's letter to Catherine Gansevoort Lansing 12 Oct 1876 mentions a set of Chaucer 'in eight vols.' as being the 'same edition as mine—Bell's'. Cf. No. 139.

139. ———. Poetical Works . . .

Edited with a Memoir by Robert Bell
. . . London, Parker, 1854–56. 8 v.
Melville's efforts to secure a set of
Chaucer for Abraham Lansing in
addition to No. 140 are described in
his letters to Catherine Gansevoort
Lansing of 26 Sep and 12 Oct 1876
and 5 Sep 1877. This set was bought
for Lansing by Melville. Cf. No.
138.

140. ———. [Poetical Works . . . ?]
Edition unknown. In his letter of 27
Aug 1876 to Catherine Gansevoort
Lansing, Melville reports that he has
bought 'a good set' of Chaucer for
$4.00 (used) and ordered it sent to
Abraham Lansing.

141. ———. The Riches of Chaucer,
in Which His Impurities Have Been
Expunged, His Spelling Modernised
. . . Obsolete Terms Explained. Also
Have Been Added a Few Explanatory
Notes, and a New Memoir of the Poet.
By C. C. Clarke. London, Wilson,
1835. 2 v.; rebound in 1.
'H. Melville'. (NYPL–GL)

141a. Cheap Repository Tracts:
Entertaining, Moral, and Religious. By
Hannah More and Others. A New Revised Edition . . . New York, American Tract Society, [18–]. 8 v. Maria
Gansevoort Melville's holding: v. 1, 2,
3, 5, 6, 8 only[?].
    V. 8: 'Maria [Gansevoort] Melville';
v. 1, 2, 3, 6: 'Maria'. (Stolen from
the collection of Mrs. Meredith M.
Jack, Haverford, Pa.)

142. Chesterfield, Philip Dormer
Stanhope, 4th Earl of. Principles of Po-
liteness, and of Knowing the World
. . . Methodised and Digested under
Distinct Heads, with Additions, by the
Rev. Dr. John Trusler . . . To Which
Is Now First Annexed a Father's Le-
gacy to His Daughters: By the Late
Dr. Gregory, of Edinburgh . . .
Portsmouth, N. H., Printed by
Melcher and Osborne, 1786.
    'Allan Melvill's Property *May the 29
1792*'; 'Hic Liber Pertinet ad Allan
Melvill . . . 1794 . . .'; 'John S Mel-
vill's Book January 1 *1800*'.
Marked. (HCL)

143. Child, Francis James, ed. English
and Scottish Ballads . . . Boston, Little, Brown, 1854–57. 8 v.
    V. 1 (1854): 'H Melville, Sep 1859'.
V. 2: 'H Melville Car. to N. Y.' V.
4: 'H. Melville Car to N. Y.' Annotated. (V. 1, 4, 7 examined by
Raymond Weaver; present location
unknown. V. 2, 3, 5, 6, 8 in HCL)

143.1. Child, Lydia Maria (Francis).
Memoirs of Mme. de Staël, and of
Madame Roland . . . New Edition,
Revised and Enlarged. New York,
Francis, 1847.
    'Mme De Stael Roland &c' borrowed
from NYSL by Allan Melville, Jr,
24 Apr–7 May 1850.

143a. 'Christmas Book.'
    Unidentified. 7 Oct 1859: '1 Christ-
mas Book to Allan Melville [$.]56'
(HCL–H, 31 Mar 1862). The Harper
catalogue for 1859 lists Charles Dic-
kens's *Christmas Tales* (comprising
'A Christmas Carol,' 'The Chimes,'
'The Cricket on the Hearth,' 'The
Battle of Life,' and 'The Haunted
Man') in muslin @ 75¢; Abraham
Oakey Hall's *Old Whitey's Christ-
mas Trot* @ 50¢ and 60¢; James
Kirke Paulding's *Book of St.
Nicholas* @ 62½¢; and William
Makepeace Thackeray's *The Rose
and the Ring* @ 75¢. No Harper re-
print of an English *Christmas Book*
published in London in 1859 is
listed.

143b. 'Christmas Story.'
Unidentified. In his letter to Abraham Lansing of 2 Jan 1877 (NYPL–GL) Melville wrote: 'I liked that Christmas Story you sent me, especially in the opening portion— the good old Dutch Saint's lamentation over these "degenerate days" which we account such an "advance." '

144. Churchill, Charles. The Poetical Works . . . With Copious Notes and a Life of the Author, by W. Tooke . . . Boston, Little, Brown, 1854. 3 v.
V. 1: 'H Melville Ap. 1862 N. Y.' Annotated. (V. 1 examined by Raymond Weaver; present location unknown. V. 2, 3 in HCL)

Cicero, Marcus Tullius: see No. 147.

145. Clark, Justin Wright. "Major Thomas Melvill. A Sketch of His Life. [In the 'Columbian Centinel' of October 30, 1832.]" [brackets in the original].
'Herman Melville, from Mrs. [Samuel] Downer [Nancy Melvill D'Wolf] May 1883.' (HCL) A second copy (HCL) is annotated by Mrs. Melville.

146. Clarke, Marcus Andrew Hislop. For the Term of His Natural Life . . . [London, Bentley, 1885?].
The gift of 'a volume which . . . opens in a manner to arrest one's attention' is acknowledged in Melville's letter of 29 Mar 1888 to James Billson. The book is identified by

Billson's penciled note on the holograph copy in the collection of H. Bradley Martin, who has authorized its citation; the note is lacking in Billson's transcript of the letter, which is in HCL. The volume is mentioned again as 'the book' in Melville's letter of 7 Apr.

147. Classical Library. New York, Harper, [18–]. 37 v.
19 Mar 1849: '1 Classical Library, 37 v. [$]12 23' (HCL–H, 10 Sep 1849).* The set consisted of the following: v. 1, 2: Xenophon. The Anabasis. Translated by Edward Spelman . . . v. 3, 4: The Orations of Demosthenes, Translated by Thomas Leland . . . v. 5: Sallust. Translated by William Rose . . . v. 6, 7: Caesar. Translated by William Duncan . . . v. 8–10: Cicero. The Orations Translated by Duncan, the Offices by Cockman, and the Cato and Lælius by Melmoth . . . v. 11, 12: Virgil. The Eclogues Translated by Wrangham, the Georgics by Sotheby, and the Aeneid by Dryden . . . v. 13: Aeschylus. Translated by the Rev. R. Potter . . . v. 14: Sophocles. Translated by Thomas Francklin . . . v. 15–17: Euripides. Translated by the Rev. R. Potter . . . v. 18, 19: Horace. Translated by Philip Francis . . . Phaedrus: With the Appendix of Gudius, Translated by Christopher Smart . . . v. 20, 21: Ovid. Translated by Dryden, Pope, Congreve, Addison, and Others . . . v. 22–23: History of

*Harper's Classical Library was 'called Harper's Family Classical Library when priced at $16.50 per set. Later it sold at a higher price—75 cents a volume. There were 37 volumes. This Classical Library is not to be confused with Harper's New Classical Library, which was reprinted from Bohn's, and listed at $1.50 a volume' (letter of 23 Mar 1948 from the library of Harper and Brothers, New York).

the Peloponnesian War. Translated from the Greek of Thucydides. By William Smith . . . v. 24–28: Livy. Translated by George Baker . . . v. 29–31: Herodotus. Translated by the Rev. William Beloe . . . v. 32–34: Homer. Translated by Alexander Pope . . . v. 35: Juvenal. Translated by Charles Badham . . . Persius. Translated by . . . Sir W. Drummond . . . v. 36: Pindar. Translated by the Rev. C. A. Wheelwright . . . Anacreon. Translated by Thomas Bourne . . . v. 37: The Three Dialogues of M. T. Cicero on the Orator, Translated . . . by W. Guthrie . . .

148. Cobb, Lyman. The Reticule and Pocket Companion, or Miniature Lexicon of the English Language . . . New York, Harper, 1849.

> 23 Jul 1849: '1 Miniature Lexicon, tucks [$.]75' (HCL–H, 10 Sep 1849). 'Herman Melville 1849 to his sister Augusta Melville'. (BeA)

149. Codman, John. Sailors' Life and Sailors' Yarns, by Captain Ringbolt [pseud.]. New York, Francis, 1847.

> Melville presumably obtained a reviewer's copy of this book, which he reviewed for the *Literary World* 1, no. 6 (6 Mar 1847), 105–106.

150. Coffin, Robert Barry. Castles in the Air, and Other Phantasies. By Barry Gray [pseud.] . . . New York, Putnam, 1883.

> 'To Herman Melville with regards of Barry Gray. Mar 31 / 83.' (HCL)

151. ———. Matrimonial Infelicities, with an Occasional Felicity, by Way of Contrast. By an Irritable Man. To Which Are Added, as Being Pertinent to the Subject, My Neighbors, and Down in the Valley. By Barry Gray

[pseud.]. New York, Putnam, 1883.

> 'To Herman Melville, with regard [*sic*] of Barry Gray.' 'Robert Barry Coffin' in Melville's hand on title page. (HCL)

152. ———. My Married Life at Hillside. By Barry Gray [pseud.] . . . New York, Putnam, 1883.

> 'To Herman Melville with regards of R. B. Coffin'. (HCL)

153. ———. Out of Town: A Rural Episode. By Barry Gray [pseud.] . . . New York, Putnam. 1883.

> 'To the Author of Typee—from Barry Gray.' (HCL)

154. Coleridge, Samuel Taylor. Biographia Literaria; or, Biographical Sketches of My Literary Life and Opinions . . . From the Second London Edition . . . New York, Wiley and Putnam, 1847 *or* 1848. 2 v.

> 8 Feb 1848: '1 Biographia Literari [*sic*] 2 vols clo—[$]1 50' (HCL–W, 1 Jul 1848).

155. ———. Notes and Lectures upon Shakespeare and Some of the Old Poets and Dramatists; with Other Literary Remains . . . Edited by Mrs. H. N. Coleridge. London, Pickering, 1849. 2 v.

> 'Coleridge's Shakespear 1.2' charged to Lemuel Shaw by BoA 27 Nov 1852–8 Jan 1853; Melville was in Boston 22 Nov–13 Dec.

156. Collins, William. The Poetical Works . . . Boston, Little, Brown, 1854. #

> 'H. Melville. April 1862 N.Y.' (Examined by Raymond Weaver; present location unknown)

Collins, William: see also No. 464.

156a. Collins, William Wilkie. No Name.

Elizabeth Shaw Melville's letters of 8 Mar and 16 Apr 1863 to Augusta Melville (NYPL–GL) mention her reading of 'No Name' as serialized in No. 241, copies of which she was forwarding from Pittsfield to Gansevoort, N.Y.

Congreve, William: see No. 358.

157. The Continental Annual, and Romantic Cabinet, for 1832. With Illustrations by Samuel Prout . . . Edited by William Kennedy . . . London, Smith, Elder, [1832]. #
'Mr; and Mrs: Hawthorne from Herman Melville, Aug. 1, 1850' (City Book Auction, Catalogue 213, 24 Oct 1942, Lot 333). The date 1850 is an error; Melville and Hawthorne first met on 5 Aug 1850. Melville visited Hawthorne on 1 Aug 1851 (*The American Notebooks,* pp. 447–448).

157a. 'Continental Guide[?]'.
Unidentified. Melville bought a 'Continental Guide[?]' at Galignani's in Paris (HCL–J, 3 Dec 1849; not listed in HCL–L).

158. Cooke, Philip Pendleton. Froissart Ballads, and Other Poems . . . Philadelphia, Carey and Hart, 1847.
2 Dec 1847: '1 Froissarts Ballads— [$.]75' (HCL–W, 1 Jul 1848).

158.1. Cooper, James Fenimore. The Last of the Mohicans; a Narrative of 1757. By the Author of 'The Pioneers.' Philadelphia, H. C. Carey & I. Lea, 1826. 2 v.
V. 1: 'Augusta Melville'. Marked; clipping dated '1874' on flyleaf of v. 1. (NL)

158a. ———. The Prairie; a Tale.
9–17 Jan 1834: Gansevoort Melville read 'the Prairie, [and] was very

well pleased with it . . .' (GMJ)

159. ———. The Red Rover. A Tale . . . New York, Putnam, 1849.
Melville presumably obtained a reviewer's copy of this edition, which he reviewed for the *Literary World* 6, no. 163 (16 Mar 1850), 276–277.

160. ———. The Sea Lions; or, The Lost Sealers . . . New York, Stringer and Townsend, 1849. 2 v.
Melville presumably obtained a reviewer's copy of this edition, which he reviewed for the *Literary World* 4, no. 117 (28 Apr 1849), 370.

Coventry, John [pseud.]: see Palmer, John Williamson (Nos. 396.1, 396.2).

160a. Cowley, Abraham. The Works . . . V. 1, 2: 10th ed. [of the first part]; v. 3: 9th ed. of the 2nd part, and 4th ed. of the 3rd part. London, Tonson, 1707, and Harper, 1711. 3 v. Rebacked.
V. 1: 'H. Melville March 21st 1862 N. Y.'; v. 2, 3: 'H. Melville'. Annotated. (Fleming)

161. Cowper, William. Poems . . .
Edition unidentified. 28 Aug 1846: '1 Cowpers Poems Mor. Ex Del^d Brother [Allan Melville, Jr.] [$]3 50' (HCL–WP, 1 Jan 1847).

162. Coyne, Joseph Stirling. The Old Chateau; or, A Night of Peril. A Drama, in Three Acts . . . London, Lacy, [18–]. (Lacy's Acting Edition of Plays, v. 15.)
'An Old Chateau' borrowed from NYSL 22 Nov–4 Dec 1890. For another play borrowed from NYSL see No. 297.

163. Cranch, Christopher Pearse. The Bird and the Bell, with Other Poems . . . Boston, Houghton, Mifflin, 1890.

'Cranch Poems' borrowed from NYSL 8–10 Jan 1891.

164. Crawford. Francis Marion. A Cigarette-Maker's Romance . . . London, Macmillan, 1890.
'Cigarette Makers Romance' borrowed from NYSL 19–24 Nov 1890.

165. Croker, Thomas Crofton. Legends of the Lakes; or, Sayings and Doings at Killarney. Collected Chiefly from the Manuscripts of R. Adolphus Lynch . . . London, Ebers, 1829. 2 v.
'Legends of the Lakes 1 & 2' charged to Lemuel Shaw by BoA 9–14 Mar 1846; Melville was in Boston 4–12 Mar.

166. Cruchley, George Frederick. Cruchley's Picture of London, Comprising the History, Rise, and Progress of the Metropolis to the Present Period . . . A Route for Viewing the Whole in Seven Days: To Which Is Annexed a New and Superior Map . . . Eleventh Edition. London, Cruchley, 1847.
'Cruchley' borrowed from George L. Duyckinck before Melville's departure for Europe in Oct 1849; returned with Melville's letter of 2 Feb 1850 to Evert Duyckinck, in which the book is mentioned. NYPL–L lists the 1847 edition.

167. Cruger, Julie Grinnell (Storrow), 'Mrs Van Rensselaer Cruger.' A Diplomat's Diary, by Julien Gordon [pseud.]. Philadelphia, Lippincott, 1890.
'Diplomats Diary' borrowed from NYSL 14–21 May 1891.

168. ———. A Successful Man, by Julien Gordon [pseud.] . . . Philadelphia, Lippincott, 1891.
'Successful Man' borrowed from NYSL 21–27 Mar 1891.

168a. Cummins, Maria Susanna. The Lamplighter. Boston, J. P. Jewett & Co., 1854.
Augusta Melville, in a letter of 31 Mar 1854 to her sister Frances (NYPL–GL), reports that their neighbor Sarah Morewood is to lend her a copy: 'So you will have an opportunity of being introduced to him [the title character] at Arrowhead.'

169. Cundall, Frank. The Landscape and Pastoral Painters of Holland: Ruisdael, Hobbema, Cuijp, Potter . . . New York, Scribner and Welford, 1891.
(HCL)

170. Curiosities of Modern Travel: A Year Book of Adventure for 1844 [–48]. London, Bogue, 1844–48. 5 v. Melville's holding: 1846[?] only.
12 Dec 1846: '1 Curiosities Modern Travel [for 1846?] [$]1 50' (HCL–WP, 1 Jan 1847).

171. Cuvier, Georges, Baron. The Animal Kingdom Arranged in Conformity with Its Organization, by the Baron Cuvier . . . With Additional Descriptions of All the Species Hitherto Named, and of Many Not Before Noticed, by Edward Griffith . . . and Others . . . London, Whittaker, 1827–43. 15 v. Melville's holding: v. 10 only, The Class *Pisces,* with Supplementary Additions, by E. Griffith and C. H. Smith. 1834.
'Herman Melville from Allan Melville'; 'Pittsfield, Mass: January 1st 1851.' Annotated. (BeA)

172. Cyrano de Bergerac, Savinien. [The Comical History of the States and Empires of the Worlds of the Moon and Sun . . . Newly Englished by A.

Lovell. London, Rhodes, 1687. 2 pts. in 1 v.?]

'Bergerac Voyage to the Moon' borrowed from Evert Duyckinck in 1849, on or after 20 Jul (NYPL–BL). The suggested title is the only entry for this author in NYPL–L.

D

173. Dana, Richard Henry. Two Years before the Mast. A Personal Narrative of Life at Sea . . . New York, Harper, 1840.

Melville's letter of 1 May 1850 to Dana states that he first read the book 'after my first voyage,' apparently between its publication and his signing for a whaling cruise in Dec 1840.

174. Dante Alighieri. The Vision; or Hell, Purgatory, and Paradise . . . Translated by the Rev. Henry Francis Cary, M.A. A New Edition, Corrected. With the Life of Dante, Chronological View of His Age, Additional Notes, and Index. London, Bohn, 1847. #

22 Jun 1848: '1 Cary's Dante— [$]2.12' (HCL–W, 1 Jul 1848). 'Herman Melville.'; p. xlviii: 'Pacific Ocean Sunday afternoon Sep. 22. 1860.'; p. 1: 'A. D. 1858'. Annotated. (Sold 22 Nov 1985 by Christie's New York: Lot 84)

D'Anvers, N. [pseud.]: see No. 55.

175. Darwin, Charles Robert. Journal of Researches into the Natural History and Geology of the Countries Visited during the Voyage of H. M. S. Beagle round the World, under the Command of Capt. Fitz Roy, R. N. . . . New

York, Harper, 1846. 2 v.

10 Apr 1847: '1 Darwin's Voyage [$].72' (HCL–H, 1 Aug 1847). The fragment listed as No. 75 may be from one of these volumes.

176. Davenant, Sir William. The Works . . . London, Henry Herringman, 1673.

'Davenant [added: '1673'] folio' bought in London, Nov 1849, for 10 shillings (HCL–J, 17 Nov 1849; HCL–L). 'Herman Melville London, December 1849. (New Year's Day, At sea)' '1850 [added in pencil]'; p. 191: '1772/1872'. Annotated. (Mott: Catalogue 215, 1986: Lot 110)

177. Defoe, Daniel. The Fortunate Mistress . . .

Edition unidentified. 8 Feb 1848: '1 De Foes Fortunate Mistress—[$.]75' (HCL–W, 1 Jul 1848).

178. ———. History of the Plague in London, 1665; to Which Is Added The Great Fire of London, 1666, by an Anonymous Writer. The Storm, 1703. With The Essay, in Verse. The True-Born Englishman: A Satire. London, Bohn, 1881. #

Described as signed and annotated (Dauber & Pine Bookshops, Inc., Catalogue 7, 1926, Lot 471)

178a. De Grey, Thomas. The Complete Horse-Man and Expert Ferrier. In Two Books . . . The Fourth Edition, Corrected with Some Additions. London, Lowndes, 1670. #

Bookplate: 'Richard Manning [Hawthorne's uncle]'; '1814'; 'Nath[aniel] Hawthorne 1832 [Hawthorne's hand]'; 'To Herman Melville 1851 [Melville's hand]'. Annotated by unknown hand; marked by Melville. Cf. No. 194, given Melville by

Hawthorne on 14 Mar 1851. (Dietrich)

Democratic Review: see No. 531.

Demosthenes: see No. 147.

179. Dendy, Walter Cooper. The Philosophy of Mystery . . . New York, Harper, 1845.
'Allan Melville [Jr.]—purchased in Troy Dec 1845 to read in the cars to Boston.' Contains clipping from the *New-York Tribune,* 23 Jan 1850: a letter to the editor on 'Those strange noises at Rochester, &c.' (Formerly in the collection of Miss Agnes Morewood; present location unknown)

180. De Quincey, Thomas. Confessions of an English Opium Eater. London, Taylor and Hessey, 1822 or later edition.
Edition unidentified. 'Confessions of Opium-Eater' bought 'at last' in London for 1 shilling 6 pence, begun immediately, and read enthusiastically (HCL–J, 22, 23 Dec 1849; HCL–L).

180a. Dickens, Charles. Dealings with the Firm of Dombey and Son, Wholesale, Retail, and for Exportation.
Helen Maria Melville, in a letter of 25 Dec 1846 to her sister Augusta (NYPL–GL), reports, 'We have been much amused this evening with the eighth chapter of "Dombey & Son," which appears in the [Albany] Argus.'

181. ———. The Personal History and Experience of David Copperfield, the Younger . . . New York, Putnam, 1850. 2 v.
'David Copperfield' borrowed by 'Miss Melville' from Evert Duyck-inck in 1850, after Sep (NYPL–BL: 65th listing for 1850). Lemuel Shaw is known to have purchased a copy—perhaps that which Elizabeth Shaw Melville took to Pittsfield: Augusta Melville, in a penciled note added to a letter of 6 Jan 1851 to her sister Helen (NYPL–GL), reports that 'Lizzie' on returning from Boston 'brought us "David Copperfield" '; her letter of 16 Jan to Mary Blatchford (NYPL–GL) notes, 'We have just begun reading it aloud.'

182. ———. The Posthumous Papers of the Pickwick Club . . .
Edition unknown. Melville 'read a chapter in Pickwick' while en route to Europe in 1849 (HCL–J, 20 Oct 1849). It is not known whether he owned this book (cf. No. 76) or borrowed it, possibly from the ship's library (cf. No. 315).

Dickens, Charles: see also No. 143a.

183. Diderot, Denis. Synonymes français, par Diderot, D'Alembert, et de Jaucourt . . . Paris, Favre, An IX [1800–01].
'A[llan] Melville'. (BeA)

183a. Diogenes Laërtius. The Lives and Opinions of Eminent Philosophers . . . Literally Translated by C. D. Yonge, B.A. London, Bohn, 1853. Rebound.
'H Melville'. Binding uniform with Nos. 14a, 14b. Annotated. (HCL)

184. Disraeli, Isaac. Amenities of Literature, Consisting of Sketches and Characters of English Literature . . . A New Edition, Edited by His Son, the Right Hon. B. Disraeli . . . London, Routledge [etc.], 1859. 2 v.
V. 1, 2: 'H Melville'. V. 1: '26.th Feb. 1862 N. Y.' Marked. (NYPL–O)

185. ———. The Calamities and Quarrels of Authors: With Some Inquiries Respecting Their Moral and Literary Characters, and Memoirs for Our Literary History . . . A New Edition, Edited by His Son, the Right Hon. B. Disraeli . . . London, Routledge [etc.], 1860.
   'H. Melville'. Marked. (NYPL–O)

186. ———. Curiosities of Literature . . . A New Edition, Edited, with Memoir and Notes, by His Son, the Right Hon. B. Disraeli . . . London, Routledge [etc.], 1859. 3 v.
   V. 1, 2, 3: 'H Melville'. V. 1: 'Feb 26 1862 N. Y.' Annotated. (NYPL–O)

187. ———. The Literary Character; or, The History of Men of Genius, Drawn from Their Own Feelings and Confessions; Literary Miscellanies; and An Inquiry into the Character of James the First . . . A New Edition, Edited by His Son, the Right Hon. B. Disraeli . . . London, Routledge [etc.], 1859.
   'H Melville Feb 26 1862 N. Y.' Annotated. (NYPL–O)

Dobell, Sydney Thompson: a list of books formerly belonging to Frances Melville Thomas, compiled by her daughter Mrs. Metcalf, includes a copy of Dobell's *Poems* (Boston, 1860). This book, which is without inscription, marking, or annotation, is bound uniformly with two others which had previously belonged to Elizabeth Thomas, sister-in-law of Frances Melville Thomas; Mrs. Osborne, another daughter of the Thomases, believed the book to have come from her aunt rather than from Melville.

187a. Doddridge, Philip. Some Remarkable Passages in the Life of the Honourable Col. James Gardiner, Who was slain at the battle of Preston-Pans, September 21, 1745; with an Appendix, relating to the Antient Family of the Munro's of Fowlis. 5th Edition. London, Buckland [etc.], [after 1763].
   'G. M [Gansevoort Melville?]'; 'H Melville New York'. (NL)

188. Dodsley, Robert, ed. A Select Collection of Old Plays . . . A New Edition: With Additional Notes and Corrections, by the Late Isaac Reed, Octavius Gilchrist, and the Editor. London, Prowett, 1825–27. 12 v.
   On 1? Feb 1862 Melville, ill in New York, sent a messenger to Evert Duyckinck with a letter requesting the loan from Duyckinck's 'set' of 'some of those volumes of the Elizabethan dramatists . . . except Marlowe, whom I have read' (cf. No. 348); the loan is not recorded in NYPL–BL, however. This edition is listed in NYPL–L, although in Duyckinck's undated 'Memoranda of Books &c' (NYPL–D) are given 'Dodsley's Collection of Old Plays 13 [*sic*] vols' and 'Supplement to Dodsley 6 vols'.

189. The Dollar Magazine. New York, 1848–51. Melville's term of subscription: 1851 only [?].
   Melville was probably a subscriber in 1851, when he mentioned the magazine in letters of 12 Feb and 26 Mar to Evert Duyckinck and 1? Jun to Nathaniel Hawthorne.

Drake, Francis S.: see No. 498.

190. Draper, John William. Thoughts on the Future Civil Policy of America . . . Fourth Edition. New York, Harper, [1865].
   11 Jul 1866: '1 Civil Policy [$]1.67' (HCL–H, 24 Jul 1866).

191. Dryden, John. The Poetical Works . . . with Illustrations by John Franklin. Second Edition. London, Routledge, 1854.
'H. Melville Pittsfield Mass.'; 'Presented to Mrs. J R. Morewood.' (Rosenbach)

192. Dullea, Owen John. Claude Gelée le Lorrain . . . New York, Scribner and Welford, 1887.
Marked. (HCL)

193. Dumas, Alexandre. Le Collier de la Reine . . .
Edition unknown. 25 Jan 1857: 'Read   Dumas's   "Diamond Necklace"—Excellent, Cagliostro's talk in opening chapter' (HCL–J).

194. Duncan,   Archibald.   The Mariner's Chronicle; Being a Collection of the Most Interesting Narratives of Shipwrecks, Fires, Famines, and Other Calamities Incident to a Life of Maritime Enterprise . . . Philadelphia, Humphreys, 1806. 4 v.
V. 1–4: 'Richard Manning [uncle of Nathaniel   Hawthorne]   1814'; 'Nath[aniel] Hawthorne, Salem, 1832.'; 'To H Melville Pittsfield March 14. 1851 [Melville's hand]'. Cf. No. 178a. (HCL)

194a. Dunlap, William. Memoirs of the Life of George Frederick Cooke . . . New York, Longworth, 1813. 2 v. Holding of Allan Melville, Jr.: v. 1 [?].
V. 1: 'A Melville from James Scull[?]'; 'A Melville'. (V. 1 only: BeA)

195. Duplessis, Georges. The Wonders of Engraving . . . Illustrated with Ten Reproductions in Autotype; and Thirty-Four Wood Engravings, by P. Sellier. London, Low and Marston, 1871.

'Mrs. Herman Melville. N. Y. June 13, 1875 [Melville's hand].' (HCL)

Duyckinck, Evert Augustus: see Nos. 75a, 189, 326, 558a.

196. D'Wolf, John. A Voyage to the North Pacific and a Journey through Siberia, More than Half a Century Ago . . .   Cambridge,   Mass.,   Welch, Bigelow, 1861.
'Herman Melville Esq. with the regards of John D'Wolf [Melville's uncle].' (HCL)

197. ———. A Voyage to the North Pacific . . . Cambridge, Mass., Welch, Bigelow, 1861.
'Mrs Maria G[ansevoort] Melville with the Affectionate regards of John D'Wolf.'; 'George Griggs, from S[ophia] T[hurston] M[elville (Mrs. Allan Melville, Jr.)].' (BeA; another copy, inscribed in turn to 'Miss [Frances] Priscilla [Melville]' and 'Mr. [John C.] Hoadley', is in NYPL–GL)

E

197a. Eagle Hill; or, Selections in Prose and Verse. Chiefly Original. Prepared for the American Sunday-School   Union   . . .   Philadelphia, American   Sunday-School   Union, [c1848].
'Florence Melville on her birth day Gansevoort, 2nd September, 1865— From Grandmother [Grandmamma?] Melville [Maria Gansevoort Melville].' (BeA)

198. Eastlake, Sir Charles L. Contributions to the Literature of the Fine Arts . . . London, Murray, 1848.
'Eastlake's Literature of the Fine

Arts' charged to Lemuel Shaw by BoA 27 Jan–8 Mar 1849; Melville was in Boston 30 Jan–10 Apr.

199. ———. Materials for a History of Oil Painting . . . London, Longman [etc.], 1847.
'Eastlake's Oil Painting' charged to Lemuel Shaw by BoA 21 Jun–13 Jul 1848; Melville was in Boston 12 Jul–after 17[?] Jul.

200. The Edinburgh Review, or Critical Journal. Edinburgh [etc.], 1803–1929. Borrowed by Melville: v. 41 (1824–25), v. 47 (1828).
'2 vols Ed Review' borrowed from Evert Duyckinck in 1849, on or after 20 Jul (NYPL–BL; NYPL–L lists the volumes for 1802–77). Ch. 36 of Melville's *White-Jacket* (1850) draws upon two articles in the *Review,* one on 'Abolishment of Impressment' (v. 41, pp. 154–181), the other on Admiral Collingwood (v. 47, pp. 385–418). Melville quotes from the latter (p. 405) in *White-Jacket,* p. 150, but erroneously cites the *Review* for 1824 instead of 1828.

200a. Edwards, Amelia Ann Blandford. Debenham's Vow. New York, Harper, 1870.
'Debham Vow' borrowed from NYSL 10 Oct–5 Nov 1890.

201. Eliot, George, pseud., i. e. Marian Evans, afterwards Cross. Adam Bede . . . New York, Harper, 1859.
13 Oct 1859: '1 Adam Bede [to Allan Melville, Jr.] [$.]75' (HCL–H, 31 Mar 1862).

202. Ellis, George Edward. Sketches of Bunker Hill Battle and Monument: With Illustrative Documents. Second Edition. Charlestown, Mass., Emmons, 1843.
'With the kind regards of Amos Lawrence March 9. 1846'; 'Herman Melville Boston.' (HCL)

202.1. Ellis, Sarah (Stickney). Hearts and Homes, or Social Distinction; a Story. New York, D. Appleton & Co., 1850.
Augusta Melville's letter of 25 Nov 1850 to Mary Blatchford (NYPL–GL) discusses 'Hearts & Homes.' 'At last I have read that long talked of book, & I can now say that Mrs Ellis has actually written a story worth reading. . . .'

202a. Elwood, Anne Katharine (Curteis). Memoirs of the Literary Ladies of England, from the Commencement of the Last Century . . . Philadelphia, Zieber, 1845.
'Miss Augusta Melville from her brother Gansevoort Melville Washington D C March 1845.' (NYPL–GL)

203. Emerson, Ralph Waldo. The Conduct of Life . . . Second Edition. London, Smith, Elder, 1860.
'J A Purves 1/3/61 Manchester [lined out]'; 'H Melville Nov. 1870 N.Y.' Annotated. (HCL)

204. ———. Essays . . . [4th ed.] Boston, Munroe, 1847.
'H Melville March 22^d 1862 N. Y.' Annotated. (HCL)

205. ———. Essays: Second Series . . . Third Edition. Boston, Munroe, 1844.
'H Melville March 22^d 1861 N. Y.' The date 1861 is an error for 1862 (cf. No. 204); Melville was in Washington, D.C., on 22 Mar 1861. Annotated. (HCL)

206. ———. Poems . . . Seventh Edition. Boston, Phillips, Sampson, 1858.
'Herman Melville from his brother

176

Entries 206-213

in law Samuel S. Shaw 1859'. Annotated. (UVL–B)

206a. ———. Representative Men: Seven Lectures . . . Boston, Phillips, Sampson, 1850.
While visiting the Hawthornes in early Sep 1850, Melville 'one morning . . . shut himself into the boudoir & read Mr Emerson's Essays' (*Log* 2: 925, quoting Sophia Hawthorne's letter of Oct(?) 1850 to Elizabeth Peabody). On *Representative Men* as the book—or one of the books—that Melville probably read at this time, see Sealts, 'Melville and Emerson's Rainbow,' pp. 269–270 and n. 49, p. 383.

207. Ethel's Story: Illustrating the Advantages of Cheerfulness. By the Child's Friend . . . Philadelphia, Perkenpine and Higgins, [1856?].
'Fanny Melville from Malcolm Melville. Xmas 1865'. (Formerly in the collection of Mrs. Walter B. Binnian; present location unknown)

Euripides: see No. 147.

208. Evans, Arthur Benoni. The Cutter, in Five Lectures upon the Art and Practice of Cutting Friends, Acquaintances, and Relations . . . Boston, House, 1808.
'A[llan] Melville'. Marked. (NYPL–GL)

209. Evans, John (1767–1827). Shakspeare's Seven Ages: or, The Progress of Human Life; Illustrated by a Series of Extracts in Prose and Poetry, Introduced by a Brief Memoir of Shakspeare and His Writings . . . Embellished with Eight Copperplate Engravings. London, Arnold, 1831.
'Cushing Mitchell's'; 'Allan Melville [Jr.]'; 'A. Melville.' (BeA)

Evening Hymn, The: see Burns, James Drummond, comp. (No. 99a).

F

210. Faber, Frederick William. Hymns Selected from Frederick William Faber, D.D. Northampton, Mass., Bridgman and Childs, 1867.
'E[lizabeth] S[haw] Melville from Mrs. Brittain—Pittsfield Sept 20 1867—'. Annotated by Mrs. Melville. (HCL)

211. Family Library. Stereotype Edition. New York, Harper, 1830–[18–].
Specific volumes unknown. 10 Apr 1847: '3 vols. Family Library 36 [$]1.08' (HCL–H, 31 Jul 1847). The fragment listed as No. 75 may be from one of these volumes.

211a. Fauriel, Claude Charles. History of Provençal Poetry . . . Translated from the French . . . by G. J. Adler. New York, Derby & Jackson, 1860.
An alphabetical list of subscribers includes 'Melville, Herman, Mass.' (p. iv).

212. Fénelon, François de Salignac de la Mothe-. [The Adventures of Telemachus, Son of Ulysses.]
Edition unknown; presumably an English translation. 'Telemachus' bought in Paris for 'about 2 francs' (HCL–J, 4 Dec 1849; HCL–L).

213. ———. Fenelon's Treatise on the Education of Daughters: Translated from the French, and Adapted to English Readers, with an Original Chapter, "On Religious Studies." By the Rev. T. F. Dibdin . . . Albany, Backus and Whiting, 1806.

'A[llan] Melville'; 'Augusta Melville'; 'Miss Augusta Melville'. (NYPL–GL)

214. Ferguson, James. An Easy Introduction to Astronomy for Young Gentlemen and Ladies . . . First American from the Seventh London Edition . . . Philadelphia, Dornin, 1805.
'A[llan] Melville'. (NYPL–GL)

215. Fergusson, Robert. The Works . . . Edited, with Life of the Author and an Essay on His Genius and Writings, by A. B. G[rosart]. London, Fullarton, 1857.
'H Melville Feb 17 1862 N. Y.' Marked. (NYPL–O)

216. Field, David Dudley, ed. A History of the County of Berkshire, Massachusetts; in Two Parts. The First Being a General View of the County; the Second, an Account of the Several Towns. By Gentlemen in the County, Clergymen and Laymen. Pittsfield, Printed by S. W. Bush, 1829.
'H Melville. Pittsfield July 16. 1850.': to Allan Melville [Jr.] 1863'. Contains clipping from the Pittsfield *Sun*, 18 Jul 1850. (BeA)

Fitz-Adam, Adam [pseud.]: see No. 565, ed. Edward Moore.

217. FitzGerald, Edward. Works . . . Reprinted from the Original Impressions, with Some Corrections Derived from His Own Annotated Copies . . . Boston, Houghton, Mifflin, 1887. 2 v.
'Fitzgeralds Works 1.2.' borrowed from NYSL 1–18 Apr 1890.

218. ———. Polonius: A Collection of Wise Saws and Modern Instances . . . London, Pickering, 1852.
'H Melville Jan. 14, '75 N. Y.'; 'Eleanor M[elville] Thomas [Mrs.

Metcalf]. From Grandma [Mrs. Melville].' On the title page Melville has supplied the author's name: 'by Edward Fitzgerald ("Omar Khayyam")'. Annotated. (HCL)

FitzGerald, Edward: see also Nos. 391, 392.

Fletcher, John: see Nos. 53, 358.

Ford, John: see No. 358.

219. Forsyth, Joseph. Remarks on Antiquities, Arts, and Letters during an Excursion in Italy, in the Years 1802 and 1803 . . . Third Edition. London, Murray, 1824. 2 v.
Annotated. (NYPL–O)

Franco, Harry [pseud.]: see No. 86a.

219a. Franklin, Sir John. Narrative of a Second Expedition to the Shores of the Polar Sea, in the Years 1825, 1826, and 1827 . . . London, Murray, 1828, *or*, Philadelphia, Carey, Lea, and Carey, 1828.
Gansevoort Melville, in a letter of 23 May 1829 to his mother (NYPL–GL), reports that he is 'now reading Franklin's second journey to the Polar Sea.'

220. Frothingham, Octavius Brooks. Boston Unitarianism, 1820–1850. A Study of the Life and Work of Nathaniel Langdon Frothingham . . . A Sketch. New York, Putnam, 1890.
'Boston Unitarianism' borrowed from NYSL 30 Jan–5 Feb 1891.

221. Fuller, Thomas. The Holy State, and the Profane State . . . A New Edition. With Notes, by James Nichols. London, Tegg, 1841.
'Fuller's Holy & Profane State' borrowed from Evert Duyckinck 13 Apr 1849 (NYPL–BL).

G

222. Gardner, Augustus Kinsley. Old Wine in New Bottles: or, Spare Hours of a Student in Paris . . . New York, Francis, 1848.
'Herman Melville Esq. with the compliments of the author'. Contains clipping of reviews of the book, with Melville's note: 'The above was placed here by the donee, not the donor.' 'Gansevoort, N. Y. Feb. 1915 C. E. Breckenridge I got this from Miss Sarah Jane Vanderwerker to whom it was given by the Melvills.' Annotated. (HCL)

223. Gautier, Théophile. The Romance of the Mummy. From the French of Theophile Gautier, by Mrs. Anne T. Wood. With an Introduction, by William C. Prime . . . New York, Bradburn, 1863.
'Romance Mummy' borrowed from NYSL 20–31 May 1890.

223a. Gessner, Salomon. The Death of Abel . . . Translated from the German . . . By Mrs. Collyer. With Memoirs of the Author. To Which Is Added, The Death of Cain, in Five Books . . . A Sequel to the Death of Abel; Likewise, The Life of Joseph . . . In Eight Books. And Death, a Vision, or, The Solemn Departure of Saints and Sinners . . . By John Macgowan . . . London, Kelly, 1838. Gospel Poems . . . by J. H. Solomons . . . Cambridge, Printed for the Author, by Talbor, 1843. The Three Churches, "Catholic and AEcumenical," with a Table of the Two Beasts and the False Prophet. A New Edition with Notes. By R. B. Sanderson . . . London, Ridgway, 1843. 3v., rebound in l.
Possibly Melville's. Title page carries the inscription 'Cloth lett[ers?]

M[elville?]' in handwriting that appears to be Melville's; the shelfback title, in gilt, is 'Death of Abel'; see Wyn Kelley, 'Melville's Cain.' (BCHS)

223b. Gibbon, Edward. The History of the Decline and Fall of the Roman Empire . . .
Edition unidentified; either owned or borrowed by Melville. In his letter to John C. Hoadley of 'Saturday in Easter Week 1877' (31 Mar) Melville stated that his enclosed poem ('The Age of the Antonines') was 'suggested by a passage in Gibbon (Decline & Fall) Have you a copy? Turn to *"Antonine"* &c in index.' HCL–J, 8 Mar 1857, indicates Melville's earlier familiarity with Gibbon. Miss Margaret Morewood told Jay Leyda that she recalled a set of Gibbon at Arrowhead.

224. Gilchrist, Alexander. Life of William Blake, "Pictor Ignotus". With Selections from His Poems and Other Writings, by the Late Alexander Gilchrist . . . Illustrated from Blake's Own Works, in Fascimilé by W. J. Linton, and in Photolithography; with a Few of Blake's Original Plates . . . London, Macmillan, 1863. 2 v. #
'H. Melville, June 4, '70, N. Y.' Described by J. H. Birss, 'Herman Melville and Blake'; present location unknown.

224a. Gobat, Samuel. Journals of Three Years' Residence in Abyssinia . . . [New York, Dodd, 1850?].
Either owned or borrowed by Melville. In 1857, meeting Gobat in Jerusalem as recorded in HCL–J among notes on 'Christian Missions &c in Palestine & Syria,' Melville wrote: 'His Journal is published. Written in a strikingly unaffected

style—apostolically concise & simple' (*Journal*, 1856–1857, ed. Horsford, p. 156).

225. Godwin, William. The Adventures of Caleb Williams, or, Things as They Are . . . Revised and Corrected. With a Memoir of the Author. London, Bentley, 1849.
'Caleb Williams (1 vol)' obtained in London from Richard Bentley, 1849 (HCL–L), probably on 19 Dec (for date, cf. No. 54).

226. ———. Baldwin's Fables; Ancient and Modern. Designed for Youth. New Haven, Conn., Babcock, 1820.
'Thomas Melville Lansingburgh'. (NYPL–GL)

227. Goethe, Johann Wolfgang von. Goethe's Werke . . . Originalausgabe. Wien, Kaulfuss und Armbruster, 1816–21. 26 v. Borrowed by Lemuel Shaw: v. 14 only.
'Goethe 14' (*Die Wahlverwandtschaften*) charged to Lemuel Shaw by BoA 21 Jul–14 Oct 1854; Melville was in Boston sometime in Jul (for date, cf. No. 411).

228. ———. The Auto-Biography of Goethe. Truth and Poetry: From My Own Life . . . Bohn's Standard Library, Nos. 31, 43; v. 1, 2 of Bohn's edition of Goethe's Works. Nos. 31, 43: Auto-Biography . . . Translated by John Oxenford. No. 43: Letters from Switzerland and Travels in Italy . . . Translated by Rev. A. J. W. Morrison . . . London, Bohn, 1848, 1849.
HCL–L lists both 'Autobiography of Goethe (Bohn)' and 'Letters from Italy (Goethe Do. [Bohn])', 6 shillings; Goethe's letters from Italy constitute pp. 237–450 of No. 43. The purchase date was probably 24 Dec 1849, when Melville left London after buying unnamed 'books' (HCL–J, 24 Dec 1849). No. 31: present location unknown (Hayford, 'Melville's German Streak,' shows that the copy of No. 31 now in BeA cannot have been Melville's). No. 43: 'Herman Melville Bought at Bohn's Dec 25 [i.e., 24]. 1849.' Marked. (BeA)

229. ———. Iphigenia in Tauris. A Drama in Five Acts . . . Translated from the German. By G. J. Adler, A.M. New York, Appleton, 1850. #
'Herman Melville, Esq., with the many regards of the Translator.'; 'Received Jan. 8th, 1851. Pittsfield.' (The Book Corner, 251 Fifth Ave., New York, unnumbered catalogue [19–], Lot 96).

230. ———. Wilhelm Meister's Apprenticeship and Travels . . . 3 v. Edition unknown. 'Wilhelmeister 3 vols' borrowed from Evert Duyckinck in 1850 (NYPL–BL: 23rd listing for 1850); NYPL–L lists only a translation in 2 v. (Boston, 1851).

231. Goldsmith, Oliver. The Deserted Village . . . New York, Cassell, Petter, and Galpin, [187–?].
'Miss Fanny Melville Xmas, 1876 New York.' (BCHS)

232. ———. The Vicar of Wakefield: A Tale . . . New York, Wiley and Putnam, 1845.
Cover lacking. 'Herman Melville May 7th.. 47:'. (BeA)

232a. Goody Two Shoes. The History of Goody Two-Shoes. Embellished with Plates. To which is Added, The Fisherman's Son. New York, N. B. Holmes, 1826.
Laid in is a note inscribed by the late Mrs. Walter B. Binnian: 'This is very valuable for some Herman

Melville collection'. Possibly a gift to Melville himself (b. 1819) as a child, or to one of his own children. His first child, Malcolm, was born in Feb 1849; there is an allusion to 'Goody Two Shoes' in Melville's 'Hawthorne and His Mosses' (1850). (BCHS)

Gordon, Julien [pseud.]: see Cruger, Julie Grinnell (Nos. 167–168).

233. Gower, Lord Ronald Charles Sutherland-. The Figure Painters of Holland, by Lord Ronald Gower . . . New York, Scribner and Welford, 1880.
    Annotated. (HCL)

233a. 'Grace C. E.'
    Unidentified. 'Grace C. E. [Grace Church Episcopal?]' borrowed from NYSL 25 Oct–5 Nov 1890. Neither the Library nor Grace Church in New York has clues to the identity of this title, unless it is one of the church year-books (not now in NYSL).

233b. Grattan, Thomas Colley. Jacqueline of Holland; a Historical Tale . . . [New York, Harper, 1831?].
    18 Jan 1834: borrowed by Gansevoort Melville 'from Atheneum Library' at Albany (GMJ).

Gray, Barry [pseud.]: see Coffin, Robert Barry (Nos. 150–153).

234. Greeley, Horace. Hints toward Reforms, in Lectures, Addresses, and Other Writings . . . New York, Harper, 1850.
    21 May 1850: '1 Greeley's Hints [$.]75' (HCL-H, 29 Apr 1851).

234.1. [Grey, Elizabeth Caroline.] The Bosom Friend. A Novel. By the Author of ''The Gambler's Wife'' . . . New York, Harper & Brothers, 1845. #
    'Miss Fanny Melville New York'. (LHS)

234.2. ———. Magdalen and Marcia; or, The Rectory Guest . . . New York, Stringer & Townsend, 1849. #
    'Fanny Melville from Helen G'. (LHS)

Greylock, Godfrey [pseud.]: see Smith, Joseph E. A. (Nos. 478, 479).

234a. Griffin, Richard, ed. Specimens of the Novelists and Romancers, with Critical and Biographical Notices of the Authors . . . New York, Langdon, 1831. 2 v.
    5 Jan 1834: Gansevoort Melville read in Griffin 'an extract from a novel by Thomas Skinner Surr entitled Winter in London . . . a tale called The Founder of a Family' (GMJ).

234b. Grimm, Jakob Ludwig Karl. German Popular Stories, with Illustrations after the Original Designs of George Cruikshank. Edited by Edgar Taylor, with Introduction by John Ruskin. London, Hotten, 1868.
    [In Melville's hand:] 'Miss Fanny Melville. Xmas. 1874. N.Y.' (BUL)

235. Grote, George. A History of Greece . . . London, Murray, 1846–56. 12 v. Borrowed by Lemuel Shaw: v. 1 only.
    'Grote's Hist. of Greece 1' charged to Lemuel Shaw by BoA 25 Nov 1854–16 Jan 1855; Melville was in Boston 28 Nov–[?].

Guidebooks: see Nos. 77, 78, 86.1, 157a, 166, 375, 376, 377, 378, 379, 402, 434a, 533, 538.

H

236. Habington, William. Habington's Castara, with a Preface and Notes, by Charles A. Elton . . . Bristol, Gutch, [1812].
'H. Melville Dec. 9. '70. N. Y. Vide A. Hallam—Remains [No. 237a]— P. 216 ['I would in particular name Habington's "Castara," as one of those works which make us proud of living in the same land, and inheriting the same associations, with its true-hearted and simple-minded author'].' Annotated. (PUL)

Hall, Abraham Oakey: see No. 143a.

237. Hall, Basil. Schloss Hainfeld; or, A Winter in Lower Styria . . . Edinburgh, Cadell, 1836.
'Hall's Schloss' charged to Lemuel Shaw by BoA 27 Jun–25 Aug 1848; Melville was in Boston 12 Jul–after 17[?] Jul.

237a. Hallam, Arthur Henry. Remains in Verse and Prose . . . With a Preface and Memoir . . . Boston, Ticknor and Fields, 1863.
Either owned or borrowed by Melville: cf. of the citation in No. 236, acquired 9 Dec 1870.

238. Hare, Julius Charles. Guesses at Truth, by Two Brothers. Third Edition, First Series. London, Taylor and Walton, 1847. Second Edition, with Large Additions, Second Series. London, Taylor and Walton, 1848. 2 v.
'Guesses at Truth 1.2' charged to Lemuel Shaw by BoA 26 Jun–16 Jul 1852; Melville was in Boston 3–6 and 13–16 Jul.

Harland, Marion [pseud.]: see

Terhune, Mary Virginia (Hawes) (No. 510).

Harper's Classical Library: see No. 147.

Harper's Family Library: see No. 211.

239. Harper's Fifth Reader . . . New York, Harper, 1889.
25 Sep 1889: copy sent with note from the publisher (HCL) acknowledging Melville's permission to include an extract from *Moby-Dick* and a biographical sketch.

240. Harper's Monthly Magazine, New York, 1850–. Melville's term of subscription: Oct 1851–Mar 1859.
30 Sep 1851: 'Magazine: 1 yr. [$]2' (HCL–H, 25 Nov 1851). 15 Nov 1852: 'Magazine 1 year [$]2' (HCL–H, 21 Mar 1853). 12 Apr 1855: 'S^r to Magazine 3 yrs., com May N° 55 [Melville noted here: 'Charged to May 1856'] [$]6' (HCL–H, 6 Mar 1856). 21 Jan 1858: 'Subs^n to Magazine, one year [Melville noted here: '(to May 1857)'] [$]2' (HCL–H, 8 Sep 1859). 16 Aug 1859: '[Subs^n to] Mag., 2 y. to [Maria Gansevoort Melville] [Melville, noted here: '(to May 1859)'] $4' and 'to H Melville [Melville noted here: 'Error', adding below: 'To May 1859—stopped in March '59)'] $4' (HCL–H, 8 Sep 1859). That the Melvilles were again reading *Harper's Monthly* in 1863 is indicated by a letter from Elizabeth Shaw Melville to Augusta Melville, 11 Feb 1863 (NYPL–GL): 'The "Harpers Monthly" that Herman sent you was a duplicate number— so you can keep it as long as you like—When the volume is complete we will send you the lot—so you can read the "Serials" together—'. A partial collection of Melville's

contributions to Nos. 240 and 413, assembled in a binder by his wife, is in HCL.

241. Harper's Weekly; a Journal of Civilization. New York, 1857–1916. Melville's term of subscription: 1859–61, in the name of his mother; 1861–63. Bound volumes: 5–9 (1861–65). #
20 Jun 1859: 'Subs^n to Wkly, 2 y. to Mrs. M[aria] G[ansevoort] Melville [$]3.34' (HCL–H, 8 Sep 1859). 7 Oct 1859: 'Weekly, N^{os} 105–122 to Mrs MGM [$].54' (HCL–H, 31 Mar 1862). 6 Jul 1861: 'Weekly, one year [$]1.80' (HCL–H, 31 Mar 1862). 19 Oct 1865: '4 vols. Weekly [$]18.67' (HCL–H, 20 Oct 1865). 11 Jan 1866: '1 vol Weekly $4.67' (HCL–H, 24 Jul 1866). That in 1863 and 1864 the Melvilles were forwarding copies of the *Weekly* to Augusta and Maria Gansevoort Melville at Gansevoort, N.Y., is indicated in family correspondence (NYPL–GL): letters to Augusta from Elizabeth Shaw Melville, 8 and 22 Mar, 16 Apr 1863); letter to Cathering Ganesvoort Lansing from Maria Gansevoort Melville, 9 Sep 1864 (Herman had sent the number for 3 Sep, in which she found 'a most melancholy picture, headed Compromise with the South. Dedicated to the Chicago Convention'). Five bound volumes, last reported in the collection of the late Mrs. E. Barton Chapin, are inscribed as follows in Melville's hand: v. 5 (1861): 'Malcolm Melville N. Y. Xmas. 1865'; v. 6: 1862): 'Stanwix Melville New York—Xmas 1865'; v. 7 (1863): 'Bessie Melville New York. Xmas 1865'; v. 8 (1864): 'Fanny Melville N. Y. Xmas. 1865'; v. 9 (1865): '*Dolly* [Mrs. Melville] New York. 60 E. 26th Xmas 1765.'

242. Hart, Joseph C. The Romance of Yachting: Voyage the First . . . New York, Harper, 1848.
Melville read but refused to review Hart's 'crucifying Romance of Yachting' for the *Literary World*, as explained in a detailed letter to Evert Duyckinck of 14 Nov 1848 (NYPL–D): 'Take it back, I beseech . . .' Either the copy Melville read or a separate copy has survived: the New York bookplate of his brother Allan is inside its front cover and the penciled name 'Melville' in the hand of one of their sisters is on the first blank recto; there is no other annotation or marking. (Haack)

243. Hartley, David. Observations on Man, His Frame, His Duty, and His Expectations. In Two Parts . . . London, Johnson, 1801. 3 v.
'Hartley on Man 1.2.3' borrowed from NYSL 17 Jan–22 Feb 1848.

244. Hawthorne, Julian. Nathaniel Hawthorne and His Wife; a Biography . . . 3rd ed. Boston, Osgood, 1885. 2 v.
'Herman from Lizzie [Mrs Melville] June 1885'. (HCL)

245. Hawthorne, Nathaniel. The Blithedale Romance . . . Boston, Ticknor, Reed, and Fields, 1852.
'Mrs. Herman Melville 105 East 18th st—'; 'Mrs Herman Melville' and a date (?) '—' erased from title page. Presumably the copy of the first American edition (published 14 Jul 1852) which Hawthorne ordered sent to Melville (letter of 7 Jul 1852 to W. D. Ticknor) and which Melville acknowledged in a letter to Hawthorne, 17 Jul 1852. (HCL)

245a. ———. Grandfather's Chair: A History for Youth . . . Boston, E. P. Peabody; New York, Wiley & Putnam, 1841, *or,* Second Edition, Revised and

Enlarged. Boston, Tappan and Dennet, 1842.

Referring to Melville's visit to the Hawthornes on 22 Jan 1851, Augusta Melville in a letter of 24 Jan 1851 to her sister Helen (NYPL–GL) reports that 'Mrs Hawthorne sent Malcolm [Melville] a beautiful book, "The Grandfather's Chair." '

246. ———. The House of the Seven Gables, a Romance . . . Boston, Ticknor, Reed, and Fields, 1851.
'Herman Melville, from Nath[l] Hawthorne [Melville's hand].'; 'April 11th 1851 Friday evening. S[ophia] A. H[awthorne] [Mrs. Hawthorne's hand].'; 'Lenox, Mass. [Mrs Melville's hand]'. Marked. Contains magazine clipping. (HCL)

247. ———. The Marble Faun: or, The Romance of Monte Beni . . . Boston, Ticknor and Fields, 1860. 2 v.
'M[r] Herman Melville with the best wishes of his friend and neighbour S[arah] A. M[orewood]. 1860'; in v. 1 Melville added: 'Pittsfield.' June, [*sic*]'. Annotated. Read on Melville's *Meteor* voyage, which had begun on 30 May 1860; v. 2, 136, is annotated '(Lat. 41° South Atlantic)'. (HCL)

248. ———. Mosses from an Old Manse . . . New York, Wiley and Putnam, 1846. 2 v. in 1.
'H. Melville. From Aunt Mary [Mrs. Thomas Melvill]. Pittsfield. July 18. 1850'; inside the front cover is fixed a bit of moss, with the following inscription: 'This moss was gathered in Salem, and therefore I place it here for a frontispiece. P.S. It may be objected that this is sea-moss; —but then, it only went to sea—like many young mortals—in its youth, and to my certain knowledge has been ashore ever since.' Added in

pencil: 'August 1850.'; v. 1, p. 189: 'May 1865'. Annotated. (HCL)

249. ———. Our Old Home. A Series of English Sketches . . . Boston, Ticknor and Fields, 1863.
'H. Melville Jan 8th 1868 N. Y.' Title page, beneath author's name: '(May 19, 1864)' (the date of Hawthorne's death). Annotated. (HCL)

250. ———. Passages from the American Note-Books . . . Boston, Ticknor and Fields, 1868. 2 v.
V. 2: 'H. Melville June 8 '70 N. Y.' Marked; annotated by Mrs. Melville. (HCL)

251. ———. Passages from the English Note-Books . . . Boston, Fields, Osgood, 1870. 2 v.
Marked. (HCL)

252. ———. Passages from the French and Italian Note-Books . . . Boston, Osgood, 1872. 2 v.
V. 1: 'H. Melville March 23, '72 N. Y.' Marked. (HCL)

253. ———. The Scarlet Letter, a Romance . . . Boston, Ticknor, Reed, and Fields, 1850.
'H. Melville July 1870 N. Y.' (HCL)

254. ———. Septimius Felton; or The Elixir of Life . . . Boston, Osgood, 1872.
'Herman from Lizzie [Mrs. Melville] Aug 1–1872'. (HCL)

255. ———. The Snow-Image, and Other Twice-Told Tales . . . Boston, Ticknor and Fields, 1865.
'H. Melville Jan 6. '71 N. Y.' Marked. (HCL)

256. ———. Tanglewood Tales, for Girls and Boys; Being a Second Wonder-Book . . . Boston, Ticknor,

Reed, and Fields, 1853.
'Master Malcolm Melville, A New Year's Present From his Uncle, John C. Hoadley, Pittsfield, Jany 1. 1854.' (HCL)

257. ———. True Stories from History and Biography . . . Boston, Ticknor, Reed, and Fields, 1851.
'Malcolm Melville, from Mrs. Hawthorne [Melville's hand].' (HCL)

258. ———. Twice-Told Tales . . . Boston, American Stationers Co., 1837.
'Hawthorne's Tales.' borrowed from Evert Duyckinck in 1849, on or after 20 Jul (NYPL–BL).

259. ———. Twice-Told Tales . . . First Series. Boston, Munroe, 1845.
'Herman Melville, from Nath[l] Hawthorne, Jan 22 1850 [Melville's hand].'; Katharine G. Bin-The date 1850 is an error for 1851; the two had first met in Aug 1850; see also No. 260. Marked. (HCL)

260. ———. Twice-Told Tales . . . Volume II. Boston, Munroe, 1842.
'Herman Melville, from Nath[l] Hawthorne [Melville's hand]'; 'Katharine G. Binnian'. Referring to Melville's visit to the Hawthornes on 22 Jan 1851, Augusta Melville in a letter of 24 Jan 1851 to her sister Helen (NYPL–GL) reports, 'Mr Hawthorne presented Herman with a copy of his "Twice told Tales" in two volumes'; see also No. 259. Annotated. (HCL)

261. ———. A Wonder-Book for Girls and Boys . . . With Engravings by Baker from Designs by Billings. Boston, Ticknor, Reed, and Fields, 1852.
'Master Malcolm Melville from M[r] Hawthorne Nov: 7th 1851 [Melville's hand].' (HCL)

Hawthorne, Nathaniel: see also No. 387.

262. Haydon, Benjamin Robert. Life of Benjamin Robert Haydon, Historical Painter, from His Autobiography and Journals. Edited and Compiled by Tom Taylor . . . New York, Harper, 1853. 2 v.
7 Apr 1854: '1 Haydon [$]1 31' (HCL–H, 6 Oct 1854).

263. ———, and William Hazlitt. Painting and the Fine Arts: Being the Articles under Those Heads Contributed to the Seventh Edition of the Encyclopædia Britannica, by B. R. Haydon . . . and William Hazlitt . . . Edinburgh, Black, 1838. #
Described as containing 'Melville's full name in lead pencil' (letter of 29 Oct 1947 from Mr. Albert Mordell, the former owner); present location unknown.

263a. Hazlitt, William. Criticisms on Art: and Sketches of the Picture Galleries of England . . . London, Templeman, 1843. ≠
'H. Melville May 11 '70 N. Y.' Annotated (sold 22 Nov 1985 by Christie's New York: Lot 85).

263b. ———. Lectures on the English Comic Writers. From the Third London Edition. Edited by His Son. New York, Derby & Jackson, 1859. ≠
'H Melville 1862 Ma[r]ch N. Y.' Annotated. (Bassett)

264. ———. Political Essays, with Sketches of Public Characters . . . London, Hone, 1819.
'Political Essays' borrowed from NYSL 18–26 Apr 1890.

265. ———. The Round Table: A Collection of Essays on Literature, Men, and Manners . . . Edinburgh, Constable, 1817. 2 v. in 1.

'H. Melville May 11 '70 N. Y.';
bookplate: '. . . ALEX[R] ORR VIETOR'.
Annotated. (YUL)

266. ———. Table Talk; or, Original
Essays on Men and Manners. Second
Edition . . . London, Colburn, 1824. 2
v.
'Table Talk 1 & 2' charged to
Lemuel Shaw by BoA 27 Jun–20
Sep 1848; Melville was in Boston 12
Jul–after 17[?] Jul.

266a. ———. Table Talk: Opinions on
Books, Men, and Things. First American Edition. New York, Wiley and
Putnam, 1845. 2 v. in 1.
'Gansevoort Melville Astor House
Room 209 May 1845'; 'H Melville';
clipping inserted 'Pitts[field]. March
1863.' Marked 'by Gansevoort
[Herman and Elizabeth Melville's
hands]'; annotated by Herman Melville. (Rovere)

Hazlitt, William: see also No. 263.

267. Hector, Annie (French). A Wo-
man's Heart. A Novel. By Mrs. Alex-
ander [pseud.] . . . New York,
Lovell, [1890].
'Womans Heart' borrowed from
NYSL 18–28 Apr 1891.

268. Heine, Heinrich. The Poems of
Heine, Complete: Translated in the
Original Metres. With a Sketch of
Heine's Life. By Edgar Alfred Bow-
ring. London, Bohn, 1861.
'H Melville March 17, 1862 H. M.'
Annotated. (NYPL–O)

269. Hemans, Felicia Dorothea
(Browne). The Poetical Works . . .
New Edition. Illustrated with Steel
Engravings. Boston, Phillips,
Sampson, 1859.
'Bessie Melville From her Father
Xmas 1862 [Melville's hand]'.
(HCL)

270. Herbert, George. The Temple
. . . The Priest to the Temple . . .
Philadelphia, Hazard, 1857.
In reply to an inquiry from George
L. Duyckinck, who had published
his *Life of George Herbert* in 1858,
Melville's letter of 14 Dec 1859 de-
scribes an unnamed book: 'Pages,
384; Price 25 cts (at least that's all I
gave for it) Publisher, Willis P.
Hazard, Phil[adelphia].—Date, 1857.
As to the size—there you have me.
But by *rule*, it is 5½ In. by 4¼, and
1 In. thick . . .'

Herodotus: see No. 147.

271. Herrick, Robert. Hesperides: or
The Works Both Humane and Divine
of Robert Herrick . . . Boston, Little,
Brown, 1856. 2 v.
V. 1: 'H. Melville Sept 1859'. V. 2:
'H Melville Pittsfield Sep. 1859'.
Marked. (V. 1 examined by
Raymond Weaver, who gave publi-
cation date as 1854; present location
unknown. V. 2 in HCL)

Hesiodus: see No. 276.

Heywood, Thomas: see No. 358.

272. Hildreth, Richard. The History of
the United States of America, from the
Adoption of the Federal Constitution
to the End of the Sixteenth Congress
. . . New York, Harper, 1851–52. 3 v.
Melville's holding: 2 v. only.
10 Nov 1851: '1 vols. 4 & 5 Hildreth [$]3' plus 'Freight p[d] on parcel
[$.]75' (HCL–H, 25 Nov 1851). This
work is a continuation of v. 1–3 of
Hildreth's *History*, which had been
published in 1849; one of the unidentified charges listed as Nos. 81
and 82 may have applied to the earlier volumes.

'Hinkleman': see No. 559.

A History of the County of Berkshire, Massachusetts: see No. 216.

273. Hoadley, John Chipman, ed. Memorial of Henry Sanford Gansevoort, Captain Fifth Artillery . . . Colonel Thirteenth New York State Volunteer Cavalry . . . Printed for Private Distribution. Boston, Rand, Avery, 1875.
'Mr & Mrs Herman Melville. with the love of Catherine Gansevoort Lansing. Albany N. Y. Dec. 1877.' One correction, not by Melville. (HCL)

274. Hoffmann, Ernst Theodor Amadeus. Nachtstücke, Herausgegeben von dem Verfasser der Fantasiestücke in Callot's Manier. Berlin, Realschulbuchhandlung, 1817 [1816–17]. 2 v.
'Hoffman's Nachstucke' charged to Lemuel Shaw by BoA 27 Nov–9 Dec 1854; Melville was in Boston 28 Nov–[?].

Hoffmann, Ernst Theodor Amadeus: see also No. 121.

275. Hoffmann-Donner, Heinrich. Slovenly Peter; or, Pleasant Stories and Funny Pictures. Translated from the German. Philadelphia, Hazard, 1851 [1850].
Mrs. Metcalf stated that this copy was long in the family: 'Mother [Frances Melville Thomas] and Aunt Bessie [Melville] knew the stories by heart.' (HCL)

Holden's Dollar Magazine: see No. 189.

275a. Hole, Samuel Reynolds. A Book about Roses, How to Grow and Show Them . . . Seventh Edition, Revised. New York, Gottsberger, 1883.
'Herman from Lizzie [Mrs. Melville] Aug 1-1884-'. Annotated. (NYPL-O)

275b. Holmes, Oliver Wendell. Urania: A Rhymed Lesson . . . Boston, Ticknor, 1846.
'Hon. Lemuel Shaw With the respect of O W Holmes'. (HCL)

276. Homerus. Homer's Batrachomyomachia, Hymns, and Epigrams. Hesiod's Works and Days. Musæus' Hero and Leander. Juvenal's Fifth Satire. Translated by George Chapman. With Introduction and Notes, By Richard Hooper . . . London, Smith, 1858.
'H. Melville from George Duyckinck Nov. 1858'; 'C[ape] H[orn] 2 [1860].' Marked. (HCL)

277. ———. The Iliads of Homer, Prince of Poets. Never Before in Any Language Truly Translated, with a Comment on Some of His Chief Places. Done According to the Greek by George Chapman. With Introduction and Notes, by Richard Hooper . . . London, Smith, 1857. 2 v.
V. 1, 2: 'H. Melville from George Duyckinck Nov. 1858'. V. 1: 'Pittsfield'; 'C[ape] H[orn] 2 [1860].' V. 2: 'Cape Horn. 2. "Meteor" & "Derby" '. Annotated. (HCL)

278. ———. The Odysseys of Homer, Translated According to the Greek, by George Chapman. With Introduction and Notes by Richard Hooper . . . London, Smith, 1857. 2 v.
V. 1, 2: 'H. Melville from George Duyckinck Nov. 1858'; 'C[ape] H[orn] 2.' V. 1: 'Pacific Ocean Oct 3^d 1860. 700 miles from San Francisco.' Annotated. (HCL)

Homerus: see also No. 147.

279. Hood, Thomas. The Poetical Works . . . [With a Memoir of the Author by Richard Monckton Milnes.] Boston, Little, Brown, 1860. 2 v.
V. 1, 2: 'H Melville Feb 14 1862

N. Y.' Marked. (NYPL–O)

280. ———. Up the Rhine . . .
Edition unknown, possibly London, 1840, or Frankfort, 1840. ' "Up the Rhine" Cologne' (HCL–L) bought at Cologne, Germany, Dec 1849.

281. Hope, Thomas. Anastasius or Memoirs of a Greek . . . [Paris, Baudry, 1831?]2 v.
'Anastasius (2 vol)' bought by Melville in Paris for '[about] 4 [francs]' (HCL–L); seized by customs officials at Dover, England, on 13 Dec 1849 (HCL–J). See Dorothee Metlitsky Finkelstein, *Melville's Orienda*, p. 55 and n.

282. ———. Anastasius; or, Memoirs of a Greek . . . London, Murray [etc.], 1836. 2 v. Reissued by Richard Bentley as Nos. 51, 52 in Bentley's Standard Novels Series.
V. 1: 'Herman Melville London, Dec 19th 1849'. V. 2: '[signature cut out] London Dec 19. 1849.' Gift from Richard Bentley (HCL–L). Marked. (HCL)

283. ———. The Costume of the Ancients . . . London, Chatto and Windus, 1875. 2 v.
(HCL)

Horatius Flaccus, Quintus: see No. 147.

284. Horne, Richard Henry. Exposition of the False Medium and Barriers Excluding Men of Genius from the Public . . . London, Wilson, 1833. ⚜
Present location unknown. Given to E. C. Stedman by Melville's widow. According to a typed copy (CUL) of her letter of 4 Feb 1892 to Stedman (the original is said to be inserted in the volume), Melville had 'much prized the book (accidentally picked up at a book-stall)'. Mrs. Melville's letter asked whether her late husband's 'surmise was correct in that the pencillings on the title page were by the author's own hand—and possibly the markings through the book—none of which were Mr. Melville's with a few exceptions in heavier lines.' Stedman's reply of 21 Feb 1892 (HCL) acknowledges the gift of Melville's copy of 'my old friend Horne's . . . "Exposition" ' and mentions its inscriptions and annotations as being Horne's own. The volume was sold at auction after Stedman's death as Lot 1431 in *The Library and Autograph Collection of Edmund Clarence Stedman*, Part II (The Anderson Auction Co., Catalogue 885, 19–20 Jan 1911).

285. ———. Gregory VII, a Tragedy [With 'An Essay on Tragic Influence'] . . . First Edition. London, Saunders and Otley, 1840. Prometheus the Fire-Bringer . . . Melbourne, Dwight, 1866. The Death of Marlowe, a Tragedy . . . London, Lacy, 1870. 3 v., rebound in 1.
E. C. Stedman's letter to Melville of 1 Feb 1888 (HCL) mentions his lending Melville 'three vols. of our old Orion's works . . . including "The Death of Marlowe". . . . I had the "tragedies" bound up together.' The titles are identified from their listing as Lot 1435 in the Stedman sale catalogue (cf. No. 284 above).

285a. Household Words. A Weekly Journal. Conducted by Charles Dickens. London, 1850–59. Augusta Melville's holding: [? Aug 1851?].
In a postscript to his letter to Evert Duyckinck of [29 Aug 1851] (NYPL–D) Melville wrote: 'Augusta tells me to say that she has received

your letter together with the Household Words . . .'

285b. Howell, James. Instructions for
Forreine Travell. English Reprints,
Edward Arber. London, 1869.
   'H Melville March 15 '70 N.Y.'
   Marked. (HCL)

286. Howells, William Dean. A
Hazard of New Fortunes . . . New
York, Harper, 1890. 2 v.
   'Hazard New Fortune 1.2.' bor-
   rowed from NYSL 31 May–13 Jun
   1890.

287. ———. The Shadow of a Dream
. . . New York, Harper, 1890.
   'Shadow Dream' borrowed from
   NYSL 15–19 Nov 1890.

288. Howitt, William. The Aristocracy
of England: A History for the People.
By John Hampden, Junr. [pseud.] . . .
[2nd ed. London, Wilson, 1846?].
   'Aristocracy of England' and 'Marlowe's Plays' bought for 5 shillings
   in Bow Street, London, in 1849
   (HCL–L), probably on 24 Dec (the
   titles are listed in HCL–L immediately before No. 228, *q. v.*).
   Lord Brougham's *Thoughts upon
   the Aristocracy of England* has also
   been suggested as the book acquired, but Henry A. Murray in his
   edition of Melville's *Pierre,* p. 435,
   n. 9.25, identifies Howitt's book as
   the probable source of information
   given by Melville.

289. ———. The Student Life of
Germany, by W. Howitt, from the
Unpublished Ms. of Dr. Cornelius.
Containing Nearly Forty of the Most
Famous Student-Songs, with the Music
. . . London, Longman [etc.], 1841.
   'Howett's [*sic*] Student's Life in
   Germany' charged to Lemuel Shaw
   by BoA 3 Jul–9 Aug 1847; Melville

was in Boston 1 Jun–c. 8–9 Jul.

290. Hugo, Victor Marie, Comte. The
Literary Life and Poetical Works of
Victor Hugo. Translated into English
by Eminent Authors . . . Now First
Collected and Edited by Henry Llewel-
lyn Williams . . . New York, Hurst,
[1883].
   Marked. (HCL)

290a. Hunt, Leigh. Rimini and Other
Poems. Boston, William D. Ticknor &
Co., 1844. #
   'H Melville Oct. 1861. New York';
   'Cedar House, Central Park.'; '(Ri-
   mini)' May 1865 [Central Park]'.
   Stamp of Chas. Miller's Book Hive,
   New York, 1859. Annotated.
   (UVL–B)

290b. ———. [Titles unidentified]
Augusta Melville's letter of 'Wednes-
day 11ᵗʰ' [1849] to Evert Duyckinck
(NYPL–D) thanks him for his gift of
'volumes' on 'Leigh Hunt. . . . selected and presented by Evert A.
Duyckinck.'

Hunt, Leigh: see also No. 325.

Hussey, Cyrus M.: see No. 323.

I

291. The Illustrated Magazine of
Art: Containing Selections from the
Various Departments of Painting,
Sculpture, Architecture, History,
Biography, Art-Industry, Manufac-
tures, Scientific Inventions and Discoveries, Local and Domestic
Scenes, Ornamental Works, etc.,
etc. New York, Montgomery,
1853–54. Melville's holding: v. 1
(1853) only.

Binding instructions in Melville's hand. Annotated. (NYPL-O)

292. Irving, Washington. A History of New York, from the Beginning of the World to the End of the Dutch Dynasty . . . by Diedrich Knickerbocker [pseud.] . . . New York, Van Winkle, 1824, 2 v. in 1.

'Knickerbocker's N. York 1 & 2' charged to Lemuel Shaw by BoA 9 Mar–6 Apr 1847; Melville was in Boston 9 Mar–[?].

292a. ———. Works . . . Philadelphia, Lea and Blanchard, 1840. 2[?] v.

V. 1: 'Herman Melville Esq from his friend Richard Lathers Winyah June 7ᵗʰ 1853'. V. 2: 'To Herman Melville Esq from his friend Richard Lathers Winyah June 7th 1853'. Marked. (HCL; NL has an identical copy of v. 1 only, inscribed 'Mrs Allan Melville from A. P. Lathers')

J

293. Jacobs, Thomas Jefferson. Scenes, Incidents, and Adventures in the Pacific Ocean; or The Islands of the Australasian Seas, during the Cruise of the Clipper Margaret Oakley, under Capt. Benj. Morrell . . . New York, Harper, 1844.

10 Apr 1847: '1 Jacob's Scenes [$]1.' (HCL-H, 1 Aug 1847). The fragment listed as No. 75 may be from this volume. Cf. also No. 372.

294. James, George Payne Rainsford. The Smuggler: A Tale . . . Leipzig, Tauchnitz, 1845.

'Augusta Melville'. (BeA)

294a. James, William, d. 1827. The

Naval History of Great Britain, from the Declaration of War by France in 1793, to the Accession of George IV . . . A New Edition . . . London, 1826 [or later edition]. 6 v.

Consulted by Melville not later than 16 Nov 1888. His notes on passages in v. 2 occur on an extratextual leaf (364) of the *Billy Budd* manuscript (HCL): see Appendix D, below.

295. Jameson, Anna Brownell (Murphy). Characteristics of Women, Moral, Poetical, and Historical . . . London, Routledge, 1870.

'Bessie Melville From her Father, Xmas 1870. New York [Melville's hand].' (HCL)

296. Jarves, James Jackson. The Art-Idea: Part Second of Confessions of an Inquirer . . . New York, Hurd and Houghton, 1864.

'Herman Melville, with kind and fraternal regards of J. C. Hoadley.—New York, March 12./ 71.' Marked. (NYPL-GL)

Jeffrey, Francis Jeffrey, Lord: see No. 359.

297. Jerrold, Douglas William. The Mutiny at the Nore. A Nautical Drama, in Two Acts . . . London, Lacy, [18–]. (Lacy's Acting Edition of Plays, v. 78.)

'Mutiny at [or &] Nore' borrowed from NYSL 31 May–13 Jun 1890. For another play borrowed from NYSL see No. 162.

298. Jewitt, Llewellyn Frederick William. The Ceramic Art of Great Britain from Pre-Historic Times down to the Present Day: Being a History of the Ancient and Modern Pottery and Porcelain Works of the Kingdom and of Their Productions of Every Class

. . . New York, Scribner, Welford, and Armstrong, 1878. 2 v.
> V. 1, in Mrs. Melville's hand: ' "Rare copy now entirely out of print and quite difficult to procure" 25.00 1903—'. (NYPL–O)

299. Johnson, Rossiter, ed. Little Classics . . . Boston, Osgood [et al.], 1874–81. 18 v. Melville's holding: v. 13, Poems Narrative . . . Boston, Houghton, Mifflin, 1881.
> 'Herman from Lizzie [Mrs. Melville] Aug 1—1882'. V. 3 of the series, in which Melville's 'The Bell-Tower' was reprinted, may have been another possible holding. (HCL)

300. Johnson, Samuel. The History of Rasselas Prince of Abyssinia . . . Philadelphia, Lippincott, 1869.
> 'Thomas Melville Philadelphia Nov 2nd 1870 J. Bogart was married at West Chester today T. M.' The history of this book after Thomas Melville's death is not known. (NYPL–O)

Johnson, Samuel: see also Nos. 84, 417a.

301. Johnston, Richard Malcolm. Widow Guthrie; a Novel . . . New York, Appleton, 1890.
> 'Widow Guthrie' borrowed from NYSL 14 Feb–2 Mar 1891.

302. Jonson, Ben. The Works of Ben Jonson, Which were formerly Printed in Two Volumes, are now Reprinted in One. To which is added A Comedy, Called The New Inn. With Additions never before Published . . . London, Herringman [etc.], 1692. Rebacked.
> 'Ben Jonson. [added: '1692'] Folio' bought in London for 13 shillings (HCL–J, 14 Nov 1849; HCL–L).
> 'Herman Melville London, December, 1849.'; '(New Year's Day,

At sea)'; '1850'. Annotated. (NYHS)

303. Judd, Sylvester. Margaret. A Tale of the Real and Ideal, Blight and Bloom; Including Sketches of a Place Not Before Described, Called Mons Christi . . . Boston, Jordan and Wiley, 1845.
> 'Judd's "Margaret" ' borrowed from Evert Duyckinck in 1850 (NYPL–BL: 41st listing for 1850).

304. Justina; or The Will. A Domestic Story . . . New York, Wiley, 1823. 2 v.; rebound in 1.
> 'Mother read this alout [sic] to me—Fanny P. Melville'; '& K G. L. [Catharine Gansevoort Lansing?] read this aloud. January, 1878. Annotated. (NYPL–GL)

Juvenalis, Decimus Junius: see Nos. 147, 276.

K

304a. Kearsley, George. Kearsley's Stranger's Guide, or Companion through London and Westminister, and the Country Round: Containing a Description of the Situation, Antiquity, and Curiosities of Every Place, within the Circuit of Fourteen Miles, together with a Map of the Surrounding Country, and a Plan of the Cities of London and Westminister, and the Borough of Southwark. London, C. and G. Kearsley, [1793?]. #
> 'Allan Melvill Paris December 15th 1807 Presented by ⟨my⟩ ↑his↓ Friend Cargill'; 'Herman Melville New York, July 6th 1850.' (Sold 2 Dec 1987 by Sotheby's. New York City. Lot 137)

305. Keats, John. The Eve of St. Agnes . . . Illustrated by Edward H.

Wehnert. London, Low and Marston, [*circa* 1860].
Annotated. (HCL)

306. Keddie, Henrietta. Childhood a Hundred Years Ago, by Sarah Tytler [pseud.] . . . With Six Chromos after Paintings by Sir Joshua Reynolds. London, Ward, 1877.
'Mrs. Herman Melville Xmas, 1886 N. Y. [Melville's hand]'. (HCL)

307. ———. Landseer's Dogs and Their Stories, by Sarah Tytler [pseud.] . . . London, Ward, 1877.
'Eleanor M. Thomas [Mrs. Metcalf] from her grandfather Herman Melville Feb. 24, 1891.' (BeA)

308. King, Charles William. The Handbook of Engraved Gems . . . London, Bell and Daldy, 1866.
'Mrs. Herman Melville Xmas 1874 N. Y.'; 'Caroline W. Stewart Nov. 29th 1908.' (NYPL–GL)

309. Kipling, Rudyard. The Light That Failed . . . Authorized Edition. New York, United States Book Company, [c1890].
'Light That Failed' borrowed from NYSL 21 May–5 Jun 1891.

310. Kirk, Ellen Warner (Olney). A Daughter of Eve, by the Author of "The Story of Margaret Kent." Boston, Ticknor, 1889.
'Daughter of Eve.' borrowed from NYSL 28 Apr–14 May 1891.

311. Kirkland, Caroline Matilda (Stansbury). Holidays Abroad; or, Europe from the West . . . New York, Baker and Scribner, 1849.
Melville 'read a little in Mrs Kirkland's European book' while en route to Europe in 1849 (HCL–J, 14 Oct 1849). It is not known whether Melville owned this book (cf. No.

76) or borrowed it, possibly from the ship's library (cf. No. 315).

312. Knight, Charles, Ed. London . . . London, Charles Knight, *or*, London, Bohn [18–]. 6 v. in 3.
Edition unidentified. 'Knight's London (3 vol oct:)' bought for 1 pound 10 shillings in London, 15 Dec 1849, and delivered three days later (HCL–J, 15, 18 Dec 1849; HCL–L). No edition published in 3 v. prior to 1851 has been located; however, Bohn's 1847 remainder catalogue lists a 6-in-3 format without specifying the imprint as either Knight's or his own.

313. Kotzebue, Otto von. A New Voyage round the World, in the Years 1823, 24, 25, and 26 . . . London, Colburn and Bentley, 1830. 2 v.
'Kotzebue's New Voyage 1 & 2' charged to Lemuel Shaw by BoA 3–19 Dec 1846; Melville was in Boston 28 Nov–7 Dec.

L

314. La Bruyère, Jean de. The Works of M. De La Bruyere. In Two Volumes. To Which Is Added the Characters of Theophrastus. Also the Manner of Living with Great Men; Written after the Manner of Bruyere, by N. Rowe . . . London, Bell, 1776. 2 v.
V. 1, 2: 'H Melville N. Y. Sep. 1862'; bookplate: 'Elizabeth Berney, Relict, Bracon Ash, Norfolk.' V. 1: 'A[lexander] O[rr] V[ietor]'. Annotated. (YUL)

314a. La Fontaine, Jean de. Fables . . . With Illustrations from Designs by J. J. Grandville. Translated from the French by Elizur Wright, Jr. New

York, Miller, [^c1879].
    Marked. One marginal correction.
(HCL)

315. Lamb, Charles [The Works
. . . ?]
    Title and edition unidentified. Mel-
ville's letter of 1 May 1850 to R. H.
Dana notes that while en route to
Europe in Oct 1849 he 'had found a
copy of Lamb in the ship's
library—& not having previously
read him much, I dived into him, &
was delighted. . . .'

316. ———. The Works . . . A New
Edition. London, Moxon, 1848.
    'Charles Lamb's works (octavo)' ob-
tained in London 'From Mr. Mo-
xon' (HCL-J, 20–21 Nov 1849;
HCL-L; letter to R. H. Dana, 1
May 1850, cited in No. 315). Be-
sides No. 317, Moxon had published
three other volumes: *The Essays of
Elia; Rosamund Grey, Essays and
Poems; The Letters of Charles
Lamb,* with a sketch of his life by
Thomas Noon Talfourd.

317. ———. Final Memorials of
Charles Lamb; Consisting Chiefly of
His Letters Not Before Published,
with Sketches of Some of His Companions. By Thomas Noon Talfourd.
. . . London, Moxon, 1848. 2 v.
    HCL-L; 'To Herman Melville, Esq.
with the Publisher's regards.'; 'London, Nov. 21. 1849.' Annotated.
(PUL)

318. ———. Specimens of English
Dramatic Poets, Who Lived about the
Time of Shakspeare. With Notes. By
Charles Lamb . . . New York, Wiley
and Putnam, 1845. 2 pts. in 1 v.
    6 Mar 1849: '1 Lambs D Poets—[$]1
00' (HCL-W, 13 Feb 1849, apparently added when the account was
settled on 12 Apr 1849).

319. La Motte-Fouqué, Friedrich
Heinrich Karl, Freiherr de. Undine,
and Sintram and His Companions.
From the German : . . New York,
Wiley and Putnam, 1845.
    'Undine & Sintram' charged to
Lemuel Shaw by BoA 19 Mar–6 Apr
1847; Melville was in Boston 9
Mar–[?].

La Motte-Fouqué, Friedrich Heinrich
Karl, Freiherr de: see also No. 121.

319a. Lamson, David Rich. Two
Years' Experience Among the Shakers
. . . West Boylston, The Author, 1848.
    Augusta Melville, in a letter of 16
Jan 1851 to Mary Blatchford
(NYPL-GL), reports 'reading a very
curious book, entitled "Two Years
Among the Shakers." Did you ever
meet with it? How is it possible for
reasonable persons to believe so
much utter nonsense.—'

319b. Landor, Walter Savage. The
Works . . . ?
    Either owned or borrowed by Mel-
ville. His annotation in No. 174, p.
xlviii, quotes somewhat inaccurately
from Petrarca's words to Boccaccio
concerning Dante, in 'First Day's
Interview,' *The Pentameron* (first
published in 1837).

320. Lanzi, Luigi Antonio. The History of Painting in Italy, from the
Period of Revival of the Fine Arts to
the End of the Eighteenth Century;
Translated from the Italian . . . By
Thomas Roscoe . . . New Edition, Revised. London, Bohn, 1847. 3 v.
    'Vasari & Lanzi 7 vols' borrowed
from Evert Duyckinck, Nov 1859
(NYPL-BL). Cf. No. 534.

321. La Rochefoucald, François, Duc
de, Prince de Marcillac. Reflections
and Moral Maxims . . . With an Intro-

ductory Essay by Sainte-Beuve and Explanatory Notes. London, Hotten, [187–]. Rebound.

Annotated. (NYPL–O)

322. Lavater, Johann Caspar. Essays on Physiognomy . . .

Edition unidentified. 'Lavater's Physiognomy' bought in London for 10 shillings, 21 Nov 1849, and delivered the following day (HCL–J; HCL–L).

323. Lay, William. A Narrative of the Mutiny, on Board the Ship Globe, of Nantucket, in the Pacific Ocean, Jan. 1824. And the Journal of a Residence of Two Years on the Mulgrave Islands; with Observations on the Manners and Customs of the Inhabitants. By William Lay . . . and Cyrus M. Hussey . . . New London, Conn., Lay and Hussey, 1828.

Attached to the front flyleaf is a letter from Thomas Macy to T. G. Coffin, 'Nantucket 1 m 9.1851' (cf. No. 134). sending the book 'as a present to Judge Shaw'. 'Hon^e Lemuel Shaw presented by his friend Thos Macy 1 m̄ 1851'; 'Herman Melville from Chief Justice Shaw 1851. Pittsfield.' Marked. (Rosenbach)

'Lays & Legends of the Rhine': see No. 404.1.

324. Lazarillo de Tormes.

Edition unidentified. 'Lazarillo De Tormes' borrowed from Evert Duyckinck in 1850 (NYPL–BL: 45th listing for 1850); not in NYPL–L.

325. Leigh Hunt's Journal; a Miscellany for the Cultivation of the Memorable, the Progressive, and the Beautiful. London, 1850–51. Melville's holding: 1850 only?

Writing Evert Duyckinck from Pittsfield, 12 Feb 1851, Melville observed: 'The society here is very much pleased with Leigh Hunt's magazine.—What a quizzical thing that is of the Duel—the man who was wounded in certain *important* parts.' His reference is to a parody of Carlyle published in the first issue, 7 Dec 1850 (Davis and Gilman, p. 122, n. 2). The *Journal* is not listed in either NYPL–BL or NYPL–L).

325a. Leonard, Levi W. The Literary and Scientific Class Book, Embracing the Leading Facts and Principles of Science . . . Keene, N. H., 1825 [or later edition].

'I now . . . read in the Scientific class book [in the Introductory Department of the New-York Male High School]' (Melville to Catherine Van Schaick Gansevoort, 11 Oct 1828). Tyrus Hillway suggests the probable identification.

Lewis, Matthew Gregory: see No. 54.

326. The Literary World. New York, 1847–53. Melville's term of subscription: 1847[?]–Feb 1852.

Melville contributed occasional reviews to this journal from early in 1847 to 1850 (cf. Nos. 88, 149, 159, 160, 242, 248, 397), and was probably a regular subscriber—at least during the period of Evert Duyckinck's editorship—until he canceled his subscription in a letter of 14 Feb 1852. Receipt of copies is mentioned in other letters to Duycknick of 5 Apr 1849, 16 Aug 1850, and 12 Dec 1850.

327. The Living Age [Littell's Living Age] . . . Boston, 1844–1941.

'Little's [*sic*] Living Age [v.] 3' (3 Nov–28 Dec 1844) charged to Lemuel Shaw by BoA 10–16 Mar 1847; Melville was in Boston 9 Mar–[?].

327.1. ———.

Melville discussed with J. E. A. Smith the article on Cooper, Dana, and himself reprinted from the *Dublin University Magazine* in the issue for 1 Mar 1856 (Smith, 'Herman Melville,' p. 142); Smith also quoted this article in the *Berkshire Eagle* for 8 Aug 1856.

327.2. ———.

V. 26 (6 Jul–21 Sep 1850): 'Thomas Melville'; 'Capt Melville "Meteor" 1860'. Later used as a scrapbook; numerous clippings are mounted on many pages. (NYPL–GL)

Livius, Titus: see No. 147.

327a. Lockhart, John Gibson. Reginald Dalton. By the Author of Valerius, and Adam Blair . . . [New York, Duyckinck, 1823?].

18 Jan 1834: borrowed by Gansevoort Melville 'from Atheneum Library' at Albany; read on 21 Jan and begun again on 24 Jan, when 'Helen Maria [Melville] lent it to Aunt Mary Gansevoort' (GMJ).

328. Loftie, William John. Views in North Wales, from Original Drawings by T. L. Rowbotham . . . with Descriptive Notes . . . Second Edition. London, Wrad, 1875.

Presumably Bessie Melville's: cf. Nos. 329, 330. (HCL)

329. ———. Views in Scotland, from Original Drawings by T. L. Rowbotham . . . with Descriptive Notes . . . Second Edition. London, Ward, 1875.

'Miss Bessie Melville Xmas, 1886 N. Y. [Melville's hand]'. (HCL)

330. ———. Views in the English Lake District, from Original Drawings by T. L. Rowbotham . . . with Descriptive Notes . . . Second Edition.

London, Ward, 1875.

'Miss Bessie Melville N. Y. May 22^d 1887 [Melville's hand].' (HCL)

330a. London. 'Old Map of London (1766)'.

Edition unidentified. In HCL–J, 18 Dec 1849, Melville wrote: 'Looked over a lot of ancient maps of London. Bought one (A. D. 1766) for 3 and 6 pence. I want to use it in case I serve up the Revolutionary narrative of the beggar' (No. 407, the basis of Melville's *Israel Potter*). In HCL–L this is listed as 'Old Map of London (1766)'.

331. The London Carcanet. Containing Select Passages from the Most Distinguished Writers. From the Second London Edition. New York, Peabody, 1831.

'Herman Melville.' stamped on cover in gold: label inside front cover: 'ALBANY ACADEMY. To Herman Melville the first best in his class in . . . [erasure]. T. ROMEYN BECK, *Principal*.'; bookplate: '. . . ALEX^R ORR VIETOR'. An article in the Albany *Argus* for 6 Aug 1831 mentions Melville's award: the first premium in the second class in ciphering books in the fourth department. Annotated. (YUL)

332. Longfellow, Henry Wadsworth. Evangeline, a Tale of Acadie . . . Fifth Edition. Boston, Ticknor, 1848.

'Mr Herman Melville from his sincere friend H[ope] S[avage] Shaw [Mrs. Lemuel Shaw, his stepmother-in-law]'. (HCL)

332a. ———. Voices of the Night. Boston, Redding and Company, 1845. ✳

'Fanny Melville from her brother Gansevoort June 1845'. (LHS)

Longfellow, Henry Wadsworth: in No.

439, p. 29, is an annotation by Melville citing Longfellow's 'Excelsior.'

The Looker-On: see No. 126.

Loti, Pierre [pseud.]: see Viaud, Julien (No. 536).

333. Lytton, Edward George Earle Lytton Bulwer-Lytton, 1st Baron. The Pilgrims of the Rhine. By the Author of "Pelham," "Eugene Aram," &c. . . . New Edition. London, Tilt, 1840.
'Herman Melville From his Friend S[arah] A. [Mrs. J. R.] Morewood Jan. 1st 1854'. (NYPL–O)

334. ———. Zanoni . . . [New York, Harper, 1842. 2 v.?]
Gift from Mrs. J. R. Morewood, acknowledged in Melville's letter of 12? Sep 1851: ' "Zanoni" is a very fine book in very fine print—but I shall endeavor to surmount that difficulty.'

M

335. Macaulay, Thomas Babington Macaulay, 1st Baron. The History of England from the Accession of James II . . . New York, Harper, 1849–61. 5 v. Melville's holding: v. 1, 2 only.
30 Mar 1849: '2 c vos. Macaulay 15 [$.]30' (HCL–H, 10 Sep 1849). The firm's 1850 catalogue lists v. 1 and 2 only, at the following prices per volume: library ed. 8vo. muslin, 75¢; sheep extra, 87½¢; calf backs and corners, $1.00; cheap ed. 8vo, paper, 25¢.

336. ———. The History of England from the Accession of James II . . . New York, Harper, 1849–61. 5 v. Melville's holding: v. 1, 2 only.
2 Apr 1849; '1 Macaulay, 2 v. ½ c[al]f

[$]3 75' (HCL–H, 10 Sep 1849). Cf. No. 335.

337. ———. The History of England from the Accession of James II . . . New York, Harper, 1849–61. 5 v. Melville's holding: v. 1, 2 only.
25 Apr 1849: '1 [Macaulay] 2 v. mus[lin]. [$]1 20' (HCL–H, 10 Sep 1849). Cf. No. 335.

Macaulay, Thomas Babington Macaulay, 1st Baron: see also No. 359.

338. McCarthy, Justin. The Ladies' Gallery; a Novel, by Justin McCarthy, M.D., and Mrs. Campbell-Praed . . . Chicago, Rand, McNally, 1889.
'Ladies Gallery' borrowed from NYSL 2–14 Mar 1891.

339. Macdonnel, D. E. A Dictionary of Quotations, in Most Frequent Use, Taken Chiefly from the Latin and French, but Comprising Many from the Greek, Spanish, and Italian, Languages; Translated into English. With Illustrations Historical and Idiomatic. Fifth Edition, Revised and Very Considerably Enlarged . . . London, Wilkie and Robinson, 1809.
'A[llan] Melville'; 'Gansevoort Melville London 1846'. (HCL)

Macgowan, John: see No. 223a.

340. Macgregor, John. The Rob Roy on the Jordan, Nile, Red Sea, and Gennesareth, &c. A Canoe Cruise in Palestine and Egypt, and the Waters of Damascus . . . With Maps and Illustrations. New York, Harper, 1870.
1 Nov 1870: '1 Rob Roy [$]1.67' (HCL–H, 2 Nov 1870).

340a. Machiavelli, Niccolò. The Florentine Histories. Edition unknown; possibly the translation by C. Edwards Lester, New York, Paine and Burgess, 1845, 2 v.
In a note dated 'Thursday afternoon'

accompanying a letter of 4 Dec 1851 from Helen Melville to their sister Augusta (NYPL–GL), Melville asked Augusta to bring back to Pittsfield from New York 'Machiavelli's Florentine history which Allan [Melville] borrowed from me.'

341. Mackay, Charles. The Lost Beauties of the English Language: An Appeal to Authors, Poets, Clergymen, and Public Speakers . . . New York, Bouton, 1874.
'Frances C. Thomas [Mrs. Osborne].' (NYPL—O)

342. ———, ed. Songs of England. The Book of English Songs . . . London, Houlston and Wright, [1857].
'H Melville N. Y. Oct 15th 1860.' (Melville was in San Francisco on this date.) Annotated. (HCL)

Mackintosh, Sir James: see No. 359.

343. Macpherson, James. Fingal, an Ancient Epic Poem, in Six Books: Together with Several Other Poems, Composed by Ossian the Son of Fingal. Translated from the Galic Language, by James Macpherson . . . The Second Edition. London, Becket and De Hondt, 1762.
'H. Melville 1848 N. Y.' Annotated. (PUL)

344. Macpherson, Robert. Vatican Sculptures, Selected, and Arranged in the Order in Which They Are Found in the Galleries, Briefly Explained . . . London, Chapman and Hall, 1863.
'Mr Herman Melville from the author Rome May 4 1866'. Marked (?). (HCL)

345. Macy, Obed. The History of Nantucket; Being a Compendious Account of the First Settlement of the Island by the English, together with the Rise and Progress of the Whale Fishery; and

Other Historical Facts Relative to Said Island and Its Inhabitants. In Two Parts . . . Boston, Hilliard, Gray, 1835.
'Herman Melville from his friend Thos Macy 7 1/m [7 Jan] 1852'; bookplate of Anna Scott Chambliss. Annotated. Contains newspaper clipping. (Reese)

346. Maistre, Xavier, Comte de. A Journey round My Room . . . Translated from the French, with a Notice of the Author's Life. By H. A. New York, Hurd and Houghton, 1871. #
'H Melville' (Abrams)

347. Mangan, James Clarence. Poems . . . With Biographical Introduction by John Mitchel. New York, Haverty, 1859.
'J. G. Hefferman, 1st Nov '59.' [inscription lined out]; 'H Melville Feb 15. 1862 N. Y.' Annotated. (HCL)

348. Marlowe, Christopher. The Dramatic Works . . . with Prefatory Remarks, Notes, Critical and Explanatory. By W. Oxberry. London, W. Simpkin, R. Marshall, C. Chapple, [1820?]. Contains eight plays separately paged: *The Jew of Malta* (1818), *Edward the Second* (1818), *Dr. Faustus* (1818), *Lust's Dominion* (1818), *The Massacre of Paris* (1818), *Tamburlaine,* I and II (1820), *Dido Queen of Carthage* (n.d.).
'Aristocracy of England' and 'Marlowe's Plays' bought for 5 shillings in Bow Street, London (HCL–L), probably on 24 Dec 1849; the titles are listed immediately before No. 228 (*q.v.*). 'H. Melville London, December 1849.' Annotated. (HCL)

Marlowe, Christopher: see also Nos. 188, 358.

349. Marsh-Caldwell, Anne (Caldwell). Angela. A Novel. By the Author of

"Emilia Wyndham" . . . New York, Harper, 1848.
'Angela' borrowed from Evert Duyckinck after Jul 1848 (NYPL–BL; not in NYPL–L).

350. Martineau, Harriet. The Hour and the Man. A Historical Romance . . . [London, Moxon, 1841. 3 v.?]
Gift from Mrs. J. R. Morewood, acknowledged in Melville's letter of 12? Sep 1851: 'The "Hour & the Man" is exceedingly acceptable to me.'

351. Marvell, Andrew. The Poetical Works . . . With a Memoir of the Author. Boston, Little, Brown, 1857.
'H. Melville Boston Feb. 1860.' Annotated. (HCL)

Massinger, Philip: see No. 358.

351a. Mathews, Cornelius. Chanticleer; A Thanksgiving Story of the Peabody Family. Boston, Munsey, 1850.
Augusta Melville, in a letter of 6 Jan 1851 to her sister Helen (NYPL–GL), reports that 'Mr Matthews sent Herman a copy of his new book—"The Peabody Family" '.

352. ———. The Various Writings . . . New York, Harper, 1863 [i.e., 1843].
Bookplate: 'Allan Melville [Jr.], New York.' Holograph cutting: 'Yours / what there is left Cornelius Mathews.'; 'Augusta [Melville]'. Annotated [not by Herman Melville]. (NYPL–GL)

352a. Maxwell, John S. The Czar, His Court and People: Including a Tour in Norway and Sweden. New York, Baker and Scribner, 1848.
'Maxwells Czar' borrowed from NYSL by Allan Melville, Jr., 29 May 1850–4 Jan 1851.

353. Mayo, Sarah Carter (Edgarton). The Flower Vase; Containing the Language of Flowers and Their Poetic Sen-

timents . . . Lowell, Mass., Powers and Bagley, 1844.
'Miss Elizabeth [Shaw—later Mrs. Herman Melville] Jany 1, 1844'. Marked. (Formerly in the collection of Mrs. Walter B. Binnian; present location unknown)

353a. Mayo, William Starbuck. The Berber; or, The Mountaineer of the Atlas, a Tale of Morocco. New York, Putnam, 1850.
Augusta Melville, in a letter of 27 Aug 1850 to Mary Blatchford (NYPL–GL), mentions reading, 'at two sittings,' 'Dr Mayo's new work—"The Berber." . . . It is very different from that wild "Kaloolah". . . .'

354. Mead, Lucia True (Ames). Memoirs of a Millionaire . . . Boston, Houghton, Mifflin, 1889.
'Memoirs of Millionaire' borrowed from NYSL 26–30 Apr 1890.

355. Melville, Sir James. The Memoires of Sir James Melvil of Hal-Hill . . . Now Published from the Original Manuscript. By George Scott . . . London, Boulter, 1683. #
Allan Melvill's copy, bearing the autograph of his great-grandfather, was examined by Raymond Weaver (*Herman Melville*, p. 50); present location unknown.

356. The Men of the Time; or, Sketches of Living Notables . . . New York, Redfield, 1852.
'H. Melville Sept 29, 1868 N. Y.' Marked. (HCL)

356a. Menken, Ada Isaacs. Infelicia. New York, H. L. Williams, 1868. #
'H. Melville'. Examined at Indiana University about 1952 by Earl Tannenbaum; present location unknown (letter from Mr. Tannenbaum, 5 Nov. 1962).

357. Menzel, Wolfgang. The History of Germany, from the Earliest Period to the Present Time . . . Translated from the Fourth German Edition, by Mrs. George Horrocks . . . London, Bohn, 1848–49. 3 v.

'Manzell's Hist. of Germany 3' charged to Lemuel Shaw by BoA 9 Sep 1854–14 Feb 1855; Melville was in Boston 28 Nov–[?].

357a. Mercier, Henry James. Life in a Man-of-War, or Scenes in 'Old Ironsides' during Her Cruise in the Pacific. By a Fore-Top-Man . . . Philadelphia, Bailey, 1841.

Either owned or borrowed by Melville. 'The writer has to thank the light-hearted author of a book called ''Scenes in Old Ironsides'' for supplying corroborative hints for some few scenes' (Melville's semifinal fair copy of the preface that appeared in the first English edition of *White-Jacket*; the manuscript, now in HCL, is reproduced and transcribed in *White-Jacket*, pp. 494–497).

358. The Mermaid Series. The Best Plays of the Old Dramatists. London, Vizetelly *or*, Unwin, 1887–19[?]. [?] v. Melville's exact holding or borrowing unknown.

Arthur Stedman's introduction to his 1892 edition of Melville's *Typee*, p. xxix, states that Melville during his last days occupied himself with 'readings in the ''Mermaid Series'' of old plays, in which he took much pleasure.' The following numbered volumes in the series were published in 1891 or before: v. 1: Christopher Marlowe (but cf. Nos. 188, 348); v. 2: Thomas Otway; v. 3: John Ford; v. 4, 5: Philip Massinger; v. 6: Thomas Heywood; v. 7: William Wycherley; v. 8: Nero and Other Plays; v. 9, 10: Beaumont and Fletcher (but cf. No.

53); v. 11: William Congreve; v. 12: John Webster and Cyril Tourneur; v. 13, 14: Thomas Middleton; v. 15: James Shirley. Other volumes, which were unnumbered, were also available.

Middleton, Thomas: see No. 358.

358a. Milton, John. Paradise Lost: A Poem in Twelve Books . . . London, A. Law, W. Miller, and R. Cater, 1795.

'Thomas Melvill'; 'T. Melvill, Boston [printed]'; 'Lucy Melvill's.'; 'Kate M. Hoadley, From her Aunt Lucy, . . . Oct. 1870—'; 'Given in August, 1930 to the Gansevoort-Lansing Collection by Miss Charlotte Hoadley V H P[altsits]'. (NYPL–GL)

358b. ———. The Poetical Works . . . with Notes, and a Life of the Author. Boston, Hilliard, Gray, 1836. 2 v. #

V. 1, 2: 'H. Melville N. Y. 1849'; 'C[ape] Horn 1860'. V. 1: '1868'. V. 2: 'Pacific Ocean N. L. 15°—Sep. 21st 1860'. Annotated. (Sold 27 Mar 1984 by Phillips, New York: Sale No. 529, Lot 45)

359. [The Modern British Essayists. Philadelphia, Carey and Hart, 1847–49. 8 v.?]

16 Feb 1849: '1 set British Essayists—[$] 18 00' (HCL–W, 13 Feb 1849, item added on 12 Apr 1849 when the account was settled). The 'set' suggested above—the identification offers certain difficulties—included eight numbered volumes: v. 1 (1847 *or* 1849): Thomas Babington Macaulay, 1st Baron Macaulay. Essays, Critical and Miscellaneous . . . v. 2 (1847): Sir Archibald Alison, Bart. Miscellaneous Essays . . . v. 3 (1848): Sydney Smith. The Works . . . v. 4 (1848): John Wilson. The Recreations of Christopher North [pseud.] . . . v. 5 (1848): Thomas Carlyle. Critical and

Miscellaneous Essays . . . v. 6 (1848): Francis Jeffrey, Lord Jeffrey. Contributions to the Edinburgh Review . . . v. 7 (1848): Sir James Stephen. Critical and Miscellaneous Essays . . . Sir Thomas Noon Talfourd. Critical and Miscellaneous Writings . . . With Additional Articles Never Before Published in This Country . . . v. 8 (1848): Sir James Mackintosh. The Miscellaneous Works . . . In addition, an unnumbered volume published by Carey and Hart in 1841 was advertised in some catalogues as part of the set: Sir Walter Scott, Bart. Critical and Miscellaneous Essays . . . Collected by Himself . . .*

360. Mollet, John William. Meisonnier . . . New York, Scribner and Welford, 1882.
(HCL)

361. ———. The Painters of Barbizon: Corot, Daubigny, Dupré . . . New York, Scribner and Welford, .890.
(HCL)

362. ———. The Painters of Barbizon: Millet, Rousseau, Diaz . . . New York, Scribner and Welford, 1890.
(HCL)

363. ———. Rembrandt . . . New Edition. London, Sampson Low, 1882.
(HCL)

364. ———. Sir David Wilkie . . . New York, Scribner and Welford, 1881.
(HCL)

365. Monkhouse, William Cosmo. Turner . . . New York, Scribner and Welford, 1879.
(HCL)

366. Montaigne, Michel Eyquem de. The Complete Works . . . Comprising; The Essays (Translated by [Charles] Cotton); The Letters; The Journey into Germany and Italy; Now First Translated; A Life, by the Editor . . . William Hazlitt [1811–93]. London, John Templeman, 1842, *or* the 'Second Edition' [i.e., second impression], London, C. Templeman, 1845.
18 Jan 1848: '1 Shakespear c[al]f and '1 Montagne [*sic*]—[$]9 25' (HCL–W, 1 Jul 1848). Aretta J. Stevens, 'The Edition of Montaigne Read by Melville,' concludes that Melville bought either the 1842 or more likely the 1845 impression of Hazlitt's edition.

367. Montalba, Anthony Reubens'. Fairy Tales from All Nations . . . With Twenty-Four Illustrations by Richard Doyle. New York, Harper, 1850 [1849?].
21 Dec 1849: '1 Fairy Tales [$.]66' (HCL–H, 22 Feb 1850). 'Catherine Gansevoort from couzin [*sic*] Allan

*Roorbach's *Bibliotheca Americana* gives two listings under 'British Essayists' published by Cary and Hart: one in 16v. 12mo cloth @ $16.00 and the other in 8 v. cloth @ $12.00; the résumés of the contents of each set differ from one another but include all the authors given in the entry above. Listings in other catalogues of the period, exclusive of expensive editions, are a Philadelphia edition in 9 v. @ $12.00 and a London edition of the eighteenth-century British essayists in 3 v. @ $7.00 for cloth and $12.00 for half morocco. Although none of these exactly corresponds to the entry in HCL–W, the Carey and Hart edition completed in 1849 seems the most likely identification, as Melville later borrowed sets of the eighteenth-century essayists (Nos. 126, 494). The discrepancy in price may be explained by reason of special binding, or even as a clerical error.

Melvile [*sic*], Jan 1st 1850'. (NYPL–GL

368. Montalembert, Charles Forbes René de Tryon, Comte de. The Life of Saint Elizabeth, of Hungary, Duchess of Thuringia . . . Translated by Mary Hackett. The Introduction Translated by Mrs. J. Sadlier . . . New York, Sadlier, 1870.
'Kate Gansevoort Lansing from Cousin Herman.'; 'Oct. 4th 1875.' Marked (annotation not in Melville's hand). (NYPL–GL)

368a. Montefiore, Joshua. A Commercial Dictionary: Containing the Present State of Mercantile Law, Practice and Custom . . . The First American Edition . . . Philadelphia, James Humphreys, 1804. 3 v. #
V. 1-3: 'Allan Melvill'; printed stickers reading 'Alan Melvill [Jr.].' (Sold Fall 1986 by The Americanist, Pottstown, Pa., Catalogue 138, Lot 95)

Moore, Edward: see No. 565.

369. Moore, Thomas. Life of Lord Byron: With His Letters and Journals . . . Boston, Little, Brown, [1853?]. 6 v. 6 v 10 Vols
V. 1: 'H Melville'; 'Life & Works $7 for 16 vols.' Binding uniform with No. 112. Jay Leyda, citing notations of prices in other volumes bought during Melville's visit to New York in Feb and Mar 1862 (Nos. 184–187, 370, 487), suggests (in a letter of 17 Jul 1948) that Nos. 112 and 369 were also acquired at that time; Melville quoted Byron's *Don Juan* in a letter of 25 May 1862 to his brother Thomas following his return to Pittsfield. Annotated. (HCL)

370. ——. The Poetical Works . . . Collected by Himself . . . With a

Memoir . . . Boston, Little, Brown 1856 [1854?]. 6 v.
V. 1, 2, 3, 5, 6: 'H Melville.' V. 1: 'Feb 15, 1862 N. Y.' V. 2: 'Oct 25, 1862 N. Y.' V. 3 annotated. (V. 1, 3, 5, 6,: HCL. V. 2,4: examined by Raymond Weaver, who gave publication date as 1854; present location unknown)

More, Hannah: see No. 141a.

371. Morgan, Sydney (Owenson), Lady. The Wild Irish Girl; a National Tale . . . Fourth American Edition. New York, Scott, 1807.
'Maria Gansevoort [Melville's mother] 1808'. (NYPL–GL)

372. Morrell, Benjamin. A Narrative of Four Voyages to the South Sea, North and South Pacific Ocean, Chinese Sea, Ethiopic and Southern Atlantic Ocean, Indian and Antarctic Ocean. From the year 1822 to 1831 . . . New York, Harper, 1832.
10 Apr 1847: '1 Morrell's Voyages [$]1.20' (HCL–H, 1 Aug 1847). The fragment listed as No. 75 may be from this volume. Cf. also No. 293.

373. Morse, Jedidiah. A Prayer and Sermon, Delivered at Charlestown, December 31, 1799; on the Death of George Washington . . . With an Additional Sketch of His Life. By Jedidiah Morse, D.D. . . . To Which Is Prefixed, an Account of the Proceedings of the Town on the Melancholy Occasion; Written by Josiah Bartlett, Esq. . . . Charlestown, Mass., Printed by Etheridge, 1800.
'A[llan] Melville'. (NYPL–GL)

374. Murphy, John Mortimer. Sporting Adventures in the Far West . . . New York, Harper, 1880.
18 Feb 1880: '1 Murphy's Adventures, [$]1' (HCL–H, 19 Feb 1880).

375. Murray, John, publisher. Handbook for Travellers in Central Italy, Including the Papal States, Rome, and the Cities of Etruria, with a Travelling Map. London, Murray, 1843.

Probably the guidebook for 'Central Italy' borrowed from George L. Duyckinck before Melville's departure for Europe in Oct 1849 (Melville to Evert Duyckinck, 2 Feb 1850). Title not listed in NYPL–L. Mrs. Melville in a memorandum cited 'Murray's Handbook of Central Italy' along with No. 86.1; see Sealts, *The Early Lives of Melville*, p. 175.

376. ———. Hand-Book for Travellers in France: Being a Guide to Normandy, Brittany; the Rivers Loire, Seine, Rhône, and Garonne; the French Alps, Dauphiné, Provence and the Pyrenees . . . With Five Travelling Maps. Third Edition, Revised. London, Murray, 1848.

Murray 'offered to give me some of his "Hand Books" as I was going on the continent. So he sent me to the house his Book of the Continent & for France' (HCL–J, London, 16 Nov 1849). HCL–L lists 'Guide Book for France'.

377. ———. Hand-Book for Travellers in Northern Italy; States of Sardinia, Lombardy and Venice, Parma and Piacenza, Modena, Lucca, Massa-Carrara, and Tuscany as far as the Val d'Arno. With Travelling Map and Plans. Third Edition, Corrected to the Present Time. London, Murray, 1847.

Probably the guidebook for Northern Italy borrowed from George L. Duyckinck before Melville's departure for Europe in Oct 1849 (Melville to Evert Duyckinck, 2 Feb 1850); on 20 Oct he 'read account of Venice in Murray' (HCL–J). Title not listed in NYPL–L.

378. ———. [A Hand-Book for Travellers on the Continent: Being a Guide through Holland, Belgium, Prussia, and Northern Germany, and along the Rhine, from Holland to Switzerland . . . With an Index Map. Sixth Edition, Corrected and Augmented. London, Murray, 184–?].

'Book of the Continent' sent Melville by John Murray, London (HCL–J, 16 Nov 1849: see No. 376); HCL–L lists '[Guide Book for] Germany'.

379. ———. Murray's Handbook for Modern London . . . Or, London as It Is. London, Murray, 1851.

'Hand Book of Mod. London' charged to Lemuel Shaw by BoA 3–24 Apr 1852; Melville was in Boston after 16 Apr–before 2 May.

380. Murray, Lindley. The English Reader: or, Pieces in Prose and Poetry, Selected from the Best Writers . . . [2nd Canandaigua edition] Canandaigua, N. Y., J. D. Bemis, 1819.

Title page lacking; edition identified by the late Merrell R. Davis; see Gilman, *Melville's Early Life and Redburn*, p. 307, n. 44. 'H. Melville'[s] Book.' Marked. (NYPL–GL)

Musaeus: see No. 276.

381. Musaeus, Johann Karl August. Volksmärchen der Deutschen; mit einem Vorwort von F. Jacobs. Neue Auflage. Gotha, Ettingersche Buchhandlung, 1826. 5 v.

'Musau's Volksmarchen 3.4' charged to Lemuel Shaw by BoA 18 Oct–16 Dec 1854; Melville was in Boston 28 Nov–[?].

Musaeus, Johann Karl August: see also No. 121.

382. The Musical Gem; a Collection of Modern and Favourite Songs, Duets, and Glees, Selected from the Works of the Most Celebrated Composers. Adapted for the Voice, Flute, or Violin. Three Volumes in One. 1. Vocal Companion. 2. British Minstrel. 3. Flowers of Song. London, Bohn, 1845.
'Mucical [*sic*] Gem' charged to Lemuel Shaw by BoA 29 May–16 Jul 1852; Melville was in Boston 3–6 and 13–16 Jul.

383. My Own Treasury. An Illustrated Gift-Book for Young Persons. Edited by Mark Merriwell [pseud.]. . . New York, Wiley and Putnam, 1847.
30 Dec 1846: '1 My Own Treasury gilt [for Brother] [$]1 25' (HCL–WP, 1 Jan 1847). 'Miss Kitty Gansevoort from her cousin Allan Melville Jany 1. 1847.' (NYPL–GL)

N

383a. Néel, Louis Balthazard. Voyage de Paris à Saint-Cloud . . . #
Described in notes by the late R. S. Forsythe (cf. No. 86a) as 'Voyage de Paris a Saint-Cloud—by Neel, flyleaf, "H. Melville."' Present location unknown.

384. The New England Primer; Containing the Assembly's Catechism; the Account of the Burning of John Rogers; a Dialogue between Christ, a Youth, and the Devil; and Various Other Useful and Instructive Matter. Adorned with Cuts. With a Historical Introduction, by Rev. H. Humphrey . . . Worcester, Howland, [183–?].
'H Melville March 6th 1851. Pittsfield. Mss: [*sic*]'. (HCL)

384a. Nichols, George Ward. The Story of The Great March. From the Diary of a

Staff Officer. By Brevet Major George Ward Nichols, Aid-de-Camp to General Sherman . . . New York, Harper, 1865.
18 Aug 1865: '1 Sherman's March. [$]1.17' (HCL–H, 20 Oct 1865). Ward's book, listed at $2.00 in the 1865 Harper catalogue, was advertised at $1.75 in *Harper's Weekly* for 26 Aug 1865.

385. Nicolini, Giovanni Battista. History of the Jesuits: Their Origin, Progress, Doctrines, and Designs . . . London, Bohn, 1854.
'Nicolinis Hist. of Jesuits (Bohn)' charged to Lemuel Shaw by BoA 2 Sep 1854–14 Feb 1855; Melville was in Boston 28 Nov–[?].

386. Norton, Caroline (Sheridan). Poems . . . Boston, Allen and Ticknor, 1833.
'Helen Maria Melville from her brother Gansevoort 1841.' (BeA)

O

The Observer: see No. 126.

387. O'Connor, Evangeline Maria (Johnson). An Analytical Index to the Works of Nathaniel Hawthorne, with a Sketch of His Life. Boston, Houghton, Mifflin, 1882.
'H. Melville Paid[?]'. Marked. (HCL)

387a. Oken, Lorenz. Elements of Physiophilosophy . . . London, Printed for the Ray Society, 1847.
Apparently owned or borrowed by Melville: a quotation from p. 186 is inscribed in his hand on the flyleaf of a copy of *The Whale* (now in NYPL–B) which he presented to John C. Hoadley, 6 Jan 185[4]. See Herbert Cahoon, *Herman Melville*, p. 12.

388. The (Old) Farmer's Almanack . . . Established in 1793, by Robert B. Thomas . . . Boston, 1793–. Melville's holding: 1877 only?

The edition for 1877 is probably referred to in Melville's letter of 2 Jan 1877 to Abraham Lansing, which mentions ordering an almanac 'from Boston.' V. H. Paltsits, ed., *Family Correspondence*, p. 45, nn. 85, 86, suggests the probable identification of Nos. 388 and 553.

389. Oliphant, Margaret Oliphant (Wilson). Effie Ogilvie; the Story of a Young Life . . . New York, Harper, 1886.

'Effie Ogilvie' borrowed from NYSL 28 Apr–14 May 1891.

390. Olney, Jesse. Practical System of Modern Geography; or A View of the Present State of the World . . . Accompanied by a New and Improved Atlas . . . Twenty Second Edition. New York, Robinson, Pratt, 1836.

'Nancy Mowry'; [possibly in Melville's hand:] 'Present from A. Rider June 1/63.' Annotated [not by Melville]. This text, according to William H. Gilman, was used in the Fourth Department of the Albany Academy, where Melville was a student in 1830–31 and 1836–37. (HCL)

391. Omar Khayyām. Rubáiyát of Omar Khayyám, the Astronomer-Poet of Persia. Rendered into English Verse. First American from the Third London Edition. Boston, Houghton, Osgood, 1878.

Melville's note opposite title page: 'Edward Fitzgerald, Indian service, translator.' Marked. Contains clipping. (HCL)

392. ———. Rubáiyát of Omar Khayyám, the Astronomer-Poet of Persia; Rendered into English Verse by Edward Fitzgerald, with an Accompaniment of Drawings by Elihu Vedder. Bos-

ton, Houghton, Mifflin, [ᶜ1886].

A portrait of Vedder and a review of *Letters and Literary Remains of Edward Fitzgerald* (New York *Evening Post,* 8 Aug 1889) inserted. (HCL)

393. ———. Rubáiyát of Omar Khayyám . . .

On 15 Feb 1886, according to a memorandum by Mrs. Melville, James Billson sent Melville a ' "semi-manuscript" copy . . . translated by Fitzgerald' (see Sealts, *The Early Lives of Melville,* p. 172); her husband in his letter of 2 Apr 1886 to Billson referred to the 'unique form' of this 'semi-manuscript "Omar" '. Billson himself, in a letter of 21 Aug 1935 to Prof. Willard Thorp (NL), explained that his friend the poet James Thomson 'had Omar Khayyam in M.S. form in his own hand writing. At that time, there were no correct copies available here & I copied from his M.S. & lent it to the Book editor at the Secular Hall [at Leicester, England] who made a large number of copies which he sold at a trifling cost. It was one of these I sent to Melville.'

394. Oneida Historical Society at Utica. Memorial of the Centennial Celebration of the Battle of Oriskany, August 6, 1877. Published by the Oneida Historical Society. Utica, N. Y., Roberts, 1878.

Catherine Gansevoort Lansing in a letter to Abraham Lansing, 24 Mar 1878 (NYPL–GL), mentioned that she 'last Eveg gave the Oriskany & Schuylerville [No. 491b] Centennial Volumes' to 'Cousin Herman.' (BeA has a copy, without inscription or marking, that came from the estate of Helen Morewood, a granddaughter of Allan Melville)

394a. See Addenda, p. 228.

395. Orsay, Harriet Anne Frances

(Gardiner), Comtesse d'. Clouded Happiness. A Novel. Translated from the French . . . New York, Harper, 1853.
> 16 Aug 1859: '1 Clouded Happiness to A[llan] Melville [Jr.] [$.]30' (HCL–H, 8 Sep 1859).

Otway, Thomas: see No. 358.

Ovidius Naso, Publius: see No. 147.

P

396. Palmer, Edward Henry. The Desert of the Exodus; Journeys on Foot in the Wilderness of the Forty Years' Wanderings; Undertaken in Connection with the Ordnance Survey of Sinai and the Palestine Exploration Fund . . . With Maps and Numerous Illustrations from Photographs and Drawings Taken on the Spot by the Sinai Survey Expedition and C. F. Tyrwhitt Drake. New York, Harper, 1872.
> 17 Jun 1872: '1 Exodus $2 10' (HCL–H, 17 Jun 1872); '1 Exodus; 1 Robertson [No. 427] $3 15' (HCL–H, 12 Feb 1875).

396.1. Palmer, John Williamson. After His Kind. By John Coventry [pseud.]. New York, Holt, 1886.
> In his letter of 23 Mar 1889 to Palmer thanking him for his 'letter and gift' (Nos. 396.1, 396.2), Melville wrote: ' "After his Kind" . . . I have as yet . . . been able but to dip into. . . .'

396.2. ———. The Golden Dagon; or, Up and Down the Irrawaddi. By an American. New York, Dix, Edwards, 1856, or later edition.
> In his letter of 23 Mar 1889 to Palmer (see No. 396.1), Melville wrote: 'To night my wife will conclude the reading to me of "Up & Down the Irrawaddy." Those stirring adventures in scenes so orientally novel make the book unique to me, and have interested me more than any volume I have read for a long time.'

396a. 'Panorama of the Rhine.' Edition unidentified. 'Panorama of the Rhine. [Cologne]' (HCL–L) obtained in Cologne, Germany, Dec 1849; antedates the 'New Panorama of the Rhine from Mayence to Cologne' published in 1854 by D. Kapp, Mayence.

396b. Pardoe, Julia. The Confessions of a Pretty Woman . . . New York, Harper & Brothers, 1846. ⚓
> 'Helen, Augusta & Fanny Melville Aug^{st} 3^{d} 1846'. (LHS)

397. Parkman, Francis. The California and Oregon Trail: Being Sketches of Prairie and Rocky Mountain Life . . . New York, Putnam, 1849.
> Melville probably obtained a reviewer's copy of this book, which he reviewed for the *Literary World* 4, no. 113 (31 Mar 1849), 291–293.

Paulding, James Kirke: see No. 143a.

398. Pepys, Samuel. Memoirs . . . Comprising His Diary, from 1659 to 1669, and a Selection from His Private Correspondence. Edited by Richard Lord Braybrooke. With a Short Introduction and Memoir by John Timbs . . . London, Warne, [187–].
> 'Abraham Lansing from Herman Melville with his sincere regards April 3, 1872 New York'. (NYPL–GL)

399. Perkins, Edward T. Na Motu: or, Reef-Rovings in the South Seas . . . New York, Pudney and Russell, 1854.
> 'Edward Haight Esq with the respects of the Publishers' [lined out]; 'E[O lizabeth] S[haw] Melville Nov. 1886'; 'Mrs. Herman Melville 105 East 18th st

New York'. A quotation copied in ink from the London *Athenaeum*, 11 Nov 1854, comparing Perkins and Melville, is pasted to the flyleaf. Also contains clipping from *Putnam's Magazine*, Oct 1854. (NYPL–O)

400. Perry, Bliss. The Broughton House . . . New York, Scribner, 1890.
'Broughton House' borrowed from NYSL 20–31 May 1890.

Persius Flaccus, Aulus: see No. 147.

Phaedrus: see No. 147.

401. Phillips, William. An Elementary Introduction to the Knowledge of Mineralogy . . . New York, Collins, 1818; *or,* Third Edition, Enlarged. London, Phillips, 1823; *or,* An Elementary Treatise on Mineralogy . . . Fifth Edition from the Fourth London Edition, by R. Allen . . . With Numerous Additions to the Introduction. By Francis Alger . . . Boston, Ticknor, 1844.
'Phillips' Mineralogy' charged to Lemuel Shaw by BoA 7–28 Mar 1849; Melville was in Boston 30 Jan–10 Apr.

402. The Picture of London for 1818 . . . Nineteenth Edition. London, Longman [etc.], 1818.
'Allan Melvill—London June 4th 1818.'; stamp: 'A. MELVILL.' (BeA)

403. Piles, Roger de. The Art of Painting, with the Lives and Characters of above 300 of the Most Eminent Painters . . . Translated from the French . . . To Which Is Added, An Essay towards an English School. The Third Edition: In Which Is Now First Inserted the Life of Sir Godfrey Kneller, by the Late B. Buckeridge . . . Who Wrote the Greatest Part of the English School. London, Payne, [1754?].
'Art of Painting' charged to Lemuel Shaw by BoA 21 Jun–18 Jul 1848; Melville was in Boston 12 Jun after 17[?] Jul.

404. Pilkington, Laetitia (Van Lewen). The Celebrated Mrs. Pilkington's Jests: or The Cabinet of Wit and Humour. To Which Is Now First Added, a Great Variety of Bon Mots, Witticisms, and Anecdotes of the Inimitable Dr. Swift . . . The Second Edition . . . London, Nicoll, 1764.
'A[llan] Melville'. (NYPL–GL)

Pindarus: see No. 147.

404.1. Planché, James Robinson. Lays and Legends of the Rhine. With Illustrative Views from Sketches Made on the Spot . . . London, Goulding & D'Almaine, 1832.
'Lays & Legends of the Rhine' (HCL–L) obtained at Coblenz, Germany, 10 Dec 1849.

404.2. Plutarchus. Morals . . .
Edition unidentified. Writing to his sister Helen Maria (Mrs. George Griggs) in 1854, Melville evidently suggested that she read one of the component essays; in her reply of 29 May 1854 (NYPL–GL) she wrote: 'Plutarch on the Cessation of the Oracles' [i.e., 'Why the Oracles Cease to Give Answers'] must be a work of deep interest, but, I'll take your word for it, having no ambition to peruse the same.' (In 1851 Melville had quoted a sentence from Philemon Holland's translation of the *Morals,* first published in 1603, in the 'Extracts' section of *Moby-Dick.*)

404a. Poe, Edgar Allan. The Works of the Late Edgar Allan Poe, with a Memoir by Rufus Wilmot Griswold and Notices of His Life and Genius by N. P. Willis and J. R. Lowell. New York, Blakeman and Mason, 1859. *#*
'H Melville 1860'; 'To My Wife New Year's Day—1861'. Annotated. Contains clipping about 'The Raven' and other works. (From a list of books

formerly belonging to Frances Melville Thomas, compiled by her daughter, Mrs. Metcalf; present location unknown)

404b. The Poetry of Love, from the Most Celebrated Authors, with Several Original Pieces. Selected by the Editor of "Poetry of the Affections." Philadelphia, Thomas Wardle, 1844.

'For Louise Iffland from Aunt Abbie'; 'Fanny from Herman N. Y. June 1868 [Mrs.Melville's hand]'; 'This book belonged to Fanny Melville, a niece of General Gansevoort. Miss Sarah J. Vanderwerker was a friend of Miss Melville and Miss Sarah presented this book to me Mrs Joseph Dodd on Dec 12$\underline{th}$ 1915 while I was calling at her house. The Gen died about 1840 at Gansevoort. N.Y.' (Fleming)

405. Pope, Alexander. The Poetical Works . . . with a Life, by Rev. Alexander Dyce . . . Boston, Little, Brown, 1856. 6 v.

Erased annotation in v. 3 (V. 1, 2 examined by Raymond Weaver; present location unknown. V. 3 is in HCL)

Pope, Alexander: see also No. 147.

406. Porter, Jane. Thaddeus of Warsaw . . . Flatbush, Riley, 1809. 4 v. in 2. 'Augusta Melville'. (BeA)

407. Potter, Israel Ralph. Life and Remarkable Adventures of Israel R. Potter, (a Native of Cranston, Rhode-Island.) Who Was a Soldier in the American Revolution . . . after Which He Was Taken Prisoner by the British, Conveyed to England, Where for 30 Years He Obtained a Livelihood . . . by Crying *"Old Chairs to Mend"* . . . [By Henry Trumbull.] Providence, Trumbull, 1824, or later edition.

The basis of Melville's *Israel Potter* (1855, following serialization). Ac-

quired at some time before the reference of 18 Dec 1849 in HCL–J to 'the Revolutionary narrative of the beggar' (cf. No.330a). The Northwestern-Newberry edition of *Israel Potter*, pp. 286–394, reproduces the first edition of the *Life*. 'Melville's own edition,' the editors conclude, 'remains uncertain'; the copy of the first edition now in HCL, though given by Mrs. Metcalf, was never Melville's own. It evidently came to her 'not through family inheritance but by purchase, whether by herself or by another person' (pp. 285, 284).

408. Praed, Winthrop Mackworth. The Poems . . . Revised and Complete Edition. With a Memoir by the Rev. Derwent Coleridge . . . New York, Widdleton, 1866. 2 v.

V. 1, 2; 'H. Melville Aug: 4 '69 N. Y.' V. 1: Augusta Melville Aug. 9th 1869. from her brother Herman.'; 'Abraham Lansing, from his Cousin Fanny [Melville] April 1876'. V. 2: 'Fanny Melville Aug. 9th 1869 from her brother Herman.' (NYPL–GL)

409. Protestant Episcopal Church in the U.S.A. Book of Common Prayer. The Book of Common Prayer, and Administration of the Sacraments; and Other Rights and Ceremonies of the Church, According to the Use of the Protestant Episcopal Church in the United States of America: Together with the Psalter, or Psalms of David. New York, Harper, 1845 or later edition.

25 May 1849: '2 Prayer, 18 mo. roan [$]1 20' (HCL–H, 10 Sep 1849).

410. ———. Book of Common Prayer. The Book of Common Prayer . . . New York, Appleton, 1849.

'Herman Melville Pittsfield Sept 25–'50'; in Mrs. Melville's hand: 'from his Aunt Mary Melville'. (HCL)

411. Pullan, Matilda Marian (Chesney). The Modern Housewife's Receipt Book: A Guide to All Matters Connected with Household Economy . . . With Receipts Tested by John Sayer . . . The Medical and Other Portions of the Work Revised by J. Baxter Langley . . . London, Aird and Hutton, 1854.

'Lizzie [Mrs. Melville] from Herman Boston. July. 1854'; 'Katharine G. Binnian.' (HCL)

412. Pulling, Frederick Sanders. Sir Joshua Reynolds . . . London, Sampson Low, 1880.
(HCL)

413. Putnam's Magazine. Original Papers on Literature, Science, Art, and National Interests. New York, 1853–70. Melville's term of subscription uncertain.

V. 5 (Jan–Jul 1855) is in HCL. Melville probably subscribed to the magazine, to which he contributed 1853–56; his *Piazza Tales* (1856) included some of his contributions set from 'corrected magazine sheets' (Melville to Dix and Edwards, 16 Feb 1856). A collection of other contributions to Nos. 240 and 413, assembled in a binder by Mrs. Melville, is in HCL; a clipping from *Putnam's* is preserved in No. 399.

Q

414. Quarles, Francis. Emblems, Divine & Moral; The School of the Heart; and Hieroglyphics of the Life of Man . . . A New Edition, with a Sketch of the Life and Times of the Author. London, Tegg, 1866.

'Miss Bessie Melville Xmas 1871, N. Y. [Melville's hand]'. (HCL)

Quarles, Francis: in 1923 BeA received from Mrs. Alfred Morewood another book that may once have belonged to Herman Melville, although this is not indicated in the record of accession ('F. Quarles. Enchiridion pub. Mosely'); the volume itself is no longer in the library.

415. Quincy, Josiah. Figures of the Past; from the Leaves of Old Journals . . . Boston, Roberts, 1883.

'Figures of Past' borrowed from NYSL 15 Nov–9 Dec 1890.

415a. Quinze historiettes illustrées pour les petits enfants. Mayence, Scholz, [185–].

[Mrs. Melville's hand:] 'From father [Lemuel Shaw] to Jenny [Jane Dempsey Melville] 1859'. (HCL)

416. The Quiver of Love. A Collection of Valentines, Ancient and Modern; with Illustrations in Colours from Drawings by Walter Crane and K. Greenaway. London, Ward, 1876.

'Bessie Melville from her Mother May 22^d 1885'. (NYPL–O)

R

417. Rabelais, François. [The Works . . . Translated from the French. With Explanatory Notes by Duchat, Ozell, and Others . . . London, Smith, Miller, 1844. 4 v. ?]

'Rabelais Vol 2.' borrowed from Evert Duyckinck in Jan or Feb 1848; 'vol 3' and 'vol 4' borrowed after mid-Feb 1848 (NYPL–BL; Davis, *Melville's Mardi*, pp. 63–64). The 1844 edition is not listed in NYPL–L, which gives among applicable entries only an 1838 Edinburgh edition of *The Romance of Gargantua and Pantagruel* in 1 v. The charge for 'Vol 2.' is the first Melville entry in NYPL–BL.

417a. Rambler, The. Issued by Samuel Johnson. Nos. 1–208, 20 Mar 1749/50–14 Mar 1751–52.

Visiting Evert Duyckinck in 1860, Melville applauded 'the plain speaking of Johnson in the *Rambler*' (*Log* 2: 613, quoting Duyckinck's diary for 26 and 31 Jan 1860).

418. Reach, Angus Bethune. London on the Thames; or, Life above and below Bridge . . . London, Published at the Office of the Puppet-Show 334 Strand, [184–?].

Associated with No. 474. (HCL)

419. Reade, Charles. It Is Never Too Late to Mend. A Matter of Fact Romance . . . Boston, Ticknor and Fields, 1856. 2 v.

'Never too late to mend 1.2' charged to Lemuel Shaw by BoA 9–30 May 1857; Melville was in Boston after 20 May–after 21 Jun.

420. The Recreation. A Gift Book for Young Readers. The Sixth of the Series. Edinburgh, Menzies, 1846.

12 Dec 1846: '1 Recreation [$]1 50' (HCL–WP, 1 Jan 1847). This volume contains considerable material on whaling.

Retzsch, Moritz: see Nos. 440 and 441.

421. Reynard the Fox. Translated by the Late Thomas Roscoe. London, Warne, [18–].

(HCL)

422. Reynolds, Jeremiah N. Voyage of the United States Frigate Potomac, under the Command of Commodore John Downes, during the Circumnavigation of the Globe, in the Years 1831, 1832, 1833, and 1834 . . . New York, Harper, 1835.

7 May 1847: '1 Potomac [$]2 40' (HCL–H, 1 Aug 1847).

423. Reynolds, Sir Joshua. The Literary Works . . . To Which Is Prefixed a Memoir of the Author; with Remarks on His Professional Character, Illustrative of His Principles and Practice. By Henry William Beechy . . . New and Improved Edition . . . London, Bohn, 1855. 2 v.

V. 1, 2: 'H. Melville'. V. 1: 'Dec. 1870 N. Y.' Annotated. (NYPL–O)

424. Richter, Johann Paul Friedrich, Flower, Fruit and Thorn Pieces: or, The Married Life, Death, and Wedding of the Advocate of the Poor, Firmian Stanislaus Sibenkäs . . . Translated from the German by Edward Henry Noel . . . London, Smith, 1845. 2 v.

'Jean Paul's Flower Pieces' borrowed from Evert Duyckinck in 1850 (NYPL–BL: 10th listing for 1850).

425. ———. Titan: A Romance . . . Translated by Charles T. Brooks . . . Boston, Ticknor and Fields, 1862, 1863, *or,* 1864. 2 v.

Copy, edition unspecified, presented to Melville in Apr 1864 by Brig. Gen. Robert O. Tyler; cf. Melville's letter to Lt. Col. Henry Sanford Gansevoort, 10 May 1864: 'And Gen Tyler . . . say that I agree with him about "Titan." The worst thing that I can say about it is, that it is a little better than "Mardi" The Terence [No. 509] I highly value; indeed both works, as memorials of the hospitalities of an accomplished General. . . .'

Richter, Johann Paul Freidrich: see also No. 121.

Ringbolt, Captain [pseud.]: see Codman, John (No. 149).

426. Roberts, Morley. In Low Relief. A Bohemian Transcript. New York, Appleton, [1890?].

'In Low Relief' borrowed from NYSL 19–30 Jan 1891.

427. Robertson, Frederick William. Life, Letters, Lectures, and Addresses . . . New York, Harper, 1870; *or*, Sermons . . . New York, Harper, 1870.
17 Jun 1872: '1 Robertson [$]1 05' (HCL-H, 17 Jun 1872); '1 Exodus [No. 396]: 1 Robertson $3 15' (HCL-H, 12 Feb 1875). Both the *Life* and the *Sermons* were listed at $1.50.

428. Robinson, Henry Crabb. Diary, Reminiscences, and Correspondence . . . Selected and Edited by Thomas Sadler . . . Boston, Fields, Osgood, 1869. 2 v.
V. 1, 2: 'H. Melville'. V. 1: 'July, '70 N. Y.' Annotated. (HCL)

428.1. Rochon, Alexis Marie de. An Abridgement of a Voyage to Madagascar . . . London, Westley, 1821.
J. W. Francis, in a letter of 3 Nov 1852 to Melville (NYPL-GL), thanks him 'most fully, for the curious volume Rochon's Voyage to Madagascar.'

428a. Roget, Peter Mark. Thesaurus of English Words and Phrases . . . London, Longmans, Green, 1883.
(HCL)

428b. Rollin, Charles. The Ancient History of the Egyptians, Carthaginians, Assyrians, Babylonians, Medes, and Persians, Macedonians, and Grecians. Translated from the French. Possibly New York, Long, 1828, 4 v.
Helen Maria Melvill, in a letter of 23 May 1829 to Maria Gansevoort Melvill (NYPL-GL), writes: 'Mrs Pointdexter has requested me to get Rollins Ancient History but Papa does not wish to get it (being a very expensive book[)] without your consent.'

429. Rousseau, Jean Jacques. Confessions . . . 2[?] v.

Edition unidentified. The 'much desired copy' of 'Rousseau [*sic*] Confessions' bought in London for 11 shillings (HCL-J, 15 Dec 1849; HCL-L); note on Rousseau near end of HCL-J cites '2^d Vol'.

430. Ruskin, John. Modern Painters . . . London, Smith, Elder, 1846-60. 5 v.
'Modern Painters 2' charged to Lemuel Shaw by BoA 21 Jun-18 Jul 1848; Melville was in Boston 12 Jul-after 17[?] Jul.

431. ———. Modern Painters . . . First American from the Third London Edition. Revised by the Author. New York, Wiley, 1860-62. 5 v.
V. 1: 'H. Melville from A[llan?] Melville'; bookseller's mark: '1865'. V. 2 annotated; v. 5 marked. (NYPL-O)

432. Russell, William Clark. Horatio Nelson and the Naval Supremacy of England . . . With the Collaboration of William H. Jaques . . . New York, Putnam, 1890.
'Eleanor M. Thomas [Mrs. Metcalf] from Grandma [Mrs. Melville] Feb 1895'. (Formerly in the collection of Mrs. Henry K. Metcalf; present location unknown)

433. ———. An Ocean Tragedy . . . London, Chatto and Windus, 1890. 3 v.
V. 1, in Mrs. Melville's hand: 'Herman Melville from the Author'. A proof-copy of the dedication to Melville (HCL) bears a note of 9 Jan 1890 stating that this edition would be published in Mar 1890. (HCL)

S

434. Sa'di. The Gûlistân, or Rose-Garden; by Musle-Huddeen Shaik Sâdy, of Sheeraz. Translated from the Original,

by Francis Gladwin, Esq. A New Edition. London, Kingsbury, Parbury, and Allen, 1822.
'W. Bulkeley Glasse[?]'; 'H. Melville Sep 29, 1868 N. Y.'; bookplate: '. . . ALEX[R] ORR VIETOR'. Annotated. (YUL)

434a. Sailing Directions for the Eastern Portion of the Mediterranean Sea. Embracing the Adriatic or Gulf of Venice, the Albanian and Grecian Coasts, the Grecian Archipelago, and the Coasts of Syria and Egypt, the Black Sea, and the Seas of Marmora and Azov . . . London, Imray, 1852 [or later edition].
27 Dec 1856: 'Saw in "Sailing Directions" brief account of Jaffa . . .' (HCL–J). Howard C. Horsford, who has identified Melville's allusion, suggests also his use of other volumes of *Sailing Directions* as well as of guidebooks for tourists. Their descriptions of local topographic features observable from the sea may thus account for 'just the brief kind of familiarity' with coastal features that is found in certain of his writings (letters of 16 Feb, 4 Apr 1951).

Sallustius Crispus, Caius: see No. 147.

435. Salt, Henry Stephens. The Life of James Thomson ("B. V.") with a Selection from His Letters and a Study of His Writings . . . London, Reeves and Turner, 1889.
'To Herman Melville from H. S. Salt'; according to Mrs. Melville's memoranda, 'Mr Salt sent his "Life of James Thomson" Feb. 2[d] 1890' (see Sealts, *The Early Lives of Melville*, p. 172). Mounted inside the front cover is an envelope containing clippings about Thomson, including an article by James Billson from the Liverpool *Daily Post* of 10 Feb 1885. Marked. (HCL)

435a. ———. The Life of James Thomson ("B. V.") . . . London, Reeves and Turner, 1889.
Arthur Stedman, in a letter to Salt of 4 May 1892 (NL), stated: 'Mrs. Melville has given me the copy of the life of James Thomson which her husband purchased before you sent him one. He paid $3.75 for it at a time when he was a very poor man.' Present location unknown.

Salt, Henry Stephens: see also No. 455.

436. Saltus, Edgar Evertson. Balzac . . . Boston, Houghton, Mifflin, 1884.
'Herman from Lizzie [Mrs. Melville] Aug 1—1885—'. Marked. (NYPL–O)

436.1. Samuels, Samuel. From the Forecastle to the Cabin. New York, Harper, 1887.
'For M[r]. Herman Melville from his friends H & B [Harper & Brothers?]. May 27, 1887.' Marked. (BCHS)

Sanderson, R. B.: see No. 223a.

436a. Sandys, George. A Relation of a Journey Begun An. Dom.: 1610 . . . [5th ed.] London, Sweeting, 1652.
Either owned or borrowed by Melville. His reference in HCL–J, 26[?] Jan 1857, to 'page 124 of Saunders' was first identified by Robert S. Forsythe, review of Weaver, ed., *Journal* . . . p. 93; see *Journal*, 1856–57, ed. Horsford, pp. 139–140, n. 7.

437. Schiller, Johann Christoph Friedrich von. Schiller's Sämtliche Werke . . . Wien, Gerold, 1819–20. 18 v.
'Schiller 6' charged to Lemuel Shaw by BoA 16 Dec 1854–15 Jan 1855; Melville was in Boston 28 Nov–[?]. During Melville's later visits to Boston of 21 Nov–8 Dec 1857 and 10 and 19 Feb 1858 Shaw was charged with 'Schiller's Works 1.3', 19 Oct 1857–20

Feb 1858, and 'Schiller 1–3', 30 Oct–5 Dec 1857; one of these charges must refer to No. 437, in German, and the other to No. 438, in English. It seems likely that No. 437 was withdrawn on 19 Oct and that No. 438 was subsequently obtained as an aid in translation.

438. ———. Works . . . London, Bohn, 1847–51. 4 v.

See No. 437 concerning works of Schiller charged to Lemuel Shaw by BoA in 1857–58.

438a. ———. The Ghost-seer! From the German of Schiller. London, Colburn and Bentley, 1831 (divided between Nos. 9 and 10 of their Standard Novels series)? *or,* London, Bentley, 1849. 2 v.?

Either owned or borrowed, by Melville or by a member of his family. That part of the story printed in No. 9 of the Standard Novels series was bound so as to follow Mary Shelley's revised *Frankenstein* (see Check-List, No. 467); Jay Leyda notes that the story appeared also in the same series of the Romanticist, and Novelist Library (1840, ed. by William Hazlitt) that included Jeremiah N. Reynolds's *Mocha Dick; or, The White Whale of the Pacific* (letter of 9 Apr 1951). On 4 Jan 1851, Melville's sister Augusta, in a letter to Mary Blatchford (NYPL–GL), reported that in 'reading aloud' the Melvilles had 'finished Schiller's "Ghost Seer" '; Melville himself later 'remembered that much of the fearful interest of Schiller's Ghost-Seer hangs upon being followed in Venice by an Armeain [i.e., Armenian]' (HCL-J, 15 Dec 1856).

439. ———. The Poems and Ballads . . . Translated by Sir Edward Bulwer Lytton, Bart. With a Brief Sketch of the Author's Life . . . Leipzig, Tauchnitz, 1844.

'H. Melville N. Y. 1849.'; 'C[ape] Horn 1860'. Annotated. (NYPL–O)

440. ———. Eight Sketches to Schiller's Fridolin, or The Message to the Forge. By Moritz Retzsch. With a Few Explanations, by C. A. Boettiger. Stuttgart, Cotta, 1857.

'Herman Melville Esqr. with the regards of E[llen] M[arett] Gifford.' Annotated. (BeA)

441. ———. Schiller's Pegasus in the Yoke, with Explanations of the Illustrations. By Moritz Retzsch. Stuttgart, Cotta, 1857.

'Herman Melville Esqr. with the kind regards of E[llen M[arett] Gifford'; [in Melville's hand:] 'March 1870. N. Y.' (BeA)

442. Schindler, Anton Felix. The Life of Beethoven, Including His Correspondence with His Friends, Numerous Characteristic Traits, and Remarks on His Musical Works. Edited by Ignace Moscheles . . . London, Colburn, 1841. 2 v.

'Life of Bethoven [*sic*] 1.2' charged to Lemuel Shaw by BoA 20 Feb–6 Mar 1858; Melville was in Boston 19–23 Feb.

443. Schopenhauer, Arthur. Counsels and Maxims; Being the Second Part of . . . Aphorismen zur Lebensweisheit . . . Translated by T. Bailey Saunders, M.A. London, Sonnenschein, 1890.

'Counsels & Maxims' borrowed from NYSL 5–12 Feb 1891.

444. ———. Counsels and Maxims; Being the Second Part of . . . Aphorismen zur Lebensweisheit . . . Translated by T. Bailey Saunders, M.A. London, Sonnenschein, 1890.

Probably acquired after 12 Feb 1891, when No. 443 was returned to NYSL. Annotated. (HCL)

445. ———. Religion: A Dialogue, and Other Essays . . . Selected and Translated by T. B. Saunders, M.A. 2nd ed. London, Sonnenschein, 1891.
Annotated. (HCL)

446. ———. Studies in Pessimism, a Series of Essays . . . Selected and Translated by T. Bailey Saunders, M.A. Second Edition. London, Sonnenschein, 1891.
Marked. (HCL)

447. ———. The Wisdom of Life; Being the First Part of . . . Aphorismen zur Lebensweisheit . . . Translated with a Preface by T. Bailey Saunders, M.A. Second Edition. London, Sonnenschein, 1891.
Marked. (HCL)

448. ———. The World as Will and Idea . . . Translated from the German by R. B. Haldane, M.A., and J. Kemp, M.A. . . . Second Edition. London, Trübner, 1888. 3 v.
Marked. (HCL)

449. Scogan, John. Scoggin's Jests; Full of Witty Mirth, and Pleasant Shifts . . . London, Thackeray and Deacon, 1796.
'Scoggins' Jests' borrowed from Evert Duyckinck in 1850 (NYPL–BL: 24th listing for 1850).

450. Scoresby, William. An Account of the Arctic Regions, with a History and Description of the Northern Whale Fishery . . . Edinburgh, Constable, 1820. 2 v.
'Scoresbys Arctic Regions 1.2' borrowed from NYSL 29 Apr 1850–14 Jun 1851. Copies of Nos. 450 and 451 were also charged to Lemuel Shaw by BoA 30 Dec 1850–16 Jan 1851, although Melville is not known to have visited Boston at that time.

451. ———. Journal of a Voyage to the Northern Whale Fishery; Including Re-searches and Discoveries on the Eastern Coast of West Greenland . . . in . . . 1822 . . . Edinburgh, Constable, 1823.
'[Scoresbys] N Whale Fishery' borrowed from NYSL 29 Apr 1850–14 Jun 1851. On Lemuel Shaw's withdrawal of this title from BoA see No. 450.

451.1. Scott, Leader. The Renaissance of Art in Italy: An Illustrated History. New York, Scribner and Welford, 1883.
'Maria G. Morewood. This book is selected from her Uncle Herman's Library by her aunt E[lizabeth]. S[haw]. M[elville].' (BeA)

451a. Scott, Sir Walter, Bart. The Lay of the Last Minstrel . . . Edinburgh, Black, 1855.
'Augusta Melville from her friend Howard Townsend October 1857'. (BeA)

452. ———. Peveril of the Peak . . . Boston, Parker, 1823; *or,* Edinburgh, Black, 1887.
'Peveril of the Peak' borrowed from NYSL 13–23 Jun 1890.

453. ———. Quentin Durward; a Romance . . . Boston, Parker, 1823.
'Quentin Durward' borrowed from NYSL 13–23 Jun 1890.

454. ———. Tales of a Grand-Father, First Series, Being Stories Taken from Scottish History. Exeter, N. H., Williams, 1833. 8 v.
V. 1: 'Gansevoort Melville Aug 1836'; 'Augusta Melville's *Book* . . .'; 'Thomas Melville'. (Names also appear in v. 2–8.) (BeA)

Scott, Sir Walter, Bart.: see also No. 359.

455. The Scottish Art Review. Glasgow, 1888–89. Melville's holding: v. 2, no. [?]

(Jun–Dec 1889), only.

J. W. Barrs, in a letter of 13 Jan 1890 (HCL), advised Melville that he had forwarded a copy of the issue containing H. S. Salt's article on Melville, which he discussed at some length.

456. Sedgwick, Elizabeth Buckminster (Dwight), 'Mrs Charles Sedgwick.' A Talk with My Pupils . . . New Edition. New York, Hopper, 1863.

'To Eleanor [Thomas (Mrs. Metcalf)] and Frances [Thomas (Mrs. Osborne)] from Grandma [Mrs. Melville] 1896'. (Formerly in the collection of Mrs. Henry K. Metcalf; present location unknown)

456a. 'Self Teacher—1834.' #
Described by the late R. S. Forsythe (cf. No. 86a) as 'Self-Teacher—1834 Flyleaf. "Herman G. Melville from his aff uncle Peter Gansevoort Albany Nov. 1837." Also "H .G. M." & "Allan Melville [Jr.]'—'. This is the only known attribution to Melville of a middle name or initial. Cf. No. 497. Present location unknown.

457. Seneca, Lucius Annaeus. The Workes . . . Both Morall and Naturall . . . Translated by Tho. Lodge. [The Life of L. A. Seneca Described by J. Lipsius.] London, Stansby, 1614.

Melville's signature on title page. Annotated. Formerly in the collection of Carl Haverlin, New York City, whose library in California was destroyed by fire on 4 Jan 1954. Described by Mr. Haverlin in letters of 31 Oct and 21 Nov 1947, 5 Sep 1962.

458. ———. Seneca's Morals by Way of Abstract. To Which Is Added, a Discourse under the Title of An After-Thought. By Sir Roger L'Estrange . . . Fifteenth Edition. London, Strahan [etc.], 1746.

'Thomas Melville from Herman Melville My Dear Tom, This is a round-of-beef where all hands may come & cut again. Jan: 26th 1854. Pittsfield. Mass:'. Marked. (NYPL–GL)

459. Sévigné, Marie (de Rabutin-Chantal), Marquise de. The Letters of Madame de Sévigné to Her Daughter and Friends. Edited by Mrs. Hale . . . Boston, Roberts, 1869.

'Miss Fanny Melville, from her uncle. A[mos] Nourse'. (NYPL–O)

459.1. Sewell, Elizabeth Missing. The Earl's Daughter. New York, Appleton, 1850.

Augusta Melville, in a letter of 29 Aug 1850 to Mary Blatchford (NYPL–GL), mentions reading ' "The Earl's Daughter" ' . . . from the graceful pen of Miss Sewell, . . . fully imbued with her deep religious feeling & gentle refinement.'

459a. Shakers. A Summary View of the Millennial Church, or United Society of Believers, Commonly Called Shakers. Comprising the Rise, Progress and Practical Order of the Society . . . Second Edition, Revised . . . Albany, Van Benthysen, 1848.

'H. Melville Shaker Village (Hancock, Mass:) July 21st 1850. Bought of Nathan Holland.' Annotated. (UVL–S)

460. Shakespeare, William. The Dramatic Works of William Shakespeare; with a Life of the Poet, and Notes, Original and Selected . . . Boston, Hilliard, Gray, 1837. 7 v. Rebacked.

Evidently the newly purchased 'edition in glorious great type' mentioned in Melville's letter from Boston, 24 Feb 1849, to Evert Duyckinck. Annotated. (HCL)

460a. ———.

Title and edition unidentified. 18 Jan 1848: '1 Shakespear clf' and '1 Montagne [*sic*]—[$]9 25' (HCL-W, 1 Jul 1848). Davis, *Melville's* Mardi, p. 63, n. 6, suggests that the charge may be for No. 464.

461. ———. A Book of Reference to Remarkable Passages in Shakespeare. With a Separate Index to Each Play. By Susanna Beever . . . London, Bull, Simmons, 1870.
'Miss Bessie Melville. May 22, 1877. New York'. (NYPL–O)

462. ———. Pearls of Shakespeare: A Collection of the Most Brilliant Passages Found in His Plays. Illustrated by Kenny Meadows. London, Blackwood, [1873].
'Miss Fanny Melville Xmas, 1873 N. Y. [Melville's hand]'. (HCL)

462a. ———. [Shakespeare]. [Plays.] *#* Vincent Starrett reports that about 1910, in the Chicago bookshop of Tom Knight, he examined 'an odd volume of an Early American set, a 16mo, containing perhaps three plays' of Shakespeare, with Melville's 'signature (and an address)' on the flyleaf (letters of 1 Feb, 14 Feb 1951).

463. ———. '2 Plays . . .'
Titles and editions unidentified. A 'pocket Shakespeare' bought in London (HCL–J, 17 Dec 1849); listed in HCL–L as '2 Plays of Shakspeare', 2 pence.

464. ———. The Poetical Works . . . With the Life of the Author. Cooke's Edition . . . London, Cooke, [17–]. The Poetical Works of William Collins. With the Life of the Author. Cooke's Edition . . . London, Cooke, [17–). 2 v. in 1.
'Fanny Melville from her brother Herman Pittsfield May 19. 1862' (cf. Nos. 470, 515); possibly identical with No. 460a. Annotated. (NYPL–GL)

465. ———. Shakespeare's Sonnets. Boston, Ticknor and Fields, 1865.
'H Melville Jan 20 '71. N. Y.'; 'Katharine G. Binnian.' Marked. (HCL)

Shakespeare, William: see also Nos. 71, 209.

466. Shelley, Jane Gibson, Lady, ed. Shelley Memorials: From Authentic Sources . . . To Which Is Added, an Essay on Christianity, by Percy Bysshe Shelley: Now First Printed. Boston, Ticknor and Fields, 1859.
'H. Melville April 22, 1868. N. Y.' Marked. (HCL)

467. Shelley, Mary Wollstonecraft (Godwin). Frankenstein: or, The Modern Prometheus. By the Author of "The Last Man" . . . Revised, Corrected, and Illustrated with a New Introduction, by the Author. London, Bentley, 1849.
'Frankenstein [(1 vol)]' obtained from Richard Bentley in London, 1849 (HCL–L), probably on 19 Dec (for date, see No. 54). See also No. 438a.

468. Shelley, Percy Bysshe. Essays, Letters from Abroad, Translations and Fragments . . . Edited by Mrs. Shelley . . . New Edition. London, Moxon, 1852. 2 v.
V. 1: 'H. Melville 1873 N. Y.' Marked. (HCL)

469. ———. The Poetical Works . . . Edited by Mrs. Shelley. With a Memoir by James Russell Lowell . . . Boston, Little Brown, 1857. 2 v. #
'H Melville Ap. 9th 1861 Pittsfield'. Annotated. (Examined by Raymond Weaver; present location unknown)

Shelley, Percy Bysshe: see also Nos. 466, 520.

470. Shenstone, William. The Poetical Works . . . With the Life of the Author,

and a Description of the Leasowes. Cooke's Edition . . . London, Cooke, [17–].
'Fanny Melville from her brother Herman Pittsfield May 19. 1862' (cf. Nos. 464 and 515). (NYPL–GL)

471. Sheridan, Richard Brinsley. The Plays . . . With an Introduction by Henry Morley . . . Eighth Edition. London, Routledge, 1887.
Annotated. (NYPL–O)

472. Sherlock, Thomas. A Letter from the Lord Bishop of London, to the Clergy and People of London and Westminster; on Occasion of the Late Earthquakes. London; printed: Boston, Draper, 1750.
'Allan Melvill [great-grandfather of Herman Melville?] June 26 1750'. (NYPL–F)

Sherman, William Tecumseh: see No. 384a.

Shirley, James: see No. 358.

473. Smith, Abigail (Adams). Journal and Correspondence of Miss Adams, Daughter of John Adams, Second President of the United States. Written in France and England, in 1785. Edited by Her Daughter. New York, Wiley and Putnam, 1841–42. 2 v.
'Miss Adam's [sic] Journal (1–2)' borrowed from NYSL 21–27 Mar 1891.

474. Smith, Albert Richard. The Natural History of the Ballet-Girl . . . Illustrated by A. Henning. London, Bogue, 1847.
'Lizzie [Mrs. Melville] from Herman June 13th 1886 N. Y. [Melville's hand]'; added by Mrs. Melville: '(set of four' [with Nos. 120, 418, 475])'. (HCL)

475. ——. The Natural History of the Gent. . . . London, Bogue, 1847.
Associated with No. 474. (HCL)

476. Smith, Elizabeth Elton. The Three Eras of Woman's Life . . . New York, Harper, 1836. 2 v. in 1.
'Augusta Melville'. (NYPL–GL)

477. Smith, Elizabeth Thomasina (Meade). Heart of Gold . . . Authorized Edition. New York, United States Book Company, [c1890].
'Heart of Gold' borrowed from NYSL 8–9 Apr 1891.

478. Smith, Joseph Edward Adams. Taghconic; or Letters and Legends about Our Summer Home. By Godfrey Greylock [pseud.]. Boston, Redding, 1852.
Described briefly in Melville's letter of 25 Oct 1852 to Nathaniel Hawthorne. Whether Melville owned or borrowed this edition (cf. No. 479) is not known. On 6 Oct his mother had sent a copy to Peter Gansevoort with an accompanying letter (NYPL–GL) stating that Melville had declined requests to contribute. Another copy, paperbound, is in NL, inscribed 'Augusta Melville, with the Love of her Brother, John C. Hoadley, Pittsfield, April 23d 1855—'.

479. ———. Taghconic; the Romance and Beauty of the Hills. By Godfrey Greylock [pseud.]. Boston, Lee and Shepard, 1879.
'Kindly presented by Godfrey Greylock 1879'. Annotated by Mrs. Melville.* (HCL)

Smith, Sydney: see No. 359.

*In HCL, though not strictly within the scope of this listing, is a copy of Smith's *The Poet among the Hills. Oliver Wendell Holmes in Berkshire* (Pittsfield, Mass., 1895), presented to Mrs. Melville by the author.

480. Smollett, Tobias George. The Adventures of Roderick Random . . . The Tenth Edition. London, Gardner [etc.], 1778. 2 v.; *or*, London Cochne, 1831.
'Roderick Random.' borrowed from Evert Duyckinck in 1850 (NYPL–BL: 9th listing for 1850).

Solomons, J. H.: see No. 223a.

Sophocles: see No. 147.

481. Southey, Robert. The Life of Nelson . . . New York, Harper, 1855.
'This book is kept for reference from "Billy Budd"—(unfinished) [Mrs. Melville's hand]'. Annotated. (HCL)

482. ———. Oliver Newman: A New-England Tale (Unfinished): With Other Poetical Remains . . . London, Longman [etc.], 1845 #
'Uncut . . . Autograph of Herman Melville on a fly-leaf' (*Catalogue of the Library of . . . Thomas Jefferson McKee*, Part VI, sold 12 and 13 May 1902, New York, John Anderson Jr, Lot 5488). (Newark Galleries, Inc., Catalogue 132, 19 Feb 1931, Lot 178)

Southey, Robert: see also No. 556.

483. Spenser, Edmund. The Poetical Works . . . The Text Carefully Revised, and Illustrated with Notes, Original and Selected, by Francis J. Child . . . Boston, Little, Brown, 1855. 5 v.
V. 1: 'H Melville April 9th 1861 Pittsfield'; 'Helen M[elville] Griggs Pittsfield May 15, 1862'. Marked (BeA)

484. Springer, John S. Forest Life and Forest Trees: Comprising Winter Camp-Life among the Loggers, and Wild-Wood Adventure. With Descriptions of Lumbering Operations on the Various Rivers of Maine and New Brunswick . . . New York, Harper, 1851.
9 Feb 1852: '1 Forest Life, m[uslin] [$.]56' (HCL–H, 21 Mar 1853). (Another *Forest Life*, by Caroline Kirkland, 1842, was not published by Harper.)

485. Squier, Ephraim George. Waikna; or, Adventures on the Mosquito Shore. By Samuel A. Bard [pseud.]. With Sixty Illustrations. New York, Harper, 1855.
28 Aug 1855: '1 Waikna: 1 Panama [No. 528] [$]1 30' (HCL–H, 6 Mar 1856).

486. Staël-Holstein, Anne Louise Germaine (Necker), Baronne de. Corinne; or, Italy . . . Translated by Isabel Hill; with Metrical Versions of the Odes by L. E. Landon; and a Memoir of the Authoress. London, Bentley, 1833 or later edition.
'Corinne [(1 vol)]' obtained in London from Richard Bentley, 1849 (HCL–L), probably on 19 Dec (for date, see No. 54). Melville had heard his fellow-travelers discussing the book while en route to Europe (HCL–J, 27 Oct 1849).

487. ———. Germany . . . With Notes and Appendices, by O. W. Wight . . . New York, Derby and Jackson, 1859. 2 v.
V. 1: 'H. Melville March 4th 1862 N. Y.' V. 2: 'H. Melville Ap 1862 N. Y.' Annotated (HCL)

488. Stanley, Arthur Penrhyn. Sinai and Palestine in Connection with Their History . . . New Edition, with Maps and Plans. New York, Widdleton, 1863.
'H Melville'; 'H Melville Ap. 4.'70 N. Y.' Annotated. (NYPL–O)

488a. Stedman, Edmund Clarence. Poets of America. Boston and New York, Houghton, Mifflin, 1885.

Stedman's letter to Melville, 1 Feb 1888 (HCL): 'as you said so much of Whitman, I will run the risk of showing you my chapter on him.' Leyda, *Log* 2: 810, takes the 'chapter' to be a manuscript; Davis and Gilman, p. 288, n. 9, suggest *Poets of America,* noting Melville's reference to 'your own book' in his letter of 20 Oct 1888 accompanying books being returned to Stedman.

Stephen, Sir James: see No. 359.

489. Stephens, Frederic George. A Memoir of George Cruikshank . . . and an Essay on the Genius of George Cruikshank by William Makepeace Thackeray. New York, Scribner and Welford, 1891.

Marked. (HCL)

490. Sterne, Laurence. The Life and Opinions of Tristram Shandy, Gent. . . .

'Last night' Melville, in London, read 'a few chapters in Tristram Shandy, which I have never yet read' (HCL-J, 16 Dec 1849). It is not known whether Melville owned this book (cf. No. 76) or borrowed it; it is not listed in HCL-L.

490a. Stevens, John Hathaway. The Duty of Union in a Just War: A Discourse, Delivered in Stoneham, (Massachusetts,) April 8, 1813, Being the Day of the State Fast . . . Albany, Buel, 1814.

'For Allen [*sic*] Melville Esqre'. (HCL)

490b. Stoddard, Charles Warren. Poems. San Francisco, Roman, 1867.

'I have read with much pleasure the printed Verses you sent me, and,

among others, was quite struck with the little effusion entitled "Cherries & Grapes" ' (Melville to Stoddard, 20 Jan 1867).

491. Stoddard, Richard Henry. The Lion's Cub; with Other Verse . . . New York, Scribner, 1890.

'Lions Cub' borrowed from NYSL 19–21 Jan 1891.

491a. Stone, William Leete (1792–1844). Life of Joseph Brant—Thayendenegea: Including the Border Wars of the American Revolution . . . [New York, Dearborn, 1838. 2 v.?]

Either owned or borrowed by Melville: cf. his letter to Evert Duyckinck of 7 Nov 1851: his newborn son will probably be named Stanwix—'for some account of which, Vide *Stone's Life of Brandt* [*sic*]'. A presentation copy of the edition suggested above, from the author to Peter Gansevoort, is in NYPL–GL.

491b. Stone, William Leete (1835–1908). Memoir of the Centennial Celebration of Burgoyne's Surrender, Held at Schuylerville, N. Y., under the Auspices of the Saratoga Monument Association, on the 17th of October, 1877. Prepared by William L. Stone, Secretary of the Association. Albany, Munsell, 1878.

Her gift 'last Eveg' of 'the Oriskany [No. 394] and Schuylerville Centennial Volumes' to Melville is mentioned by his cousin Catherine Gansevoort Lansing in a letter of 24 Mar 1878 to her husband, Abraham Lansing (NYPL–GL).

492. Stories from Scripture, on an Improved Plan. Old Testament. Boston, Munroe and Francis, 1827.

'Elizabeth K[napp] Shaw [later Mrs. Melville] Presented by her Mother

1830'. (Formerly in the collection of Mrs. Walter B. Binnian; present location unknown

Surr, Thomas Skinner: see No. 234a.

T

Talfourd, Sir Thomas Noon: see Nos. 317, 359.

493. The Tatler; or, Lucubrations of Isaac Bickerstaff, Esq. [pseud.] . . . London, Tonson [etc.], 1764. 4 v. Melville's holding: v. 1–3 only. 'Melville'. (HCL)

494. The Tatler; a Daily Journal of Literature and the Stage. London, Onwhyn, 1830–32. 4 v.
'Tatler [4 v.], Observer [No. 126], Looker On [No. 126] 10 vols' borrowed from Evert Duyckinck in Jan 1860, for Melville's 'winter reading at Pittsfield' (NYPL–BL; Duyckinck's diary, NYPL–D, 26–31 Jan 1860; NYPL–L lists 'Tatler, A Daily Journal, 4 vols. London, 1830–32.'). Cf. No. 126.

494a. Tayler, Charles Benjamin. The Records of a Good Man's Life. New York, W. Van Norden, 1832, or later edition.
S. Newman, in a note of 5 Feb 1849 to Augusta Melville (NYPL–GL), reports the return (by 'Robert') of Augusta's copy of 'the Record of a Good Man's Life'.

495. Taylor, Bayard. Views A-Foot; or, Europe Seen with Knapsack and Staff . . . New York, Wiley and Putnam, 1846. 2 v. in 1.
12 Dec 1846: '1 Views Afoot 2 parts [$]1—' (HCL–WP, 1 Jan 1847).

495.1. Taylor, Sir Henry. Notes from

Life in Seven Essays . . . Boston, Ticknor, Reed, and Fields, 1853.
'18 cts. H Melville New York Oct 27th 1861'; bookplate of John F. Dillon. Annotated. (UVL–B)

495a. Taylor, Jeremy. The Rule and Exercise of Holy Dying . . . Boston, Little, Brown, [1864?]. ✣
'H. Melville Jan. 16. 1869. N. Y.' Marked. An editorial note is dated Boston, 10 Nov 1864. (Once examined by Charles J. Olson—letter of 2 Jun 1950; present location unknown)

496. Taylor, John (1694–1761). The Scripture Doctrine of Original Sin Proposed to Free and Candid Examination . . . London [?], 1701 [sic; i.e., 1740 or later edition—possibly 1741]. ✣
Described as 'Herman Melville's copy with a presentation inscription in his hand on flyleaf, dated 1851, and an interesting note in his hand, in pencil, on titlepage' (Alfred F. Goldsmith, Catalogue 63, 1931, Lot 125). T. Walter Herbert, 'Calvinism and Cosmic Evil in *Moby-Dick*,' p. 1613, n. 4, finds it 'almost certain' that Melville's copy 'contained the supplement to the first edition' of 1740 and must therefore have been one of five later editions: 1741, 1746, 1750, 1767, or 1845. In a letter of 13 Nov 1967, noting that the edition of 1741 is described in the British Museum *Catalogue* as incorrectly dated '1761', he conjectures that the compiler of the Goldsmith catalogue made the further error of copying '1701' for '1761'.

497. Taylor, John Orville. The District School . . .
Edition unidentified. In his letter to Peter Gansevoort, 31 Dec 1837, Melville acknowledges his uncle's gift of several books, naming 'John O Taylors "District School"' and

commenting upon it at some length. Cf. No. 456a.

Taylor, Tom: see No. 262.

498. Tea Leaves: Being a Collection of Letters and Documents Relating to the Shipment of Tea to the American Colonies in the Year 1773, by the East India Tea Company. Now First Printed from the Original Manuscript. With an Introduction, Notes, and Biographical Notices of the Boston Tea Party, by Francis S[amuel] Drake. Boston, Crane, 1884.
'Herman Melville from his wife Nov. 1886'. One correction in Mrs. Melville's hand. Marked (?). (HCL)

499. Tegg, William. Wills of Their Own, Curious, Eccentric, and Benevolent, Collated and Arranged by William Tegg . . . London, Tegg, 1876.
'Fanny Melville March 2. '76. N. Y. [Melville's hand]'. (HCL)

500. Tegnér, Esais. Frithiof's Saga, or The Legend of Frithiof. By Esais Tegnér. Translated from the Swedish. London, Baily, 1835; *or,* Frithiof, a Norwegian Story, from the Swedish of Esais Tegnér. By R. G. Latham . . . London, Hookham, 1838.
'Frithiof's Saga' borrowed from Evert Duyckinck after mid-Feb 1848 (NYPL–BL, the 4th book charged to Melville; Davis, *Melville's* Mardi, p. 64); Duyckinck owned both editions listed.

500a. Tennant, William. Anster Fair. A Poem . . . [1st ed.] Edinburgh, Cockburn, 1812. #
Described as containing the 'autograph of Herman Melville, in pencil, dated N. Y., 1875, on back of title. There is also a presentation inscription on the page of Preface, to Allan Melville, from his friend Robert Swan, together with the latter's

autograph' (Anderson Galleries, Inc., Catalogue 1652, 17–18 Apr 1922, Lot 396).

501. Tennyson, Alfred Tennyson, Baron. The Holy Grail and Other Poems . . . Boston, Fields, Osgood, 1870.
'Herman Melville [Mrs. Melville's hand]'. (HCL)

502. ———. The Holy Grail, and Other Poems . . . Boston, Fields, Osgood, 1870.
(NYPL–O)

503. ———. The Holy Grail, and Other Poems . . . Boston, Tilton, 1870.
'Fanny Melville from Her Father Xmas 1870 New York [Melville's hand]'. Marked. (HCL)

503a. ———. In Memoriam. London, Moxon, 1850 [?].
Augusta Melville's letter of 20 July 1850 to Evert Duyckinck (NYPL–D) thanks him for 'Tennyson's new poem.'

504. ———. In Memoriam. London, Moxon, 1850.
'Tennyson's In Memoriam' borrowed from Evert Duyckinck in 1850 (NYPL–BL: 37th listing for 1850). Cf. No. 503a.

505. ———. In Memoriam. Boston, Ticknor and Fields, 1865.
'H. Melville Jan 27 71 N. Y.'; 'To Bessie, May 22^d 1871 N. Y.' Annotated. (NYPL–O)

506. ———. Maud, and Other Poems . . . Boston, Ticknor and Fields, 1855.
(NYPL–O)

507. ———. The May Queen . . . London, [?], 1868. #
Described as containing an inscription 'in Herman Melville's Autograph Handwriting, presenting [it] to his Sister, Fanny,' together with

No. 70, an 1858 edition of Bloomfield's *Farmer's Boy* (American Book Auction, Catalogue 61, 26 Jan 1945, Lot 196).

507a. ———. Poems . . . London, Effingham Wilson, 1830, *or* London, Moxon, 1833 [1832] [?].
Mrs. Frances Wickes informed Henry A. Murray that Melville once presented a copy of Tennyson's early poems to her grandmother, née Mary Parmelee; the copy was lost 'in the express' many years ago. Gilman, *Melville's Early Life*, p. 104 and p. 326, n. 69, proposed 1838–39 as the date of Melville's friendship with Mary Parmelee. That the book 'contained only a few poems,' as Mrs. Wickes advised Gilman, 'suggests the 1830 or 1833 edition. . . .'

507b. ———. Poems . . . Boston, Ticknor, 1842. 2 v.
V. 2: 'Augusta Melville, from Mrs. M. Blatchford Dec: 19th 1844.' V. 1: 'Given to Thomas Melville after the death of his sister Augusta, 1876'. V. 1, 2: 'Eleanor Melville Thomas [Mrs. Metcalf]. from her Aunt Kate [Mrs. Thomas Melville]. January 1898.' Marked. (Formerly in the collection of Mrs. Henry K. Metcalf; present location unknown)

508. ———. The Poetical Works . . . Boston, Ticknor and Fields, 1861. 2 v.
V. 1, 2: 'H Melville'. V. 1: 'Aug 14th 1861 Albany.' Contains annotated clipping. (NYPL–O)

509. Terentius Afer, Publius. The Comedies . . . Literally Translated into English Prose, with Notes. By Henry Thomas Riley . . . To Which Is Added the Blank Verse Translation of George

Colman. New York, Harper, 1859.
Copy (edition unspecified) presented to Melville in Apr 1864 by Brig. Gen. Robert O. Tyler; cf. Melville's letter to Lt. Col. Henry Sanford Gansevoort, 10 May 1864: 'The Terence I highly value' along with No. 425; 'indeed both works, as memorials of the hospitalities of an accomplished General. . . .'

510. Terhune, Mary Virginia (Hawes). With the Best Intentions; a Midsummer Episode, by Marion Harland [pseud.]. New York, Scribner, 1890.
'With Best Intentions' borrowed from NYSL 14–25 May 1891.

511. Thackeray, William Makepeace. Ballads . . . Boston, Ticknor and Firlds, 1856.
'H. Melville Sep 22, '74 N. Y.' (HCL)

511a. ———. The Great Hoggarty Diamond. New York, Harper, 1848[?].
Augusta Melville's letter of 'Thursday Eveg' [1848 or after] to Evert Duyckinck (NYPL–D) thanks him for 'The Great Hogarty [*sic*] Diamond.'

512. ———. Vanity Fair. A Novel without a Hero . . . New York, Harper, 1848.
1 Sep 1848: '1 Vanity Fair, mus. [$.]94' (HCL–H, 10 Sep 1849). Listed in Harper catalogue @ $1.25 muslin.

Thackeray, William Makepeace: see also Nos. 143a, 489.

513. Thiele, F. The Mysteries of Berlin; from the Papers of a Berlin Criminal Officer. Translated from the German, by C. B. Burckhardt . . . New York, Colyer, 1845.
'Mysteries of Berlin' charged to Lemuel Shaw by BoA 8–19 Mar 1847; Melville was in Boston 9 Mar–[?].

514. Thompson, Waddy. Recollections

of Mexico . . . New York, Wiley and Putnam, 1846.

30 Dec 1846: '1 Thompsons Mexico Nov 27th by ['Brother'—i.e., Allan Melville, Jr.] [$.]75' (HCL–WP, 1 Jan 1847).

515. Thomson, James (1700–1748). The Poetical Works . . . With His Last Corrections, Additions, and Improvements. With the Life of the Author. Cooke's Edition . . . London, Cooke, [17–].

'Fanny Melville from her brother Herman Pittsfield May 19. 1862' (cf. Nos. 464 and 470). (NYPL–GL)

516. ———. The Poetical Works . . . Boston, Little, Brown, 1854. 2 v. ⚓
V. 1: 'H. Melville N. Y. July 3ʳᵈ 1861'.
V. 2: 'H. Melville July 30, 1861'. Annotated. (Examined by Raymond Weaver; present location unknown)

517. Thomson, James (1834–1882). The City of Dreadful Night, and Other Poems . . . London, Reeves and Turner, 1880.
'Herman Melville From Mr James Billson Leicester England Jan 1885'. Marked. (HCL)

518. ———. Essays and Phantasies . . . London, Reeves and Turner, 1881.
'Herman Melville from Mr James Billson Leicester England Oct 7–1885'. Annotation erased; marked. (HCL)

519. ———. Satires and Profanities [With a Preface by G. W. Foote.] . . . London, Progressive Publishing Company, 1884.
Gift of this volume and No. 518 (sent 7 Oct 1885) acknowledged in Melville's letter of 20 Dec 1885 to James Billson.

520. ———. Shelley, a Poem: With Other Writings Relating to Shelley . . . To Which Is Added an Essay on the Poems of William Blake, by the Same Author. [Ed. Bertram Dobell.] [Lon-

don], Printed for private circulation, by Whittingham, 1884.
Apparently the item referred to in Mrs. Melville's memoranda as 'Thomsons "Essay on Shelley" ' which James Billson sent to Melville on 4 Dec 1888 (see Sealts, *The Early Lives of Melville,* p. 172); she described it as 'long out of print and very scarce—a copy at "Scribners["] was 7.00—'. Melville's letter of 31 Dec 1888 to Billson acknowledges a 'book' containing an essay on Blake.

521. ———. Vane's Story, Weddah and Om-el-Bonain, and Other Poems . . . London, Reeves and Turner, 1881.
According to Mrs. Melville's memoranda, James Billson 'sent . . . "Vane's story" . . . Oct 1884' (see Sealts, *The Early Lives of Melville,* p. 171). Melville's letter of 1 Dec 1884 to Billson, acknowledging the gift of a volume of poems, reported that 'The "Weddah and Om-el-Bonain" gave me more pleasure than anything of modern poetry that I have seen in a long while.'

522. ———. A Voice from the Nile, and Other Poems . . . With a Memoir of the Author by Bertram Dobell. London, Reeves and Turner, 1884.
'to Herman Melville from J. W. Barrs as a small tribute of of [*sic*] admiration to Typee & Omoo. Feb 15/86'. Annotated by Barrs; marked by Melville. (PUL)

Thomson, James (1834–1882): see also No. 435.

523. Thomson, William McClure. The Land and the Book; or, Biblical Illustrations Drawn from the Manners and Customs, the Scenes and Scenery of the Holy Land . . . New York, Harper, 1859. 2 v.
16 Aug 1859: '1 Land & Book, fullmor-

to A[llan] Melville [Jr.] $4.50' (HCL–H, 8 Sep 1859). This may have been a special edition; this title was listed at $6.00 for half morocco extra.

524. Thoreau, Henry David. A Week on the Concord and Merrimack Rivers . . . Boston, Munroe, 1849.
'Thoreau's Merrimack' borrowed from Evert Duyckinck in 1850 (NYPL–BL: 40th listing for 1850).

525. Thornbury, George Walter. Lays and Legends; or Ballads of the New World. [1st ed.] London, Saunders and Otley, 1851; *or,* Songs of the Cavaliers and Roundheads, Jacobite Ballads, etc. London, Hurst and Blackett, 1857.
E. C. Stedman's letter to Melville of 1 Feb 1888 (HCL) mentions his lending Melville a volume of 'Walter Thornbury's Ballads. The book is one which I doubt if you have seen, as I never have been able to procure another copy.' Cf. Lots 3041 and 3042 in *The Library and Autograph Collection of Edmund Clarence Stedman,* Part III (The Anderson Auction Co., Catalogue 887, 24–25 Jan 1911).

Thucydides: see No. 147.

Tieck, Ludwig: see No. 121.

526. Tillotson, John, comp. Gems of Great Authors; or, The Philosophy of Reading and Thinking . . . London, Gall and Inglis, [1880].
'Bessie Melville from her Father [Mrs. Melville's hand]'. (HCL)

526a. Todd, John. Index Rerum: or Index of Subjects; Intended as a Manual, to Aid the Student and the Professional Man, in Preparing Himself for Usefulness . . . Third Edition. Northampton, Mass., Butler, 1836 and subsequent years. Gansevoort Melville's holding: 4? vols.

V. for 1836: 'Gansevoort Melville'; v. for 1837: 'Gansevoort Melville N[ew] Y[or]k February 17—1840 *"Office"* Vol 4'. Annotated. (BeA holds only the volumes for 1836 and 1837 of this commonplace book)

527. ———. The Student's Manual; Designed by Specific Directions, to Aid in Forming and Strengthening the Intellectual and Moral Character and Habits of the Student . . . Seventh Edition. Northampton, Mass., Butler, 1837.
'Allan Melville March 1839.'; stamp: 'ALLAN MELVILLE.' Annotated. (BeA)

528. Tomes, Robert. Panama in 1855. An Account of the Panama Rail-Road, of the Cities of Panama and Aspinwall, with Sketches of Life and Character on the Isthmus . . . New York, Harper, 1855.
28 Aug 1855: 'I Waikna [No. 485]: 1 Panama [$]1 30' (HCL–H, 6 Mar 1856).

Tourneur, Cyril: see No. 358.

Trumbull, Henry: see No. 407.

529. Tucker, Abraham. An Abridgement [by William Hazlitt] of The Light of Nature Pursued . . . Originally Published . . . under the Name of Edward Search, Esq. London, Johnson, 1807. #
'Richard Lathers Esq from his friend Herman Melville. Pittsfield Aug: 1853.' (American Art Association-Anderson Galleries, Catalogue 4296, 28–29 Jan 1937, Lot 359).

530. Tupper, Martin Farquhar. Proverbial Philosophy: A Book of Thoughts and Arguments, Originally Treated . . . [New York, Wiley and Putnam, 1846. 2 v. in 1. ?]
8 Sep 1846: '1 Proverbial Phil^y fancy ['Del^d Brother'—i.e., Allan Melville, Jr.] [$]1 25' (HCL–WP, 1 Jan 1847).

530a. Turnbull, John. A Voyage Round

the World, in the Years 1800, 1801, 1802, 1803, and 1804: in which the Author visited Madeira, the Brazils, Cape of Good Hope, the English Settlements of Botany Bay and Norfolk Island; and the Principal Islands in the Pacific Ocean. With a Continuation of Their History to the Present Period . . . 2nd Edition. London, Maxwell, 1813. ⧧
'Herman Melville April 10ᵗʰ 1847. New York.'; stamp: 'S[AILORS']. S[NUG]. HARBOR. STATEN ISLAND.' (SBL)

Tytler, Sarah [pseud.]: see Keddie, Henrietta (Nos. 306, 307).

U

531. The United States Democratic Review. Washington, 1838–40; New York, 1841–59. Borrowed by Melville: 'vol [?]'. 'Democrat Review vol [?]' borrowed from Evert Duyckinck in 1850 (NYPL–BL: 38th listing for 1850). NYPL–L lists 23 v., '1837–52'.

532. United States Exploring Expedition, 1838–1842. United States Exploring Expedition. During the Years 1838, 1839, 1840, 1841, 1842. Under the Command of Charles Wilkes, U. S. N. . . . In Five Volumes, and an Atlas. Philadelphia, Lea & Blanchard. 1845, 6 v.
17 Apr 1847: 'I Wilkes U.S. Exploring Expedition 6 Volˢ Sheep [$]21.00' (HCL–WP, 1 Jul 1847). Presumably the issues numbered 2B or 3 plus the *Atlas*, 17B, in Daniel C. Haskell, *The United States Exploring Expedition*, pp. 37–41, 46–47. Haskell's 2B and 17B were 'unofficial' issues of a thousand copies each; the 'official' issues printed for the use of Congress (nos. 1, 17) were of only a hundred copies. Haskell, pp. 21–22, notes also that those classed as 'official' carry no

publisher's imprint, that their original binding was dark green morocco while the unofficial issues 'were usually bound in black cloth,' and that 'the official issue does not assign a number to the atlas . . . while the unofficial does, calling it vol. 6.' Roorbach's *Bibliotheca Americana, 1820–1852*, lists Lea & Blanchard's 6-v. edition at $25.

'Up the Rhine': see No. 280.

V

533. Valery, Antoine Claude Pasquin, known as. Historical, Literary, and Artistical Travels in Italy, a Complete and Methodical Guide for Travellers and Artists . . . Translated with the Special Approbation of the Author, from the Second Corrected and Improved Edition by C. E. Clifton. With a Copious Index and a Road-Map of Italy. Paris, Baudry, 1852.
'Herman Melville'; 'H Melville, Florence.' Melville was in Florence 23–29 Mar 1857 (HCL–J). Annotated. (NYPL–O)

534. Vasari, Giorgio. Lives of the Most Eminent Painters, Sculptors, and Architects: Translated from the Italian . . . With Notes and Illustrations Chiefly Selected from Various Commentators. By Mrs. Jonathan Foster . . . London, Bohn, 1850–52. 5 v. Borrowed by Melville: 4 [?] v.
'Vasari & Lanzi 7 vols' borrowed from Evert Duyckinck in Nov 1859 (NYPL–BL; not in NYPL–L). Cf. No. 320 (3 v.).

534a.———. Lives . . . see Addenda, p. 228.

535. Vase, Gillan. Through Love to Life; a Novel. New York, Harper, 1889.
'Through Love to Life' borrowed

from NYSL 30 Apr–9 May 1890.

Vergilius Maro, Publius: see No. 147;
Melville's annotation in No. 160a, I, 74,
cites Dryden's translation of the *Aeneid*.

536. Viaud, Julien. Rarahu; or, The
Marriage of Loti, by Pierre Loti [pseud.]
. . . London, Paul, 1890.
    J. W. Barrs, in a letter to Melville of 13
Jan 1890 (HCL), mentioned Pierre
Loti's account of his twelve months in
the South Pacific: 'I hope shortly to
get the volume when, if it interests me,
I will post it to you.'

536a. 'Views of Paris.'
Unidentified. 'Views of Paris. (R. R.
Station)' obtained in Paris, 1849
(HCL–L).

537. Voltaire, François Marie Arouet
de. Histoire de Charles XII. Roi de
Suede . . . Nouvelle édition stéréotype,
soigneusement revue et corrigée sur les
meilleures impressions, par M. Catty
. . . Londres, Vernor, Hood et Sharpe,
1808.
    'A[llan] Melvill'. (NYPL–GL)

538. Voyage descriptif et philosophique
de l'ancien et du nouveau Paris. Miroir
fidèle . . . Paris, Chez l'auteur, 1815.
    Allan Melvill's copy. (BeA)

W

539. Waddington, Samuel, ed. The Sonnets of Europe; a Volume of Translations
Selected and Arranged, with Notes . . .
New York, White and Allen, 1886.
    'Maria G. Morewood from the li-
brary of her uncle Herman Melville
1891 [Mrs. Melville's hand]'; 'Edgar F. Romig 1/5/29'. Marked.
(Last reported in the collection of

Miss Eleanor Romig, then of Wellesley, Mass.)

540. Wade, John. British History,
Chronologically Arranged; Com-
prehending a Classified Analysis of
Events and Occurrences in Church and
State; and of the Constitutional, Politi-
cal, Commercial, Intellectual, and Social
Progress of the United Kingdom, from
the First Invasion by the Romans to A.
D. 1847 . . . Fifth Edition. London,
Bohn, 1847.
    'Wade's British History' charged to
Lemuel Shaw by BoA 26 May–16 Jun
1860; Melville was in Boston *circa*
26–30 May.

541. Wakefield, Priscilla (Bell). An Introduction to Botany, in a Series of
Familiar Letters, with Illustrative Engravings . . . Third Edition. London,
Darton and Harvey, 1803.
    'Allan Melvill'. (NYPL–GL)

542. Walford, Lucy Bethia (Colqu-
houn). Pauline . . . New York, [Holt?],
1874.
    'Pauline' borrowed from NYSL 4 Dec
1890–2 Jan 1891.

543. Walker, H. H. The Comédie
Humaine and Its Author, with Transla-
tions from the French of Balzac . . .
London, Chatto and Windus, 1879.
    Annotated. (NYPL–O)

543a. Walpole, Horace, Earl of Orford.
Anecdotes of Painting in England. Reprint of the Edition of 1786. London,
Alexander Murray, 1871.
    'H. Melville Jan. 5 '72 N.Y.' Card en-
closed: 'Miss Eleanor Melville
Thomas 63 Montrose Avenue South
Orange [N.J.]' inscribed 'I am sending
one of Grandfather Melville's books,
with warm Christmas greetings. The
markings are his. E. M. T.'; the reci-

pent, Rev. Samuel Hines Bishop, is identified in Mrs. Metcalf's *Herman Melville,* p. 293. (NL)

544. ———. The Castle of Otranto: A Gothic Story . . .

Edition unidentified. 'Castle of Otranto' bought in London for 1 shilling, probably between 15 and 17 Dec 1849. The purchase, not mentioned in HCL–J, is listed in HCL–L between No. 429, bought on 15 Dec, and No. 463, bought on 17 Dec; *The Castle of Otranto* is also included in No. 54, which Melville probably acquired on 19 Dec.

545. ———. Letter Addressed to the Countess of Ossory, from the Year 1769 to 1797 . . . Now First Printed from Original Mss. Edited, with Notes, by the R[t.] Hon. R. Vernor Smith . . . London, Bentley, 1848. 2 v.

'Letter's of [*sic*] Ossory 2' charged to Lemuel Shaw by BoA 27 Jan–24 Feb 1849; Melville was in Boston 30 Jan–10 Apr.

546. Warren, Samuel. The Moral, Social, and Professional Duties of Attorneys and Solicitors . . . New York, Harper, 1849.

19 Dec 1848: '1 Warren's Duties [$.]60' (HCL–H, 10 Sep 1849).

547. ———. Now and Then . . . New York, Harper, 1848.

In Mrs. Melville's hand: 'Augusta Melville from her brother Herman'; 'Augusta'. (NYPL–GL)

548. Washington, George. The last Will and Testament of Gen. George Washington. Boston, Russell and Manning & Loring, 1800.

'Allan Melvill March 12th 1800'; '. . . A Melvill'. (NYPL–GL)

549. ———. The President'a Address

to the People of the United States on His Declining Another Election. Amherst, N. H., Cushing, [1796]. 'A[llan] Melville'. (NYPL–GL)

Washington, George: see also No. 373

549a. Watts, Isaac. The Improvement of the Mind; or, A Supplement to the Art of Logic . . .

2 Mar 1834: begun by Gansevoort Melville (GMJ).

Webster, John: see No. 358

550. Webster, Noah. An American Dictionary of the English Language . . . New York, Harper, 1846 or later edition.

10 Apr 1847: '1 Webster's Dictionary $2.80' (HCL–H, 1 Aug 1847). The Goodrich revision of Webster is listed in the Harper catalogue for 1847 @ $3.50. The fragment listed as No. 75 may be from this volume, although it apparently came from a cheaper edition.

551. ———. An American Dictionary of the English Language . . . New York, Harper, 1846 or later edition.

15 Nov 1847: '1 Webster's Dictionary $2.80' (HCL–H, 1 Feb 1848). The duplication of No. 550 by Nos. 551 and 552 suggests that Melville took advantage of his professional discount to secure additional dictionaries for relatives or friends.

552. ———. An American Dictionary of the English Language . . . New York, Harper, 1846 or later edition.

16 Nov 1848: '1 Webster's Dictionary [$]2 80' (HCL–H, 10 Sep 1849). Cf. Nos. 550, 551.

553. Webster's Calendar: or, The Albany Almanac . . . Albany, 1786–1907. Melville's holding: 1877 only?

From Melville's letter to Abraham

Lansing, 2 Jan 1877, it appears that the almanac had been a Christmas gift from the Lansings: '. . . the Almanac—I should have been sorry to have forgotten it. . . . I relish looking over it mightily.' V. H. Paltsits, ed., *Family Correspondence*, p. 45, nn. 85, 86, suggests the probable identification of Nos. 388 and 553.

554. Wellington, Arthur Wellesley, 1st Duke of. The Words of Wellington. Collected from His Despatches, Letters, and Speeches, with Anecdotes, etc. . . . Compiled by Edith Walford [Blumer]. New York, Scribner, Welford, 1869.
'Mr. Stanwix Melville Xmas, 1871 N. Y. [Melville's hand]'. (HCL)

555. Wells, William Vincent. Explorations and Adventures in Honduras, Comprising Sketches of Travel in the Gold Regions on Olancho, and a Review of the History and General Resources of Central America . . . New York, Harper, 1857.
'Well's [*sic*] Honduras' charged to Lemuel Shaw by BoA 1 Oct–5 Dec 1857; Melville was in Boston 21 Nov–8 Dec.

556. White, Henry Kirke. The Poetical Works and Remains . . . With Life by Robert Southey . . . New York, Appleton, 1857.
'H Melville Apl 3^d 1862 N. Y.' Marked. (HCL)

556.1a. White, Joseph Blanco. Extracts from Blanco White's Journal and Letters . . . Boston, W. Crosby and H. P. Nichols, 1847; *or*, The Life of . . . Joseph Blanco White, Written by Himself. Ed. John Hamilton Thom. London, J. Chapman, 1845. 3 v.
Melville's letter of 18 Nov 1856 to Henry Arthur Bright thanks him for his kind perseverance concerning

"Blanco White." ' Davis and Gilman, pp. 186–187, n. 6, suggest these possible identifications.

556.1b. White, Richard Grant. National Hymns. How They Are Written and How They Are Not Written. New York, Rudd & Carleton, 1861. #
Described as 'Presentation copy from Herman Melville to Fanhy M. Raymond, with numerous pencilled marginal notes in her hand' (Anderson Galleries, Catalogue 1682, 21 Nov 1922, Lot 1201).

556a. Whitney, Adeline Dutton Train. Faith Gartney's Girlhood . . . [Boston, Loring, 1863?].
21 Dec 1865: letter from Maria Gansevoort Melville to Catherine Gansevoort (NYPL–GL): 'We have been reading aloud, "Faith Gartneys Girlhood," "The Gayworthys," by the same author—Helen brought us "The clever woman of the Family" [No. 567]—which we are now reading in the eve^g aloud—.'

556b. ———. The Gayworthys: A Story of Threads and Thrums . . . [Boston, Loring, 1865?].
See No. 556a.

557. Whittier, John Greenleaf. The Chapel of the Hermits, and Other Poems . . . Boston, Ticknor, Reed, and Fields, 1853.
'Miss Hellen [*sic*] Melville, Pittsfield, Mass. With the respectful and affectionate regards of J. C. Hoadley, July 25th, 1853.' (NYPL–GL)

Wilkes, Charles: see No. 532.

558. Willmott, Robert Eldridge Aris. A Journal of Summer Time in the Country . . . New York, Appleton, 1852.
Augusta Melville, in a letter of 14 Nov 1852 to Evert Duyckinck (NYPL–D),

acknowledges his gift of a 'book on "Summer Time" '.

558a. ———. The Poets of the Nineteenth Century. Selected and Edited by the Rev. Robert Aris Willmott . . . With English and American Additions, Arranged by Evert A. Duyckinck . . . Illustrated with One Hundred and Thirty-Two Engravings, Drawn by Eminent Artists. New York, Harper, 1858.
18 Jun 1859: '1 Poets, fullmor. to A[llan] Melville [Jr.] [$]3 85' (HCL–H, 8 Sep 1859). This volume is listed in the 1859 Harper catalogue at $5.50 for 'full Turkey Morocco.'

Wilson, John ('Christopher North'): see No. 359.

559. [Winckelmann, Johann Joachim. The History of Ancient Art, Translated from the German . . . By G. Henry Lodge . . . Boston, Osgood, 1849–73. 4 v. Borrowed by Lemuel Shaw: v. 2?]
'Hinkleman's [sic] Hist. of Mod. art' charged to Lemuel Shaw by BoA 3–24 Apr 1852; Melville was in Boston after 16 Apr–before 2 May. No work of this title was in BoA; Winckelmann's work on *ancient* art seems a likely identification. V. 2, published in Boston by Munroe, 1849, was the only volume available in 1852.

559a. Wise, Henry Augustus. Los Gringos: or, An Inside View of Mexico and California, with Wanderings in Peru, Chili, and Polynesia. New York, Baker and Scribner, 1849.
HCL–J, London. 15 Dec 1849: 'I also spoke to him [Richard Bentley] about Lieut: Wise's book, & he is to send for it.' Anderson, *Melville in the South Eeas*, p. 465, n. 23, suggests that Melville asked Bentley, his London publisher, to secure a copy for him;

another possibility is that Melville was urging Bentley to publish an English edition. Bentley's London edition is dated 1849.

560. Wood, Ellen (Price), 'Mrs. Henry Wood.' The Mystery. A Story of Domestic Life . . . Philadelphia, Peterson, [c 1862].
'Mystery' borrowed from NYSL 9–18 Apr 1891.

561. Woods, Katherine Pearson. Metzerott, Shoemaker . . . New York, Crowell, [c 1889].
'Metzeroff [sic]' borrowed from NYSL 13–21 Mar 1891.

562. Worcester, Joseph Emerson. A Primary Pronouncing Dictionary of the English Language . . . Boston, Hickling, Swan, and Brewer, 1859.
'Fannie Melville 104 East 26th St New York City'. Annotated. (Formerly in the collection of Mrs. Walter B. Binnian; present location unknown)

563. Wordsworth, Christopher. Greece: Pictorial, Descriptive, and Historical . . . Second Edition. London, Orr, 1844.
'H. Melville May 71 N. Y.' Marked. (HCL)

563a. Wordsworth, William. The Complete Poetical Works . . . Together With a Description of the Country of the Lakes in the North of England . . . Edited by Henry Reed. Philadelphia, James Kay, Jun. and Brother; Boston, James Munroe and Company; Pittsburgh, C. H. Kay & Co., 1839. Rebound.
Melville's signature on the title page was lost by trimming during rebinding. 'Pacific Ocean, Sep. 14th 1860 5°50″ *N.L. Gulf of Mexico* 〈Oct.〉 Nov. 6th 1860 Steamer "North Star" ' Annotated. (Woodstock)

564. The Works of Eminent Masters, in Painting, Sculpture, Architecture, and Decorative Art . . . London, Cassell, 1854. 2 v. in 1.
'H. Melville Dec '71 N. Y.' Annotated. (HCL)

565. The World. By Adam Fitz-Adam [pseud. of Edward Moore, ed.] . . . A New Edition. London, Dodsley, 1767[?]. 4 v. Melville's holding: v. 2 only (1767), containing numbers 53–104. (HCL)

Wycherley, William: see No. 358.

X   Y   Z

Xenophon: see No. 147.

566. Yankee Doodle. New York, 1846–47. Melville's association: 1847 only [?].
Melville was a contributor to and member of the staff of this humorous weekly in 1847.

567. Yonge, Charlotte Mary. The

Clever Woman of the Family . . . New York, Appleton, 1865.
See No. 556a.

Zschokke, Heinrich: see No. 54.

ADDENDA

394a. Opie, Amelia (Alderson). Detraction Displayed. London, Rees, Orme, Brown, and Green, 1828. #
Bookplate of Ralph Hamilton; 'Melville' (Herman Melville's hand]; printed label: 'H. Scofield.' (Serendipity)

534a. Vasari, Giorgio. Lives of the Most Eminent Painters, Sculptors, and Architects: Translated from the Italian . . . With Notes and Illustrations Chiefly Selected from Various Commentators. By Mrs. Jonathan Foster . . . London, Bohn, 1849–52 (v. 2: 1855). 5 v. #
V. 1: 'H Melville 1 March 1862 N. Y.'; v. 2-5: 'H Melville'. Annotated. (Whitburn)

Analytical Index to the Check-List

In the following index, the various numbers designating entries in the Check-List have been grouped in numerical order within appropriate categories and subdivisions. These are:

> Books owned that have survived
>> Names of owners within Melville's lifetime, arranged alphabetically
>>> Present locations (abbreviated as in the Check-List)
> Books owned that have apparently not survived
>> Names of owners during Melville's lifetime
>>> Sources of information by which the books and their owners are known
> Books either owned or borrowed
>> Names of owners or borrowers
>>> Sources of information by which the books and their borrowers are known
> Books borrowed
>> Names of borrowers
>>> Sources from which borrowed

Except in the case of books given by Melville to his wife and children, index numbers of titles belonging to more than one relative during Melville's lifetime are listed under the names of each of the owners, and are printed each time in *italics*. (Examples: No. *103*, which once belonged to Melville's father, Allan Melvill, and was later bought at second hand by Herman Melville; No. *66*, which belonged in turn to Priscilla Melvill and, after her death, to her cousins Herman Melville and Augusta Mclville.) Totals and

subtotals for the number of entries in each subdivision appear in aprenth-
eses following the appropriate headings; these totals include italicized items
each time they occur.

Books Owned That Have Survived

Griggs, George, brother-in-law (2)
 BeA (1): *197*
 NYPL–GL (1): *3*

Griggs, Helen Maria Melville, sister (6)
 BeA (2): *386, 483*
 LHS (1); *396b*
 NL (1): *107*
 NYPL–GL (2): 63, *557*
 NYPL–GL (1): 63)

Hoadley, Catherine Melville, sister (1)
 NYPL–GL (1): *358a*

Hoadley, John C., brother-in-law (8)
 NYPL–B (1): *137*
 NL (1): *478*
 NYPL–B (1): *137*
 NYPL–GL (4): *21b, 197, 296, 557*
 Unlocated (1): *100*

Melvill, Allan, great-grandfather (1)
 NYPL–F (1): *472*[?]

Melvill, Allan and Maria Gansevoort,
parents (46?)
 BeA (7), 183, 194a *197* 197a, 402, 538
 HCL (10?): 8, 12[?], 21c, *103*, 132,
  142, *339*, 490a, *493*[?], *565*[?]
 NL (1): 62a
 NYPL (1): *57*
 NYPL–F (1?): *472*[?]
 NYPL–GL (20?): *3*, 6, 12[?], 60, *63*,
  69, 86, 118, 131, 208, *213*, 214,
  304, 371, 373, 404, 537, 541, 548,
  549

Sotheby (1): *304a*

Unlocated (5): 141a, 286a, 355, *500a*,
529

Melvill, Priscilla, aunt (2)
 NYPL–GL (1): *197*
 Unlocated (1): *73a*

Melvill, Priscilla, cousin (1)
 HCL (1): *66*

Melvill, Thomas, grandfather (1)
 NYPL–GL (1): *358a*

Melville, Allan, brother (14?)
 BeA (4)? *171*, 209, *216*, 527
 Haack (1): 242
 NL (1): 292a ('Mrs. Allan Melville')
 NYPL–GL (3): *117, 352*, 383
 NYPL–O (1?): *431*[?]
 Unlocated (4): 11a, 179, *368a, 456a*

Melville, Augusta, sister (21)
 BeA (7):*7*, 73, 148, 294, 406, 451a,*454*
 HCL (2): *66, 99a*
 LHS (2): 87.1, *396b*
 NL (2): *107*, 158.1
 NYPL–GL (7): *21b, 202a, 213, 352,
  408, 476, 547*
 Unlocated (1): *507b*

Melville, Elizabeth Shaw ('Dolly,' 'Liz-
zie'), wife (31?)
 BCHS (1): 12a
 HCL (17?); 61, 99a, 120, 135, 145,
  195, 210, 245, 273, 275b, 306, 411,
  415a, 418, 474, 475, 479[?]
 NYPL–GL (2): 50, 308
 NYPL–O (2): 130, 399
 Unlocated (9); 108, 109, 110, 111,
  115, *241*, 353, 456, 492

Melville, Elizabeth ('Bessie'), daughter
(12)
 HCL (8): 5, 269, 295, 328, 329, 330,
  414, 526
 NYPL–O (3): 416, 461, 505
 Unlocated (1): *241*

Melville, Frances Priscilla, sister (17)
 BeA (1): *7*

BCHS (1): 231
BUL (1): 234b
HCL (4): 4, 462, 499, 503
NYPL–O (1): 96
Unlocated (3): *207, 241,* 562

Other books kept in the family (4)
BeA (1): 307
HCL (2): 275, 421
Unlocated (1): 456

Books Owned That Have Apparently Not Survived

Griggs, Helen Maria Melville (1?):
428b[?]

Melville, Allan (1): *131a*

Melville, Augusta (8): 6a, *155a,* 285a,
290b, 494a, 503a, 511a, 558

Melville, Herman (91 + ?):
Acquired in Europe, 1849 and
1856–57, according to HCL–J
and/or HCL–L (25): 9, 54, 84, 90,
157a, 180, 212, 225, 280, 281, 288,
312, 316, 322, 330a, 376, 378, 396a,
404.1, 429, 463, 467, 486, 536a, 544
Bought for Abraham Lansing, as reported in correspondence (2): 139,
140
Brought on lecture tour in 1859, as
recorded in notebook (1+): 83
Destroyed, or destroyed except for
fragments (11+): *73a,* 74, 75, 75a,
76, 79a, 95, 101a, 105, *128,* 457
Given to J. W. Francis (1): 428.1
Given to Mary Parmelee (1): 507a
Given to Arthur Stedman (1): 435a
Magazines: known subscriber (3):
240, 241, 326
Magazines: owned at least one
number (4): 1, 128a, 325, 455
Magazines: probable subscriber (3):
189, 413, 566
Mentioned by others as owned by or
given to Melville (8?): 211a, 239,
340a, 351a, 394, 404.2, 491b,
536[?]

Mentioned in Melville's letters or
journal as owned, exclusive of
HCL–L (22+): 51, 80, 138, 143b,
146, 270, 334, 340a, 350, 388, 393,
396.1, 396.2, 407, 425, 490b, 497,
509, 519, 520, 521, 533
Presumably furnished Melville (1): 8a
Probably acquired in Italy in 1857
(1): 86.1
Review copies known to have been
obtained by Melville (1): 88
Review copies probably obtained by
Melville (4): 149, 159, 160, 397
Review copies read and presumably
returned by Melville (2): 79, 242

Melville, Herman and/or Allan (51+)
Bought from Harper and Brothers, as
charged in HCL–H (35+): 81, 82,
127, 143a, 147, 175, 190, 201, 211,
234, 262, 272, 293, 335, 336, 337,
340, 372, 374, 384a, 395, 396, 409,
422, 427, 484, 485, 512, 523, 528,
546, 550, 551, 552, 558a
Bought from John Wiley, as charged
in HCL–W (8): 102, 154, 158, 177,
318, 359, 366, 460a
Bought from Wiley and Putnam, as
charged in HCL–WP (8): 13, 161,
170, 420, 495, 514, 530, 532

Melville, Malcolm (1): 245a

Melville, Thomas (1): *128*

Other (5): 101a, 120b, *131a,* 180a, 275

Books Either Owned or Borrowed

Griggs, Helen Maria Melville (1): 327a

Melvill(e), Maria Gansevoort (4): 116a, 556a, 556b, 567

Melville, Augusta (4): 202.1, 319a, 353a. 459.1

Melville, Gansevoort (5): 107a, 158a, 219a, 234a, 549a

Melville, Herman (26?)
 Cited in annotation (3): 237a, 319b, 387a

Cited in manuscripts (2): 294a, 357a
 Mentioned by others as known by Melville (4) 71a, 327.1, 358, 417a
 Mentioned in HCL–J as read by Melville (10): 78a, 182, 193, 224a, 311, 434a, 436a, 438a, 490, 559a
 Mentioned in letters as read by Melville (6): 173, 223b, 325a, 404.2, 478, 491a,
 Other (1): 556.1a

Books Borrowed

Melville, Allan (3)
 From NYSL (3): 120a, 143.1, 352a

Melville, Augusta (2?)
 From Evert A. Duyckinck (1?): 181[?]
 From Sarah Morewood (1): 168a

Melville, Gansevoort (2)
 From Athenaeum Library, Albany (2): 233b, 327a

Melville, Herman (96+)
 From 'son' of Owen Chase (1): 133
 From Evert A. Duyckinck (29): 14, 38, 89, 91, 92, 121, 122, 123, 126, 172, 188, 200, 221, 230, 258, 303, 320, 324, 349, 417, 424, 449, 480, 494, 500, 504, 524, 531, 534
 From George L. Duyckinck (5): 77, 78, 166, 375, 377
 From Nathaniel and Sophia Hawthorne (1 or more): 206a

From NYSL (55): 2, 10, 39, 40, 41, 42, 43, 44, 45, 46, 47, 59, 67, 68, 85, 99, 106, 162, 163, 164, 167, 168, 200a, 217, 220, 223, 233a, 243, 264, 267, 286, 287, 297, 301, 309, 310, 338, 354, 389, 400, 415, 426, 443, 450, 451, 452, 453, 473, 477, 491, 510, 535, 542, 560, 561
 From ship's library (1): 315
 From Edmund Clarence Stedman (3): 285, 488a, 525
 From an unidentified library (1): 294a

Shaw, Lemuel (35):
 From BoA, during Melville's visits to Boston (35): 98, 124, 136, 155, 165, 198, 199, 227, 235, 237, 238, 266, 274, 289, 292, 313, 319, 327, 357, 379, 381, 382, 385, 401, 403, 419, 430, 437, 438, 442, 513, 540, 545, 555, 559

APPENDICES

Appendix A

Other Books Advertised as Melville's

Between 1962 and 1972 at least twelve books were advertised as volumes from Melville's library in catalogues issued by the Bodley Book Shop of New York City. My letters to the proprietor (Samuel Loveman) requesting information before the publication of *Melville's Reading* (1966) received no answer, but I had the opportunity to examine two of these volumes which were in other hands at that time, and I have since seen photocopies of the inscription in two more. In my opinion, none of the inscriptions I have seen is in the handwriting of Herman Melville, and I doubt that these books were ever part of his library.

Under the circumstances, I have not been persuaded that any of the books that Bodley has advertised should be included in the alphabetical Check-List in Part II of this study, but as a matter of record I am listing their titles here in their own alphabetical order, with citation of their respective listings in the various Bodley catalogues I have seen. (There may have been others.) The descriptions are quoted, with some normalization, from these catalogues; e.g., entries are by author and title, and words in all capitals are printed here in capitals and lower case.

1. Barrell, George, Jr. The Pedestrian in France and Switzerland. 312 Pages. 8vo, original cloth. New York, G. B. Putnam [*sic*], 1853. First Edi-

237

tion . . . Very Scarce and Extremely Delighted Reading. Herman Melville's Copy, with his Autograph Signature on the Front End-Leaf, and his Markings Throughout the Text. The Passages He Has Chosen Are Worthy of Scrutinizing and Study. [Catalogue 60, 1970: Lot 194]

2. Bible. La Sainte Bible. Qui Contient le Vieux et le Nouveau Testament, et les Livres Apocryphes. 1550 Pages. . . . Neuchatel, 1771. Herman Melville's Copy . . . , with his Autograph Signature on the Front End-Leaf. [Catalogue 30, 1962: Lot 24]

3. Carleton, William. Farm Legends. Poems. Illustrated by Winslow Homer, Darley, etc. 4to, original gilt-decorated cloth. New York, 1876. Herman Melvelle's Copy with his Autograph Signature on the Half-title [Catalogue 59, 1969: Lot 241]

4. Chadwick, John W. ['Minister of the Second Unitarian Church of Brooklyn, N.Y.'] The Bible Today. 324 Pages. 8vo, cloth. New York, 1879. First Edition. Herman Melville's Copy, with his Autograph Signature on the Front Flyleaf, and His Pencilled Markings (of Surpassing Interest) Throughout the Text. Chadwick—Actually an Agnostic—was a Friend of Ralph Wald[o] Emerson. [Catalogue 60, 1970: Lot 31]

5. Curtis, Herbert Pelham. Arabian Days' Entertainments. Illustrated. 434 Pages. 8vo, cloth. Boston, 1858. First edition. A rare American, Facetious Continuation of the 'Arabian Nights.' Herman Melville's Copy. With his Autograph Signature on the Title-page and his Markings Throughout the Text. [Catalogue 59, 1969: Lot 17]

6. Hyde, John. Mormonism: Its Leaders and Designs. New York, 1857. Herman Melville's Pencilled Autograph Signature on the Front Flyleaf, and his Numerous Markings. . . . Under the Portrait of Joseph Smith Jr. he has noted: 'Son of Joe I.' [Catalogue 32, 1962: Lot 184; Catalogue 35, 1962: Lot 132; Catalogue 38, 1963: Lot 127]
This volume has been presented to the Harvard College Library.

7. Percival, James. The Wonders of the World. Comprising the Most Remarkable Curiosities of Nature and Art . . . Charleston 1836. Herman Melville's Copy, with his Autograph Signature in Pencil on the Title-Page and his Numerous Markings. One of the Heaviest Scored Sections is that Devoted to Whaling. . . . Against the Engraving of a Waters[p]out, Melville has Pencilled the Word: 'True!' [Catalogue 32, 1962: Lot 185; Catalogue 34, 1962: Lot 199]

8. Platt, I. [John Platts, 1775–1837]. The Book of Curiosities. Containing Ten Thousand Wonders and Curiosities in Nature and Art . . . Philadelphia, 1857. Herman Melville's Copy, with his Autograph Signature on the Front Flyleaf and Several Markings with Two or Three Jotted Words, against passages on Whaling, Sea-Serpents, etc. [Catalogue 36, 1962: Lot 153]

INSCRIPTIONS, AUTHENTIC OR OTHERWISE

The inscriptions reproduced here are taken from copies of: (a) William Carleton, *Farm Legends* (No. 3 above), by courtesy of J. W. P. Frost, Eliot, Maine; (b) John Hyde, *Mormonism* (No. 6 above), by permission of the Houghton Library, Harvard University; (c) Harriet Spofford, *The Amber Gods* (No. 11 above), by courtesy of Kenneth Walter Cameron, from his 'A Melville Letter and Stray Books from His Library,' p. 49; and (d) William Hazlitt, *Criticisms on Art* (Check-List, No. 263a), by courtesy of Christie's New York. 'H. Melville' followed by the date and place of purchase is the usual form of Melville's autograph signature in those books that he acquired during his later years.

9. Read, Thomas Buchanan. A Summer Story, Sheridan's Ride and Other Poems. 8vo, original cloth, gilt top, uncut. Philadelphia, 1865. Herman Melville's copy, with His Autograph Signature on the Front Flyleaf, and His Markings Throughout the Text. Beside the first stanza of 'The Western Vine,' Melville has pencilled the Wo[r]d 'Wine.' 'Sheridan's Ride[']—Buchanan's [*sic*] Most Famous Poem, Melvil[l]e has underscored in Several Places. His Own Poem Beginning with 'Shoe the Steed with Silver' was on the Same Subject. [Catalogue 32, 1962: Lot 186; Catalogue 37, 1963: Lot 141; Catalogue 53, 1966: Lot 113 (adds 'contains A. Edward Newton's bookplate.')]

10. Sears, Robert. The Wonders of the World in Nature, Art, and Mind . . . New York, 1844. Herman Melville's Copy, with his Autograph Signature on the Front Flyleaf and his Markings on the Margins of Various Subjects: American Caves; Escurial of Spain; Piazza del Populo in Rome; Whaling, etc. On the latter he has commented: 'Accurate.' [Catalogue 36, 1962: Lot 154]

11. Spofford, Harriet Elizabeth (Prescott). The Amber Gods and Other Stories. Boston, 1863. 8vo. Original cloth. Herman Melville's Copy, with His Pencilled Autograph Signature on the Title-Page. [Catalogue 59, 1969: Lots 119 and 203]

12. 'Toby.' The American Tour of Messrs Brown, Jones and Robinson. What They Saw and Did in the U. S., Canada and Cuba. By TOBY. With Several Hundred Woodcut Illustrations by the [P]seudonymous Artist. 4to . . . New York, Appleton and Co., 1872. Original Edition. Herman Melville's Copy, with His Autograph Signature on the Title-page. Incidentally—'Toby' is One of the Characters in Melville's South Sea Books—An Actual Character and His Close Friend. Rare.

The books I have examined are Nos. 6 and 9: the Hyde and the Read.

In 1971, Kenneth W. Cameron in 'A Melville Letter and Stray Books from His Library' reprinted four of the descriptions (Nos. 3, 5, 9, 11: the Carleton, Curtis, Read, and Spofford) 'largely as given in the bookseller's catalogue,' commenting that the books 'are listed here because they do not appear in Sealts' *Melville's Reading* and deserve, doubtless, to be added . . . if the autographs are genuine' (p. 47). The article includes a reproduction of the title page of the Spofford volume (p. 49).

In 1980 Bodley also advertised at $100.00 'AN ORIGINAL SAILOR-DRAWING IN PENCIL BY HERMAN MELVILLE SIGNED AND DATED 1845,' describing it as follows:

Melville, Herman. An Original Drawing in Pencil by Herman Melville, Measuring 18 x 12 Inches. Drawn on Stiff Contemporary Board, this depicts a Sailor in Uniform on a Hip [*sic*]. Drawn at Full Length with a

Suggestion of Rigging in the Background. Signed with Melville's Initials and Dated ' '45', the Charm of this Amateur Drawing, lies in the Precision of the Period-Naval Costume and the Complete Sincerity depicted in the Young Sailor's Features. THIS DRAWING IS LIKELY ENOUGH, RE-MINISCENT OF MELVILLE'S FIRST VOYAGE ON THE WHALER 'ACUSHNET,' WITH THE TOBY OF 'TYPEE,' WHEN HE DES[E]R-TED IN THE MARQUESAS, TO GATHER MATERIAL FOR HIS FIRST SOUTH SEA NOVEL. UNIQUE. [Catalogue 60, 1970: Lot 177]

Readers will form their own judgment concerning this item as well as the books offered by Bodley.

Appendix B

Other Books Bought By Melville's Relatives

1. Books Imported by Allan Melvill, 1805

Among Allan Melvill's accounts in the Gansevoort-Lansing Collection of the New York Public Library is an invoice of 5 July 1805 listing forty French works charged to his account. As he was an importer by trade, the books were probably purchased for sale rather than for his own use; no further reference to any of these volumes has been found among the family papers. Their titles are therefore listed here, for convenient reference, rather than in Part II above. Figures following the individual entries indicate numbers of volumes.

'Cartes des Campagnes en Italy & en Allemagne', 'Rousseau 37 Vol.', 'Corneille 8', 'Molière 6', 'Encyclopedie des Arts & Sciences 23 & Les planches seperés', 'Jeune Anarchasis & planches 7 Vol', 'Boileau 5 Vol.', 'Regnard 4', 'Voltaire 70', 'Mably 15', 'Virgile 4', 'Histoire des Peuples des Dieux 8', 'Synonymes de Rabaud 4', 'Memoires de Sully 12', 'Bibliorum Sacrorum 8', 'Divers Romans brochés', 'Chef d'oeuvres dramatiques 1', 'Lettres de la Suisse 2', 'Grand tour 4', 'Dictionnaire de la Fable 2', 'Helvetius 5', 'Guide des Voyageurs 2 Vol.', 'Telemaque 2', 'Josephus 1', 'Guides Amateurs 3', 'histoires des peuples des Dieux 10', 'Discription de Paris 8', 'Voyage en Suisse 2', 'Machiavel 2', 'Racine 3', 'Finances 2', 'Maladies Syphilitiques 1', 'Papes Sixte IV 2', 'Siege de Calais 2', 'Conn: de la mer Noire 2', 'Code Prussien 5', 'Regne de Guillaume II 2', 'Esprit de l'Encyclopedie 13', 'Code des Prisses 2', 'Revolution de Suede, Romaine, Portugal 6'

The invoice totals 3,300 livres, less discount—this would have been approximately $600 in American money.

2. Books Owned by Major Thomas Melvill, Jr., 1822–1836

Now in the Berkshire Athenaeum, Pittsfield, Massachusetts, are several volumes once owned by Major Thomas Mellvill, Jr., that Herman Melville may well have seen at Broadhall before his uncle left Pittsfield for Galena, Illinois, in June 1837. They are a recent gift from Miss Jean F. Melvill, a great granddaughter of Major Melvill.

> (1) Joseph Collyer, *The History of England, from the Invasion of Julius Cæsar to the Dissolution of the Present Parliament,* 14 vols., London, J. Johnson and W. Goldsmith, 1774 ('Thos. W. Melvill—1821', 'Thomas Melvill Jun.'); (2) Lindley Murray, *English Grammar Adapted to the Different Classes of Learners* . . . , from the 28th English edition, Utica, New York, William Williams, 1822; (3) *Helen and Maria,* Parts I, II, and III, Boston, Wait, Greene & Co., 1828 (bought on 12 April 1832); (4) *Quotations from the British Poets, Being a Pocket Dictionary of Their Most Admired Passages,* New York, Charles Wells, 1836.

The following titles are listed on a statement of Major Melvill's account with Phineas Allen of Pittsfield as of 24 May 1824 (HCL), the relevance of which was pointed out to me by Jay Leyda in a letter of 3 June 1951.

> 11 Nov 1814: '1 English Reader, dld your Son .75' [Cf. Check-List, No. 380: Lindley Murray, *The English Reader*]. 27 Jun 1815: '1 Brown's Bible 17.00'. 19 Jul 1815: '1 Memoirs of Jefferson 2 vols. $5.00' [returned 15 Feb 1816]; '1 Faber on the Prophecies, 3.00' [George Stanley Faber, *A Dissertation on the Prophecies* . . . Fifth ed., revised and corrected (London, Rivington, 1814)]; '1 Scott's Lord of the Isles, 1.00' [Sir Walter Scott, *The Lord of the Isles, a Poem* (Boston, Wells & Lilly, 1815)]; '1 Morse's Universal Geography, 7.50' [Jedediah Morse, *The American Universal Geography* . . . Sixth ed. (Boston, Thomas and Andrews, 1812)]. 15 Feb 1816: returned a Bible @ $8.00 and 'Memoirs of Jefferson' @ $4.65. 6 Apr 1816: '1 Pike's Arithmetic $2.50' [Nicholas Pike, *A New and Complete System of Arithmetick* . . . (New York, Duyckinck, 1816?)]. 17 Apr 1816: '1 Dickinson's Compilation 1.50' [Rodolphus Dickinson, *A Compilation of the Laws of Massachusetts* . . . (Boston, Mallory, 1811?)]. 3 Mar 1817: '1 Bible, dld your Son, 1.00'. 3 Jan 1818: '1 Johnson's Captivity .75'; '1 Indian Wars, 87 1/2'; '1 Ashe's Travels, 1.37 1/2' [Thomas Ashe, *Travels in America, Performed in the Year 1806* . . . (London, Philips, 1809?)]. 24 Jun 1818: '1 Murray's Exercises .63' [Lindley Murray, *English Exercises?*]. 13 Jun 1822: '1 Common Prayer 1.25'. 28 Dec 1822: '1 Woodbridge's Geog. & Atlas 1.38' [William Channing Woodbridge, *Rudiments of Geography* . . . *Accompanied with an Atlas* . . . (Hartford, Goodrich, 1821)]. 10 Apr 1823: '3 Spelling Books .60'.

Leyda's notes on later book bills of Major Melvill found in the Shaw Collection of the Massachusetts Historical Society, generously furnished in his letter of 11 April 1951, mention the following:

11 Jul 1831: '2 Times of our Saviour 1.25'; '3 Ware on Christian Character 1.12' [Henry Ware, *On the Formation of the Christian Character* (Cambridge, Mass., Hilliard and Brown, 1831)]. 13 Jul 1831: '1 Stewart's Visit 2 Vols. $2.00' [Charles Samuel Stewart, *A Visit to the South Seas, in the U.S. Ship Vincennes, during the Years 1829 and 1830* . . . (New York, Haven, 1831), 2 v.]. 3 Sep 1831: '1 Mothers Book .75'; '2 Ware on Ch[ristian] Character .68"'; '2 Gannett's Sermon .17' [Rev. Ezra Stiles Gannett?]; '1 Teachers Gift .50' [*The Teacher's Gift. For 183–* (Boston, 183–)?]. 12 Apr 1832: 'I Helen & Maria .15' (now in the Berkshire Athenaeum); '1 History of New England .50' [Francis Lister Hawks, *The History of New England* . . . By Lambert Lilly, Schoolmaster . . . (Boston, Hyde, 1831)].

3. Books Bought by Lemuel Shaw

Jay Leyda, in a letter of 11 April 1951 citing receipted bills in the Shaw Collection of the Massachusetts Historical Society, noted Shaw's regular renewals of his subscriptions to periodicals and his purchase not only of many law books but also of a number of other works such as travel narratives that might have attracted the notice of his son-in-law. The following titles are books of this sort.

22 May 1826: '1 Flints Travels 2.25 at dis[count] 1.75' [Timothy Flint, *Recollections of the Last Ten Years, Passed in Occasional Residences and Journeyings in the Valley of the Mississippi* . . . (Boston, Cummings, Hilliard, 1826)]. 25 Apr 1829: [binding of] '1 vol Goldsmiths A[nimated] Nature 1.75'. 14 Dec 1831: '1 Paulding's Cruise .62' [Hiram Paulding, *Journal of a Cruise of the United States Cruiser Dolphin among the Islands of the Pacific Ocean; and a Visit to the Mulgrave Islands, in Pursuit of the Mutineers of the Whaleship Globe* . . . (New York, Carvill, 1831); cf. Check-List, No. 323]. 11 Jun 1832: '1 Atwaters Tour .75' [Caleb Atwater, *Remarks Made on a Tour to Prairie du Chien; Thence to Washington City, in 1829* . . . (Columbus, Ohio, Whiting, 1831)]. 26 Dec 1835: 'Godwin on Atheism' [Benjamin Godwin, *Lectures on the Atheistic Controversy* . . . (Boston, Hilliard, Gray, 1836)]; 'The Foreign Quarterly Review [1835]'; 'Parley's Magazine for 1836'. 15 Dec 1835: 'Studies in Poetry 1.25'. 11 Sep 1850: 'Bayley's Poet[ical] Works 2.50' [Joanna Baillie, *Complete Poetical Works* (Philadelphia, Carey & Lea, 1832)?]. 23 Sep 1850 and 23 Oct 1850: 'Cruikshank Copperfield .12' [possibly Charles Dickens, *The Personal History* . . . *of David Copperfield;* cf. Check-List, No. 181]. 11 Nov 1850: 'Ajax .25'. 19 Nov 1850: 'Footprints 1.25' [*Footprints: or, Fugitive Poems* . . . (Philadelphia, Penington, 1843)?]. 26 Dec 1850: 'Stars and

Earth .25' [Felix Eberty, *The Stars and the Earth; or, Thoughts upon Space, Time, and Eternity* . . . (Boston, Crosby and Nichols, 1849)]. 2 Jan 1851: 'Night Side of Nature 1.25' [Catherine Crowe, *Night Side of Nature*, 1848)].

4. Augusta Melville's List of 'Books to be purchased'

Among the Melville Family Papers in the Gansevoort-Lansing Collection, New York Public Library, is an undated list, in Augusta Melville's hand, headed 'Books to be purchased'. The ten entries, some evidently made at different times, are as follows:

'1 Religious Consolation' [a compilation by Rev. Ezra Stiles Gannett, Boston, 1836]; '2 Mary N[oel] McDonald's Poems' [i.e., by Mary Noel (Bleeker) Meigs, New York, 1844]; '3 Woodland Gleanings' [by Robert Tyas, London and Edinburgh, 1837, or later edition]; '4 [The] Virginia Housewife' [or, Methodical Cook, by Mary Randolph. Washington, 1824, or later edition] '—50 cts'; '5 True Politeness for ladies & gentlemen' [two handbooks of etiquette, both New York, ^c1847, or later editions: 'for Ladies. By an American Lady,' and 'for Gentlemen. By an American Gentleman']; '6. [William] Motherwell's Poems' [Narrative and Lyrical. Boston, 1841 or later edition]; '7. A [The] New Timon' [A Romance of London, by Bulwer Lytton, 1846]; '8 "The Young Ladies Guide" to &c' [Harvey Newcomb, The Young Lady's Guide to the Harmonious Development of Christian Character. Boston, ^c1839, or later edition]; '9 Six Lectures on the Uses of the Lungs by Dr. [Samuel Sheldon] Fitch' [New York, 1847, or later edition]; '10 Sir Edward Graham' [or, Railway Speculators, by Catherine Sinclair. New York, 1850]; '11' [no entry].

Appendix C

The Ship's Library of the *Charles and Henry*

From the bill submitted in December 1840 by Andrew M. Macy to Charles and Henry Coffin of Nantucket, owners of the whaleship *Charles and Henry*, the late Wilson L. Heflin was able to identify the thirty-seven books and two magazines Macy had provided for the ship's library. 'The short titles recorded in this bill are sometimes most difficult to identify fully,' in the words of Professor Heflin, 'but with the use, as Melville would say, of the "best authorities," ' he arrived at the probable listing that follows. It is reprinted from his 'New Light on Herman Melville's Cruise in the *Charles and Henry*,' pp. 11–13, 15, by permission of Edouard A. Stackpole (the discoverer of Macy's bill) and the Nantucket Historical Association.

'Moral Tales' (2 copies, 30c)—Samuel Griswold Goodrich [Peter Parley], *Moral Tales*, Boston, E. Littlefield, 1840 (Another title: *Moral Tales: or, A Selection of Interesting Stories. By the Author of Peter Parley*. New York, Naffs and Cornish, 1840).

'Jack Halyard,' 40c—William Samuel Cardell, *Story of Jack Halyard, the Sailor Boy, or, The Virtuous Family*. Designed for American children in families and schools. 30th ed., with appropriate questions, by M. T. Leavenworth, Philadelphia, U. Hunt, 1835.

'Young Christian,' 75c—Jacob Abbott, *The Young Christian: or, A Familiar Illustration of the Principles of Christian Duty*. Stereotype ed., Boston W[illiam] Peirce, 1835. (Also Revised Edition, New York, American Tract Society, 1835.)

'Family Library' (4 selections, $2.00)—Probably selections from Harper's Family Library, which contained 105 volumes in the fall of 1840.
'Constantinople & Athens,' 75c—Rev. Walter Colton, *Visit to Constantinople and Athens*, Boston, Crocker & Brewster, 1836. (Also published in New York, 1836, by Leavitt, Lord & Co.)

'American Revolution,' 33c—Many possibilities. A likely one: William Shepherd, *History of the American Revolution . . .* 1st American Ed. with Notes, Boston, Stimpson, 1832.

'Shipwreck on Desert Island,' 58c—Probably *The Shipwreck: or The Desert Island. A Moral Tale*, Philadelphia, J. Kay, Jun. & Brother, 1840.

'Holden's Narrative,' 20c—Horace Holden, *A Narrative of the Shipwreck, Capitivity, and Sufferings of Horace Holden and Benj. H. Nute: Who Were Cast Away in the American Ship Mentor, on the Pelew Islands, in the Year 1832: And For Two Years Afterwards Were Subjected to Unheard of Sufferings Among the Barbarous Inhabitants of Lord North's Island*, Boston, Weeks, Jordan, 1839. (Also Boston, Russell, Shattuck and Co., 1836.)

'Strive & Thrive,' 50c—Mrs. Mary (Botham) Howitt, *Strive and Thrive: A Tale . . .* Boston, J. Munroe and Company, 1840.

'History of Banking,' 25c—Possibly Richard Hildreth, *The History of Banks: To Which is Added, A Demonstration of the Advantages and Necessity of Free Competition in the Business of Banking*, Boston, Hilliard, Gray & Company, 1837.

'Hope on, Hope Ever,' 50c—Mrs. Mary (Botham) Howitt, *Hope on! Hope Ever! or, The Boyhood of Felix Law*, Boston, James Munroe and Company, 1840.

'Victims of Gaming,' 42c—*The Victims of Gaming; Being Extracts from the Diary of an American Physician*, Boston, Weeks, Jordan & Co., 1838.

'Graham's Lecture,' 50c—Sylvester Graham, *A Lecture to Young Men on Chastity*, 6th stereotype ed., Boston, George W. Light, 1839.

'Home,' 33c–*Probably* [Catharine Maria Sedgwick,] *Home, Domestic Tales*, Boston, James Munroe and Co., 1837, 12th ed.

'Scenes in Nature,' 62c—[Mrs. Jane (Halimand) Marcet,] *Scenes in Nature; or, Conversations for Children, On Land and Water*, Boston, Marsh, Capen, Lyon, and Webb, 1840.

'Merchant's Widow,' 25c—Mrs. Barbara (Wreaks) Hoole Hofland, *The Merchant's Widow, and Her Family*, Boston, Printed by Munroe & Francis, at Their Juvenile Library, No. 4 Cornhill [182–?].

'Life of Harrison,' 37c—Probably Richard Hildreth, *The People's Presidential Candidate; or The Life of William Henry Harrison, of Ohio*, Boston, Weeks, Jordan and Company, 1840. 3rd ed.

Child's Robinson Crusoe,' 63c—Possibly *The Children's Robinson Crusoe; or, The Remarkable Adventures of an Englishman, Who Lived Five Years on an Unknown and Uninhabited Island of the Pacific Ocean*, By a Lady [Eliza Ware (Rotch) Farrar] . . . Boston, Hilliard, Gray, Little, and Wilkins, 1830. (Another possibility: *The Life and Adventures of Robinson Crusoe; From the Original Work of Daniel Defoe. A New Edition Carefully Adapted to Youth* [by S. G. Goodrich?] Illus. by engravings. New York, Pub. by C. Wells, 1836. ['Purified from every thought and expression which might sully the mind . . . of youth.']

'Oberlin,' 25c—Possibly Johann Friedrich Oberlin, *Memoirs* . . . with an introduction [by Henry Ware, Jr.], Cambridge, Hilliard & Brown, 1832. (Other possibilities: *Life of John F. Oberlin*, American Sunday School Union; and Oberlin, pseud., *A Letter on the Unitarianism of the First Three Centuries of the Christian Era*, Meadville, 1830.)

'Young Rover,' 38c—[John H. Amory,] *The Young Rover*, Boston, James B. Dow, 1836.

'Fireside Piety,' 42c—Jacob Abbott, *Fire-Side Piety, or, The Duties and Enjoyments of Family Religion*. Boston, Crocker and Brewster, 1834. (Also New York, Appleton & Co., 1834.)

'Young Man from Home,' 37c—Rev. John Angell James, *The Young Man from Home*, New York, American Tract Society, 1839. (Also New York, Appleton & Co., 1840.)

'Are You a Christian,' 10c—[John Lowell], *Are You a Christian or a Calvinist? or, Do You Prefer the Authority of Christ to That of the Genevan Reformer? Both the Form and Spirit of These Questions Being Suggested by the Late Review of American Unitarianism in the Panoplist and By the Rev. Mr. Worcester's Letter to Mr. Channing. To Which Are Added, Some Strictures on Both Those Works. By A Layman*. Boston, Wells and Lilly, 1815.

'Readings in History,' 30c—Unidentified.

'Pencil Sketches,' 30c—Eliza Leslie, *Pencil Sketches; or, Outlines of Character and Manners*, Philadelphia, Carey, Lea & Blanchard. (There were three series of these, the third series being published in 1837.)

'Poor Jack,' 45c—Captain Frederick Marryat, *Poor Jack*, New York, N. C. Nafis, 1840. (Also Philadelphia, Carey and Hart, 1840.)

'Harrison versus Van Buren,' 12c—Very likely Richard Hildreth, *The Contrast: or William Henry Harrison versus Martin Van Buren*, Boston, Weeks, Jordan & Company, 1840. (Cover title: William Henry Harrison versus Martin Van Buren.)

'Cabinet of Literature,' 37c—Possibly *The Cabinet of Literature, and Monthly Miscellany, Containing History, Biography, Voyages, Travels, Curiosities of Nature and Art, Poetry, Music, Elegant Extracts, Select Anecdotes, Passing Events, etc., etc.,* New York, A. R. Crain & Co., 1833–.

'Fire Side Book,' 38c—Possibly *The Fireside Book, A Miscellany.* With a Plate of Abbotsford. Philadelphia, Printed for the Trade, 1837.

'Washington,' 50c—Difficult to identify. If a biography, there are many possibilities, including lives by J. K. Paulding, 1836, and Jared Sparks, 1832, but most likely it was Mason Locke Weems, *The Life of George Washington,* Philadelphia, J. Allen, 1840.

'People's Own Book,' 25c—Hugues Felicité Robert de Lamennais, *The People's Own Book,* Tr. from the French by Nathaniel Greene. Boston, C. C. Little & J. Brown, 1839. (Also, Boston, E. Littlefield, 1840.)

'Coronal,' 37c—Mrs. Lydia Maria (Francis) Child, *The Coronal. A Collection of Miscellaneous Pieces, Written at Various Times,* Boston, Carter and Hendree, 1832.

'Paul and Virginia,' 25c—Jacques-Henri Bernardin de Saint-Pierre, *Paul and Virginia.* Many editions. Possibly that translated 'from the French' . . . by Helen Maria Williams, Boston, Lilly, Wait & Co., 1834.

'Abbott's Magazine,' 87c—Probably *The Religious Magazine and Family Miscellany,* edited by Jacob Abbott, Boston.

'Family Magazine,' 88c—Probably *The Family Magazine; or Monthly Abstract of General Knowledge* . . . v. 1–8, Apr 20, 1833–1840/41, New York, Redfield & Lindsay, 1834–40.

Total $16.24

Appendix D

The Library Call Slips

During the last five or six years of his life Melville made use of at least two New York libraries for his current reading and for reference materials needed in his writing of that period, notably *Billy Budd, Sailor*, the novel left in manuscript at his death on 28 September 1891. One of these, the New York Society Library, is known; its surviving records of the period list by date and title the fifty-one works charged to him during 1890 and 1891. Still to be determined are the questions of what other library or libraries he may also have used during his late years, the precise dates of such use, and the possibility that records may survive of other books actually charged to him.

A passage in *Billy Budd, Sailor* (Chicago, 1962), pp. 54–55, affords a convenient introduction to the particulars of the matter at hand. In *Billy Budd*, discussing the Nore Mutiny of 1797 in the British Navy, Melville directly quotes one of the sources he drew upon for historical background: the British naval historian William James, author of *The Naval History of Great Britain*, 6 vols., which appeared in various London editions during Melville's lifetime. James's treatment of the mutiny at the Nore, Melville goes on to say, 'is less a narration than a reference, having to do hardly at all with details. *Nor are these readily to be found in the libraries* [italics added].' Melville's statement implies

251

that he had sought information in other authors as well as in James, and in more than one locality. Since from other evidence it is known that this passage of *Billy Budd* (Leaves 53, 54 of the manuscript, now in HCL) was in fair copy not later than 16 November 1888, which is before his membership in the New York Society Library became effective, one infers at the outset that he was using some other library or libraries for reference purposes during the period between 1885/86 and the autumn of 1888.

Among other possibilities, the New-York Historical Society reports no mention of Melville on its registers for this period; though he had lectured there in earlier years, he was never a member (letter of 14 October 1960 from James J. Heslin, Director, the New-York Historical Society). The Lenox Library he had at least visited during the 1870's, as we know; the Astor Library listed James's *Naval History* in its printed catalogue of 1880. But wherever Melville may actually have *read* James's *Naval History*, he took a series of notes from its second volume on two library call slips that came from neither the Astor Library nor the Lenox, though the slips bear no printed identification of their origin. The call slips, now fastened to Leaf 364 of the *Billy Budd* manuscript, are headed 'Reference Department,' and there are instructions on the verso addressed to 'Members.' Neither the Astor Library nor the Lenox was departmentalized before their subsequent consolidation as the New York Public Library. Moreover, the term 'Members,' which would exclude a public institution, suggests a private subscription library. (That of a college or university is a possibility, but though an academic library might well serve 'members' of its community, the usage appears strained; moreover, Melville was without academic affiliations.) Of the subscription libraries of New York, two can be ruled out at once. The New York Society Library, of which he became a member after the allusion to James was written, was apparently not using call slips during the years in question (letter of 28 July 1948 from Mrs. F. G. King of the New York Society Library); the New York Mercantile Library, which has no record of his possible membership, was using slips of a different size and wording (letter of 2 March 1949 from Miss Florence S. Garing, Librarian, the Mercantile Library). Still another private institution must therefore be the source of the call slips—an institution that in the period 1885–1888 maintained a 'Reference Department' for the use of its 'Members.'

Of the remaining possibilities, one is especially intriguing. This is the Apprentices' Library of the General Society of Mechanics and Tradesmen, which since 1878 had been located in Mechanics' Hall at 18 East 16th Street—not far from Melville's residence at 104 East 26th Street. This library, which during the 1880's contained approximately

THE LIBRARY CALL SLIPS

Two library slips, recto, mounted on Leaf [87a]364 of the manuscript of Melville's *Billy Budd, Sailor,* bearing Melville's notes from William James, *The Naval History of Great Britain.* (By permission of the Houghton Library, Harvard University.)

2 464

Books contained in the Library and not found upon

the shelves of the Reference Department, can be consulted

by filling up this blank, givi⬛⬛⬛ author's name and title *M 146*

of the book.

**Members, after finishing with the work,
will please return it to the clerk, and see
that the order upon which it was delivered
is returned to them before leaving the
Library.**

Books contained in the Library and not found upon

the shelves of the Reference Department, can be consulted

by filling up this blank, givi⬛⬛⬛ author's name and title

of the book

**Members, after finishing with the work,
will please return it to the clerk, and see
that the order upon which it was delivered
is returned to them before leaving the
Library.**

Verso of the library call slips.

75,000 volumes, included the De Milt Library 'for reference,' from which, according to an earlier printed catalogue of 1865, books could not be taken 'except by special permission.' This same catalogue mentions the use of 'blank forms'—i.e., call slips—to be filled in with the title of the work wanted by a reader, the date of application, and the reader's 'signature and the number of his folio'; Melville's 'Reference Department' slips call for folio, title, name of reader, and residence, specifying that 'Books applied for on this slip cannot be taken out of the Library.' Written book-orders were still in use as late as 1888, according to the printed Finding-List issued by the library in that year. Before 1 August 1886 persons not members of the General Society of Mechanics and Tradesmen could obtain reading privileges at the Apprentices' Library for $2.00 per year; after that date the library was made free without restriction. Melville might well have been a reader there both before and after it became a free library, and after that time, of course, the Reference Department (the De Milt Collection) might simply have continued using existing call slips reading 'Members' until the supply was exhausted.

The character of the Apprentices' Library (now located at 20 West 44th Street in New York) has changed considerably in more recent years. Many of its former holdings have been disposed of; there are apparently no surviving ledgers or other records listing persons to whom books were charged in the 1880's; nor are there call slips from that period that might be compared with those on which Melville made his notes from James. It has therefore proved impossible to secure any information at the library itself which might establish whether or not Melville was ever a reader or borrower there.

There is, however, another piece of evidence to be considered that may eventually yield further results. On the verso of one of the call slips bearing the notes from James are two penciled notations also in Melville's hand—'2464' and 'M146'—that deserve further scrutiny. It would be extremely useful to learn what each represents: 'the number of the [reader's] folio' in the ledgers of a particular library, the call number of a specific book, or whatever. Several librarians with whom this matter has been discussed have immediately suggested the possibility that 'M146' is a Cutter number, but a check of various editions of Cutter's tables dating from the 1880's has yielded no significant results. Another approach to the problem has been in terms of the several printed catalogues issued by the Apprentices' Library, which is still not ruled out as one of the institutions used by Melville.

1. The printed catalogue of 1865 issued by the Apprentices' Library included in its alphabetical listing of each title a number (call

number? accession number? shelf number?) of one to four digits. An inspection of this catalogue located a '2463' and a '2465' but not a '2464.'

2. During the period 1871–1879, Jacob Schwartz, then the Librarian of the Apprentices' Library, contrived a more elaborate system of book classification (thereby provoking a controversy among librarians reflected in pages of the *Library Journal* at the time). The *Finding-List* of the library published in 1888 uses this system, explaining that the classification includes a class letter plus up to four figures, and sometimes a title letter as well. 'M' is used in the *Finding-List* to designate books of 'Mental and Moral Science'; in earlier printed catalogues of the library it had indicated works of general literature. In none of the listings, however, does 'M146' appear among the subclassifications.

3. Under a later librarian, H. W. Parker (father of a still later librarian), a simpler system of classification was introduced; see his *Library Classification and Numbering System* (1901; 3rd ed., 1926). An inspection of several books in the present library relevant to *Billy Budd* revealed no vestigial classification symbols from an earlier period of accession that might be of significance.

4. It has not been established whether the Apprentices' Library ever included a set of James's *Naval History*; the title does not appear in any of the earlier printed catalogues examined nor in the present card catalogue, but the mere absence of such a listing is of course not conclusive. Moreover, Melville need not have read James in the same library from which he obtained the call slips, nor do '2464' and 'M146' necessarily pertain either to the *Naval History* or to the library from which the call slips came.

In summary, the library or libraries where Melville obtained the call slips and took his notes from Vol. II of James's *Naval History* are still unidentified, and the significance of the penciled notations '2464' and 'M146' has not been explained. The Apprentices' Library may indeed have been the source of the call slips, since no more likely possibility has been established, but there is apparently no conclusive evidence to show that the call slips either did or did not come from that library, that the Apprentices' Library did or did not contain a set of James's *Naval History*, or that Melville did or did not use the library's facilities. Put another way, it might be said that the following questions remain to be answered conclusively:

From what library did the call slips come?

If the library can be identified, did it in the period 1886–1888 have a set of James's *Naval History of Great Britain*?

If this set survives, does it contain symbols corresponding to Melville's '2464' or 'M146'?

What is the significance of these notations?

Is there any surviving record of a relationship between Melville and this library, such as membership, payment for reading privileges, charges by date and title, etc.?

Works Cited

This listing does not include booksellers' catalogues cited in individual entries within the Check-List of Books Owned and Borrowed, in Part II above.

Anderson, Charles Roberts. *Melville in the South Seas*. New York: Columbia University Press, 1939.

Barber, Patricia. 'Two New Melville Letters.' *American Literature* 49 (November 1977): 418–421.

Bell, Millicent. 'Pierre Bayle and *Moby Dick*.' *PMLA* 66 (September 1951): 626–648.

Bercaw, Mary K. *Melville's Sources*. Evanston, Ill.: Northwestern University Press, 1987.

Berthold, Dennis. 'Factual Errors and Fictional Aims in *White-Jacket*.' *Studies in American Fiction* 11 (Autumn 1983): 233–239.

Bezanson, Walter E. Historical Note. *Israel Potter: His Fifty Years of Exile*. By Herman Melville. Vol. 8 of *The Writings of Herman Melville*. Pp. 173–235.

————. Introduction. *Clarel: A Poem and Pilgrimage in the Holy Land*. By Herman Melville. New York: Hendricks House, 1960. Pp. ix–cxvii.

————. 'Melville's Reading of Arnold's Poetry.' *PMLA* 69 (June 1954): 365–391.

Birss, J. H. 'Herman Melville and Blake.' *Notes and Queries* 166.18 (5 May 1934): 311.

Blair, Walter, and Harrison Hayford. Editors' Introduction. *Omoo: A Narrative of Adventures in the South Seas*. By Herman Melville. New York: Hendricks House, 1969. Pp. xvii–lii.

Bond, William H. 'Melville and *Two Years Before the Mast*.' *Harvard Library Bulletin* 7 (Autumn 1953): 362–365.

Boston Athenaeum. *Catalogue of the Library . . . , 1807–1871*. 5 vols. Boston: [The Boston Athenaeum], 1874–1882.

Branch, Watson, Hershel Parker, and Harrison Hayford, with Alma A. Mac-Dougall. Historical Note. *The Confidence-Man: His Masquerade*. By Herman Melville. Vol. 10 of *The Writings of Herman Melville*. Pp. 255–357.

Breinig, Helmbrecht. 'The Destruction of Fairyland: Melville's "Piazza" in the Tradition of the American Imagination.' *ELH: A Journal of English Literary History* 35 (June 1968): 254–283.

Bryant, John. 'Melville and Charles F. Briggs: *Working a Passage* to *Billy Budd*.' *English Language Notes* 22 (June 1985): 48–54.

——, ed. *A Companion to Melville Studies*. Westport, Conn.: Greenwood Press, 1986.

Cahoon, Herbert. *Herman Melville: A Check List of Books and Manuscripts in the Collections of The New York Public Library*. New York: New York Public Library, 1951.

Cameron, Kenneth Walter. 'A Melville Letter and Stray Books from His Library.' *ESQ: Journal of the American Renaissance* 63 (Spring 1971): 47–49.

Cannon, Agnes Dicken. 'On Translating *Clarel*.' *Essays in Arts and Sciences* 5 (July 1976): 160–180.

Charvat, William. 'Melville's Income.' *American Literature* 15 (November 1943): 251–261.

Coffler, Gail H. *Melville's Classical Allusions: A Comprehensive Index and Glossary*. Westport, Conn.: Greenwood Press, 1985.

Cohen, Hennig. Introduction. *The Battle-Pieces of Herman Melville*. New York: Thomas Yoseloff, 1964. Pp. 11–28.

Cowen, Walker. 'Melville's "Discoveries": A Dialogue of the Mind with Itself.' *The Recognition of Herman Melville: Selected Criticism Since 1846*. Ed. Hershel Parker. Ann Arbor: University of Michigan Press, 1967. Pp. 333–346.

——. *Melville's Marginalia*. Dissertation Harvard University, 1965.

——. 'Melville's Marginalia: Hawthorne.' *Studies in the American Renaissance: 1978*. Ed. Joel Myerson. Boston: Twayne Publishers, 1978. Pp. 279–302.

Davis, Merrell R. *Melville's Mardi: A Chartless Voyage*. New Haven, Conn.: Yale University Press, 1952.

——, and William H. Gilman. Introduction and notes to *The Letters of Herman Melville*. New Haven, Conn.: Yale University Press, 1960. Pp. xv–xxviii and *passim*.

Davis, Susan. 'More for the NYPL's Long Vaticans.' *Melville Society Extracts* 57 (February 1984): 5–7.

De Marco, John, and Carolyn DeMarco. 'Finding the New Melville Papers.' *Melville Society Extracts* 56 (November 1983): 1–3.

Duban, James. 'The Translation of Pierre Bayle's *An Historical and Critical Dictionary* Owned by Melville.' *Papers of the Bibliographical Society of America* 71 (3rd Quarter 1977): 347–351.

Finkelstein, Dorothee Metlitsky. *Melville's Orienda*. New Haven, Conn.: Yale University Press, 1961.

Foley, Brian. 'Herman Melville and the Example of Sir Thomas Browne.' *Modern Philology* 81 (February 1984): 265–277.

Forsythe, Robert S. Review of Raymond Weaver, ed., *Journal up the Straits*, by Herman Melville. *American Literature* 8 (March 1936): 93.

Foster, Elizabeth. 'Another Note on Melville and Geology.' *American Literature* 22 (January 1951): 479–487.

———. Historical Note. *Mardi and a Voyage Thither*. By Herman Melville. Vol. 3 of *The Writings of Herman Melville*. Pp. 657–681.

———. Introduction. *The Confidence-Man: His Masquerade*. By Herman Melville. New York: Hendricks House, 1954. Pp. xliii–xcv.

———. 'Melville and Geology.' *American Literature* 17 (March 1945): 50–65.

Frank, Stuart M. *Herman Melville's Picture Gallery: Sources and Types of the "Pictorial" Chapters of* Moby-Dick. Fairhaven, Mass.: Edward J. Lefcowicz, 1986.

Freeman, F. Barron. 'The Enigma of Melville's "Daniel Orme." ' *American Literature* 16 (November 1944): 208–211.

Garner, Stanton. 'The Melville Who Awaits Discovery.' *Melville Society Extracts* 53 (February 1983): 2.

———. 'Melville's Scout Toward Aldie.' *Melville Society Extracts* 51 (September 1982): 5–16; 52 (November 1982): 1–14.

———. 'The Picaresque Career of Thomas Melvill, Junior.' *Melville Society Extracts* 60 (November 1984): 1–10; Part II, 62 (May 1985): 1, 4–10.

Gilman, William H. *Melville's Early Life and* Redburn. New York: New York University Press, 1951.

———. 'Melville's Liverpool Trip.' *Modern Language Notes* 61 (December 1946): 543–547.

Glenn, Barbara. 'Melville and the Sublime in *Moby-Dick*.' *American Literature* 48 (May 1976): 165–182.

Gollin, Richard, and Rita Gollin. 'Justice in an Earlier Treatment of the *Billy Budd* Theme.' *American Literature* 28 (January 1957): 513–515.

Gretchko, John M. J. 'Remnants of the U. S. Census, 1850–1880.' *Melville Society Extracts* 62 (May 1985): 15–16.

Haskell, Daniel C. *The United States Exploring Expedition, 1838–1842, and Its Publications, 1844–1874*. New York: New York Public Library, 1942.

Hawthorne, Nathaniel. *The American Notebooks*. Ed. Claude M. Simpson. Vol. 8 of *The Centenary Edition*.

———. *The Centenary Edition of the Works of Nathaniel Hawthorne*. Ed.

William Charvat et al. 16 vols. to date. Columbus: Ohio State University Press, 1962–.

———. *The Letters, 1843–1853*. Ed. Thomas Woodson, L. Neal Smith, Norman Holmes Pearson. Vol. 16 of *The Centenary Edition*.

Hayford, Harrison. 'Melville's German Streak.' [Forthcoming]

———, and Merton M. Sealts, Jr. Editors' Introduction. *Billy Budd, Sailor*. By Herman Melville. Chicago: University of Chicago Press, 1962. Pp. 1–39.

———, and Walter Blair. Editors' Introduction. *Omoo: A Narrative of Adventures in the South Seas*. By Herman Melville. New York: Hendricks House, 1969. Pp. xvii–lii.

Hays, Peter L., and Richard Dilworth Rust. ' "Something Healing": Fathers and Sons in *Billy Budd*.' *Nineteenth-Century Fiction* 34 (December 1979): 326–336.

Heffernan, Thomas Farel. 'Herman Melville's Annotations and Markings in His Copy of Owen Chase's *Narrative*.' *Stove by a Whale: Owen Chase and the Essex*. Middletown, Conn.: Wesleyan University Press, 1981. Appendix A, pp. 184–209.

Heflin, Wilson L. 'Melville and Nantucket.' *Proceedings of the Nantucket Historical Association*, 1951: 22–30.

———. 'New Light on Herman Melville's Cruise in the *Charles and Henry*.' *Historic Nantucket* 22 (October 1974): 6–27. Reprinted as a pamphlet by the Melville Society.

Herbert, T. Walter. 'Calvinism and Cosmic Evil in *Moby-Dick*.' *PMLA* 84 (October 1969): 1613–1619.

Higgins, Brian. 'Herman Melville.' *The Transcendentalists: A Review of Research and Criticism*. Ed. Joel Myerson. New York: Modern Language Association of America, 1984. Pp. 348–361.

Hillway, Tyrus. 'Melville's Education in Science.' *Texas Studies in Literature and Language* 16 (Fall 1974): 411–425.

———. 'Melville's Geological Knowledge.' *American Literature* 21 (May 1949): 232–237.

Hirsch, Penny L. 'Melville's Spenser Edition for *The Encantadas*.' *Melville Society Extracts* 50 (May 1982): 15–16.

Howard, Leon. Historical Note. *Typee: A Peep at Polynesian Life*. By Herman Melville. Vol. 1 of *The Writings of Herman Melville*. Pp. 277–302.

———, and Hershel Parker. Historical Note. *Pierre or, The Ambiguities*. By Herman Melville. Vol. 7 of *The Writings of Herman Melville*. Pp. 365–410.

Howes, Jeanne C. 'Melville's Sensitive Years.' In Howard P. Vincent, *Melville and Hawthorne in the Berkshires*. Pp. 22–41.

Huntress, Keith. 'Melville's Use of a Source for *White-Jacket*.' *American Literature* 17 (March 1945): 66–74.

———. 'A Note on Melville's *Redburn*.' *New England Quarterly* 18 (June 1945), 259–260.

Keep, Austin Baxter. *History of the New York Society Library*. New York: DeVinne Press, 1908.

Kelley, Wyn. 'Melville's Cain.' *American Literature* 55 (March 1983), 24–40.

Kennedy, Frederick J. 'Dr. Samuel Jones and Herman Melville.' *Extracts / An Occasional Newsletter* (The Melville Society) 32 (November 1977): 3–7.

———, and Joyce Deveau Kennedy. 'Additions to *The Melville Log*.' *Extracts / An Occasional Newsletter* (The Melville Society) 31 (September 1977): 4–9.

Kring, Walter D., and Jonathan S. Carey. 'Two Discoveries Concerning Herman Melville.' *Proceedings of the Massachusetts Historical Society* 87 (1975): 137–141.

Kulkarni, H. B. *Moby-Dick: A Hindu Avatar. A Study of Hindu Myth and Thought in* Moby-Dick. Logan, Utah: Utah State University Press, 1970.

Levin, Michael E. 'Ahab as Socratic Philosopher: The Myth of the Cave Inverted.' *ATQ: The American Transcendental Quarterly* 41 (Winter 1979): 61–73.

Leyda, Jay. *The Melville Log: A Documentary Life of Herman Melville 1819–1891* (1951). With a New Supplementary Chapter. New York: Gordian Press, 1969. 2 vols.

———, ed. *The Complete Stories of Herman Melville*. New York: Random House, 1949.

Lydenberg, H. M. *History of the New York Public Library*. New York: New York Public Library, 1923.

MacDougall, Alma A. 'The Chronology of *The Confidence-Man* and "Benito Cereno": Redating Two 1855 Curtis and Melville Letters.' *Melville Society Extracts* 53 (February 1983): 3–6.

McElderry, B.R., Jr. 'Three Earlier Treatments of the *Billy Budd* Theme.' *American Literature* 27 (May 1955): 251–257.

———, ed. *Narrative of the Most Extraordinary and Distressing Shipwreck of the Whaleship Essex.* By Owen Chase. New York: Corinth Books, 1963. Supplementary Accounts of Survivors and Herman Melville's Notes, pp. 117–136.

McKay, George L. *American Book Auction Catalogs, 1713–1934; a Union List.* New York: New York Public Library, 1937.

McNeilly, Dorothy V. B. D. R. 'The Melvilles and Mrs. Ferris.' *Extracts / An Occasional Newsletter* (The Melville Society) 28 (November 1976): 1–9.

Mansfield, Luther S. *Herman Melville: Author and New Yorker: 1844–1851*. Dissertation University of Chicago 1936.

———, and Howard P. Vincent. Introduction. *Moby-Dick or, The Whale.* By Herman Melville. New York: Hendricks House, 1952. Pp. ix–xxxiii.

Matthews, Pamela R. 'Four Old Smokers: Melville, Thoreau, and Their Chimneys.' *ATQ: American Transcendental Quarterly* 51 (Summer 1981): 151–164.

Matthiessen, F. O. *American Renaissance: Art and Expression in the Age of Emerson and Whitman.* New York: Oxford University Press, 1941.

Melville, Elizabeth Shaw. Memoranda (May 1861–February 1902). In Merton M. Sealts, Jr., *The Early Lives of Melville*. Pp. 167–177.

Melville, Gansevoort. 'An Albany Journal by Gansevoort Melville.' Ed. Jay Leyda. *Boston Public Library Quarterly* 2 (October 1950): 327–347.

Melville, Herman. *Billy Budd, Sailor: An Inside Narrative*. Ed. Harrison

Hayford and Merton M. Sealts, Jr. Chicago: University of Chicago Press, 1962.

———. *Clarel: A Poem and Pilgrimage in the Holy Land.* Ed. Walter E. Bezanson. New York: Hendricks House, 1960.

———. *The Collected Poems of Herman Melville.* Ed. Howard P. Vincent. Chicago: Packard and Company (Hendricks House), 1947.

———. *Journal of a Visit to London and the Continent . . . 1849–1850.* Ed. Eleanor Melville Metcalf. Cambridge, Mass.: Harvard University Press, 1948.

———. *Journal of a Visit to Europe and the Levant October 11, 1856–May 6, 1857.* Ed. Howard C. Horsford. Princeton, N.J.: Princeton University Press, 1955.

———. Letter to Simeon E. Baldwin, 17 November 1889. Reproduced in *Melville Society Extracts* 58 (May 1984): 7.

———. Letter to G. P. Putnam & Sons, 27 March 1879. Reproduced in 'Collecting Melville et al.' *Melville Society Extracts* 66 (May 1986): 14.

———. *The Letters of Herman Melville.* Ed. Merrell R. Davis and William H. Gilman. New Haven, Conn.: Yale University Press, 1960.

———. *Moby-Dick. An Authoritative Text, Reviews and Letters by Melville, Analogues and Sources, Criticism.* Ed. Harrison Hayford and Hershel Parker. New York: W. W. Norton, 1967.

———. 'A New Melville Letter.' *Melville Society Extracts* 64 (November 1985): 11.

———. 'Two New Melville Letters.' Ed. Patricia Barber. *American Literature* 49 (November 1977): 418–421.

———. *The Writings of Herman Melville.* Ed. Harrison Hayford, Hershel Parker, and G. Thomas Tanselle. Evanston and Chicago: Northwestern University Press and the Newberry Library, 1968–. 9 vols. to date: 1. *Typee: A Peep at Polynesian Life* (1968); 2. *Omoo: A Narrative of Adventures in the South Seas* (1968); 3. *Mardi and a Voyage Thither* (1970); 4. *Redburn: His First Voyage* (1969); 5. *White-Jacket: or The World in a Man-of-War* (1970); 7. *Pierre or The Ambiguities* (1971); 8. *Israel Potter: His Fifty Years of Exile* (1982); 9. The Piazza Tales *and Other Prose Pieces, 1839–1860* (1987); 10. *The Confidence-Man: His Masquerade* (1984).

Metcalf, Eleanor Melville. *Herman Melville: Cycle and Epicycle.* Cambridge, Mass.: Harvard University Press, 1953.

Monteiro, George. 'Melville and Camões: A Working Bibliography.' *Melville Society Extracts* 64 (November 1985): 14–15.

Moore, Maxine. *That Lonely Game: Melville,* Mardi, *and The Almanac.* Columbia: University of Missouri Press, 1975.

Murray, Henry A. Introduction. *Pierre.* By Herman Melville. New York: Hendricks House, 1949. Pp. xiii–ciii.

———, Harvey Myerson, and Eugene Taylor. 'Allan Melvill's Bye-Blow.' *Melville Society Extracts* 61 (February 1985): 1–6.

———, and Eugene Taylor. 'From Mocha to Moby.' *Melville Society Extracts* 64 (November 1985): 6–7.

New York Society Library. *Alphabetical and Analytical Catalogue of the New*

York Society Library. New York: R. Craighead, Printer, 1850.

Palmer, R. R. 'Herman Melville et la Révolution Française.' *Annales Historiques de la Révolution Française* 26 (July–September 1954): 254–256.

Paltsits, Victor Hugo, ed. *Family Correspondence of Herman Melville 1830–1904 in the Gansevoort-Lansing Collection*. New York: New York Public Library, 1929.

Parker, Hershel. Historical Note. *Redburn: His First Voyage*. By Herman Melville. Vol. 4 of *The Writings of Herman Melville*. Pp. 315–352.

——, and Leon Howard. Historical Note. *Pierre or The Ambiguities*. By Herman Melville. Vol. 7 of *The Writings of Herman Melville*. Pp. 365–410.

Pavese, Cesar. 'The Literary Whaler' (1932). *Sewanee Review* 68 (Summer 1968): 407–418.

Peckham, Morse. 'Hawthorne and Melville as European Authors.' In Howard P. Vincent, ed. *Melville and Hawthorne in the Berkshires*. Pp. 42–62.

The Rebellion Record: A Diary of American Events, with Documents, Narratives, Illustrious Incidents, Poetry, etc. Ed. Frank Morris. 11 vols. New York: G. P. Putnam, 1861–1863; D. Van Nostrand, 1864–1868.

——. *Supplement—First Volume*. New York: G. P. Putnam; H. Holt, 1864.

Reynolds, Larry J. 'Melville's Catskill Eagle.' *Melville Society Extracts* 64 (November 1985), 11–12.

Rogin, Michael Paul. *Subversive Genealogy: The Politics and Art of Herman Melville*. New York: Alfred A. Knopf, 1983.

Roorbach, Orville Augustus. *Bibliotheca Americana. Catalogue of American Publications . . . from 1820 to 1852*. New York: O. A. Roorbach, 1852.

——. *Supplement . . . from October, 1852, to May, 1855*. New York: O. A. Roorbach, 1855.

——. *Addenda . . . from May, 1855, to March, 1858*. New York: Wiley & Halsted [etc.], 1858.

——. *Vol. IV . . . from March, 1858, to January, 1861*. New York: O. A. Roorbach, 1861.

Roper, Gordon. Historical Note. *Omoo: A Narrative of Adventures in the South Seas*. By Herman Melville. Vol. 2 of *The Writings of Herman Melville*. Pp. 319–344.

Rosenbach, Abraham Simon Wolf. *Books and Bidders; the Adventures of a Bibliophile*. Boston: Little, Brown and Company, 1927.

Runden, John P. 'Columbia Grammar School: An Overlooked Year in the Lives of Gansevoort and Herman Melville.' *Melville Society Extracts* 46 (May 1981): 1–3.

Sealts, Merton M., Jr. 'A Correspondence with Charles Olson' (1982). In *Pursuing Melville*. Pp. 93–151.

——. *The Early Lives of Melville: Nineteenth-Century Biographical Sketches and Their Authors*. Madison: University of Wisconsin Press, 1974.

——. 'The Ghost of Major Melvill' (1957). In *Pursuing Melville*. Pp. 67–77.

——. Historical Note. *The Piazza Tales and Other Prose Pieces 1839–1860*. By Herman Melville. Vol. 9 of *The Writings of Herman Melville*. Pp. 457–533.

——. 'Innocence and Infamy: *Billy Budd, Sailor*' (1986). In John Bryant, ed. *A Companion to Melville Studies*. Pp. 407–430.

————. 'Melville and Emerson's Rainbow' (1980). In *Pursuing Melville*. Pp. 250–277.

————. 'Melville and Richard Henry Stoddard.' *American Literature* 43 (November 1971): 359–370.

————. 'Melville and the Platonic Tradition' (1982). In *Pursuing Melville*. Pp. 278–336.

————. 'Melville and Whitman.' *Melville Society Extracts* 50 (May 1982): 10–12.

————. *Melville as Lecturer*. Cambridge, Mass.: Harvard University Press, 1957.

————. 'Melville's Burgundy Club Sketches' (1958). In *Pursuing Melville*. Pp. 78–90.

————. 'Melville's Chimney, Reexamined' (1969). In *Pursuing Melville*. Pp.171–192.

————. 'Melville's "Neoplatonical Originals." ' *Modern Language Notes* 67 (February 1952): 80–86.

————. *Pursuing Melville 1940–1980: Chapters and Essays*. Madison: Univeristy of Wisconsin Press, 1982.

Smith, Joseph Edward Adams. 'Herman Melville' (1891–1892). In Merton M. Sealts, Jr., *The Early Lives of Melville*. Pp. 119–149.

Spivey, Herman E. Review of Sealts, *Melville's Reading* (1966). *Papers of the Bibliographical Society of America* 61 (1st Quarter 1967): 67–68.

Stedman, Arthur. 'Herman Melville' in *Appleton's Annual Cyclopaedia . . . 1891* (1892). In Merton M. Sealts, Jr., *The Early Lives of Melville*. Pp. 149–154.

————. Introduction. *Typee: A Real Romance of the South Seas* (1892). By Herman Melville. In Merton M. Sealts, Jr., *The Early Lives of Melville*. Pp. 154–166.

Stevens, Aretta J. 'The Edition of Montaigne Read by Melville.' *Papers of the Bibliographical Society of America* 62 (2nd Quarter 1968), 130–134.

Sweeney, Gerard M. *Melville's Use of Classical Mythology*. Amsterdam: Rodopi N.V., 1975.

Tanselle, G. Thomas. 'Two Melville Association Copies: The Hubbard *Whale* and the Jones *Moby-Dick*. Part I: The Hubbard Whale.' *The Book Collector: Collector's Piece* 8 (Summer 1982): 170–186.

Thorp, Willard. *Herman Melville: Representative Selections, with Introduction, Bibliography, and Notes*. New York: American Book Co., 1938.

————. 'Herman Melville's Silent Years.' *University Review* 3 (Summer 1937): 254–262.

————. Historical Note. *White-Jacket or The World in a Man-of-War*. By Herman Melville. Vol. 5 of *The Writings of Herman Melville*. Pp. 403–440.

————. 'Redburn's Prosy Old Guidebook.' *PMLA* 53 (December 1938): 1146–1156.

Tilton, Eleanor M. 'Melville's "Rammon": A Text and Commentary.' *Harvard Library Bulletin* 13 (Winter 1959): 50–91.

Titus, David K. 'Herman Melville at the Albany Academy.' *Melville Society Extracts* 42 (May 1980): 1, 4–10.

Vargish, Thomas. 'Gnostic *Mythos* in *Moby-Dick*.' *PMLA* 81 (June 1966): 272–277.

Vincent, Howard P. *The Tailoring of Melville's* White-Jacket. Evanston, Ill.: Northwestern University Press, 1970.

———. *The Trying-Out of* Moby-Dick. Boston: Houghton Mifflin Company, 1949.

———, ed. *Melville and Hawthorne in the Berkshires: A Symposium*. Kent, Ohio: Kent State University Press, 1968.

———, and Luther S. Mansfield. Introduction. *Moby-Dick or, The Whale*. By Herman Melville. New York: Hendricks House, 1952. Pp. ix–xxxiii.

Wallace, Robert K. 'Melville's Prints and Engravings at the Berkshire Athenaeum.' *Essays in Arts and Sciences* 15 (June 1986): 50–90.

———. 'New Evidence for Melville's Use of Turner in *Moby-Dick*.' *Melville Society Extracts* 67 (September 1986): 4–9.

Weaver, Raymond M. *Herman Melville: Mariner and Mystic*. New York: George H. Doran Company, 1921.

Wegelin, Oscar. 'Herman Melville as I Recall Him.' *The Colophon* n.s. 1 (Summer 1935): 21–24.

Wilson, James C. 'Melville at Arrowhead: A Reevaluation of Melville's Relations with Hawthorne and with His Family.' *ESQ: A Journal of the American Renaissance* 30 (4th Quarter 1984): 232–244.

Wright, Nathalia. 'Biblical Allusion in Melville's Prose.' *American Literature* 12 (May 1940): 185–199.

———. *Melville's Use of the Bible*. Durham, N.C.: Duke University Press, 1949.

Yannella, Donald. 'Writing the "*other* way": Melville, the Duyckinck Crowd, and Literature for the Masses.' In John Bryant, ed. *A Companion to Melville Studies*. Pp. 63–81.

General Index

This is an index of proper names, including the names of authors and the titles of their works but not publishers' imprints. The secondary listings in the Check-List of Books Owned and Borrowed, pp. 149–228 of Part II, have been indexed selectively, to include published studies that identify certain titles and editions; documentation within the secondary listings that involves family papers of the Melvilles, Gansevoorts, and Duyckincks is not indexed here, though correspondence outside their respective circles has been taken into account. The General Index does not duplicate the Analytical Index to the Check-List, pp. 229–233 above, which lists by entry numbers those books known to have been owned and borrowed by Melville and by members of his family and which also indicates the known locations of surviving books.